Praise for

THE WAR ON
ALCOHOL

"All good history is as much about the present as it is about the past. McGirr invites readers to hear in our own era the echoes of conflict over the prohibition of intoxicants, over the role of moral entrepreneurs in imposing a single cultural standard on a multicultural society, over the costs of xenophobia, over state policing of private behavior, and over the abuses of state power. . . . [F]or readers not well versed in Prohibition and its aftermath, *The War on Alcohol* is a terrific introduction as well as a terrific read." —ERIC C. SCHNEIDER,
Washington Independent Review of Books

"McGirr shifts our attention from gangsters and flappers to policemen and agency chiefs in order to explain the critical role of Prohibition in the creation of the modern American state. Histories of temperance often stop in 1919, with the unlikely passage of the 18th Amendment. McGirr picks up where these stories leave off, exploring the daunting political problems and personal casualties that come with trying to enforce this strange new law." —BEVERLY GAGE,
The Nation

"An important book that warrants a place at the forefront of Prohibition histories. General readers will love it, and scholars will find much to ponder." —*KIRKUS REVIEWS,* starred review

"[McGirr] takes a fresh and fascinating look at Prohibition, arguing that it should not be viewed as a failed experiment, but as one of the defining political and social movements of the 20th century."
—NICHOLAS GRAHAM,
Library Journal, starred review

"Both sobering and enlightening, McGirr's work gives Prohibition and its consequences a much-needed reexamination that provides insights relevant to today's War on Drugs." —PUBLISHERS WEEKLY

"McGirr makes two major contributions to the historical record. First, she vividly shows how enforcers targeted immigrant and black communities. . . . Second, McGirr tells us that Prohibition gave birth to big government—an argument that could have a major impact on how we read American political history. . . . [O]ur present-day nativists would do well to heed McGirr's meticulous reconstruction of a time in which oppressed people fought back and helped build a coalition that dominated American politics for 40 years." —JAMES A. MORONE,
New York Times Book Review

"In this remarkable book, Lisa McGirr transforms our understanding of Prohibition and its legacy. Moving beyond familiar tales of speakeasies and gangland violence, she shows how this episode contributed to the expansion of the authority of the modern American state and the origins of mass imprisonment. No history could be more timely."

—ERIC FONER,
author of Gateway to Freedom

"McGirr's book, fascinating and deeply researched, offers a startlingly fresh argument for why so many of our current problems—from the war on drugs to mass incarceration—grow out of Prohibition. Anyone who wants to understand the 1920s, 1930s, and 2000s should read this book." —JONATHAN ALTER,
author of The Defining Moment

"This is not just the best book ever written about the era of Prohibition; it is a landmark history of modern America. With splendid insight and illuminating details, Lisa McGirr demonstrates that the war on alcohol was the health of the state." —MICHAEL KAZIN,
author of American Dreamers

THE WAR ON
ALCOHOL

ALSO BY LISA McGIRR

Suburban Warriors:
The Origins of the New American Right

THE WAR ON
ALCOHOL

PROHIBITION AND THE RISE
OF THE AMERICAN STATE

LISA McGIRR

W. W. NORTON & COMPANY

Independent Publishers Since 1923

New York • London

For information about permission to reproduce selections from this book,
write to Permissions, W. W. Norton & Company, Inc.,
500 Fifth Avenue, New York, NY 10110

For information about special discounts for bulk purchases, please contact
W. W. Norton Special Sales at specialsales@wwnorton.com or 800-233-4830

Manufacturing by Quad Graphics, Fairfield
Book design by JAM Design
Production manager: Devon Zahn

Library of Congress Cataloging-in-Publication Data

McGirr, Lisa, 1962–
The war on alcohol : prohibition and the rise of the American state / Lisa McGirr.
— First Edition.
pages cm
Includes bibliographical references and index.
ISBN 978-0-393-06695-1 (hardcover)
1. Prohibition—United States. 2. United States—History—20th century. I. Title.
HV5089.M354 2016
363.4'10973—dc23
2015028038

ISBN 978-0-393-35352-5 pbk.

W. W. Norton & Company, Inc.
500 Fifth Avenue, New York, N.Y. 10110
www.wwnorton.com

W. W. Norton & Company Ltd.
15 Carlisle Street, London W1D 3BS

2 3 4 5 6 7 8 9 0

FOR SVEN

CONTENTS

LIST OF ILLUSTRATIONS

PREFACE

WHEN FRANKLIN D. ROOSEVELT TOOK OFFICE ON MARCH 4,
1933, with the global economy on the brink of collapse, he called Congress into special session. The new president inaugurated the New
Deal's activist one hundred days by urging quick passage of the Emergency Banking Act to rescue the financial system and the Economy Act
to cut salaries of government employees and veteran's benefits. On his
eighth day in office, Roosevelt forwarded his third major policy initiative, after proclaiming to a small group of advisors, "It's time the country did something about beer." That very night he drafted his plea to
Congress for its legalization, declaring "action at this time to be of the
highest importance."[1]

When the clerk read Roosevelt's statement on the floor of Congress,
cheers rang out. Less than thirty hours later, the "beer bill" sailed
through the House. The commodity banned for close to fourteen years
was relegalized on April 6. At the nadir of the nation's economic catastrophe, beer took its place in the vanguard of New Deal measures. That
night a festooned truck escorted by a police detail pulled up to the

White House, delivering two crates of the city's new brew: "President Roosevelt, the first real beer is yours," announced a large banner. Crowds braved the rain and the midnight hour to cheer at the White House gates. The years of national alcohol Prohibition were laid to rest. Eight months later, the Twenty-First Amendment rescinded the Eighteenth Amendment, bringing to an end the boldest effort to remake private behavior in the nation's history.[2]

Around the country, the celebratory mood that welcomed the end of the war on alcohol was chastened by the daunting task of recovery and the massive crisis of unemployment. In the following two years, Roosevelt and Congress unleashed the largest burst of policy innovation the federal government has ever seen. The once preoccupying war on alcohol came to appear as but a footnote to the main drama of the New Deal and the regulatory state it spawned. Roosevelt's popular beer bill is ignored in most historical accounts of the New Deal's opening days. So too are the contributions of the war on alcohol to the development of the American state and to politics in twentieth-century America.[3]

On one level, this is not surprising. The Eighteenth Amendment was, after all, one of the nation's most significant policy debacles: after less than fifteen years it became the first, and it remains the only, constitutional amendment to be rescinded. The admission by one former antiliquor crusader that Prohibition was "stupidly wrong" and had led to an "utter disregard for law" epitomized a widely accepted verdict by the time of repeal. Such a devastating pratfall, however, distracted contemporaries and later chroniclers from the significant but largely unacknowledged mark left on America's still-developing state by this social experiment. This book restores national Prohibition to its critical role in the building of the modern American state.[4]

For the most part, Great Depression contemporaries let Prohibition simply drop from public consciousness. A few, however, did plumb its failure for deeper lessons. In 1934, the radical artist Ben Shahn, while employed by the Public Works of Art Project, an early New Deal ini-

tiative, painted eight works on national Prohibition for a mural project
to be displayed in New York's Central Park. Each painting rendered a
different dimension of the "noble experiment," from federal enforcement, illicit bootlegging, and gangland killings to the religious reformers at the core of the campaign. When officials rejected Shahn's sketches,
they provided no reason for their decision; perhaps they considered the
witty, biting commentary on the recently failed government effort
backward looking compared to the muscular optimism of mainstream
New Deal art. Federal arts workers, including Shahn himself in his
larger body of work, honed in on the dignity of the common man and
championed a more heroic vision of the government as his supporter
and friend. Shahn's series on the government's great disciplinary experiment held different, potent lessons on the self-aggrandizing dynamics
of the penal state and antinarcotics activity.[5]

The generation of historians writing soon after the New Deal and
World War II did not entirely ignore Prohibition but they overwhelmingly emphasized its failings. The majority shared liberal New Deal
reform sensibilities, and they drew a sharp separation between the New
Deal and the war on alcohol that preceded it. They found the origins
of the New Deal coalition not in debates between wets and drys but in
the material dislocations of the Great Depression. They linked New
Deal policy makers to earlier economic regulatory efforts from the
income tax to the Federal Trade Commission, not to the institutional
rigors of running a massive expansion of the federal enforcement establishment. The influential historian Richard Hofstadter wrote—in a
post–World War II dismissal that became gospel—that the Eighteenth
Amendment was "a farce," a vestigial remnant of the World War I
reform "debauch" and its crusading "village" cast of mind. He relegated it to "a symbol of the moral overstrain of the preceding era, the
butt of jokes, a perennial source of irritation, a memento of the strange
power of crusades of absolute morality to intensify the evils they hope
to destroy." Such "preposterous restrictions" were, Hofstadter implied,
completely ineffectual. Historians writing after Hofstadter mostly fol-

lowed this viewpoint, concluding, as one account did, "there was never any serious effort to enforce national Prohibition until the early thirties, and by that time it was too late."[6]

A later generation of historians broke with Hofstadter's dismissal of the Progressive reform impulse behind the Eighteenth Amendment, but they continued to marginalize it in other ways. Convinced that the amendment was essentially dead on arrival, most scholars have focused on the struggle to pass such an impractical project, neglecting as predetermined its flawed implementation and eventual failure. Some scholars even interpreted Prohibition as a "symbolic crusade" whose real aim was to affirm the cultural dominance of Yankee Protestantism. Even those few historians who focused on the Prohibition years devoted most of their attention to the repeal effort among influential elites or the farcical attempts to enforce Prohibition in wet jurisdictions.[7]

Filling the vacuum, there developed an entire genre of sensationalist books and movies set in the Prohibition years. They featured a colorful cast of bootleggers and gangsters, from Chicago's Al Capone to Ohio's George Remus. In these narratives, bootleg liquor flows freely, cultural rebellion flowers in the back rooms of speakeasies, and criminal entrepreneurs make and lose fabulous fortunes and sometimes their lives. These fragmentary portraits of the Prohibition years have had an outsized impact on both popular and scholarly understandings of the "roaring" twenties, or the Jazz Age. Taken together, they have obscured one of America's greatest experiments in state building and its lasting institutional and ideological effects. The selective focus of these chronicles on elite groups and the national level, moreover, buries the highly differential impact of the law on distinct social groups, many of whom face parallel challenges to this day.[8]

·   ·   ·

THIS book tells a more consequential story—one closely attuned to the ways in which social class, ethnicity, race, gender, and religiosity powerfully shaped not just the passage of the Eighteenth Amendment but also its more than decade-long unfolding across the nation. *The War on Alcohol* charts the battles waged over Prohibition between different social groups from its unfolding to its demise. The seemingly uniform impact of the national law actually took on a very different cast in distinct settings, from metropoles like Chicago and New York to small towns and cities such as Herrin, Illinois, and Richmond, Virginia. In these varied settings the Prohibition drama features a new cast of characters—policy entrepreneurs and religious reformers, local and state enforcement agents, immigrant workers, ethnic politicians, and struggling rural whites and African-Americans. Through these ordinary Americans we see the effects of Prohibition on everyday experience. This approach also recasts our understanding of broader historical developments, including the political awakening of the religious right, the electoral realignment that launched the New Deal, and the emergence of the twentieth-century federal penal state. As the story unfolds, it will become clear that the war on alcohol was no mere distraction with few lasting consequences: Prohibition remade national party politics and imprinted the path of American state development into distinctive and permanent molds.

The war on alcohol was a prime example of a recurring theme of United States mass politics. The nation's powerful traditions of evangelical Protestantism and its freewheeling brand of expansive capitalism emerged in tandem—and in tension with one another. This combination of forces periodically fueled moral crusades among men and women unsettled by social conflict and change. These reformers turned to the state to stabilize the social order, and secure their place within it, with strong doses of coercive moral absolutes. Their monumental anxieties over industrial capitalism, mass immigration, and the increasingly large and potentially volatile proletarian populations congealed around the campaign against the saloon and the liquor traffic. The nation's first "narcotics" war focused these myriad grievances on the liquor trade and the social ills it purportedly engendered.

Imbued with resonant themes of Protestant evangelicalism, the one-hundred-year-old temperance movement found its white knight in the growing power of the nation-state during the Progressive Era and World War I. Antiliquor crusaders turned toward the radical solution of a national ban by the federal government in the early twentieth century, and rode a wave of institution building, regulatory reforms, and constitutional activism to power. Without the potent elixir of moral panic from the Prohibition army, Progressive reformers might have adopted significantly more moderate and gradualist forms of liquor control as a cure for the "saloon problem." But many urban Progressives, scientific experts, social workers, and settlement-house workers, including luminaries such as Jane Addams, instead embraced the momentum and vigor of the crusaders' more absolutist approach. After the outbreak of World War I in Europe, the clamor for efficiency, ending waste, and war preparedness made the radical reform unstoppable. Its parentage of moral crusaders and efficiency-minded Progressive reformers built their successful coalition in a united fight against public working-class drink in the saloon. That early logic set the stage for the type of enforcement that followed.

The enforcement of Prohibition was notable for its magnitude and its selectivity. Not surprisingly for a movement led at its core by the well-heeled Protestant Anti-Saloon League, enforcement hit working-class, urban immigrant, and poor communities hardest. It was, after all, enacted to discipline their leisure in the first place. *The War on Alcohol* charts the repercussions of selective enforcement in two distinct geographical regions. It first examines the reshaped landscape of drink in Chicago, among the city's heavily ethnic working-class population. Here we see how and why the enforcement of Prohibition proved a powerful grievance for men and women already hostile to the law itself. The closure of saloons, the violence of organized crime, costly and sometimes poisoned bootleg liquor, and the law's identification as an attack on immigrant culture provided these men and women a stronger shared identity across their distinctive groups. The sporadic early opposition took on a more consequential cast when ethnic political brokers leveraged the cause of Prohibition opposition to awaken in their voting base a new national political consciousness.

Selective enforcement had different but just as significant repercussions for poor communities elsewhere. Exploring the thicket of enforcement in Virginia, *The War on Alcohol* reveals the harsh and frequently deadly realities of enforcement for poor men and women in socially and racially stratified communities in the south. Southern law enforcement officials, like authorities elsewhere, used Prohibition to police communities already identified as prone to "criminality." The vast market that supplied illegal liquor was tawdry, corrupt, and violent—its operation smoothed by the frequently porous boundaries between enforcement officials and suppliers. At the same time, Prohibition law enforcement was anything but a dead letter. In the poor communities that bore its brunt, it contributed to a crisis of overcrowded court dockets and prisons.

By one gross measure, the popular image of Prohibition is correct. The partial enforcement of Prohibition did little to stem the oceans of liquor supplied by the black market to thirsty Americans. In many places, men and women flagrantly violated the law. Among them, a small, affluent group of self-proclaimed avant-garde challenged the constricting norms they associated with Prohibition in a new world of vibrant, experimental, and permissive leisure. *The War on Alcohol* charts the nightlife revolution at its epicenter—New York—and the cultural earthquake that radiated outward to smaller towns and cities through the new media of mass culture. Much to the dismay of its advocates, Prohibition, as we will see, proved a cultural accelerant to the more permissive norms of a newly emergent corporate middle class.

Faced with flagrant violations, permissive sexual norms, and interracial mixing—hallmarks of the experimental world of nightlife leisure—Prohibition's foot soldiers did not signal retreat. Instead they counterattacked under a new banner of law and order. Already anxious over Catholicism, immigration, religious modernism, labor strife,

shifting gender norms, and African-American militancy in the aftermath of World War I, a multipronged army of citizen enforcers
launched the first incarnation of the twentieth-century religious right.
These citizen enforcers, including the large temperance organizations
and the Ku Klux Klan, utilized the Eighteenth Amendment, the Volstead Act—the law passed to enforce Prohibition—and its state equivalents to wage a broad assault on the "enemies" of white Protestant
nationalism.

The Eighteenth Amendment and the Volstead Act in fact enabled
the Klan's rise to power. In southern Illinois we see an example of how
the Klan won droves of recruits battling bootlegging and "lawlessness,"
using violence and intimidation to wage war against threats to 100 percent Americanism. This example was mirrored elsewhere on smaller
scales. Klan vigilantism, in turn, provoked controversy and countermobilization, even among former allies in the war on alcohol. The
Klan's meteoric growth then ended in equally rapid decline. Faced
with the unintended consequences of Prohibition, many men and
women began to rethink their commitments to the war on alcohol, but
they did not altogether reject the state's right to police and punish the
use of other recreational narcotics.[9]

The rise and power of the Klan was only the most egregious of the
many affronts that Prohibition posed to urban immigrant, and heavily
Catholic, working-class men and women. These grievances sharpened
their politicization, forging them into a potent political bloc. When a
candidate from the "sidewalks of New York"—Al Smith—hoisted the
banner of Prohibition repeal in 1928, they coalesced around the national
Democratic Party as never before. By charting the grassroots political
mobilization of these men and women in urban industrial communities
from Chicago to Pittsburgh, we will see that opposition to the war on
alcohol laid the foundation for the ethnic urban working-class base that
Franklin D. Roosevelt rode to the White House.

Lawlessness, corruption, violence, and cultural rebellion eroded
support for Prohibition, and the Great Depression sealed its fate. Alco-

hol reemerged by 1933 with a diminished but no longer seriously contested place in American recreational culture. Repeal struck the law
from the books, but its effects on the nation-state proved indelible.
Scholars of twentieth-century American political development have
long mapped the sources and tributaries of the young nation's social
welfare state. Typically they move from the enactment of pensions for
Civil War veterans and mothers to Progressive Era regulatory reforms
and finally the New Deal years, leapfrogging over the 1920s, the decade
of national Prohibition, as a period of retrenchment and laissez-faire. In
doing so, they miss the contribution of the war on alcohol to the character of the twentieth-century American state—a state that has been
interventionist yet weak, heavy on coercion yet light on social welfare.
Prohibition and the wave of crime and violence it unleashed forged the
foundations of a less examined side of twentieth-century state building:
the federal penal state.[10]

Even with its vast corruption, inefficacy, and insufficient funding,
Prohibition marked the birth of a qualitatively new and enduring role
of the federal state in crime control. The massive, flagrant violations of
the law in response to the war on alcohol engendered a new public
panic over crime. For the first time, crime became a national problem,
and a national obsession. The effort to restore law and order resulted in
streamlined federal criminal record keeping, professionalized prison
administration, new prison growth, and expanded and muscular federal policing, including stronger authority and a broadened purview for
the FBI.

Herbert Hoover, whose lifetime of vigorous state building was hidden behind a reputation as an American "individualist," bolstered the
federal penal state. Hoover's approach to the wars on alcohol, crime,
and narcotics was consistent with this Quaker engineer's neoliberal
sensibility, a political philosophy that would return once more with
vigor to Washington in the latter third of the twentieth century.
Hoover favored the use of expansive state power, but for conservative
purposes. Just as early New Deal economic initiatives built on Hoover's

ideas, so too did Roosevelt embrace and extend Hoover's war on crime. Indeed, far less ambivalent about expansive federal powers, the Roosevelt administration pushed them to another level, bolstering the power and visibility of J. Edgar Hoover's fledgling FBI. Long overlooked, these continuities between the New Deal and the Hoover administration comprise some of the most durable achievements of both administrations.[11]

Despite its baleful enforcement, Prohibition and the escalating crime it sparked permanently convinced Americans to look to the federal government for solutions to new national problems. The government did not retreat from its new role in crime control after the end of the war on alcohol. Its punitive approach to recreational narcotics persisted and expanded in new directions, building on the lessons learned from federal alcohol Prohibition. The nation's nascent domestic and international drug-prohibition regime emerged symbiotically with national alcohol Prohibition. It drew upon the logic, the core moral entrepreneurs, and the beachheads of bureaucratic influence won during the antialcohol campaign. As broad support for the war on alcohol waned and then collapsed, key antiliquor crusaders turned their energies toward the less controversial war against recreational narcotic drugs. With a second twentieth-century drug war contributing to a new crisis of overcrowded prisons and uncounted social costs, there is no better time to revisit the history of national alcohol Prohibition.

THE WAR ON
ALCOHOL

1

THE MAKING OF
A RADICAL REFORM

ON DECEMBER 10, 1913, ANTILIQUOR CRUSADERS FROM EVERY
state of the union gathered in downtown Washington. The nation's
powerful temperance organizations had united in a "great Joint Committee" to demand federal action to outlaw the nation's liquor traffic.
Organized in two phalanxes, they marched to the Capitol in military
style: Brigadier General Aaron S. Daggett, a veteran of both the Civil
War and the Spanish-American war, headed up the Anti-Saloon League
Committee of 1,000. A young boy bearing an American flag and flanked
by fifty girls in prim white dresses led the Woman's Christian Temperance Union. The president of the Anti-Saloon League rallied the
marchers when they arrived at the seat of Congress and championed
their "radical" purpose. "The time has come," he blazed, for the federal
government to banish the "worst enemy of civilization"—alcohol—
from shore to shore. Georgia's WCTU temperance "cyclone" Mary
Harris Armor addressed the crusaders as well. Praising the new call for
a constitutional amendment to end the liquor traffic, she boldly predicted that national prohibition would be the law of the land "by 1920."[1]

Alabama congressman Richmond P. Hobson, later nicknamed by some the "father of Prohibition," greeted the men, women, and children gathered on the Capitol steps on that brisk December day. With a military bearing, and so strikingly handsome that he had earned a reputation as a Victorian Don Juan as a young man—"America's Most Kissed Man-Ever" according to one biographer—Hobson lauded the crusaders for their "loftiest motives of patriotism in the service of our country and the interests of humanity." Hobson, an ardent prohibitionist, had authored a resolution in favor of a constitutional ban on liquor that he planned to introduce to Congress. He exhorted the prohibition army to press on in the war on the liquor traffic. For, as he claimed in one of his many addresses, "the principles of war are the same whether it is a war between nations or a war between civilization and its destroying foe, the liquor traffic."[2]

This was no mere rhetorical flourish. Hobson's military experience molded his approach toward the nation's war on alcohol. A steadfast champion of United States naval power and imperial ambitions in Asia, Admiral Hobson had served during the Spanish-American War in 1898. He returned home a war hero for his part in a risky but ill-fated mission to scuttle the U.S. collier *Merrimac* to blockade Cuba's Santiago Harbor. The jingoist press transformed the failed venture into the stuff of myth, a celebration of American daring and ingenuity, and Hobson became a wartime celebrity. He later served in the Philippines, where the opium trade flourished. The effort to suppress this commerce became one means by which the United States sought to exert new muscle in the region. The United States banned opium from its new possession in 1905. Hobson emerged from these experiences a strong advocate of national power, imperial expansion, and international—as well as domestic—narcotics control.[3]

The former naval commander turned politician identified intoxicating liquor too, in line with contemporary "scientific" temperance knowledge, as a "narcotic"— a "life destroyer" toxic to mind and soul. After a career in military service, he instinctively sought to bring fed-

eral power to bear on this domestic traffic just as United States diplomats, missionaries, and military commanders were beginning to do in
the global drug trade. The resolution he introduced to Congress for the
Eighteenth Amendment declared in no uncertain terms, "[A]lcohol is a
narcotic poison destructive and degenerating to the human organ-
ism . . . that lowers to an appalling degree the average standard . . . of
our citizenship . . . threatening . . . the very life of the nation."[4]

Richmond Hobson exemplified a new component and, arguably,
the critical ingredient of the decades-old prohibition effort: a distinctly
modern fusion of twentieth-century nation-state building with an
older strand of Protestant moral righteousness. The increased exertion
of national power, Hobson believed, required a strong and efficient
citizenry. This new logic, with its secular twist, widened alcohol prohibition's resonance and linked it to new cross-border—state and
national—narcotic drug control efforts. For a half century, prohibition
sentiment had drawn strength from powerful currents in evangelical
circles that viewed intoxicating liquor as a moral evil. Hobson, who
grew up in the cotton empire of Magnolia Grove, Alabama, had been
steeped in strict temperance ideals since boyhood. But now, as an advocate of strong national power, he and his allies began to view the struggle and the solution in new terms. A Protestant moral project that
sought to coerce, control, and reshape public and private behavior saw
new hope in muscular action by the federal government. This propitious marriage of state power and moral suasion would yield a dramatic
expansion of federal policing and an increase of state and local policing
in the quasi-military sphere of crime control.[5]

The 1913 campaign for a constitutional amendment was a radical
shift in strategy for the antiliquor crusade. Until then, temperance
mobilization had relied on state prohibition legislation and local-option
campaigns to ban the saloon and the sale of liquor in towns and counties. The men and women gathered in Washington that crisp morning
were veterans of those decades-long efforts. To understand their
embrace of Hobson and his new brand of moralism backed by the fed-

eral government and armed agents, we must delve into the longer history of temperance sentiment and the powerful war on alcohol it wrought.

.   .   .

TEMPERANCE reform in the United States, as in other alcohol-drenched nations in western Europe, gained strength in the nineteenth century. The culture of drink in North America ran long and deep and stretched back to colonial times. Cotton Mather referred to alcohol as "that good creature of God." Since the early years of settlement, drinking had been a customary part of workday and celebration, a vital element of both politics and private life. Indeed, throughout the American colonies—as in England—at a time when water was often impure, brackish, and dangerous to health, whiskey and other intoxicating liquors formed a staple of daily diet and nourishment."[6]

The patterns of preindustrial life, with breaks for a grog of whiskey interrupting the workday, were less at home in the increasingly market-driven world. Sobriety seemed to facilitate success in the antebellum market revolution. The movement gained traction in the 1830s and 1840s when the rising middle class adopted temperance norms as part of an ethos of self-discipline and upward mobility. The fledgling nation, temperance advocates warned, was drowning in hard liquor: annual consumption of distilled liquor surpassed five gallons per capita in 1830, an all-time national historic high. Tellingly, in 1829 the army dared not bar the recruitment or enlistment of "habitual drunkards," since the secretary of war estimated that three-quarters of the nation's laborers drank at least four ounces of distilled whiskey daily. Such drinking led the Delaware Moral Society to warn that the new nation was threatened with becoming a "nation of drunkards."[7]

European countries, from England to Germany, competed with these high per capita alcohol consumption rates and a few, such as Sweden, outpaced United States thirst for hard liquor during these years. These places sparked their own powerful temperance movements, but the dynamism of the American antiliquor crusade—and its absolutism—was unmatched in other large Western nations. The character of the temperance movement in the United States owed a debt to the nation's strong currents of evangelical Protestantism. Moral religiosity and Protestant revivalism sank deep roots in the United States—a frenetic world of capitalism and slavery. The nation's dearth of strong mediating institutions to mitigate the power of capital provided a propitious climate for entrepreneurial Protestant evangelical ministers. In this environment, staunch moral rule and strict religiosity became a means of shoring up social order and providing a firm world of felt attachments. Emotive, revivalist religiosity filled in meaning and provided a sense of order in a world lacking the established social fabrics, rootedness, and public life that structured communities in many parts of the world.[8]

The contest over drink, driven by powerful currents of evangelical Protestant perfectionism in the United States from the beginning, was more absolutist in its orientation than in most other Western countries. Temperance advocates favored total abstinence, not simply moderation. For crusading evangelical preachers, and a decidedly less pious faction of employers of growing numbers of wageworkers, any alcoholic imbibing at all constituted a social evil. Committed to redeeming souls and creating a more perfect world, the preachers and their acolytes linked liquor to temptation and sin: just one drop would lead down the path of dependency, "slavery," and destruction. A pledge to abstinence smoothed the path toward salvation. Timothy Shay Arthur's 1854 novel, and later a popular play, *Ten Nights in a Bar-Room and What I Saw There*, popularized these sentiments. In the novel, Joe Morgan, upstanding husband and father, succumbed to the temptations proffered by the profiteering saloonkeeper Silas Slade. Once responsible and hardworking, Morgan wastes his wages on drink, ignoring the desperate pleas of his wife. Debauchery follows. Morgan loses his job and destroys his family. The story ends with Morgan holding the lifeless body of his daughter killed as a result of a barroom fight after she entered the saloon to beg her father to return home. The lesson was obvious: hard work contributed to success and family happiness. Succumbing to the temptation of even one drink, on the other hand, meant certain ruin.[9]

These early temperance advocates centered on *individual* conversion. The Washingtonians, a Baltimore-based artisan society of "reformed drinkers," for example, signed a pledge to abstinence and to a life of redemption. Yet by the mid-nineteenth century, temperance reformers argued that individual conversion alone would prove insufficient to end the problem of the destructive, dangerous, and "evil" alcohol trade. They turned to local and state governments to bring rectitude on a wholesale scale. The first statewide effort was launched in Maine by Portland's energetic and public-oriented manufacturer and mayor, Neal Dow, who proclaimed, "the traffic in drink tends to more degradation and impoverishment of the people than all causes of evil combined." Dow succeeded in getting a state law passed banning "drinking Houses and Tippling Shopes" in 1851. When a band of rowdy working-class men marched to city hall to protest the ban, he ordered out the militia, shots were fired, and the war on alcohol claimed its first victim. A decade-long wave of Prohibition campaigns ensued in northern and eastern states, but all of these experiments were repealed by the time of the Civil War. Prohibition generated powerful opposition, and the controversy over slavery sidelined temperance efforts and eroded support for antiliquor measures. A new tax on alcohol established in 1862, in addition, promised much-needed revenue for the war effort. Even the energetic temperance champion Neal Dow turned his reform activism toward the battle against slavery. He eventually led Maine troops in the war for the Union, reaching the rank of brigadier general.[10]

Despite the leadership of the prohibition movement by men like Neal Dow, the temperance ethos was not solely a middle-class norm. Artisans, craftsmen, and labor leaders from the Baltimore Washingtonians to the Knights of Labor's Terence Powderly embraced temperance as a means of safeguarding independent-labor Republicanism. The whiskey bottle threatened dependency and bondage no less than profiteering employers, they believed. Powderly declared that "no workingman ever drank a glass of rum who did not rob his wife and children of the price of it." The Knights barred liquor dealers from membership. The nineteenth-century temperance movement, then, stretched across a wide swath of reform sentiment and won support from populist reformers and labor champions as well as leading African-Americans who condemned the "profiteering" liquor industry. The lead organizers of the core prohibition army, however, were middle-class Protestant religious men and women—a group who became increasingly oriented not just toward self-discipline and control but to coercive means to dry up the nation.[11]

By the late nineteenth century, these temperance reformers emerged with a new organizational capacity and a new appreciation for state-sponsored social change. The Woman's Christian Temperance Union (WCTU), established in Cleveland, Ohio, in 1874, became the most powerful female reform organization of the late nineteenth and early twentieth century. The "white ribboned" women were involved in multiple reform activities to expand women's influence in the public sphere and safeguard the family against threats brought by untrammeled industrial growth. "Home protection" became the broad, evocative banner under which these middle-class Protestant reformers labored, but their most critical mission was embodied in their name.[12]

Middle-class Protestant women, identifying themselves as guardians of family virtue, saw the abolition of liquor consumption as the linchpin in an effort to protect vulnerable women and children and discipline male, and especially working-class, breadwinners. New armies of male wageworkers labored long hours in the nation's burgeoning cotton mills, machine shops, steel foundries, and coal mines by the end of the nineteenth century. Their wives labored in their households raising children, cooking, doing laundry, and sometimes taking in boarders. They relied on their husbands' wages to make ends meet. Working-class women's budgetary challenges were compounded by spouses' periodic unemployment. Layoffs, economic downturns, and manufacturers' seasonal production cycles made bouts of unemployment common for wage earners. The saloon, well-to-do "friendly visitors" argued, added insecurity to their home lives: poor women had to fear that much-needed cash would land in a saloon. To make matters worse, inebriated husbands returning home threatened domestic violence as well as family destitution. The paternalist Protestant elite women who filled the ranks of the grassroots crusaders drew upon the well of earlier temperance ideas. Their solutions, however, no longer focused on converting individuals to an abstinent life. They sought social means to promote temperance and launched local-option campaigns and eventually statewide prohibition battles to abolish the liquor traffic.[13]

Groups of Protestant clergymen soon joined the dynamic grassroots female reformers in their war against the saloon. Steeped in the traditions of the antebellum teetotaling preachers who identified alcohol imbibing with sin, they organized the Anti-Saloon League in 1893. Backed by the vast resources of the nation's Protestant churches, and most especially the personnel and energies of revivalist Methodist clergymen, the Anti-Saloon League blossomed into a highly organized and well-heeled pressure group. While the WCTU built its strength through vibrant local chapters of female Protestant activists, the Anti-Saloon League gained recruits and financing directly through the nation's Protestant churches and their clergy. The Protestant "church in action," as they proudly declared themselves, worked in politics to reform "public morals." The Methodist church, the largest Protestant denomination, was most closely linked to the league, with many of its bishops serving as key leaders. Baptists and Presbyterians, along with the smaller Disciples of Christ and Christian Scientists, also affiliated. Lutherans and Episcopalians, on the other hand, were largely absent from the ranks of the antiliquor crusaders. The local leagues' pastors, local ministerial associations, and their thousands of congregations in towns and cities throughout the nation gave the Anti-Saloon League a ready-built institutional means of disseminating its message to a wide swath of the Protestant churchgoing public.[14]

In addition to its impressively wide base, the league was efficiently managed, modeling itself after a modern business firm. Protestant clergymen filled the league's key leadership positions and its executive board, but the organization recruited seasoned and politically astute lawyers as well. The best known, by far, was the league's general counsel, bespectacled and balding Wayne Wheeler. Diminutive in physical stature, the power he eventually commanded in Washington more than compensated. Backed by the cudgel of the league's well-organized pressure machine, Wheeler came to wield the influence of an overbearing giant. At no other moment in American history since the church-based civil authority of the Massachusetts Bay Colony in the seventeenth century did the nation's Protestant churches so effectively mobilize to build a "righteous nation" through the instrument of state power.[15]

The Anti-Saloon League built its broad and successful coalition by targeting the "saloon evil" rather than attacking personal alcohol consumption. The enticing saloon, with its swinging doors, foot railing, and long bar, whether the sawdusted and seedy establishments of small western frontier towns or eastern and midwestern urban ethnic "poor men's clubs," catered to an overwhelmingly male working-class clientele prone to boisterous and disorderly behavior. "The all important question," wrote one reformer confidently in 1905, "centers on the saloon. All lovers of sobriety and social order may agree upon this point of view."[16]

Abolishing the saloon, however, meant confronting the "profiteering" spider web of liquor businesses from distilleries and brewers to dealers. Attacking the liquor traffic, in turn, inevitably reached into controlling drink consumption outside the saloon as well. Texas senator Morris Sheppard, who in 1914 introduced the resolution that would become the Eighteenth Amendment to the Senate declaring the manufacture, sale, import, and transportation of intoxicating liquors illegal, sharply distinguished between opposition to personal drink consumption and the abolition of the liquor traffic. Without any apparent sense of contradiction, he backed the constitutional amendment, declaring, "I am not a prohibitionist in the strict sense of the word. . . . I am fighting the liquor traffic. I am against the saloon, I am not in any sense aiming to prevent the personal use of drink."[17]

A powerful animosity toward working-class drinking in the saloon, then, constituted the core unifying principle of the prohibition movement by the early twentieth century. For a swath of the largely Protestant middle class in small towns and industrial cities, the workingman's pub was a concrete space that encapsulated a host of threatening developments. Mass poverty, market disorder, crime, and vast inequalities of wealth accompanied the nation's transformation into an industrial powerhouse. The saloon was an appealing foe for self-identified "respectable" men and women. It provided one easy explanation for those ills without challenging the material underpinning of these men's and women's lives or requiring more far-reaching change to rebalance social and economic power. Excessive drink explained the "large mass of poverty" that so shocked observers of the early twentieth-century United States. As one leading antiliquor crusader put it, "Poverty in a few cases . . . is the result of unavoidable circumstances" but far more "idleness, want of forethought, and worst of all drink" were at its root. By eradicating the saloon and the traffic that sustained it, Prohibitionists could bring civic betterment, ostensibly improve the lives of working-class men and women, and affirm their cultural capital as the arbiters of public good.[18]

Antiliquor crusaders exaggerated the actual harm inflicted by the saloon, by liquor, and by the excessive influence wielded by the alcohol industry. They leapt toward a total ban of the liquor trade, a cure wholly disproportionate to the ills of the saloon and of liquor consumption. The climate of fear evoked to root out the liquor "foe" led many prohibitionists to grant intoxicating liquor, identified as a dangerous "narcotic poison," an almost magical power to do evil. In doing so, they deflected attention from the economic causes of poverty in a rapidly industrializing economy. Hobson's lectures on the Chautauqua circuit, the popular assemblies bringing nationally renowned speakers to small towns, held alcohol alone responsible for "tossing children by the thousands upon the streets and driving them into the factories and mines during the plastic period when it is so vital for themselves and for the nation that they should be receiving an education to prepare them for the higher duties of citizenship." Dethroning "King Alcohol" provided a means to discipline a particularly "corrupt" group of profiteering capitalists and the volatile collective leisure of potentially threatening poor populations, whether European immigrants in cities, native mine workers in the west, or African-Americans in the south. It was the quintessential reform of a white Protestant evangelical and largely Anglo-Saxon middle class who found their traditional mores and powers under assault in the rapidly paced world of unbridled American capitalism.[19]

.   .   .

BETWEEN 1880 and 1920 over twenty million men and women immigrated to the United States, drawn by the voracious appetite of manufacturers large and small for their labor. The largest flows of immigration took place between 1900 and World War I. In 1907 alone, over one million immigrants entered the country, the largest single year of the nation's late nineteenth and early twentieth-century massive wave. Large-scale immigration reached its highpoint in 1910, when 14.9 percent of the population was foreign-born. During the earlier nineteenth century, beginning in the 1840s, immigrants hailed largely from northern European countries such as Germany, Ireland, and Sweden. Chinese immigrants, contracted for work to build the transcontinental railways in the wake of the Civil War, contributed another flow. A successful racist campaign to end "coolie" labor, however, cut off the Asian immigrant stream with the Chinese Exclusion Act in 1882. Supplementing the stream from Germany and Ireland, immigrants in the late nineteenth and early twentieth century increasingly hailed from southern and eastern Europe. Poles, Italians, Greeks, Bohemians, Russians, and Slovakians settled in unprecedented numbers in the nation's cities, seemingly overnight. New York and Chicago, the nation's premier cities, became not only incomprehensibly large but were filled with distinctly foreign sights, smells, and dialects. In 1910, 41 percent of the close to five million inhabitants of New York City were foreign-born. In Chicago, in 1920, two-thirds of the population were either foreign-born or the children of foreign-born parents.[20]

The large population of immigrant laborers and their children settled in dense ethnic enclaves in East Coast and midwestern cities. A thick web of Catholic parishes, Jewish ethnic institutions and synagogues, Bohemian welfare organizations, and Italian social clubs transformed the built landscape. For many of these European immigrant communities, alcoholic drink was part of community life, family celebration, religious ritual, and relaxation. Diverse establishments—ranging from Boston's "Birds-in-Hand" and Milwaukee's socialist-oriented Doerfler's Saloon to Chicago's Workingmen's Exchange—were just a few of the sites of working-class drinking. The number of saloons, broadly defined, tripled in the last third of the nineteenth century.[21]

The growth of saloons spiked beer consumption. Hard-liquor consumption declined sharply throughout the nineteenth century. It halved from 1830 to 1910, from over 5 gallons per capita annually to 2.3 gallons. With that decline many of the objective debilitating effects of excessive alcohol use eased. Beer consumption, however, rose from 2.3 gallons per capita annually in 1840 to 25.9 gallons in 1910, a rise of over 1,000 percent. Alcohol consumed per capita in the United States in the early twentieth century was in line with rates in industrializing Europe. Indeed, the amount of beer consumed lagged behind the heavy consumption rates of Germany and Britain. The exponential rise in beer consumption nonetheless was a visible, noisy, and for many Americans alarming harbinger of the immigrant makeover of American cities. The working-class drinking establishments became a lightning rod for cultural and class anxieties. The men who patronized these establishments, after all, were not only working-class, they were also largely foreign and heavily Catholic. Immigrant laborers, thus, not only altered the nation's class composition but its religious and ethnic identity as well. Ethnic and religious divisions closely paralleled class cleavages in the United States. As a result, a potent alchemy of ethnic, religious, and class tensions fused in the battle over the saloon.[22]

Antiliquor crusaders attacked saloons in the nation's small towns of the west and industrial cities of the east as "cankerous sores" and a "social menace," a "foe of the wage-earner," and a contributing factor to the "bleak conditions of urban tenements." Undisciplined sexuality in the all-male saloon also raised the risk of social disease. "Respectable" women, either by proscription or custom, did not patronize saloons. Some saloons, however, had side entrances for women and private booths in back rooms, and were sites of sex trafficking. New York's Committee of Fourteen, established in 1905, worked to eradicate saloon-linked prostitution. Saloons and liquor sales, vice fighters argued, were deeply implicated in that trade. In 1912 Progressive luminary Jane Addams publicized one scientist's finding that alcohol was the "indispensable vehicle" of the "white slave traffic." Ella Boole of the Woman's Christian Temperance Union proclaimed, in turn, "There would not be any social evil," a euphemism for prostitution, "if there was no saloon evil."[23]

For politically astute reformers, the drive to rein in the saloon was also linked to the saloons' and urban proletarians' role in politics. Ethnic working-class saloons were often informal political institutions, serving as the lowest rung and neighborhood hub of the local urban political party machinery. The saloonkeepers tended to be active in the local Democratic and Republican parties—and in industrial cities where socialism gained traction saloonkeepers were active in the Socialist Party as well. In Milwaukee's vibrant center of "sewer socialism"—so named for its pragmatic brand of left politics focused on providing sewers, paved streets, and parks in working-class neighborhoods—saloons served as important havens for the party. Victor Berger, who served as an alderman in 1910 and who one year later was elected as a Socialist to Congress, dominated the lively discussions at John Doerfler's establishment, where the local Socialist organization held its regular meetings. One former Milwaukee Socialist saloon owner later recalled that his place, for all intents and purposes, was an "educational institution."[24]

It was, however, in cities with large Democratic and Republican machines that saloons served most importantly as the storefront for local partisan politics. There, ethnic ward bosses and party precinct captains kept in close personal touch with their constituents, providing much-needed services such as jobs, a rent payment, or a Thanksgiving basket in exchange for constituent loyalty on election day. In a world of anemic public provisioning, powerful municipal political machines, characterized by widespread corruption, solidified their working-class voting bases through these clientelist practices. Clientelism, the exchange of services for votes, characterized party politics in societies structured by deeply asymmetric power relations and vast income inequality, among them the United States and parts of Europe and Latin America. Antisaloon sentiment became a focal point of reformers who sought to rid cities of corrupt and "inefficient" political machines.[25]

The goal of "cleaning up" proletarian-based clientelist machines contributed to Progressive support for the saloon's eradication. Historians of the United States have labeled the late nineteenth and early twentieth century the "Progressive Era," after the energetic group of Protestant and largely elite men and women, self-identified as Progressives, and the reform wave they launched. These policy-oriented men and women were a diverse bunch. They included businessmen, social scientists, reform ministers, settlement-house workers, and labor advocates who sought to grapple with the problems wrought by urban industrialization. They worked to improve health, hygiene, and urban sanitation, to beautify their cities, and to provide social centers for immigrants. One central concern of these reformers was ending the municipal power of urban political machines. Meshed in networks of graft, kickbacks, and patronage, and providing routes for upward mobility for ethnic political brokers, this form of politics offended reformers' sense of the civic public good.[26]

The eradication of saloons, then, was also a political question. For some Progressives, this effort was imbued with a deeply antidemocratic impulse: Frances Willard, founder of the WCTU, made the linkage explicit as early as 1890: "Alien illiterates rule our cities today; the saloon is their palace; the toddy stick their scepter." Close to a quarter century later, congressman Richmond Hobson deployed these arguments in favor of constitutional prohibition: "It is the degenerate vote that has in the past overwhelmed the liberties of free people. And it is the degenerate vote in our big cities that is a menace to our institutions."[27]

If the local political practices of those northeastern and midwestern working-class men who held the vote (many of the newest immigrants did not) and saloons as spaces for politics drove support for the war on alcohol in the north, a related but distinctive set of concerns inspired the antiliquor crusade in the south. Below the Mason-Dixon line, prohibitionist crusaders also attacked the saloons of "illiterate whites," but their sharpest animus centered on "negro dives." The specter of the collective gatherings of African-Americans, many recently disfranchised, in "colored only" saloons, beyond the eye of white surveillance, haunted white Southerners. Anywhere such saloons thrived, Prohibitionists warned, they posed a "deadly menace," threatening the safety of women, of children, and of the home. Dance halls and "colored only" saloons, declared one Georgia reformer, were "veritable centers of vice, schools of iniquity, and hot-beds of crime." Another Georgia commentator, in what became a common refrain across the south, averred that "the saloon was the ravager of the negro people. It plundered them at all points, robbed them of their wages," and "fed their animalism."[28]

In the aftermath of African-American disfranchisement in the late nineteenth and early twentieth century, the contest for tight control over politically dispossessed populations heightened the drive for pro-hibition. Atlanta Baptist minister and antiliquor crusader John E. White in 1908 referred to the "feeling of insecurity" in the rural sections of the south that had become a "contagion" because of roaming "drunken negroes." A host of selectively applied laws and ordinances for petty violations, from loitering to vagrancy, already policed and criminalized African-American leisure and coerced their labor. A wave of novel and unevenly enforced dry laws in the south layered on top of these ordi-nances served as an additional means to target and discipline African-American as well as poor white leisure. The "dives" of "illiterate whites," claimed southern reformers, threatened at any time to light the tinderbox of racial and class animosities into violent "racial disor-ders." Race riots, racial pogroms, and lynch terror were an endemic feature in this system of racial domination. By scapegoating the saloon, white southern reformers explained such violence as an aberrant char-acteristic that might be controlled through saloon eradication. "Race war," White warned, "is a perilous possibility" in "any Southern com-munity with a barroom."[29]

Along with concerns over the destabilizing effects of intoxicating liquor on the South's less civilized "dangerous" classes, a parallel alarm over the use of other narcotic substances snowballed at the same time. In southern states such as Tennessee and Georgia, state policing author-ities between 1900 and 1914 warned of African-Americans "crazed by cocaine" who went on superhuman rampages of violence. "Many of the horrible crimes committed in Southern States by colored people can be traced directly to the cocaine habit," charged Colonel J. W. Watson of Georgia in 1903. Such fantastical claims, including the rumor that the effects of cocaine shielded the user against gunshot wounds, fueled the adoption of state antinarcotics legislation and buttressed southern support for the first inclusive federal antidrug law in 1914.[30]

During these same decades, scientific discourse increasingly identi-fied alcohol as a dangerous narcotic drug. At the 1909 meeting of the American Society for the Study of Alcohol and Other Narcotics, one researcher, Winfield S. Hall, professor of physiology at Northwestern University, concluded, "Alcohol is a narcotic in its drug action." Another participant suggested that alcohol be classed "in the list of dangerous drugs along with morphine, cocaine and chloral." Scientific experts emphasized its damaging "poisonous" physiological effects and its addictive qualities. Such testimonies clothed older moral antiliquor arguments with new authority, enabling them to gain wider traction. The American Society for the Study of Alcohol and Other Narcotic Drugs, the Boston-based Scientific Temperance Federation founded in 1906, the *Scientific Temperance Quarterly*, and the American Medical Association took pains to debunk conventional medical homilies that emphasized alcohol as a valuable remedy that could nourish and exert special effects on the nervous system. Antiliquor crusaders popularized and widely exaggerated these findings: the "protoplasmic poison," warned Richmond Hobson, "even in the smallest quantities," lessened the activity of the brain. It acted most strongly on the "most recently acquired facilities" to "annihilate those qualities built up through education and experience, the power of self-control and the sense of responsibility." The new scientific "facts," many of them presented to Congress, bolstered support for the war on alcohol.[31]

Antiliquor crusaders worked to educate the public about the dangers of alcohol through posters, pamphlets, graphs, and charts. Mary Hunt, director of Scientific Temperance Instruction, ensured that the nation's school textbooks by the early twentieth century disseminated to the nation's children the message of the dangers of the "seductive poison," warning that even the most moderate amounts led to ruin. Such campaigns now spread among wider circles of reformers. Elizabeth Tilton, head of the Boston Associated Charities, warned of the dangers of alcohol through a poster campaign begun out of her home in 1912. Not content with dry scientific journals, the campaign borrowed tools from the new profession of advertising to counter the success of liquor advertising in poor neighborhoods. The drink custom, the posters warned, was a bane to the requirements of a modern, ordered world—a menace to health and the enemy of efficiency. "Liquor stands for waste," proclaimed one poster. Success in a modern, mechanical age required "self-discipline, self-control, and respectability," another announced. These secular messages no longer centered on the century-old concerns over "sin." Instead, they adopted a modern, forward-looking ethos.[32]

Along with these concerns over alcohol's negative effects on health and efficiency, antiliquor crusaders drove home its social costs. Alcohol, they insisted, was responsible for "a good portion of insanity," a "large part of all crime," a "considerable part of pauperism," and "most of child misery." Worst of all, it was "a staggering economic burden." Elizabeth Tilton, speaking before the National Conference of Charities and Corrections, drove this "fact" home with frightening statistics: alcohol was "directly and indirectly responsible for 42 percent of broken homes, 45 percent of children cruelly deserted, 50 percent of crime, 25 percent of our poverty, not to mention feeble mindedness and insanity."[33]

Bold and frightening posters, graphs, charts, and pamphlets distributed by prohibition forces linked alcohol, above all, to the bête noire of all progress-loving moderns: "degeneracy." Late nineteenth-century popularizations of Darwin's theories of evolution emphasized the application of natural selection to society. "Each generation must be an improvement over the previous generation if the nation is going to comply with the law of evolution," cautioned Richmond Hobson. As the United States lurched onto the global imperial stage, anxieties over threats to the survival of the white race by the world's "colored" populations permeated social purity campaigns, social hygiene, eugenics, and the war against alcohol. "Alcohol," one scientist warned, "leads to race suicide." Another antiliquor crusader decried the perilous "wave of degeneracy . . . sweeping the land . . . so appalling in magnitude that it staggers the mind and threatens to destroy this republic." Abolishing the saloon was essential to combating that threat. Should they fail in this "mission," warned E. W. Davis, the superintendent of the Chicago district of the Illinois Anti-Saloon League, "Anglo-Saxon civilization would ultimately disappear."[34]

. . . .

THESE ideas animated the nation's war against alcohol. By 1910, as these fears gained traction, approximately 50 percent of the population had fallen under some form of liquor-prohibition legislation. Many regions had become dry through local and county ordinance. Additionally, in twelve states of the south and west, antiliquor crusaders succeeded in passing state laws by 1914. These laws were diverse: North Carolina's 1909 law allowed the sale of hard cider and limited quantities of imported liquor. Georgia's 1907 law allowed citizens to import liquor from outside the state, sparking a booming mail-order service. In general, these laws sought to reduce and control liquor consumption—particularly among socially identified "problem" populations—but not to fully suppress it. Not surprisingly, such piecemeal efforts failed to dent overall consumption rates. Even "bone-dry" states could do little to stop transportation of intoxicating liquor from neighboring wet states into their territories. To make matters worse, the geographic territory conquered by prohibitionists left large cities untouched. As Charles Stelze, a staunch advocate for a nationwide ban, argued after a full twenty-eight states had banned liquor by 1918, "We must not be deceived by 'dry territory' maps which seem to indicate that the fight is almost finished. . . . We're after men, and most of those live in unconquered territories, in cities which do not cover much land area."[35]

In the face of such unsatisfying triumphs, the leaders of prohibition campaigns came to a growing consensus: constitutional prohibition at the federal level was the only real solution. Anti-Saloon League leader Ernest Cherrington announced this bold new plan in 1913. With a series of statistics outlining shifting demographics, he illustrated the dire threat posed by populous urban centers to the mission of drying up the nation. Rural areas enjoyed better representation in Congress and in state legislatures than more populous and drink-soaked urban cen-

ters. Under demographic and political assault, with the threat of reap-
portionment looming in 1920, the federal strategy was a radical and
ambitious means of imposing alcohol prohibition on populations that
would not seek it for themselves. The political landscape would never
again be as propitious. A constitutional amendment also seemed to
promise safety in a more urban, wet political future. Once it passed,
thirty-six states would have to sign off on repeal.[36]

The adoption of a federal strategy to banish the liquor trade was not
only driven by fears of shifting demographics. Progressive reform
focused new attention on the federal government as the proper arena to
resolve problems wrought by industrial capitalism. While many Progressives had focused on reform at the municipal level, others had turned
to their states, calling for factory inspection laws, workman's compensation laws, and minimum wages for women. Still others worked to
establish a federal administrative apparatus to regulate industries—from
finance to railroads—that knit together a growing national economy. In
1906 Congress established the Food and Drug Administration to control patent medicines, regulate pharmaceuticals, and protect consumers
against impure food. That same year, concerns over diseased and rotting
meat led to the passage of the Meat Inspection Act. In 1913 the Federal
Reserve Board reformed the banking system. The Clayton Act tightened antitrust laws. The Federal Trade Commission in 1913 promised
more regulation of the nation's economy. In 1914 Congress expanded
the authority of the Interstate Commerce Commission with the Hep-
burn Act. Finally, also in 1914, the Harrison Narcotics Act established
the first broad federal antidrug legislation. This antinarcotics bill was
fueled by a fusion of regional moral panics and the State Department's
campaign for domestic legislation to bolster the government's nascent
efforts to build an international narcotics control regime.[37]

The time, in short, seemed ripe for a federal strategy to combat the
liquor "scourge." The league's savvy legislative strategist, Wayne
Wheeler, justified the drive for a constitutional amendment as part of
this broader reform trend. The resolution, he proclaimed, "is the logical

result of the tendency of the times toward a government under which the people may protect themselves from evil and wrong." Another antiliquor crusader similarly referred to the new regulatory structures for consumer protection in appealing for the Eighteenth Amendment: "The government that wisely counts it its duty to enact and enforce pure food laws to protect its citizens . . . [should] stop the most gigantic poison factory that has ever debauched citizenship." In turning toward a federal remedy, the antiliquor crusaders—too optimistically—believed that the "moment the Federal government with its strong arm destroys the sale, at that moment, the organized liquor business is destroyed."[38]

The Progressive reform era also witnessed a wave of constitutional activism not seen since the Civil War and Reconstruction. After a nearly half-century hiatus, the nation adopted four amendments within the brief period of 1913 to 1919. The Eighteenth Amendment benefited from and formed part of that wave. It was introduced in the wake of state ratification of a federal income tax and the direct election of senators. Indeed, the Prohibition amendment and the income tax, perhaps counterintuitively, shared the same political DNA. Until the establishment of the income tax, federal revenue depended upon regressive consumer taxes and the protective tariff, both disliked in the south. The income tax was intended to build a more equitable system by requiring men of great fortune, associated with the arrogance of wealth and financial power of eastern Wall Street bankers, to pay a fair share of the tax burden. It initially targeted only the uppermost income brackets, leaving untouched the incomes of the vast majority of households. Antiliquor crusaders argued that the passage of such a tax was an important precondition for the success of the war on alcohol. Providing an alternative source of federal revenue would ease dependence on the alcohol tax. The federal government drew its most substantial revenue from the protective tariff, but in 1910 the liquor tax still accounted for a substantial share, close to 30 percent. The chief cry against prohibition, argued the Executive Committee of the Anti-Saloon League, "has been that the government must have the revenue. . . . The adoption of the income tax amendment to the Federal Constitution furnishes an answer to the revenue problem." They could now press forward to achieve their "final step."[39]

Other social movements also sensed the time was ripe for federal strategies. In 1913, suffrage advocates too launched a campaign for a constitutional amendment to win the vote for women. They found support among an overlapping group of policy makers. When women's rights groups faced a hostile group of hecklers abetted by police during a parade in Washington in March 1913, it was Congressman Hobson who opened an investigation into police conduct, winning the accolades of suffrage organizations from around the country. The Prohibition resolution's cosponsor, Texas senator Morris Sheppard, who vied with Hobson for the title of the "father of Prohibition," also advocated women's suffrage and further reform legislation ranging from rural credit programs to antitrust legislation.[40]

The growing support for the antiliquor crusade within the broader reform climate did not go unnoticed by temperance organizations. The American Issue, the newspaper of the Anti-Saloon League, expressed to its readers both "surprise" and gratitude "at the favorable attitude of a large proportion of the newspapers commenting on the call for the Eighteenth amendment. . . . scores of them frankly and openly express themselves in favor of the Prohibition amendment." The Portland (Oregon) Telegram in 1913, too, noted a seismic shift: "A few years ago it was not considered quite respectable to favor the Prohibition cause. . . . In light of present day opinion, the public judgment then is almost incomprehensible. . . ." The Nashville Banner echoed those sentiments: "The world is fast awakening to the fact that the large consumption of alcoholic drinks is . . . a producer of disease, crime and poverty. . . . It is not, therefore, the religious sentiment that decries drunkenness as a sin that alone fights the sale of alcohol, both common sense and science now make war on it."[41]

New consciousness spread not just through the Anti-Saloon League's vast publishing house in Westerville, Ohio, but also through reform journals such as *McClure's*. In such venues, muckrakers, from Upton Sinclair to George Kibbe Turner, exposed the abominable conditions in unregulated industries such as meat-packing plants. They also condemned the liquor industry. Turner attacked breweries in saloon-saturated Chicago for contributing to "city savagery." He linked those saloons to the "new colonies of foreigners" and condemned brewers for plying "a population of hundreds of thousands of rough and unrestrained male laborers . . . with alcoholic liquor." With the "certainty of a chemical experiment," he warned, it would lead to "violent and fatal crime." Brewers, in their hunger for profits, were "rott[ing]" these men and their children. Progressives such as Jane Addams and Irving Fisher, Yale University professor and father of modern mathematics, also lent support for the cause. *The Survey* magazine reflected the favorable support for the radical reform among some Progressives. The reform journal carried a series of articles both for and against the Eighteenth Amendment. Robert Woods, leader of Boston's South End Settlement House, declared in favor. It was, he proclaimed, a "leading social issue."[42]

Progressive reformers, who viewed the state as an appropriate tool to rectify social and economic injustice, proved more sympathetic to a national solution to the liquor traffic than did many conservative men and women. Even conservatives with strong antiliquor sentiments proved far less willing to resort to federal power. Harvard University president Charles Eliot, asked by Richmond Hobson to lend support to the cause, refused: "I believe that alcoholism threatens the destruction of the white race . . . because it promotes disease and degeneracy . . . and should be resisted and reduced . . . by every available agency. . . . I am not yet convinced that prohibitory legislation is an available agency." Former president and future Supreme Court justice William Howard Taft also opposed the Eighteenth Amendment. He wrote to Boston's Elizabeth Tilton, "[I]t would be a direct blow to local and state governments and the integrity of our federal system. . . . [T]he exercise of jurisdiction to prohibit the liquor traffic would call for a horde of fed-

eral officials in addition to the hundreds of thousands already representing the United States government." Such a vast expansion of central
state authority was anathema to men like Taft.[43]

Elizabeth Tilton, for her part, felt no apprehensions about using the
arm of the administrative state to end the liquor traffic. Her fusion of
Progressivism, Protestant religiosity, class politics, and feminism formed
an important segment of the coalition for prohibition. Tilton's leadership in suffrage politics and the prohibition movement also debunks a
political canard long held by historians that "Northeastern urban progressives would never support total prohibition of the liquor trade," a
movement, so the story went, driven by rural rubes."[44]

Born in Salem, Massachusetts on March 13, 1869, Tilton was proud
of her long line of New England ancestors. Raised in a world of formal
gardens and seashores in the summer, in a religiously oriented
household—her father was a Unitarian minister—she relished her
childhood years and looked back fondly to the stories her mother told
of her family's "fierce anti-slavery." Tilton's mother moved the family
to Cambridge so that her sons could attend Harvard College. Ambitious and strong-willed, Tilton, like a growing minority of elite women
in the late nineteenth century, also aspired to higher education. Barred
from the prestigious all-male college, she attended and graduated in
1890 from Harvard's recently founded female "Annex," Radcliffe College. She later recalled the scorn female students braved in their quest
for higher education, which no doubt bolstered her strong support for
women's rights. It was a trip to England in 1909, however, that she
recalled as a turning point in her civic activism. She joined a stream of
men and women who traveled to Europe and brought back with them
ideas that fueled the early twentieth-century reform wave. A tour of
the slums of East London, she later recalled, made her aware of the
importance of fairer and more even economic conditions. She was particularly inspired by the militant activism of Emmeline Pankhurst and
her fellow British suffragettes.[45]

Tilton joined the Women's Trade Union League and worked in

favor of a minimum wage law for female wage earners in Massachusetts in 1911. When the law passed, she became more deeply involved in the two causes that she remained passionate about: women's suffrage and prohibition. Tilton served as the organization chairman for the Massachusetts Women's Suffrage Association in 1917 and concomitantly worked energetically as an antiliquor crusader. She was far from unique in combining suffrage activism with support for the war against the liquor traffic. Other leading suffrage advocates, such as Harriet Burton Laidlaw, member of the Equal Suffrage League and the New York State Woman Suffrage Association and chair of the New York State League of Women Voters in 1918, along with Jane Addams, strongly supported Prohibition.[46]

While the National American Woman Suffrage Association (NAWSA) did not take a position on the Eighteenth Amendment for fear of dividing its ranks, it should come as no surprise that a good number of women's rights advocates favored the ban. The liquor industry, after all, had been one of the strongest organized foes of women's suffrage, fearing that women would cast their votes for Prohibition. With the WCTU calling for the vote for women to bolster "home protection," brewers and distillers warned that women's suffrage would bring an end to "personal liberty." In addition, at a moment when many women were dependent on a husband's family wage, some women's rights advocates understood excessive drink as a gendered concern grounded in social reality. Just such a concern contributed to Tilton's prohibition activism. On many days in 1912, she traveled from her home on a quaint and quiet tree-lined street in Cambridge to Charlestown, where masses of largely Irish immigrants crowded together in small tenement flats. There she volunteered as a "friendly visitor" for a charity organization. Among the squalid details of those noisy streets, the sight of inviting saloons, with men packed three abreast, left a strong impression. In her eyes, the thriving saloons were the flip side of the impoverished conditions of women and children in crowded tenement flats. Years later, she vividly recalled standing with a group of concerned neighbors outside one apartment while a baby inside "wailed with hunger," the parents lying in a "drunken stupor."[47]

The crowded conditions of the tenements, Tilton believed, exacerbated the problems of excessive male drinking. In contrast to more well-to-do men and women who lived in spacious homes, poor women and children in small flats could quite literally not escape the reach of inebriated spouses and fathers. Tilton's elite social position and the strong temperance views nurtured during her youth led to her understanding of intoxicating liquor as the key contributor to the plight of the urban poor. Soon she was publicly speaking for the cause. By 1917, she became the chairman of the Women's Division of the Massachusetts Anti-Saloon League. By 1923, she had risen to the directorship, the only woman to obtain such a leadership position within the ranks of the antiliquor crusaders.[48]

Tilton's approach to reform was colored by a paternalist and disdainful view of immigrant working-class culture. She bristled with contempt for the "loose" habits of the "unthinking" immigrant masses, a sentiment shared by many early twentieth-century reformers. The immigrants, she claimed, "thought little but acted rashly," imperiling an older, "quality" America. With strong opinions on what constituted civic good, she hoped to inculcate her values in the immigrant masses. Through saloon eradication, Tilton, along with a wide segment of the Protestant Anglo-Saxon elite, sought to buttress their previous easy dominance against an ever more pluralist, urban, and proletarian nation.[49]

This fusion of Protestant religiosity and reform made early twentieth-century social activism somewhat distinct from later reform eras. Then, efforts to transform a nation plagued by inequality and the arrogance of wealth frequently married "Jefferson and Jesus." William Jennings Bryan, one of the era's charismatic advocates for democratic reform and evangelical religiosity, was the quintessential exemplar of this ethos. Bryan's antiliquor sentiment had been nurtured at his family's hearthside in a devout Presbyterian rural Nebraskan family. He took his first temperance pledge when he was twelve. Bryan became one of the alcohol war's most charismatic and best-known supporters. The liquor traffic put private profit above human welfare and fed upon the helpless and the masses. Its eradication, he proclaimed, "will bring the highest good to the greatest number, without any injustice for any, for it is not injustice to any man to refuse him permission to enrich himself by injuring his fellowmen." The brewers and distillers, the boy orator from the Platte claimed, "impoverish the poor and multiply their suffering." The success of the nation's war on alcohol rested on this novel coalition of urban progressives, leading agrarian reformers, and above all on the nation's evangelical Protestant churchgoers in both urban and rural areas.[50]

Additionally, the movement benefited from the strong support of prominent capitalists who provided significant financial resources. The industrial magnate John D. Rockefeller strongly backed the Anti-Saloon League, donating millions of dollars to the Prohibition crusade. Manufacturing magnate Henry Ford also supported the war against alcohol, seeing it as one means of bolstering an efficient workforce. Alcoholic drink, the common wisdom among employers held, contributed to "blue Mondays," with high absentee rates marking the beginning of the workweek. Heavy drinking left less money for other consumer goods. Manufacturers such as Lewis Edwin Theiss argued, as a result, "Until booze is banished we can never have really efficient workmen. We are not much interested in the moral side of the matter as such. It is purely a question of dollars and cents." The "managers of the big corporations" opposed drink among their employees, observed journalist Ames Brown. One industrial journal offered confirmation: "If America becomes liquor free in the next generation, as some industry leaders predict, it will probably be because of the drastic action of our industries which cannot stand by and see large profits swallowed up by alcoholism."[51]

Though the movement gained support among a wide swath of the

Protestant middle class, it is important to recall that not all businessmen, or Progressive reformers for that matter, backed the Eighteenth
Amendment. When Tilton spoke before the General Federation of
Women's Clubs of Chicago in 1915, for example, her reception was
mixed: Jane Addams encouraged her antiliquor activism, but other
women, she later recalled, were only cool and polite. The crusade in
their eyes, admitted Tilton, was too tainted with the stain of "Methodist ranting." The 1905 report of the Committee of Fifty on the Investigation of the Liquor Problem, produced by an influential group of
social scientists, policy-oriented businessmen, and university leaders,
had also warned against a total ban on the liquor industry. The committee published multiple studies establishing alcohol's damaging physiological effects and its social costs. They found that state prohibition
laws had reduced liquor consumption in areas with strong public support, but had failed to stamp out the traffic completely. Foreshadowing
later critiques of the war on alcohol, they concluded that in "districts
where public sentiment has been adverse or strongly divided," prohibition legislation fostered defiance of the law and a "generation of habitual law breakers schooled in evasion and shamelessness."[52]

So while the reform tilt provided an auspicious climate for winning
support for the war against alcohol, and prominent Progressives signed
on in support, Progressive-oriented policy reformers alone would likely
have produced liquor-control laws more in line with the measures
introduced by other industrializing nations. Sweden established a government monopoly on the sale of liquor in 1905 and the Bratt system of
rationing in 1917. Russia prohibited the manufacture and sale of vodka
as a war measure in 1914. Norway banned the sale of hard spirits in 1917
but allowed the sale of beer and light wine. Australia and New Zealand
adopted early pub-closing laws in 1917. But with the exception of tiny
Iceland and Finland, with populations in 1920 that together made up
less than the population of Massachusetts, and temporary war measures,
no western industrialized country embarked on such an ambitious
effort to permanently eradicate the traffic in hard liquor, wine, and beer

in one fell swoop. In the United States, evangelical Protestants provided the yeast fermenting the war on alcohol. They were highly
mobilized by their sense of moral anger. They were also well represented in the political process due to the structure of political participation in the early twentieth-century United States. The targets of their
reform effort—immigrants new to the country as well as disfranchised
African-Americans and poor whites—were often barred from the
national political process. Congressional apportionment, in addition,
was heavily weighted to rural regions, which were strongholds of Protestant religiosity. With the institutional openings provided by the Progressive reform spirit, Prohibitionists sought to build the momentum
necessary to reach their goal of drying up the nation.[53]

With full knowledge of their advantages, the men and women at
the leading edge of the antiliquor crusade organized themselves into a
militant fighting force to wage a "war" against the "liquor traffic."
Richmond Hobson introduced the "Hobson resolution" in the House
in 1914. The measure's language survived almost verbatim in what
would become the Eighteenth Amendment. It prohibited the manufacture, sale, transportation, import, and export of all intoxicating liquors
for beverage purposes in the United States and all territory subject to
its jurisdiction. It declared, too, that Congress and the states should
have powers to enforce the law by means of legislation. Antiliquor crusaders flooded Congress with over one million pink postcards. With
such orchestrated grassroots backing, the resolution won a majority of
House votes. It did so, however, by a razor-thin margin: 197 in favor,
189 opposed. While this was a great achievement for such a radical
reform, it fell far short of the two-thirds required to send the amendment to the states.[54]

.   .   .

THE Eighteenth Amendment, then, even at the high tide of Progressive reform was anything but a foregone conclusion. Its radical scope,
the first constitutional amendment intended to take away rather than to

safeguard liberty, as well as the transfer to the nation-state of broad new authority, generated wide skepticism. Something dramatic was necessary to win the support needed to put it over the top. The Great War, sparked by the fateful shot fired by a Serbian nationalist in Sarajevo on June 28, 1914, was that contingency.

The outbreak of world war changed everything. It stirred up a passion for national preparedness that neutralized the qualms of Prohibition's critics and it further galvanized the prohibitionist base. In Europe, the mobilization for war also led to a cacophony of novel and diverse liquor regulations among combatant nations. States at war rationed cereals and grains and limited their use in the production of alcohol. They also sought to limit its excessive use by troops. France forbid absinthe the day war broke out. Russia banned the sale of vodka in retail establishments. Belgium limited liquor sales, and most states in Australia shortened pub hours. In Britain, municipalities experimented with pub-hour restrictions too, and banned the custom of "treating." The Central Control Board in northern England initiated the Carlisle experiment establishing the state management of the retail and wholesale trade. An incessant volley of propaganda lauded these measures from the day war broke out in Europe and cheered the "heroic onslaught" against booze. The *New York Times* reported in 1915 a "Prohibition wave sweeping Britain." Reformers exaggerated the full extent of "Prohibition" in countries at war to lend authority to their call for domestic legislation, claiming that the United States now lagged behind Europe in the drive for Prohibition. The *Atlantic Monthly* reported in 1915, as a result, "The Great War has had the effect of imparting to the anti-alcohol movement what is perhaps the greatest impetus recorded in all the ages."[55]

With war raging in Europe, prohibitionists hunkered down to mobilize their troops for the final battle. Alabama's No-license League president W. G. Nice trumpeted in 1915: "We have come to a time when the antiliquor army ought to be mobilized and drilled and officered, in the large, and the squads formed into one line." Well before the United States entered the war, Prohibition legislation snowballed. Prohibitionist arguments against the "poisonous" qualities of alcohol and its contribution to a debauched and inefficient citizenry gained traction with the drive for war "preparedness." In the three years after World War I broke out in Europe, fourteen states adopted prohibition laws, more than doubling the number of prohibition states. By 1917 the number of states in the prohibition column reached twenty-six out of forty-eight states.[56]

The United States entry into the war, on April 6, 1917, widened support for the reform. Federal authority dramatically expanded as a result of war mobilization. The federal government took control of important sectors of the economy, including the railroads. Prohibition's call for the radical expansion of federal authority to banish the liquor industry seemed in line with the wider state-building effort of the war years. Arguments over the liquor industry's contribution to waste and inefficiency resonated more widely as the nation readied troops for battle. Partial prohibition measures were now advocated as a means of shoring up a disciplined fighting force. Franklin D. Roosevelt, then assistant secretary of the navy, and secretary Josephus Daniels issued an order forbidding alcohol use in the navy. Daniels also set up "dry and decent zones" around military camps to safeguard the efficiency and health of the military. These zones barred the sale of liquor to servicemen and reduced servicemen's access to prostitution. The Selective Service Act, in turn, forbade the sale of liquor to men in uniform. The antiliquor crusade now seemed part of the patriotic campaign to win the war.[57]

The prohibitionist cause had always been linked to anti-immigrant sentiment. Now the nation's large brewing companies, overwhelmingly in the hands of men of German descent, were further stigmatized as "enemies" and "traitors." The Anti-Saloon League shamelessly pandered to the hostility to all things German to win the amendment's passage. The league identified the antiliquor crusade as the ultimate patriotic act. The time had come, wrote one pamphleteer, for a split between "unquestioned and undiluted American patriots and slackers and enemy sympathizers." The most patriotic act of any legislature or citizen was to "abolish the un-American, pro-German, crime-producing, food-wasting, youth-corrupting, home wrecking, treasonable liquor traffic."[58]

Desperate to survive in the face of the onslaught, the brewing industry only made matters worse. It had begun donating large sums of money to the national German-American Alliance after the constitutional amendment was introduced. The Alliance was founded in the early twentieth century as a German-American cultural organization, but with the influx of funds from the brewing industry after 1913, it also championed the anti-Prohibition cause. It argued that Prohibition was an anti-immigrant initiative, and it waved the banner of personal liberty. But the Alliance also engaged other issues. Its Washington lobbying office, established in 1914, worked to keep the United States strictly neutral. It linked the antiliquor crusade with the war effort: "The drink question," fulminated John Schwaab of the Ohio branch of the Alliance in 1915, "is forced upon us by the same hypocritical puritans as over there are endeavoring to exterminate the German nation." Attorney general A. Mitchell Palmer condemned the industry: "The organized liquor traffic of the country is a vicious interest because it has been unpatriotic, because it has been pro-German in its sympathies and its conduct." The Senate investigated the brewer's great ally, the German-American Alliance, forcing it to disband in 1918.[59]

The campaign to provide food supplies for troops and wartime allies also meant that the nation was drying up even prior to the amendment's passage. Once the United States entered the war, it seemed to make little sense to waste grain in distilling and brewing alcohol rather than feeding the troops. Under the slogan "Shall the many have food or the few have drink?" the House passed the Lever Food and Fuel Control Act on June 23, 1917, by a vote of 365 to 5, outlawing the use of foodstuffs for distilled spirits and commandeering distilleries' spirits for redistillation and use in manufacturing wartime supplies. The Senate followed in August with a vote of 66 to 7. By December 1917, a presidential proclamation forbade brewers to brew beverages that had an alcoholic content of more than 2.75 percent, converting beer into a pale temperance beverage.[60]

With the war effort and wartime patriotism at full throttle, congressional majorities well in excess of the two-thirds requirement submitted the Eighteenth Amendment to the states on December 22, 1917. One month later, on January 8, 1918, Mississippi became the first state to ratify with the stunning legislative tally of 122 in favor and 8 opposed. Virginia, Kentucky, South Carolina, and North Dakota followed suit. On September 18, 1918, Congress introduced a plan for wartime Prohibition at the time that many states were considering ratification. In doing so, it once again linked the war against alcohol to the war effort. By January 1919, ratification was complete. Nebraska signed on as the thirty-sixth state required for ratification. (Eventually forty-six of the forty-eight states ratified, with Connecticut and Rhode Island the only two holdouts). The amendment had swept through the ratification process more quickly than any other amendment in United States history. When the Massachusetts statehouse ratified on April 2, 1918, Elizabeth Tilton "rushed out from that gallery mad with joy . . . church bells ringing. . . . We were in ecstasy." For the Boston reformer, the amendment's ratification was proof that "urbanization had not yet laid its material, beer-soaked class on the vote of America."[61]

World War I sped the process for the achievement of the Eighteenth Amendment to an extent unexpected by even its most avid supporters. When the Anti-Saloon League first introduced its goal for constitutional reform, some of its strongest supporters acknowledged that the battle would likely take a generation. Elizabeth Tilton, looking back years later, remembered that the amendment was initially raised as a mere "trial balloon" and the positive reception the temperance forces met in their bid for the amendment took them by surprise. Prohibition reformers had feared that the war would prove a distraction. Instead, while the war doomed the prospects for wider reform hopes and led to the repression of radical politics, it provided the propitious climate that pushed the Eighteenth Amendment over the top.[62]

Nor was the amendment destined to flounder as a mere constitutional ideal: The House passed a vigorous enforcement code on July 22, 1919, by a vote of 287 to 100. The Senate followed suit on September 5. Wilson's veto, owed to the bill's inclusion of wartime Prohibition, was easily overcome on October 28. The National Prohibition Act, better known as the Volstead Act, contained sixty-seven separate sections. Significantly, the code defined intoxicating beverages strictly at .05 percent alcoholic content. It made even the lightest beers and wines illegal along with hard spirits. The bill was capacious in its reach. It allowed foreign ships that carried liquor for their crews to pass through the Panama Canal but barred such ships from stopping in U.S. ports. At the same time, it provided exemptions for "sacramental wines," the manufacture of industrial alcohol, ciders and fruit juices, and physicians' prescriptions for medicinal purposes. In addition, its provisions failed to criminalize purchase, and exempted consumption within the home of pre-Volstead liquor, effectively allowing the well-to-do to stock large quantities of liquor in their homes for private consumption before the law's enactment on January 17, 1920.[63]

Despite these exemptions that would bedevil later enforcement, the antiliquor crusaders had triumphed. January 16, 1920, was their moment of deliverance. As the clocks struck midnight from New York to Los Angeles, hundreds of thousands of men and women who had been working for years and decades to make the nation dry cheered. Celebrations were held at Leavitt Street Church in Flint, Michigan, at grand bonfires in Atlanta, and at "wakes" and funerals for "John Barleycorn" in Louisville, Kentucky, and Norfolk, Virginia. Finally, "sinful ways" would be laid to rest. Demon Rum had been outlawed. "Hell will be forever for rent," cheered well-known preacher Billy Sunday. The nation had finally established a "declaration of independence from the legalized liquor traffic."[64]

.   .   .

IN adopting some form of prohibition legislation during World War I, the United States was far from unique. Partial liquor control measures, as we have seen, had been enacted by many countries during the war, and some of the new drink regulations lasted permanently. But in its effort to totally eradicate the use of intoxicating liquor, the United States stood alone among major industrialized nations. The moral fervor of evangelical Protestants had intersected with the Progressive reform wave and the institutional openings provided by the war. Combined with political representation weighted heavily to rural districts and the limited political power of the law's targets, the antiliquor crusaders were able to rewrite the Constitution and federal law. The result was one of the boldest and most radical social efforts to alter personal behavior in the nation's history and one that would have dramatic though unintended consequences for nation-state building and for politics.

2

BOOTLEG, MOONSHINE,
AND HOME BREW

ELIZABETH TILTON CHEERED WITH ANTILIQUOR CELE-
brants in Massachusetts when the Eighteenth Amendment won ratification in early 1919. Emotions of a very different sort swept the ranks of
ethnic working-class communities, the primary target of the new law.
On April 6, just across the Charles River from Tilton's quiet tree-lined
street, a crowd of fifty thousand gathered on the Boston Common to
protest the law's impending arrival. Protest organizer M. J. O'Donnell,
president of the Central Labor Union, decried the amendment as "government by a minority." State senator John J. Kearney blasted the
reform as a "trick" put over by a faction while the country was distracted by the war. Banners proclaimed, "establish Democracy at
home" and "we fought for liberty for all the world, and we want some
here at home too." The *Boston Daily Globe* declared it "one of the greatest mass meetings ever held on the Common."[1]

Baltimore, a midsize industrial city, witnessed a similar outpouring.
On June 2, 1919, a dense crowd, including veterans in military uniform, braved sweltering heat to protest the new law. The Maryland

branch of the "Anti-Prohibition League," along with the city's social clubs, fraternal orders, and labor unions, joined the parade. At least a thousand decorated cars and trucks, fourteen bands, and a Statue of Liberty float wound through the city's downtown. Reports estimated the marchers numbered between ten thousand and twenty-five thousand. A far bigger crowd, a hundred thousand, lined the parade route.[2]

Newspapers remarked on the "large numbers of women" in these demonstrations. In Baltimore, two hundred of the cars along the parade route were filled with women. In Boston too, women joined the April protest. Waitresses in fashionable hats waved banners announcing "Labor's Protest Against Prohibition." And in a later demonstration in Washington, newspapers remarked on the "prominent part . . . played by women." Evidently these women in Boston and Baltimore rejected the home protection ethos championed by Elizabeth Tilton and the WCTU.[3]

Not content to merely march, organized labor sent emissaries to Washington. The American Federation of Labor had called for the legalization of light wines and beers in a resolution at its June convention. The AFL national leadership had earlier avoided taking a stand against Prohibition, with three members of the Executive Committee supporting the Eighteenth Amendment, while Samuel Gompers, the organization's president, spoke forcefully against it. When Congress threatened to ban all intoxicating beverages under the Volstead Act—not just hard liquor but also the "workingman's beer"—the AFL aligned itself with its rank and file. Trains brought AFL convention delegates from Atlantic City to Washington in the wake of the convention. Gompers addressed the crowd, blasting the "vicious" constitutional amendment and charging that it had been "foisted" upon the nation. He called attention to the loopholes in the proposed Volstead Act that would allow the storage of pre-Volstead liquor, and focused on the inequality it ensured: "[T]he rich may have their booze for a lifetime guaranteed and the right of the worker to get a glass of beer is denied to him."[4]

In northeastern industrial cities, with their large immigrant populations, a "No Beer, No Work" campaign swept through local unions in
the spring of 1919. In Essex and Newark, New Jersey, and in New York
City, longshoremen, shipbuilders, ironworkers, and hatters endorsed
the call. The anti-Prohibition campaign made headway among Boston's laborers too: Elizabeth Tilton remarked on supporters she saw
there sporting "No Beer, No Work" buttons. Heightened labor militancy in the wake of World War I no doubt fueled these protests. Ultimately, however, organized labor faced a far more serious fight retaining
their wartime gains—higher wages and union recognition—as employers sought to return to prewar conditions. Despite his personal anti-
Prohibition sentiment, Gompers condemned the "no beer, no work"
campaign for stoking middle-class anxieties over "labor bolshevism,"
and it soon sputtered to a halt.[5]

However short-lived, the mass outpourings revealed the hostility
of ethnic, urban working-class communities to the Volstead Act even
prior to its implementation. During the following years, as the war on
alcohol encroached ever deeper into their communities, sporadic
opposition would take on a new, more politically consequential cast.
Ethnic working-class communities came to understand the law as an
attack on their leisure and personal habits and protested its consequences on their communities. Prohibition spurred an Americanization process from the bottom up, though not the kind of Americanization
that many elite Protestant reformers hoped for. As one banner at a 1921
New York protest proclaimed: "We are citizens, not inmates, which
are you?" The radical and far-reaching nature of the reform pushed
immigrant workers to clothe themselves in an all-American mantle of
patriotism and personal liberty and to mobilize in electoral politics to
claim their rights. The windy city of Chicago offers a prime example
of this process at work, and what happened there occurred in other
industrial cities.[6]

In the early twentieth century, Chicago was a city of immigrants.
Political scientist and reformer Charles Merriam called it "the world's

greatest melting pot." Foreign-born and children of the foreign-born made up 70 percent of Chicagoans in 1920. Recently arrived immigrants—Bohemian Czechs, Poles, and Italians—jostled with better established and politically entrenched Irish and Germans. Alcoholic beverages—beer, wine, or, less frequently, whiskey—were central to immigrant culture. German families met in local beer gardens. Czechs, Poles, and Slovaks held social dances at their saloons. Italians drank wine during the Festivals of Maria or Saint Rocco and at baptisms and weddings. Without "the cooling, exhilarating, and life giving glass of wine," lamented a Greek opponent of Prohibition, "we Greeks cannot give picnics, or dances, or weddings or baptisms . . . or even funerals . . . for these are habits which have been left to us by our ancestors and without which we cannot live."[7]

Drinking was also woven into the workday. In the vast stockyards of the meatpacking districts, "beer men" ran buckets of cold beer hanging from poles over their shoulders from nearby saloons to the workmen on their breaks, with beer selling at two quarts for a nickel. In a "Back of the Yards" neighborhood, on Whiskey Row, saloons were densely concentrated. In 1910, just three blocks boasted forty-six. Saloons in fact offered the only seats at a table during the lunch hour near the stockyards. After their long workday, laborers crowded in for a beer before returning to their family's tenement or bungalow in frequently cramped quarters. For the most part, saloons were not the dens of depravity of the prohibitionists' imagination. One University of Chicago Settlement House report remarked that the saloon was the "most hospitable place in the community to the non–English-speaking people. One Slovak saloon has all the Slovak papers. The intelligent saloonkeeper is the friend and counselor of his people. They meet in the back of his saloon as they would a clubhouse." For male immigrant breadwinners, the saloon functioned as a social center and source of community solidarity.[8]

In Chicago, as elsewhere, immigrant communities had organized to oppose the Anti-Saloon League and to preserve their right to "eight hours for what we will." Since the early 1900s, they had fought Sunday closing laws that not only shuttered saloons on that day but barred liquor from being served in social clubs, concert gardens, picnic grounds, and ethnic halls. In 1906 Chicago's immigrant leaders established the United Societies for Local Self-Government, representing 835 ethnic organizations, a remarkable display of transethnic unity. A year later, a new city charter threatened to cede control over liquor issues to lawmakers in the state's capital, Springfield. In response, the United Societies formed a "popular front against consolidation," joining with the Chicago Federation of Labor as well as local businesses afraid of higher taxes to block the change.[9]

In 1915, with antiliquor crusaders winning wider support as the fighting in Europe intensified, Chicago reformers renewed their drive to enforce Sunday closing laws. Immigrant communities once again mobilized opposition. They organized a mammoth parade along Michigan Avenue, the crowd at forty-four thousand people. Ethnic orders, benevolent societies, bands, and choirs paraded with "great pomp and pageantry," reported the *Chicago Daily Tribune*. Banners in many languages and music from Irish airs to Polish polkas along with Slovak and Swedish marching songs wrought a "confusion of tongues and tunes." Workers from Back of the Yards societies carried signs—"Why pick on Sunday, the working man's holiday?" Polish merchants in "silk hats and Prince Albert coats" came out too, revealing not just multicultural but cross-class support for the parade. Their erudite banners announced, "The toiler is worthy of his recreation." A coffin in an old buggy bore the inscription "Here lies our liberty."[10]

The tireless antiliquor crusader Richmond Hobson was in Chicago on the day of the march. He spoke from the pulpit of the imposing Second Presbyterian Church, built in Gothic revivalist style, and the spiritual home of some of Chicago's most prominent Protestant families. The church was located along the parade route. Inside the church, "respectable" Protestant men and women listened to Hobson's plea for an end to the liquor "evil." The din of the immigrant marchers returning home from their parade outside made a perfect study in contrasts. Hobson blasted the noisy "parade of degenerates" and urged passage of the Eighteenth Amendment, introduced into Congress a year earlier. While elite Protestant churchgoers provided strong support for the crusade, the windy city's antiliquor crusaders were vastly outnumbered by their opponents. After the amendment was ratified in 1919, a majority of Chicagoans who went to the polls expressed their opposition to the Anti-Saloon League agenda. In a 1919 city referendum that posed the question "Should Chicago become Anti-Saloon League territory?" Chicagoans voted no by a large majority, with 144,032 voters in favor and 391,360 opposed.[11]

Despite Chicago immigrants' collective opposition, the war on alcohol was not the most urgent challenge facing Chicago's economically hard-pressed majority immigrant communities. As in other industrial centers, the city's large employers were intent on rolling back worker rights extended during the war, chief among them better wages and working conditions. In 1919, in response to employers' open-shop campaigns, Chicago's industrial workers launched a powerful strike wave shutting steel mills, packinghouses, garment shops, and agricultural machine factories. Despite these mobilization efforts for better pay and union recognition, divisions between skilled workers and the mass of unskilled, manipulative employer tactics, and lack of national federation support, kept union and immigrant communities under siege.[12]

Under pressure on the shop floor, ethnic workers had an even greater need for their own spaces—from saloons to social clubs—to enjoy what sprinkling of leisure time and discretionary pay they did have. They saw the war on alcohol as a direct assault on cherished personal and community habits. Antiliquor crusaders, whose leaders included some of their own employers, went further, proclaiming that banning liquor would improve workplace efficiency and end waste. Their arguments paralleled principles of scientific management winning popularity among employers eager to increase productivity on the shop floor, and soon workers faced novel measures to speed up the pace of work at the same time that antiliquor crusaders waged their war against alcohol. The new discipline laborers experienced on the shop floor threatened to spill into the semiautonomous spaces of private life and collective leisure. Since the reform was backed by a wide swath of the Protestant elite, the liquor ban also appeared to many immigrant groups as an attack on ethnic identities and, especially, on Catholic religiosity. The fight against Prohibition was on the surface an effort to protect leisure habits, but in a world where class cleavages closely aligned with cultural, religious, and racial divisions, it resonated with the deepest fractures of the economic and social postwar order.[13]

Contempt for the law united the immigrant working-class with ethnic community leaders from shopkeepers and saloonkeepers to local politicians and brewers. On other issues facing deeply unequal Chicago, ethnic ward bosses and the city alderman often allied themselves closely with local capitalists and gave only lip service to their communities on policy initiatives for poor constituents. Their real service, however, came through informal material services, whether in the form of a rent payment, a job, or a needed permit; their base of operations frequently was a local saloon. As Prohibition began to threaten all levels of these communities, their upwardly mobile "betters" joined their working-class base in the unsuccessful attempt to protect immigrant customs against the attack of largely elite Protestant reformers.

.   .   .

SO deep were the cultural roots of drink in immigrant working-class communities in Chicago and elsewhere that these communities saw little reason to obey the ban after the Volstead Act took effect on January 17, 1920. Settlement-house workers reported that working-class men and women in Packingtown "appeared to have [no] compunction regarding post-prohibition drinking." Social workers in other places too echoed this view. With existing inventories dwindling and increasingly muscular enforcement, Prohibition nonetheless began to reshape their leisure worlds and their neighborhoods. Reformers cheered many of these changes but ethnic working-class men and women mourned the growing costs of the law to their neighborhoods and their traditional comforts.[14]

The first and most visible casualty of the war on alcohol was the neighborhood saloon, once so ubiquitous it seemed a virtual extension of the city sidewalk. Opponents and supporters of Prohibition marshaled statistics to endless debate for or against the new law. But both sides agreed the law almost single-handedly killed the institution of the saloon. The need to solve the saloon "problem" had been the essential seed for the snowballing support for national Prohibition. And reformers' push over the years for high-license laws, local ordinances, and state liquor-prohibition laws, had already weakened saloons, especially in small cities and in rural towns. By the early 1900s, saloons also faced competition from nickelodeons and dance halls as well as professional and amateur sports for the leisure time of working-class men and women. These alternative entertainments lessened the attraction of the all-male saloon, particularly among younger men and women. Nonetheless, the saloon still thrived in cities like New York, Chicago, Pittsburgh, and other large urban centers populated by great numbers of immigrant workers.[15]

After Prohibition, the institution of the saloon fell into a steep decline from which it never recovered. In Chicago, the best-known of the city's many saloons was the Workingmen's Exchange. With a thirty-foot walnut bar, the large establishment had served as one base of operations for alderman Mike Kenna, informally known as a "Lord of the Levee." His saloon provided free lunches and nickel beer, and favors to patrons and constituents. There, and at another saloon, he solidified his political position based on webs of corruption and graft, doling out patronage and servicing poor constituents. Kenna freely conceded that he "customarily" provided "peddlers' permits" to poor men and women looking for work, so they could eke out a livelihood marketing small wares on the streets without paying the required fee.

His quite literal Workingmen's Exchange was so successful that it served 175,000 kegs of beer before closing its doors for good in February 1920, after a last paroxysm selling "near beer," a beverage marketed as a replacement for beer but derided as tasteless. The Exchange was but the most notorious among the many drinking establishments that shut their doors, permanently changing the urban landscape.[16]

To reformers, shuttering saloons was a great achievement. Indeed, the war on alcohol did sever a tight linkage between saloons and municipal politics. In its place sprouted far more egregious ties forged between politicians and organized crime, but saloons no longer served as central sites for the operation of Democratic and Republican municipal political machines. A Prohibition supporter acknowledged that although drinking continued, nonetheless "what everyone must admit is the patent fact that the strangle-hold which the saloon had on our politics and much of our industrial and social life has been broken." A Chicago settlement-house worker put it succinctly: the illegal "drinkery is not a political center."[17]

As the saloon vanished, so too did its signature boisterous public drunkenness that so offended middle-class sensibilities. Drinking by working-class ethnics may not have disappeared, but increasingly it moved to clandestine spaces. Mary McDowell, founder of the University of Chicago Settlement House, remarked: "Before Prohibition there was noisy drinking on Saturday nights up and down the alleys . . . we do not have this now." Similar changes occurred in other cities. A Boston reformer noted that "there was a great number of open saloons in the West End, then Prohibition came, at once the streets were cleared of drunkards, and in fact of people." Even Eighteenth Amendment supporters who acknowledged rising crime rates celebrated the quieter streets that resulted. A Sioux City, South Dakota, social worker declared "[W]e have more crime now . . . [but] there is much less disorder, due to the absence of drunken people on the streets and in public places." Lillian Wald, New York's Henry Street Settlement House founder, cheered that despite the city's many speakeasies, the scenes of brewers' trucks delivering their barrels of beer on Saturday nights, with workers cashing their checks and whittling away family money, "has disappeared from one end of the country to the other." With it, she contended, "has gone the Sunday brawls and the tragic Monday mornings when in the factory workshop, tearful women came to beg for advances on their husband's wages."[18]

Surveys of saloon properties documented their fate. Reformers reported that Prohibition transformed even Whiskey Row behind the Chicago stockyards. In a symbolic inversion, several of the packing companies helped establish a day nursery on the site of seven former saloons. Two other saloon properties reopened as restaurants; two more became grocery stores; one turned into a clothing store. In 1923, a study of Chicago's Central District took stock of a four-block area that had thirty saloons in 1917. Ten properties showed no signs of life. Two had been torn down. Six were cheap "eating places." There were also three grocery stores, a drug store, a picture studio, a secondhand shop, a hotel, an undertaker's parlor, and an auto supply shop. Hardly a utopian transformation, but antiliquor crusaders welcomed these changes. The closure of three "flourishing saloons" on one busy corner, said one settlement-house worker, "greatly improved the general tone" of the neighborhood. Saloons, meantime, disappeared in other cities too: Charles Cooper, president of the Kingsley Settlement House, remarked on the transformation of a row of buildings in Pittsburgh "from a solid row of saloons to a 'decent street' containing a movie theater and an A&P store."[19]

While many saloon owners shut down, unwilling to bear the risks of operating illegally, others tried to remain open under Prohibition. Some did so legally by serving "near-beer," but rarely successfully. Working-class men did not stop drinking with saloon closures, but drinking increasingly moved from the saloon into the home, private halls, and "athletic clubs." Many former saloons reopened as thinly veiled soft-drink parlors and "halls" catering to working-class clienteles. Behind signs that read "for rent," others carried on their business through a back door. Some of these businesses sold "tonics" or "bitters" that included a mixture of moonshine under another name, and, eventually, beer and whiskey as well. A Chicago Commons report noted that twenty-five to thirty neighborhood saloons had closed, but others operated "camouflag[ing] the front with the appearance of neglect, unwashed windows and an apparently vacant storefront."[20]

Staying in business under the Volstead Act required new strategies. It meant selling bootleg liquor to a known clientele in a semisecretive manner, and in affiliation with increasingly powerful criminal gangs. Sellers of bootleg liquor risked periodic police crackdowns and frequent relocations after agents padlocked suspect premises. Once closed, the affected owner lost not just sales income but also property. Under federal law, places selling liquor could be padlocked for up to one year. In 1928 federal agents in Chicago padlocked more than seven hundred properties accused of selling liquor in a city often considered "wide open" in terms of enforcement. Enforcement took a toll on illicit saloons elsewhere as well. Vice organizations, such as New York's Committee of Fourteen, filed hundreds of photos of former saloon properties in New York and New Jersey emptied of life and bared of fixtures and furnishings after enforcement raids. In Pennsylvania, by 1926, special counsel William Wright Jr., governor Gifford Pinchot's chief lieutenant in charge of enforcement, had closed 404 of the 665 worst saloons identified by enforcement officers as still operative. In Philadelphia Thomas Peak operated his saloon for two years under the Volstead Act until police and Prohibition agents cracked down, removing its bar and fixtures in a raid that turned violent, with two hundred men resisting the closure.[21]

Staying open not only meant the threat of raids, it also meant contending with the climate of violence that came with the illicit drink traffic. Police crackdowns triggered gangland fights around saloon doors. As a result, working-class saloons increasingly embodied the depraved vision of reformers' nightmares: dark, furtive spaces enmeshed in networks of corruption, crime, and violence. On Chicago's South Side, saloons, especially a few reinvented "athletic clubs," became the notorious bases for local gangs under the direction of large organized crime rings.[22]

For working-class imbibers, the war on saloons and legal breweries had effects beyond their shuttered doors. It drove up the cost of buying a drink, making social-drinking ventures less attractive. Prior to the Volstead Act, beer in a saloon was cheap; in cities like Detroit and Chicago, before World War I, it was customarily a nickel or a dime for a "schooner." In Packingtown and other working-class neighborhoods, an off-premises "growler," a small bucket of beer, went for as little as a nickel. During Prohibition, once illicit markets gained a foothold in industrial cities, the cost of beer multiplied between five- and tenfold. The price of hard liquor spiked as well. One former Illinois state representative of Bohemian descent complained that the "stuff is too high." Workers at Chicago's Hawthorne Works of General Electric testified that the high cost of liquor had cut into their household budgets.[23]

Not surprisingly, therefore, the war on alcohol did measurably reduce alcohol consumption by men and women of lower income. The underground nature of the market makes it difficult to say by precisely how much, but one study claimed drinking among workers was cut by half, whereas among the professional classes it remained unchanged. Men and women with lower incomes simply could not afford the high cost. The wife of one New Jersey shipyard worker noted this change. "There was no problem procuring illegal liquor," she remarked, but her husband "probably drinks less . . . because of the poorer quality of the liquor and its greater cost." Though estimates of liquor consumption during Prohibition varied wildly, systematic studies conducted in its wake confirm that there was an overall decline. In the immediate aftermath of the Twenty-First Amendment, consumption of alcohol was about half its 1911–1915 level. Per capita, alcohol consumption rates would not catch up with early twentieth-century levels until 1970.[24]

In the face of rising costs, working-class men and women searched out cheaper sources of liquor. While some workers splurged on moonshine from backdoor saloons, far more frequently they procured liquor from other sources. In Chicago, drugstores were one supplier. Druggists sold "medicinal" whiskey to buyers with a prescription and the deep pockets to afford the steep price tag: a pint of "medicinal whiskey" went for $40 to $60 in inflation-adjusted dollars. Only the very wealthy could afford decent-quality whiskey bought legally with a prescription; the poor had to make do with less expensive alternatives. Drugstores advertised cheap tonics, including Triner's Bitters and Hoffman drops. These concoctions were marketed for their medicinal properties and contained pure alcohol cut with commercial ether or other substances. As a Polish parish priest remarked, "[A]long the Lake Shore Drive they have liquor but the average man has to take the next best, a drug with a percentage of alcohol."[25]

The closing of saloons and the high cost of reasonable-quality liquor in a drug store drove another change. With the "price of whiskey . . . too high for the laboring class . . . they must get a cheap grade or manufacture their own whiskey or homebrew," remarked one commentator. Some laborers bought liquor in soft drink parlors, in tailor shops, and grocery stores proffering cheap moonshine, but private homes provided an important source of illegal production and consumption as well, particularly in the early years of Prohibition. Working-class families brewed beer, made homemade wine, and distilled whiskey in small-scale operations for their own consumption or for sale to neighbors, reviving and expanding the working-class custom of household liquor production. A Chicago Commons Settlement House report likened the return of home brewing to what one might see if "the great baking companies ceased baking bread. Back would come the home loaf. . . . A great industry formerly carried on in the distilleries and breweries became decentralized and went back into the home."[26]

Stores soon sprang up to supply the needs of the legions of home brewers. On one corner in Packingtown three different stores sold home-brew and distilling supplies. Hardware stores too advertised coils, copper cans, kegs, caps, and bottles for home production of beer and whiskey. Ironically, some of the new dry goods stores that reformers cheered supplied a rising demand for yeast and other items needed for alcohol production in the home. One small grocer saw his sales of yeast multiple fivefold to meet the new demand. Amateur producers manufactured crude moonshine using simple recipes. The most basic called for a mixture of yeast and sugar; another recommended combining apricots, sweet potatoes, and yeast. One police precinct near the University of Chicago Settlement House reported a 70 percent increase in the number of people making liquor in their homes.[27]

Settlement-house workers uniformly remarked on the widespread practice of home brewing in working-class households "for the family's own consumption, together with the operation of many . . . blind pigs," so called after the legendary nineteenth-century ruse of charging customers a fee to view an attraction, and serving "complimentary" alcoholic beverages in communities with Prohibition ordinances, thus evading the law. In Chicago, blind pigs were small drinking establishments, operated in first-floor flats, walkup apartments, and working-class bungalow homes.[28]

Working-class homes thus became sites not just for producing alcohol but also for its sale in "kitchen-table" drinkeries. Manufacturing crude moonshine, home-brewing beer, and fermenting wine required production and storage space—and space was precious in already crowded homes. Home brewing and distilling was also messy. For thirsty working-class men and women who did not produce themselves, but who wished to imbibe, a neighbor's nearby dwelling might provide a convenient space. The neighbor then assumed the risk (and rewards) of running the illegal operation. Women frequently produced the home brews and ran these blind pigs. With men at work, manufacturing moonshine and sometimes bootlegging it became an extension of women's household duties. Such small operations also provided a means to supplement family income. Ethnic working-class women, with their families, were marginal producers, but collectively, their small production provided one source of supply for the growing and increasingly organized criminal traffic.[29]

At the other end of the spectrum, those who set up larger illegal operations could reap vast profits. Larger producers then emerged alongside the home brewers. Jane Addams witnessed this development in one Chicago immigrant neighborhood. After the initial revival of home production during the first years of Prohibition, Addams observed, "[T]he bootlegging industry entered a new stage. In place of small home stills came the small factory." Groups of bootleggers employed men to run the larger stills they owned. "These enterprises," Addams reported to a group of settlement-house workers, "are housed in old barns, basements, the rears of store buildings, old warehouses, and the volume of business is quite large." Manufacturing and cutting operations located in poorer industrial neighborhoods or in outlying rural areas because there they attracted less attention from law enforcement. The run-down neighborhood of West Madison Street, which ran from the edge of the Loop to Halsted Street, was said to smell "like a distillery throughout the dry era."[30]

With demand high and profits abundant, the moonshine and bootleg business evolved quickly. "In no city has the bootlegging industry been so completely organized and so successful, apparently, in securing protection," lamented one Chicago Commons Settlement House report. Small home producers and blind pigs were of little interest to big-time criminal entrepreneurs, but anyone who set up larger stills, Jane Addams reported, was folded into the strong organizations or forced to shut down: "We find the exploiters trying to get control of all the stills within a given area. They offer to any man who is discovered owning a still within the area a fifty-fifty proposition. They provide police protection and selling advantages in return for half his output. If he declines, his still is broken up or if he is persistent, he is personally attacked or in the end obliged to conform or go out of business." Organized criminals expanded their penetration into poor neighborhoods, drawn by the bright promise of this highly profitable new trade.[31]

Organized-crime entrepreneurs already had experience working in the underground operations of gambling and prostitution. By 1919 they were well positioned to exploit the tremendous new opportunities created by the criminalization of the alcohol traffic. Giacomo "Big Jim" Colosimo immigrated to Chicago in 1898 and by 1910 had built a small empire of saloons, gambling establishments, and brothels. When mayor William "Big Bill" Thompson took office in 1915, he provided political protection for Colosimo's illicit sex and gambling industries. Colosimo brought in Brooklyn gangster Johnny Torrio to solidify his power against rivals. Torrio in turn brought in his own protégé from New York, Alphonsus Capone to work as his right-hand man. When Colosimo was killed in March 1920, just a few months into the "noble experiment" (rumor had it that he was reluctant to enter the alcohol trade), Torrio took over his businesses and embarked with Al Capone in the profitable bootleg traffic. The two competed with rival kingpin Dean O'Banion for control over the illegal industry for the first four years of the war on alcohol until O'Banion's murder in 1924, which set off bloody gang warfare. The next year Torrio survived an assassination attempt but left Chicago and bequeathed control of his illegal operations to Al Capone.[32]

Long before the war on alcohol, Chicago was known for widespread political graft, "boodle," and corruption. Alderman Mike Kenna, one of Chicago's "Gray Wolves," was among the many politicians who sold off lucrative city franchises in return for kickbacks, and protected the city's gambling and brothel operations from police raids. Tellingly, at one banquet held by the city's vice king, Colosimo, many of the city's police captains were in attendance. The war on alcohol, however, brought the cooperation between organized criminals and state officials to entirely unprecedented levels. With an entire industry rendered illegal and forced underground, crime bosses and judges, law enforcement agents and politicians saw a main chance. Chicago politicians admitted that they knew of a "tremendous amount of graft being collected for the protection of bootleggers . . . police, judges, and the influence of state's attorneys." Mayor Thompson was only the most notorious. He gave the city, according to the *Chicago Tribune*, "an international reputation for moronic buffoonery, barbaric crime, triumphant hoodlumism, [and] unchecked graft." [33]

Law administration, enforcement, and every level of urban politics was shot through with the influence of what became colloquially known as "boozedom." Politicians of "good repute" unabashedly attended weddings, baptisms, and christenings of organized crime kingpins. They were "not ashamed to deal with criminals," remarked the *Chicago Tribune*; indeed, "they are compelled to deal with it if they are to remain successful politicians." Senator Charles Deneen, tellingly, attended the christening of "Diamond Joe" Esposito's child in 1925 along with a number of judicial officials. And when the assistant state's attorney of Cook County was shot in a torrent of machine gun bullets in 1928, it was not because he sought to crack down on the industry, but because he allied himself with one gang faction that was attacked by another. "He drank with them, rode with them, entered speakeasies with them." Such connections between government and organized crime were a harbinger of the relationship between state officeholders and drug cartels in drug-supplying countries today. [34]

Corruption's stain touched politicians at all levels, from United States senators down to judges, justices of the peace, and the policemen on the beat. The Chicago Commons Settlement House reported that "liquor [was] obtainable directly under the protection of police." One neighborhood establishment "benefited from the protection of the police precinct next door" with patrolmen making "deliveries [of liquor] into automobiles." It was not unusual for police squads to escort beer caravans and patrolmen to ride on the trucks of organized crime rings to protect deliveries against rival gangs who might be planning to hijack valuable cargo. Police participated in the illegal trade in other ways. One Chicagoan reported on the experience of an acquaintance who opened a bootleg establishment in an out-of-the-way place. When his operation was discovered by police, they did not shut it down. Instead, they paid a visit and informed him that "they were his partners. . . . His products were delivered under their protection, and they reportedly share an income of 60,000 dollars a year," a sum of more than $800,000 in inflation-adjusted dollars.[35]

The high cost of protection, whether from police or criminal gangs or both, favored large-scale suppliers. As one Polish producer whose home still brought in ten dollars a day lamented, "I do not make enough money on moonshine to pay for protection, and so I am going into another business." According to government figures, by midsummer 1924, Torrio and Capone each pocketed $100,000 a week in protection money, over one million dollars today. Such costs and rising murderousness spelled the decline of home-scale brewing in many metropolises.[36]

Prohibition lawlessness has provided fodder for popular retellings of the exploits of colorful crime kingpins, from the activities of "scarface" Al Capone to the sensational murders of fabulously wealthy bootleggers such as George Remus. While such accounts are frequently tinged with romance and nostalgia, less emphasis has been placed on the devastating impact of organized crime networks on poor communities, where illegal liquor businesses operated with impunity. The new industry fueled an expansion of criminal webs in Chicago in the fast-deteriorating Chicago immigrant neighborhoods, often lumped together as "gangland," and on the city's largely African-American South Side. Criminal gangs controlled the large working-class enclave of Cicero just west of Chicago proper as well; it was soon dubbed "Caponetown." Surrounded by factories, the enclave served as the base for the gangster's operation. Capone operated uninhibited by police, his illegal empire smoothed by his political connections, violence, and the wet sentiments of many of Chicago's ethnic political leaders. Foremost among them stood Anton Cermak, who served as a Cook County commissioner for the mid-1920s. His solution to the power of gangland lay in rescinding the Volstead Act, upon which he placed full blame for the rise in organized crime.[37]

Poor communities in Chicago bore the brunt of the illegal alcohol trade because residents lacked the power to prevent criminal penetration. Police directed and permitted illegal activities in areas largely invisible to the city's powerful and wealthy. These neighborhoods included a "Lithuanian colony at the Southern end, part of Little Pilsen on the West, the Valley, the Ghetto . . . and the southern portion of Little Italy that bordered Hull House." Street-level gangs built alliances with larger criminal businesses running the profitable liquor trade. These local gangs served as ground-floor enforcers and the muscle in the broader struggles over territory. It was in these immigrant working-class neighborhoods that Chicago's notorious beer wars were fought. [38]

In 1923, after mayor William Dever cracked down on crime, gangs competed even more fiercely in a greatly reduced territory. Each gang strong-armed local retailers into carrying only its brand of beer. Gangsters threatened to bomb reluctant establishments, a promise made good on several occasions. Chicago's infamous 1928 "Pineapple Primary" earned its name because of the rampant bomb explosions, killings, and kidnappings during the election to intimidate rival gangs' political supporters. "Fighting for control of areas" in Chicago, lamented one settlement-house worker, "rivalries between gangs, and holding up of stills and store rooms results in violence and murder."[39]

Although poor residents abhorred the violence and crime from bootlegging rings, the product they supplied undeniably found a profitable market among them. Even the illegal activity itself brought opportunity to some. Whether by operating a still in a living-room tenement flat or peddling, delivering, or transporting bootleg liquor, poor men and women participated in the illegal trade despite the risks involved. The Chicago Commons Settlement House reported the result: boot-

legging brought an "obvious new prosperity" to "men who before Prohibition were never prosperous." Such reports were echoed in a 1925
survey from the Federal Council of Churches: "The illicit liquor traffic
has become a means of comparative opulence to many families that
formerly were on the records of relief agencies." A Polish banker in
Bridgeport, Connecticut, saw similar results: "Those who a few years
ago had to be helped by the Falcon society," a Polish benefit society,
"are now driving around in expensive automobiles." Understandably,
such profiteering by an unscrupulous few sparked resentment among
their neighbors, who after all shared in the risks as their neighborhoods
erupted in violence and criminality.[40]

These developments in vulnerable immigrant communities led to a
widespread but erroneous popular linkage of "foreigners" with criminality. The 1920s saw heightened anti-immigrant sentiment whose
stock and trade came to include frequent portrayals of noncitizens as
lawbreakers and criminals. This stereotype was later exposed by Edith
Abbott in her 1929 government study Crime and the Foreign Born. Immigrants were underrepresented in the ranks of criminals, the study found.
Foreigners were not the source of the illegal liquor trade. Instead, it was
second-generation American-born children of immigrants who were
proportionally more likely than their parents or other groups to be arrested
and charged with crime, including Volstead violations. Even an otherwise
sympathetic settlement-house observer reported: "If it is the foreigner
who manufactures, it is the American in his hotel, his club, his suburban
home, his lake front apartment who buys. It is the foreigner who is raided,
who takes the risk, who pays the fine and goes to jail, not the wealthy
customer, not the buyer who comes to his home in expensive cars." Such
stigmatizing contributed to ethnic communities' bitter opposition to
Prohibition.[41]

Compounding all these grievances, poor communities faced the
additional risk of drinking cheap, sometimes toxic bootleg liquor.
Much bootleg whiskey was made from industrial alcohol diverted from
government-licensed distilleries that manufactured large quantities of

alcohol for use in industrial products from paint to antifreeze. Bootleggers redistilled this industrial alcohol to remove the poisons intended to
make it unpalatable for human consumption. Some denaturants were
fairly easy to remove; others, such as methanol, commonly known as
wood alcohol, was one of the most deadly and the most difficult to
remove.[42]

Unscrupulous bootleggers disguised the taste and odor of contami-
nants with heavy infusions of flavor. Cutters of industrial alcohol might
also add products such as embalming fluid to give bootleg whiskey
increased kick. Such additives could have drastic effects. Poisonous
bootleg liquor could and did lead to blindness or paralysis. In 1928,
sixty New Yorkers died from wood-alcohol poisoning alone. The official count of deaths annually from wood-alcohol peaked in 1923 at 321,
but throughout Prohibition several thousands more, largely poor men
and women, are known to have died from poisoned liquor.[43]

The south too experienced an epidemic of poisonings, and there as
in the urban north poor communities were especially hard hit. "Jake
ginger," a highly potent alcoholic drink, was sold legally as a prescription medicine for stomach ailments. But during Prohibition, Jake was
adulterated by bootleggers for the illegal market, making an adulterated drink so fiery that it was often mixed with ginger ale or other
beverages, but even in small quantities the additive could cause nerve
damage. Affected drinkers lost muscle control or feeling in their legs or
limped, dragging their feet, and many victims were left permanently
paralyzed. In the wake of Prohibition, public health officials estimated
the number of Jake victims at fifty to sixty thousand. The incidents
affected enough people that the victims founded the United Victims of
Ginger Paralysis Association, an organization that claimed thirty-five
thousand members. Renditions of "Jake Leg Blues" and "Jake Walk
Papa," by blues artists white and African-American, among other commercial releases, testified to the familiarity with the ravages of the
liquor scourge.[44]

Immigrant groups and their American-born children complained about moonshine and its harmful effects. An Italian doctor interviewed by the Chicago Commons said that the health of the neighborhood was being affected to a "lamentable degree by the poisonous drinks now being consumed." Social-service and charity organizations too documented the harmful effects of poor-quality liquor, and especially the increased use of hard liquor. Hard liquor was favored in the illegal liquor trade because its more potent alcohol had a higher value per volume; it was easier to transport and to store and to hide from the eyes of authorities. While some charity organizations heralded happier homes because poor men were drinking less, others told of women coming to them for help complaining that their husbands were made "crazy" by the moonshine they were drinking and were more prone to violence and outbursts under its sway.[45]

As the "noble experiment" persisted, hostility to the law intensified in many communities. A priest of Czech origin in a largely working-class Chicago parish declared, "Prohibition is the biggest crime a person can imagine." Another priest lamented: "They give the good stuff to the sewers and the bad stuff to the people." Such anger was shared by many and erupted spontaneously into crowd action on at least one occasion when a "mob of nearly 1,000 men, women and children" in the Back of the Yards district "hissed, cursed and hurled missiles" when federal Prohibition agents destroyed twenty-eight barrels of beer in a raid on one holdout saloon. Police beat back the belligerent crowd with clubs, but not before the protesters damaged the federal raiders' car.[46]

Such crowd action was rare, but passionate resentment toward the government's enforcers was common. The Chicago Commons Settlement House interviewed forty-two residents of an Italian neighborhood that included grocers, political workers, and laborers: all uniformly expressed "very emotional" opposition to the law. Another group of ninety young men who were mostly "new to the country" overwhelmingly labeled the law "an evil." According to the settlement-house workers who interviewed them, they gave four reasons: it interfered with personal liberty; it produced poisonous, poor-quality liquor; it contrib-

uted to graft and corruption; and it increased crime and violence—
problems in plain sight in their neighborhoods.[47]

Rising hostility to the law ironically did not always translate into
hostility toward government power. Instead, the experience often led
action to consider how government might be oriented in new ways. Of
course, most immigrants wanted the war on alcohol simply to end,
with the legalization of beer and light wines, grocery-store liquor sales,
or the reopening of saloons. But a portion of these men and women
began to call for more radical change, such as a larger role for the federal government in reregulating the liquor industry or a government
monopoly of the liquor trade.[48]

Many Prohibition opponents, then, did not seek a complete devolu-
tion of federal authority to the state and local level, as the conservative
men of the Association Against the Prohibition Amendment (AAPA)
clamored for. Rather, they sought to reorient federal power in more
benign directions. As one Chicago *Danish Times* writer shot back at a
staunch prohibitionist: "Does Dr. Max really believe it is the function
of Government to regulate the habits and appetites of the people rather
than provide them with jobs so that they may produce commodities in
the form of food, clothing, shelter, etc., and enjoy the use of them?" In
this view, the government had an important role to play in the lives of
people—just not the role it was currently taking, interfering with the
minutiae of deeply embedded recreational habits.[49]

Prohibition sparked a new debate over federal power in an era of
otherwise conservative retrenchment. Its manifest successes and failures contributed to widely altered understandings of government's
purview. Despite the relatively moderate Progressive Era regulatory
apparatus—such as the Food and Drug Administration and the Federal
Trade Commission or the dramatic but brief expansion of federal power
during the First World War, the federal government was rarely visible
at a local level. National power had usually been exercised in imperial
expansion or the capture and reorganization of land and territory, from
the West to the Panama Canal. Outside of wartime, most Americans

only experienced the federal government through visits to their local post office. The federal income tax established in 1913 affected only a small number of Americans—five and one half million. National Prohibition put the spotlight on the federal government and drew countless Americans into a debate over the scope, purview, and legitimacy of federal power. To many opponents of Prohibition, the Eighteenth Amendment signaled the government's capture by a highly mobilized minority, the "tyrannical power of the Billy Sundays" as one ethnic newspaper put it. In response, opponents of the law mobilized so that they might grasp the reins of power for themselves and in the process steer the state in new directions.[50]

.   .   .

IN Chicago, these urban ethnic men and women had already displayed their collective power at the ballot box prior to the Eighteenth Amendment's enactment. Now they mobilized to voice their opposition to the Anti-Saloon League and its agenda. No political leader in Chicago did more to bring ethnic voters into the political process than Anton Cermak, leader of the city's wets. A gruff and outspoken citizen of Czech origin, he bristled with disdain for the nation's antiliquor crusaders. Cermak immigrated to the United States from Bohemia as a child, arriving in 1879. He grew up in a poor, immigrant community where heavy drinking was common. His family settled first in a Bohemian enclave of Braidwood, southwest of Chicago, where he and his father worked in the nearby soft bituminous coal fields that dotted the Braidwood landscape. While still a teenager, Cermak led an effort to demand better pay in his nonunion mine; its owners immediately fired him as a labor agitator. Soon afterward, his family moved to Pilsen, a vibrant Bohemian neighborhood of Chicago. There Cermak found skilled work on Chicago's railroads, coupling and uncoupling rail cars, setting train brakes, and inspecting equipment.

Thick-shouldered and broad-bodied, Cermak was tough enough to hold his own among the ethnic gangs that often served as the lowest rung of local political party organizations. As a leader of a local Bohemian gang, Cermak came to the attention of the local Democratic Party, which had won the loyalty of Chicago's Czech community. From his first low-level party job as a ward heeler, he worked his way up, becoming first precinct captain and then chairman. Like other politicians in early twentieth-century urban politics, he built a loyal constituency through personal service to the community, distributing coal, clothing, and sometimes rent money to needy residents. Drawing on his work in the mines as a mule skinner, he invested in a wood-hauling business that soon expanded and allowed him to buy a home in the growing Czech community of Lawndale on the west side of Chicago. In 1902 he won election to the Illinois state legislature, where he worked for neighborhood improvements such as sewers, sidewalks, and pavements.[51]

Cermak wielded power with an iron hand, freely utilizing patronage and graft when the provision of services was not enough to solidify his power. While he was never indicted, accusations dogged him throughout his career. Prohibition allowed Cermak to ride passionate wet sentiment to the leadership of a local anti-Prohibition organization. Backed by the resources of the brewing industry, Cermak used the United Societies for Local Self-Government to focus opposition to liquor-law legislation and, not least, to secure his preeminence as leader of Chicago wets. Once the amendment passed, Cermak continued to speak out against Prohibition. "In the days past," he declared, "people were warned to be on their guard against the Prohibition system, no one wished to listen to these warning voices and everyone dismissed the subject with a 'it will never happen!'" Cermak fearlessly debated Prohibition supporters, pounding his fists and expertly rousing his predominantly wet audiences to a fever pitch. One event proved so lively that an otherwise sympathetic newspaper chided the audience, imploring them to voice their dissent in more civil and respectful terms.[52]

At Cermak's urging, the Chicago City Council passed a resolution in 1920 calling on state and federal officials to amend the Volstead Act and state enforcement laws to legalize the sale of light wine and beer. He also opposed spending city funds for enforcement, quipping, "[L]et the federal government pay." In 1920, he carried his idea for a beer-and-wine amendment to the Illinois delegation of the Democratic National Committee. To his disappointment, the state delegation was too divided between wet and dry wings to unite on the issue, just as the national party was.[53]

But Cermak characteristically would not give up the fight. In 1922, at the same time that he ran for office as chair of the Cook County Board of Commissioners, effectively "mayor" of Cook County, he launched a drive for a ballot referendum calling for the amendment of the Volstead Act to allow for the manufacture, sale, and transportation of beer and light wines for home consumption. The referendum's relatively modest demands testified to the low hopes of even staunch Prohibition opponents for a complete end to it. No constitutional amendment had ever been rescinded. Practical politicians like Cermak focused, instead, on amending the Volstead Act to mitigate the law's enforcement. Still, the Anti-Saloon League—"out after his scalp" according to one newspaper—energetically worked to derail his campaign and the referendum effort.[54]

Many ethnic organizations, on the other hand, mobilized for Cermak and his amendment campaign. German grand lodges, Bohemian sokols, local gymnastic clubs, the Irish American Society of Cook County, and the Polish Fellowship League of Illinois, which included nearly every Polish organization, endorsed Cermak. The Bohemian Ladies Union and the Federated Unions of Bohemian Catholic women promised support for a mass rally backing the referendum. Ethnic newspapers urged their readers to the polls. The German *Abendpost* announced a mass meeting in support of the beer-and-wine referendum, and urged voters to elect anti-Prohibition congressmen. An influential Czech daily exhorted "citizens of this new homeland . . . [to] unite in an effort to combat the forces of fanaticism."[55]

In Chicago, a broad and united ethnic front transcended localist identities, forging an increasing collective enfranchisement as Americans. They appropriated the rhetoric of "Americanism" from their largely Protestant and disapproving opponents, redefining it from the bottom up. In October, shortly before the referendum vote, a mass anti-Prohibition gathering was held in Pilsen Park. There Czech immigrants evoked a romanticized American past and themselves as its rightful heirs: Czech women dressed as "Indian maidens" and served food to those who turned out in support. Meal and drink tickets were sold by ladies representing "liberty." Signs declared "the spirit of 1776" in opposition to what they saw as "tyranny of a minority."[56]

During the campaign, ethnic newspapers stimulated large turnouts and educated community members on the voting process. "Every one of us who has his citizenship papers . . . ought to go to register at once in order to be able to join our fighting ranks and to be entitled to use his weapon—the ballot." One Czech-language paper provided instructions to those who did not possess sufficient English on how to navigate the process: "We are convinced that there is not a single Czechoslovak citizen who would not wish to change the existing Prohibition law, and it is therefore necessary that every one of us place a cross after the word "yes." Such calls contributed to the success of the amendment: Chicago voters approved the initiative with a resounding 81 percent in favor. Turnout was particularly heavy in ethnic working-class wards.[57]

Immigrants in fact took to the voting booths in Chicago in greater numbers in the 1920s then ever before. They were drawn to the ballot at least in part by the war on alcohol. While increasing numbers of first-generation immigrants became citizens and thereby eligible to vote, the habit of actually voting did not emerge spontaneously. Voters had to see sufficient stakes to go to the polls. The two major political parties rarely offered solutions relevant to these working-class men's and women's lives on election day. The war on alcohol, however, directly affected them. When Prohibition was on the ballot, many working-class immigrants took the plunge into the political process. Once involved, this new political cohort contributed the fledgling growth of the urban ethnic wing of the Democratic Party.[58]

. . . .

WORKING-CLASS urban ethnic communities, their leaders, and their labor allies lambasted Prohibition as a "trick" put over by a small minority in a nation distracted by war. Such a narrative belied the still-powerful coalition behind the passage and ratification of the Eighteenth Amendment. Whatever its flaws as historical explanation, this narrative did accurately point to the skewed balance of power of the early twentieth century. The war on alcohol was possible only because some Americans were unevenly mobilized in the body politic. While the Protestant churches were highly organized, enjoyed national reach, and wielded great resources, poor immigrant communities had a far more tenuous relationship to politics, particularly at the national level. Many were, in fact, noncitizens and ineligible to vote; those who were eligible were disproportionate among the ranks of nonvoters. Their political loyalties were usually local in orientation and frequently mediated by ethnic ward bosses or precinct captains. Coupled with a structural overrepresentation of rural regions in Congress, not to mention disfranchisement of poor whites and African-Americans in the south, resistance by the natural opposition to Prohibition stood little chance. Ironically, only the experience of welling grievances provoked by the law could wake the sleeping tiger of new ethnic voters, drawing them into the political process and ultimately transforming the Democratic Party.

3

SELECTIVE ENFORCEMENT

ON THE EVENING OF MARCH 7, 1922, ISIDOR EINSTEIN
entered a Brooklyn cabaret, a violin case in hand, and ordered a drink.
A hesitant waiter asked his boss if he should serve the stranger. "Sure,"
the proprietor reassured him, "that's Jake the fiddler . . . he plays down
on Flatbush Avenue." The waiter served the "musician" his order and
requested that he play a tune. Einstein agreed to "Revenuer's Blues,"
opened his case, poured the evidence into a container concealed inside,
and arrested the surprised proprietor and waiter. The sly agent had col-
lared two more hapless Volstead violators in his celebrated career as
"Prohibition Agent no. 1."[1]

During the first four years of Prohibition, "Dry Hooch Hound"
Isidor Einstein and his partner Moe Smith entertained New Yorkers
with stylized busts of Volstead violators. Dressed in drag, donning
blackface, posing as statues of Buddha, or disguised in other outlandish
costumes, the federal investigators gained access to many of the places
New Yorkers drank, gathering evidence and arresting thousands of
unsuspecting bartenders, speakeasy proprietors, and bootleggers. As

their notoriety grew, the corpulent agents (Izzy weighed in at 225 pounds despite his modest height) expanded their repertoire, dressing as undertakers, fishermen, baseball or football players, icemen, even rabbis. They broke up "delightful parties" with heavy hearts—"[I]t almost made me weep," lamented Einstein. It was widely reported that Izzy didn't even carry a gun, casting enforcement as lighthearted at best and harmless at worst. New York's press celebrated the "Prohibition comedians," who shrewdly timed their raids for maximum press publicity. Their exploits made them—if the hype could be believed—the country's most successful Prohibition agents. Despite colorful newspaper copy that stretched credulity, the agents were undeniably New York's public face of Prohibition enforcement.[2]

Einstein's methods—his "theory of rum-snooping," as one paper grandly labeled it—was a rare oasis of lighthearted news in what journalists called the "driest business on earth." Popular and scholarly accounts retold these fictionalized stories of "Prohibition Agent No. 1" as fact, including Einstein's wildly exaggerated claim that during his four years as a federal agent he single-handedly arrested 4,932 violators and convicted 95 percent of them. By missing the punch line in stories written to entertain New York's largely wet readership, subsequent chroniclers have cast Prohibition itself as a joke. By one account, "there was never any serious effort to enforce national Prohibition until the early thirties, and by that time it was too late." Such interpretations capture the gaps in enforcement when it came to particular cities and social groups but obscure the serious and at times lethal nature of enforcement against select groups across the nation. As one legal scholar familiar with Prohibition's full record averred, "Prohibition is often described as a dead letter, but it was an extremely lively corpse."[3]

Federal agent William Turner, in sharp contrast to the antic-filled collarings of Izzy and Moe, approached his work with zeal and ruthlessness. Turner was in charge of enforcement in a poor rural farm region that included the remote Appalachian mountain town of Hazard, Kentucky. When Turner and his men surprised a small group of imbibers with one half-gallon jug of whiskey, one man—Bradley Bowling—ran out and took refuge behind a pile of rocks in the backyard. Williams spotted him there and, seeing him "put his hand in his pocket," fatally shot him. Turner found no weapon on Bradley's body but recovered the half gallon of whiskey.[4]

In such places, Prohibition enforcement was anything but a laughing matter. With men like William Turner leading the charge, the war on alcohol radically expanded the surveillance arm of the police at the federal, state, and local level. The newly established Prohibition Unit of the Treasury Department (the forerunner of the Prohibition Bureau), which first hired 1,550 field agents supported by a staff of another 1,500, expanded the existing policing apparatus exponentially. This number far outstripped the fledgling Bureau of Investigation, the precursor of the FBI, which had only 650 agents and support staff in 1924. Backed by this expanded policing apparatus, and the mandate of the Coast Guard and the Customs Bureau to aid in enforcement, John Kramer, the first U.S. Prohibition Commissioner, confidently declared in his first press conference, "This law will be obeyed in cities, large and small, and in villages, and where it is not obeyed it will be enforced. . . . We shall see that [liquor] is not manufactured, nor sold, nor given away, nor hauled in anything on the surface of the earth or under the earth or in the air." By the late 1920s, the Prohibition Bureau housed around 4,000 employees. Its budget of $13 million in 1930 (equivalent to over $185 million in today's dollars) dwarfed J. Edgar Hoover's Bureau of Investigation budget that same year of just over $2 million. Even by 1936, when the renamed FBI had vastly expanded its powers beyond the narrow mandate of the Prohibition agents, it still had an annual budget of only $5 million. Not surprisingly, the mushrooming government agency had soft, shallow roots and was soon beset by corruption, violence, and penetration by organized crime. Though Kramer's ambitions for a total victory were ultimately dashed, his effort toward the frankly impossible goal of abolishing liquor unquestionably rewrote the federal government's role in crime control.[5]

As expansive as its effort was, the federal government was not the only authority responsible for enforcing the Eighteenth Amendment, which charged "the several states" along with Congress with "concurrent power to enforce this article by appropriate legislation." Many states had passed their own prohibition laws during the First World War. Where some of these laws had wide loopholes, most were amended to comply with the standards of the Volstead Act. Virginia and Georgia, for example, now barred the importation of even small quantities of ardent spirits that earlier had contributed to a brisk mail-order business. All states, with the exception of Maryland, adopted laws to buttress the Volstead Act. Sixteen had even stricter bans on liquor and penalties for violators. Only a handful of states would eventually disavow a role in enforcement of the law. Forty-two states maintained their enforcement codes throughout national Prohibition, with thirty-four strengthening those laws to rein in violations. Evasion of the Eighteenth Amendment, then, was a state as well as a federal crime. The Supreme Court's 1922 ruling in *United States v. Lanza* exempted liquor-law violators from the Constitution's protections against double jeopardy due to the concurrent enforcement clause in the Eighteenth Amendment. This meant that some violators were prosecuted for the same crime twice, contributing even more to uneven policing and enforcement regionally.[6]

Across the nation's forty-eight states, and in its colonial possessions, enforcement varied widely, but in most states punishment for liquor-law violations caused serious penalties. In Massachusetts, violators could win steeply discounted fines and shortened sentences by pleading guilty in the special court "bargain days" that judges instituted to reduce vast backlogs. In West Virginia, however, there were no such back doors. The "drastic" state enactment "bristl[ed] with severe penalties." Possession of a still was a felony subject to not less than one and not more than five years in prison. Even the former confederate states, chary since Reconstruction of federal power, rallied their state agencies for national Prohibition. In 1919, Arkansas criminalized possession and storage, declaring "to manufacture or give away intoxicating liquor" a felony. In Mississippi manufacturing or distilling intoxicating liquor was also a felony "punishable by imprisonment in the state penitentiary." Texas's draconian 1919 Dean Act penalized possession with a prison term of one to five years and even criminalized liquor advertising as a felony offense. Indiana criminalized not just sale but purchase, sharply increasing the volume of arrests. Colorado's amended 1919 law outlawed "possession or personal use," as did Oregon. Such state laws were aimed at loopholes in the Volstead Act that protected consumption within the home of pre-Volstead liquor and storage in clubhouses. While tightfisted legislatures left many of these laws without sufficient or sometimes any funding, at a minimum local and state police were responsible for enforcing the law. Some states' newly established Prohibition offices—such as Virginia's—joined those officials creating another layer of enforcement.[7]

Despite its manifest gaps and imperfections, many Americans, and especially poor men and women, found themselves ensnared in one or more of Prohibition's webs, arrested, charged, fined, or incarcerated by local, state, or federal agents whose methods frequently violated constitutional protections. Prohibition policing differed by region, by rural or urban setting, and most especially by race, ethnicity, and class. An unprecedented campaign of selective enforcement lurked beneath the surface glamor of the roaring twenties that left the urbane elite sipping cocktails in swank, protected nightclubs from New York's Cotton Club to Chicago's Plantation Club, while men like Bradley Bowling died over a jug of whiskey. Uneven enforcement was the hidden reason the white, urbane upper-middle class could laugh at the antics of Izzy Einstein and Moe Smith, while Mexicans, poor European immigrants, African-Americans, poor whites in the South, and the unlucky experienced the full brunt of Prohibition enforcement's deadly reality.

Prohibitionists' historic antipathy to the ethnic, working-class saloon contributed to selective enforcement. So too did the logic of the newly profitable black market. Dwarfed by the herculean nature of their task and cowed by the sophistication and resolve of the big alcohol traders, agents at all levels naturally boosted their casebooks by sleuthing out and prosecuting small rather than large stakeholders in the trade. Enterprising and unscrupulous Americans built large illegal business empires to quench the thirst of the nation's imbibers. With vast sums of money, such networks had little trouble oiling the gears of collaboration and selective enforcement among federal, state, and local officials and liquor manufacturers and suppliers. Lacking funds for wholesale bribery, graft, and protection payoffs, small, marginal violators filled a disproportionate share of Prohibition's courtroom dockets.

. . . .

VIRGINIA, the former seat of the Confederacy and then still a bulwark of white racial domination, provides a dramatic example of these processes at work. Even before the advent of national Prohibition, the state's powerful antiliquor crusaders had successfully rallied support for prohibition. Its public officials took their antiliquor crusade seriously, but directed state policing powers almost exclusively toward a crackdown on the alcohol-laced leisure world of the poor and on marginal suppliers. Virginia's Mapp Act, the state prohibition statute, went into effect on October 31, 1916, three years before national Prohibition. The movement's triumph there owed its greatest debt to the Protestant church and, especially, the evangelical Methodists so plentiful in the state. Anti-Saloon League–affiliated ministers occupied the pulpits of all but three or four churches in the state's large Methodist Conference, which included just under two thousand churches dotting the Commonwealth's cities, small towns, and rural landscapes. With one voice, these pastors railed against the evils of excessive drink, pressing their congregants to join the Anti-Saloon cause.[8]

James Cannon Jr., the bishop of Virginia's Methodist Church Conference, exemplified the dynamism of Virginia's Prohibition forces. Now at the height of his regional influence, Cannon sought to enact his church's vision of the collective public good into law. Known for his organizational savvy, political shrewdness, and dictatorial style, the "Dry Messiah" exerted a powerful influence on matters of "public morality" in the Old Dominion. During the debate over the enforcement provisions of the Mapp Act, Cannon had a seat on the assembly floor. His presence at the state-capitol hearings testified to the still porous boundaries between church and state in Jefferson's home state. With cadres of dry enthusiasts at the grassroots level and Cannon in the lead, the evangelical movement steamrolled the vocal but outclassed opposition of the *Richmond Times-Dispatch* and local Richmond businessmen who somewhat belatedly banded together as the Association for Local Self-Government.[9]

Virginia's Association for Local Self-Government may not have had the powerful organized social base of the Methodist crusaders, but it did win significant support from a small cadre of prominent lawyers and businessmen, as well as the preordained support of stakeholders in the liquor trade. George L. Christian, former president of the Virginia Bar Association, along with Royal E. Cabell, former United States Commissioner of Internal Revenue, lent support to their efforts. Housed in the Richmond Chamber of Commerce, the organization printed broadsides, pamphlets, and, at the zenith of the campaign, a weekly newspaper. The law, they argued, would drain state coffers and lead inevitably to increased taxes. Beyond its blow to Virginians' pocketbooks, the law abrogated sacred principles of local self-government and was sure to breed hypocrisy, disrespect for law, and social unrest. Their arguments would be echoed later by the national group, the Association Against the Prohibition Amendment. The referendum battle was a contest, however, for the hearts and minds of but a small segment of Virginia's population, and one heavily biased to favor stern control of their social inferiors. Virginia's voting rolls had effectively been slashed in half in 1903 as a result of the disfranchisement of African-Americans and numerous poor whites. Virginia's 136,900 voters out of a population of close to two million residents took to the polls and sided decidedly with the drys, with a vote of 94,251 to 63,886.

This was a high turnout in Virginia's tightly constricted electoral process, about the same number that had voted during the presidential
election of 1912 just two years earlier.[10]

Cannon and religious reformers in other southern states swept away
objections raised by their opponents with arguments similar to their
brethren in the Progressive north and west. Since alcoholic spirits were
toxic substances, destructive to both mind and spirit, banishing them
was, a priori, a social good: "a policy favorable to religion, favorable to
education, favorable to industry, and favorable to the coming generation." In the south, however, antiliquor arguments added a peculiar
twist: the war on alcohol was a particularly urgent "necessity of Southern conditions in particular," specifically the "presence of eight million" African-Americans which, according to one reformer, amounted
to "the largest sociological problem any people ever had." Anxious
white elites fretted over agitation by recently disfranchised poor
African-Americans, and as economic conditions worsened on southern
farms, so did the dire possibility of resistance from poor whites increase
at the same time. Such arguments had sufficient power to overcome the
south's usual wariness over federal power to back the expansion of its
policing power. Southern states such as Virginia were at the cutting
edge of the nation's Prohibition crusade.[11]

Nine southern states passed state prohibition laws between 1907 and
1915, shortly after the imposition of disfranchisement. Saloons and bars
stood out as one of the remaining public places African-Americans
could gather without white surveillance or the supervision of "respectable" black elites, such as ministers. As such, they became a focal point
of southern anxieties: the "crime-breeding, sloth-producing saloons . . .
sold negros whiskey bottles labeled with picture[s] of nude white
women" and "tempted idle and criminal negroes . . . to commit hei-
nous offenses against unprotected women and girls." Equally problem-
atic, in elite reformers' eyes, were the dives and honky-tonks frequented
by "illiterate whites." Such hole-in-the-wall establishments prolifer-
ated in "sections where poorer whites dwell" and contributed to vio-

lent race riots. Respectable southerners were "tired" of such disturbances to southern "peace." For southern reformers, the crusade promised an "opportunity," as one supporter observed, to simultaneously control "inferior" folk and improve the social order. In an era when its "best" men and women kept silent about the public murder of African-Americans through lynching, Prohibition promised to burnish the moral authority of southern elites, realigning the "moral and patriotic elements of Southern society on the side of law." Tellingly, Mississippi, with its large population of disfranchised African-Americans, was the first state to ratify the Eighteenth Amendment and, in 1966, one of the last to rescind its state dry law. Despite their lambasting of the evils of drink, the Virginia provisions mysteriously allowed residents to import limited quantities of liquor from outside the state, an indication of how the movement targeted the drink of specific social groups.[12]

After the well-organized Protestant movement won passage of statewide prohibition in Virginia, activists did not retreat home to savor their victory. They wanted more than a paper triumph and pushed through strict enforcement legislation. Bishop Cannon's formidable power ensured that enforcement unfolded under the vigilance of organized Methodism and the Anti-Saloon League. The state's first prohibition commissioner, J. Sydney Peters, was a close ally of Cannon and was appointed at Cannon's behest by the Virginia legislature. Peters, a Methodist minister, had been a devoted soldier in the prohibition crusade, steeped in staunch prohibition sentiment since boyhood. His mother had once been president of the Virginia Woman's Christian Temperance Union. To ensure the effectiveness of the new law, his church freed Peters from pulpit obligations, allowing the reverend to accept the position of state commissioner. Given the close ties between the state enforcement arm and the moral reformers, it seemed only natural that the commission's first headquarters was the Anti-Saloon League office in Richmond. Applicants for jobs at the commission emphasized their "good moral standing" and "consistent membership in the Methodist church." One Wilbur Hamilton, for example, detailed the work he had done to win prohibition and his attendance at the "Men's Worthwhile Bible Class, in the Central Methodist Church." H. S. Sherman, minister of the Methodist Church South, wrote to "Brother Peters" directly with his suggestions about who should be hired.[13]

Financial constraints pulled the commission even closer to the well-organized crusaders. Peters's staff of paid investigators relied on a voluntary corps of 519 volunteers who kept an eye out for violations. When commission agents chased down and fired on a liquor-laden car in Richmond, killing the two occupants, outcry over the commission's amateurish overreaching rose to fever pitch. Since by this time the national law had overtaken Virginia's statewide efforts, officials held out fresh hope that success would come with a more experienced, federally empowered administrative leader. The job was handed to the state's attorney, Harry Smith, in 1922. By 1928, the office staff of the state commissioner in Richmond oversaw one hundred field agents who coordinated their work with federal field agents and local sheriffs. In Virginia, prohibition enforcement thus passed from the literally parochial orientation of Reverend Peters to the state's highest law enforcement official, marking a shift to a more professionalized and bureaucratic law enforcement apparatus with intimate ties up the federal law enforcement hierarchy.[14]

The Virginia Prohibition Commission struggled against the same headwinds that bedeviled national enforcement: tight budgets, insufficient staffing, and meager pay. The commission nonetheless worked diligently, first under Peters, then Smith, and finally his successor, attorney general John R. Saunders, to pursue the monumental task of drying out the Commonwealth. While investigators were put in charge of large regions, they were encouraged to vigorous enforcement by financial incentives to nab violators and special "fees" for stills captured and violators prosecuted.[15]

In some regions, the state's investigators confronted conditions that no incentives could overcome, especially given the far larger sums available through collusion in the trade. This was particularly true in the Blue Ridge mountains in the western part of the state. Bereft of eastern Virginia's prime agricultural land, farmers had a long history of moonshining to help eke out their subsistence. In the late nineteenth century, rural moonshiners had violently battled federal "revenuers" seeking to collect taxes from the unlicensed producers of distilled spirits across the region. While national Prohibition brought a new level of enforcement to the crusade against alcohol, it also opened up vast new markets for moonshine production. What had once been a marginal, individualistic business now became tightly organized and coordinated. In rural western areas like Franklin County, moonshiners were a critical part of the local economic establishment, operating with the collusion of local elites. The Wickersham Commission, the government commission set up by Hoover to study enforcement around the country, reported that ninety-nine out of one hundred county residents were either making or had some connection with illegal liquor. With so many stakeholders in the moonshine business, local whistle-blowers feared reprisals and were hesitant to lodge complaints. "The whole mountain region is honeycombed with moonshine," wrote one Franklin County resident to state agents in 1927. "Officers are doing nothing to stop the moonshine down here." Significantly, he added a plea that his complaint remain confidential because "it would mean the loss of my property if they know." The networks of police, judges, politicians, and community members scattered throughout the region's isolated hollows and rough roads successfully resisted efforts to disrupt their web of production and supply.[16]

The assignment to rein in violations in the Blue Ridge mountains fell to Frank Dobson. Despite the ubiquity of moonshine in his district, Dobson's thin file of reports and incomplete and often missing daily logs testify to the difficulties he faced and perhaps a resigned but safer and more profitable collusion in the trade. Dobson's superiors nonetheless praised his "good work" under conditions considered nigh impossible. Dobson's investigations frequently came to naught, and when he did break up a still and arrest its operators, his chances of winning a conviction were close to zero. The investigator advised the state commissioner in 1923, "I am sorry to report that at this time it is almost impossible to get a conviction in any case. Juries are in sympathy with the bootlegger and the moonshiner." Dobson's quixotic efforts in the "moonshine capital of the world" offers a concrete example of an abject failure of enforcement in a region with deep roots in the illicit trade in liquor, one of many pockets whose flouting of the law contributed to the popular image of Prohibition as a dead letter.[17]

In other regions of the Old Dominion, however, Prohibition enforcement was alive and more often than not, so effective as to raise alarms of government overreach rather than impotence. In 1928, Virginia officials seized nearly three thousand stills and 67,000 gallons of ardent spirits statewide. They confiscated over a thousand automobiles tied to the trade. Of the 21,706 individuals prosecuted for liquor law violations that year, the vast majority—17,127—were convicted. Prohibition also produced revenues for state coffers. Far from a threat to the state's finances, Prohibition brought in $593,489 (over $8 million in today's dollars) in 1928. While convicted violators often served merely a few months in jail, the cumulative impact of this prosecutorial vigor was large: that year, state and federal judges imposed sentences totaling 16,376 months in jail for liquor offenders.[18]

This tidal wave of arrests, convictions, fines, and sentences, not the backwoods cat-and-mouse game of Hazard, Kentucky, was the more emblematic face of Virginia's enforcement. It was an effort that became more, not less, intense over the course of the decade. During Virginia's Prohibition years, between 1916 and 1933, state and local agents amassed 147,683 arrests. Judges statewide imposed 12,676 years in total jail time and over $6 million in fines (more than $80 million in current dollars). Police seized thirty thousand stills, impounded ten thousand automobiles, and confiscated $8 million worth of other property. While the state commission had every reason to tout its success in its annual reports and may have been tempted to inflate numbers, a wider body of evidence testifies to the accuracy of this picture of vigorous Prohibition policing.[19]

Such unprecedented numbers of arrests and convictions not surprisingly overwhelmed the state's prison and jail system. Prisons were more crowded than at any time in the Commonwealth's history. Short- and long-term jail commitments more than doubled in the seven years from 1923 to 1931, spiking from 26,506 to 53,758. In 1931 there were almost seven thousand prisoners in the Commonwealth's myriad prisons, from the penitentiary to state prison "farms," a leap from just over four thousand only ten years earlier. Overcrowding led state officials to authorize the expansion and renovation of the Virginia penitentiary and to rush to completion a new building in 1929. The state established a State Farm for Defective Misdemeanants and the Prison Board purchased a tract of 170 acres in 1930 to build the first unit of the Women's State Industrial Farm, a monument to white women's role in the illicit traffic. "Few" of the existing packed institutions, remarked one observer, "had adequate facility for the proper care and segregation of the [white] women prisoners." The first unit of the segregated women's facility was filled to capacity soon after it opened. This same concern was not extended to female African-American prisoners.[20]

Overcrowded prisons meant that many violators had to serve their time on the state's notorious chain gangs, building the roads desired by Virginia's Highway Commission. State law enforcement provisions stipulated that liquor violators sentenced to jail could be ordered to serve their time on the state's convict road force. Inability to pay a fine or the costs "incident to the prosecution and conviction" could also lead to hard labor in shackles. A large number of convicted liquor-law violators—black and white—served out their time in the state's loosely regulated road camps, where prisoner infractions from insubordination to attempted escape drew corporal punishment, including the lash.[21]

Agent James T. Crute's voluminous daily logs reveal ground-level efforts that contributed to the state's hefty enforcement numbers. Crute was in charge of a relatively populous region of small cities and towns, including Barhamsville, Gloucester, and Williamsburg in the peninsular region of the state. A former lumber-mill operator and active Methodist, he was a true believer in the cause and zealous in his mission. He spent long days and, not infrequently, long nights scouring the area's dirt roads, some impassable in the rain. Local sheriffs, volunteer "posse" members, and federal agents joined him on many of these expeditions.[22]

Crute's investigations sometimes uncovered operations of astonishing sophistication. In a pre-Christmas raid on one mill owner, he discovered a state-of-the-art still located near the Gloucester courthouse. It was "the most complete still I ever saw," he reported, with a "concrete floor and walls built for the purpose, all fitted up with pipes, a pipe line from his mill to the house, the pump pushing water to a tank over the basement." On this raid, the zealous officer confiscated a seventy-five-gallon steam still and seven hundred pounds of mash, and arrested R. L Tipton and J. J. Hanson, two white men working on the premises. On another case, he uncovered an entirely subterranean manufacturing operation: "The still was in an underground room about sixteen feet long, the hole was dug out and then covered over with board. . . . The dirt [was] hauled out in the woods. . . . [F]lowers were planted on the mound over the still house. . . . One end of the still house was built above the ground, . . . [and] after raking the dirt away . . . [from] what was apparently a dirt floor . . . a trap door was found lead[ing] to the still from a flight of steps in the small house above the ground which had a lot of meat hanging up in the roof." The moonshiners, Crute, reported, would "smoke the meat when the still was in operation" to cover the smell of distilled liquor."[23]

While spectacular, busts of such large establishments were exceptional. Entrepreneurial and newly wealthy whites may have dominated the large wholesale and retail trade, but agents like Crute spent most of their time arresting small violators, a large number of whom were African-American. Like poor native-born whites, urban immigrants in Chicago, and Latinos in the Southwest, African-American men and women worked stills, made home brew, operated "blind tigers" (marginal retail establishments), and bootlegged. For poor men and women in search of employment or ways to supplement meager incomes, the underground business of drink offered alluring, if precarious, opportunities. By eliminating large capitalized producers from the liquor business, Prohibition reversed the normal economics of scale and allowed even the smallest, least efficient producers to profit.[24]

By drawing those at the lower end of the economic scale into an illicit enterprise, bootlegging and moonshining in the Jim Crow south had the unintended effect of blurring lines of segregation. Federal agents frequently noted both whites and "negroes" on the premises in their raids of still operations, and both African-Americans and whites were victims of indiscriminate and often deadly use of force by those enforcing the law. The African-American newspaper *The Pittsburgh Courier* reported with dry humor one North Carolina reference to the mixed racial composition of the illegal economy: "[I]f white and Negro preachers understood each other and worked together, as well as white and Negro bootleggers do, a large part of our interracial troubles would come to a speedy end."[25]

Beneath this veneer of racial harmony, however, was an entrenched imbalance of power that consigned whites and poor African-Americans to quite divergent roles in the subaltern economy. Poor African-Americans and whites found employment in the business of drink, but rarely as equals. One federal study of Virginia's enforcement acknowledged that blacks were frequently the employees of the white still owners, performing "the physical work in the manufacturing." Whites, as in other areas of the economy, had more access to the capital required to set up such operations and better access to enterprising enforcement officials.[26]

As employees tending to the large stills, African-Americans faced a greater risk of arrest than their white employers. When John Walker was arrested during a raid of a 350-gallon-capacity still, he told officers he was "merely an employee on wages." In Montgomery, Alabama, one grand jury remarked that all the cases brought before them "involved only negroes, while the testimony indicated that these negroes were working for white men." "It is a certainty," observed one African-American newspaper, "that a large percentage of the crimes with which the colored race is charged have to do with bootlegging for white men." Law enforcement officials in the South had neither the resources nor the will to go after the large still owners, so those caught red-handed suffered the most.[27]

James Crute's daily logs from 1922 and 1923 starkly document this pattern: African-Americans made up over half of those he charged with manufacture and possession, though to be sure some operated their own stills from their homes. The same day Crute decommissioned the underground still in Gloucester, he raided the home of African-American W. B. Turner, taking possession of a modest fifteen-gallon still and arresting several men. They attempted to escape when the raiders arrived, but were caught, jailed without bail, and later convicted. The white bootleggers operating the elaborate Gloucester still, on the other hand, were rapidly acquitted of charges.[28]

Crute was not the only inspector whose "daily reports" frequently listed "black" or "colored" next to the name of those charged. Agent A. S. Chase headquartered in Portsmouth was in charge of sleuthing out violators in Norfolk County. From June through December 1924, Chase conducted over one hundred raids. Again, African-Americans made up over half of the men and women he arrested and charged with violations. Thirty-seven-year-old Arthur Faulkner was one of them. Charged with possessing approximately two quarts of liquor, likely for personal use, Faulkner was sentenced to two months in jail and handed a $225 fine. Since the average daily income of unskilled African-American wage-earners in Virginia was less than three dollars a day in 1928, with average annual incomes totaling less than eight hundred dollars, this was an extremely onerous fine. Since Virginia's enforcement law stipulated that those who could not pay legal costs or fines could be sentenced to serve on the convict road gangs, Faulkner's possession of moonshine likely earned him months of hard labor.[29]

Because of the severity of possible fines and prison sentences, boot-leggers sometimes took extreme measures to escape sentences, abscond-ing or destroying the evidence. When Eula Andres and Vaughn Finville realized that Crute and local officers were about to raid their home, they smashed bottles and poured out liquor so that only three quarts of whiskey remained when police entered and charged them with posses-sion. Confrontations between raiding officers and violators sometimes turned deadly. John Normeley, an African-American, operated a small still in his backyard, outside the city of Richmond. Tipped off to the still, four state investigators raided Normeley's home, ordering him outside. Normeley refused and a violent confrontation followed during which he was hit over the head with the butt end of one officer's pistol. He defended himself against the assault, and the gun went off, the bul-let hitting an agent. When Normeley tried to run away, the police shot him several times in the back. His unarmed wife was shot in the head and killed. The raid that resulted in two deaths recovered one quart of whiskey and a ten-gallon copper still.[30]

Such deadly use of force against both African-American and white liquor offenders was not uncommon. In a November 1922 raid on a moonshine operation in a wooded area on the outskirts of Richmond, Crute stealthily approached two white still tenders. He called on the men to put their hands up, but they dove into a nearby thicket: "I let them have one bauble of my gun. . . . I got one man, shot in the back." A few weeks later Crute unloaded his weapon again, this time shooting an African-American still tender: "[H]e was shot at twice, as he ran into the bushes . . . he must have been shot but disappeared." Crute made no claims that the moonshiners had attacked him, reporting mat-ter of factly that he shot both men in the back as they tried to escape.[31]

Crute's logs suggest a broad official sanction for the cavalier use of force by enforcement officials. Such violence provoked attacks through-out the Prohibition years by opponents of rampant government "law-lessness." Zealous Prohibitionists reprimanded such critics as "apologists for law breakers" who "vilified, slandered, assaulted and persecuted brave gentlemen." Virginia's James Cannon believed that enforcement must take place "no matter the cost in money or men." But even the government's firebrand enforcement spokeswoman, assistant attorney general Mabel Walker Willebrandt—while defending force by officers in dealing with "a vast class of desperadoes"— condemned as "atrocious, wholly unwarranted, and unnecessary some of the killings" and pleaded for better training and more professional policing. A report by the Association Against the Prohibition Amendment questioned the official government estimate of two hundred citizens killed by government agents, putting the number far higher, in excess of one thousand "if a thorough canvass were made that included not just [killings by] Bureau agents but the many types of officers who make up the great Volstead army." A review of the myriad enforcement agencies in Virginia suggests that the numbers were far higher than even that estimate.[32]

Arrests and prosecution of offenders, however, proved highly selective. In Richmond local police openly acknowledged that violators were treated differently depending on their race, class, or "moral standing." One Richmond police court judge remarked that in terms of who gets "arrested and indicted for ardent spirits . . . it makes a vast difference in whose house liquor is found." Richmond's "cleanup squads" heavily targeted the capital city's working-class and African-American population. In 1930, Richmond was a midsized city of less than two hundred thousand inhabitants and African-Americans constituted just under one-third of that population. In 1928, however, over half of those arrested for liquor law violations were black.[33]

In Richmond the police energetically and intrusively raided private homes and apartments in poor neighborhoods. Police records indicate a veritable avalanche of arrests for liquor-law violations. In April 1923, police conducted over 131 searches, some on "selling houses," but mainly on private dwellings. During 1925 and 1926 enforcers ratcheted up their efforts. The Richmond Times-Dispatch publicized one "whirlwind crusade" by the "cleanup squad," in January of 1925, netting fifty-three quart jars of whiskey and "all negro" prisoners. In February 1925, police conducted 171 searches, again mainly on private dwellings. In one-half of those raids, "nothing was found." Given the targeting of homes rather than clubs or speakeasies, and the frequency with which officers came up empty-handed, poor and minority residents of Richmond likely felt those intrusions as an unjustified abuse of state power, if not a veritable reign of terror.[34]

In 1925 the Virginia state legislature had passed new enforcement provisions stipulating hefty special fees paid directly to local and state agents who seized stills and successfully apprehended liquor-law violators. In Richmond, the special fees led to the zealous efforts of local police who freely entered private residences and smashed down doors to catch violators. Search warrants could be issued on the basis of "information and belief," a clause police interpreted with wide latitude. Arrests were often made for "possession and storage" of small quantities of liquor that was most likely intended for personal use or for the operation of a small blind pig. African-Americans Lizzie and Fitzhugh White, a laundress and a laborer, were on the receiving end of the selective crackdown. In 1923 police searched White's home at 411 North 17th street, Richmond, and recovered a two-quart jug "half full with corn whiskey," one and a half pints of "ardent spirits," and a basket of empty bottles. The Whites were hauled down to the police station and charged with "keeping and storing ardent spirits for sale." Police found a somewhat larger stash in their raid of Robert Moseley's home at 1410 West Moore Street. Apparently Moseley was supplementing his income as a "helper" by operating a small blind pig. Police netted an unusually large haul—forty-eight "half gallon jars full of ardent spirits"—and arrested Moseley as well as Hattie Laventia and Lucy Pleasants who were at the apartment at the time of the raid. When officers invaded the home of an African-American couple, carpenter Edward Amos and his wife Clara Amos, on February 2, 1925, they uncovered a two-quart jar of whiskey and a one-pint bottle of corn liquor, most likely for personal consumption. Amos, the father of two young children, was arrested and charged with "possession, keeping, and storing."[35]

By paying, in effect, a commission for successful raids and granting warrants liberally, Virginia's law enforcement agencies experienced a qualitative change in their intrusive powers. Not surprisingly, in Richmond the city police gained new authority during the war on alcohol. The city police force had won a new headquarters in 1911 and by 1914 the police force was staffed with 125 patrolmen. But by 1929 its force doubled: 252 officers equipped with new patrol wagons policed a city with a population of approximately two hundred thousand. The city's poor communities felt the results.[36]

In Newport News, city police reacted to the new incentives by targeting poor and working-class violators, many of whom were African-American. Etta Davenport, an African-American domestic worker, evidently took advantage of the underground economy to supplement her meager income. Arrested for possession of a still, she was fined $102.50 and sentenced to a month and a half in jail. James McCoy, a laborer, spent one month in jail and paid $75 for transporting. Willie Chavis, a sometime elevator operator, paid a fine of $68 and spent one month in jail after his conviction for manufacture in 1921. For poor laborers who frequently earned only a few dollars a day, such fines were a hefty burden. The volume of liquor involved in these and many similar cases was often minuscule, frequently as modest as a pint or two. With the exception of a few pool hall proprietors, most of those arrested worked as laborers; whether carpenters or shipfitters, skilled or unskilled, black or white, those apprehended for "possession, manufacture, transport, and sale" were disproportionately poor and working-class. While white middle-class drinkers purchased, possessed, and imbibed illegal alcohol in relative safety and security, poor men and women in Virginia had good reason to fear arrest, fines, and jail time for possessing even small quantities for personal use or for sale. Local, state, and federal police applied the law unequally, obtained dubious search warrants, and used deadly force with impunity.[37]

Poor African-American Virginians' participation in the underground world of drink as consumers, producers, still tenders, and sellers, despite a disproportionate likelihood of arrest and punishment in cities such as Richmond and Newport News, suggests that for some the benefits continued to outweigh the risks. The unregulated contraband market offered an opportunity to boost income in a world of decidedly limited options in Jim Crow Virginia. African-Americans also had more urgent grievances than discriminatory enforcement. Just weeks after the February raids, a frenzied white mob of five hundred residents of nearby Waverly took twenty-two-year-old James Jordon, a lumbermill worker, from his jail cell to a vacant lot, tortured him, and hung his burnt, bullet-ridden body from a tree. That same month, the Ku Klux Klan flogged another African-American man and, days later, threatened similar treatment to an African-American couple who fended off the raiders with shotguns.[38]

Indeed, one of the novel aspects of the Eighteenth Amendment was the extent to which poor whites—carpenters, farmers, and other small-time moonshiners—were targets of southern law enforcement alongside African-Americans. Despite the disproportionate targeting of African-Americans in Virginia's cities, and the large number of arrests made by agents Chase and Crute, whites were not exempt from the law. Making up 70 percent of the state's population in 1930, even with lax enforcement in areas like Franklin County, they were the majority of those arrested for Prohibition violations. In a world structured by white supremacy, marginal rural white moonshiners, barely eking out a living, whether in Virginia, rural Kentucky, or rural areas of Arkansas, risked arrest and prison terms for their illicit operations. In the Ozarks, for example, a region populated by poor whites, the average moonshiner was apprehended not once but several times. These violators also frequently served time in prison. The *Richmond Planet*, the capital's black newspaper, sarcastically remarked that "it was a source of gratification to those American citizens of color who take the time to think and observe to note that the same treatment that has been

accorded to black citizens for more than a decade in the matter of constitutional rights and privileges is now being meted to white citizens"
as well. The concrete experience of rural poor white southerners with
the coercive arm of the law during Prohibition contributed, undoubtedly, to sharpening a libertarian "don't tread on me" proclivity. Whites
receiving treatment equivalent to African-Americans helps explain the
popular revulsion against Prohibition. The Eighteenth Amendment
placed constitutional rights, especially protection against unwarranted
search and seizure, at the forefront of public discussion nationally,
sharply broadening the public debate over the importance of safeguarding such protections beyond African-American leaders and their allies.[39]

While some took up the antistate banner as a result of Prohibition
enforcement, others, not surprisingly including African-Americans
whose own constitutional rights had long been flagrantly violated,
called for more action against long-standing social ills. Reacting to
Herbert Hoover's incessant pleas for "enforcement" and "observance,"
Edward B. Rembert, for example, wrote to the president to protest
federal *inaction*, in contrast, against lynch terror. He reminded Hoover
that it was the president's responsibility to enforce the laws: "ALL OF
THEM, not the eighteenth alone but the fourteenth amendment too."
The expanded scope of federal power provided a grounding, which
even Prohibition's opponents leveraged, to argue for the expansion and
reorientation of federal power in new directions, whether to rectify
social and economic injustice or protect citizens from lynch mobs.[40]

This did not make African-Americans wary of opposing the dire
consequences of the Eighteenth Amendment's enforcement on their
community. The widely circulated *Pittsburgh Courier* complained, "For
several years colored citizens here have suffered indignities from policemen and prohibition agents who crash into their homes unlawfully and
make liquor searches and arrests in violation of the search and seizure
provisions of the law on the pretext of quelling disorder." Prohibition
agents who violated Fourth Amendment constitutional guarantees,
they charged, should be convicted of a felony. The *Courier* backed a

proposed law restricting the enforcement activity of federal agents and local police. The coercive arm of the federal government, in other words, was a double-edged sword: it could and did impinge upon "personal liberty" and fostered new grievances, but it also inspired a growing embrace of a federal approach toward solving other social and economic injustices.[41]

.   .   .

THE logic of Prohibition put the private home at special risk. State and federal alcohol laws had driven liquor production from industrial plants to more informal structures such as mom-and-pop distilleries. As never before in U.S. history, as a result, the government invaded private homes, mostly of poorer citizens, in a widespread, systematic, and coercive campaign. Well-to-do citizens were, for the most part, exempt from draconian police actions, and in the few instances when antiliquor crusaders overreached, their wealthy targets raised a highly public ruckus in the papers and the courts. In Portland, Oregon, for example, enforcement officials for years raided private homes in the city's poor and minority neighborhoods with little outcry among the city's opinion makers. In 1924, however, police invaded the home of a well-respected corporate manager, E. J. Labbe, at an elaborate New Year's Eve ball hosted by him and his wife. Outraged partygoers watched state agents cart Labbe off to jail, along with the two bottles of whiskey he had served his guests. Suddenly, even Portland's normally dry newspapers were questioning enforcement tactics. One outraged cartoon showed hordes of police snoopers peeking in the windows of a single-family home, crawling over its rooftop, climbing down the chimney, and prying into the basement. Another cartoon depicted a couple in bed startled by the noise of two armed men who had entered their home. The husband turns to his wife: "Don't be alarmed, Dear, just some detectives searching our cellar." In the face of the outcry, officials quickly released Labbe and dropped charges. The Labbe case was exceptional, but the intensity of the response reveals widespread anxieties over the danger overzealous sleuthing posed to the privacy of the bourgeois home, even the sacred realm of the bedroom.[42]

In the overwhelming majority of cases, however, the war on alcohol targeted poor communities and brought new forms of exploitation to their neighborhoods, especially in large metropolitan centers. In the late nineteenth and early twentieth century many other forms of vice had been relegated to poor communities in the nation's great metropolises. As reformers worked to beautify their cities, policy makers, despairing of actively eliminating vice, made it a top priority to isolate it geographically. The *Pittsburgh Courier*, for example, complained about "the vice that continues to flourish unopposed in the negro district in practically every large city in the country. Police walk complacently past bootlegging joints . . . bordellos, gambling joints. . . . Most of this vice is either supported or subsidized by whites of the criminal class who have behind them the protective hand of safely bribed judges, and police officials." While private homes were more vulnerable than ever, Prohibition deepened the hold of organized criminal gangs and their corrupt official partners in poor minority neighborhoods in many American cities.[43]

By the end of the decade, as a result, many African-American opinion makers, even those who had earlier supported the war on alcohol, spoke out against Prohibition. A number of influential African-Americans had voiced opposition to the Eighteenth Amendment prior to its passage. In 1912, Booker T. Washington, who earlier had supported state Prohibition legislation, wrote to antiliquor crusader Richmond Hobson's office expressing his conviction that the law "would excite opposition on the part of the colored people throughout the country on the ground that it is class or race legislation." With the dry triumph, such criticisms escalated. The *Pittsburgh Courier* declared its opposition because the "people never had the Constitutional privilege of speaking on the question." John Mitchell, the outspoken editor of the African-American newspaper the *Richmond Planet*, bristled with contempt for the legislation from the start: "A man's home used to be his castle. Now it is the United States government's castle and the rights and privileges have been taken away." Mitchell called attention to the deaths and blindness that resulted from the consumption of poisoned wood alcohol. Such concerns, along with long-standing deep racial grievances, likely contributed to the National Association for the Advancement of Colored People's endorsement of Clarence Darrow, the prominent and outspoken Prohibition critic and civil liberties advocate, for a place on Hoover's National Commission on Law Observance and Enforcement, the government body charged with looking into the crisis of enforcement in 1929. Marcus Garvey's Universal Negro Improvement Association, with its large working-class African-American following, spoke out forcefully against the amendment. Even those voices of opinion, such as the *Amsterdam News*, that had once been strong advocates for the benefits alcohol Prohibition might bring to black communities, abandoned their support.[44]

African-Americans, of course, had long suffered authorities applying legal codes selectively to control their communities and coerce their labor. Local and state statutes against vagrancy, gambling, "crap-shoots," or "nuisance," among others, had been utilized since Reconstruction to criminalize the conduct of African-Americans in states throughout the south. In Virginia, as in other southern states, the law enforcement fee system exacerbated these trends. Sheriffs, whose salaries partially depended on fees and per diems for each person arrested and held, had an economic interest to fill their jails. Prisoners also provided a substantial private and public labor force, first through the convict lease system and, after its demise, on public building projects. To widespread local ordinances, Prohibition added a statewide and national law and a huge expansion of available funding and potential offenders. The result, not surprisingly, was a surge in the arrest, harassment, and incarceration of poor and working-class men and women.[45]

While the war on alcohol was but a new chapter in the far deeper and wider history of legal abuse and criminalization of African-Americans, so too the law provided an instrumental means of criminalizing other social groups. In East Los Angeles, the largely poor Mexican ethnic community suffered disproportionately in the liquor war. Mexican Americans accounted for 25 percent of those charged under the state's Prohibition law for liquor-law violations in 1924 despite constituting only 10 percent of the population. That very year, the renowned police reformer August Vollmer had been called in from Berkeley to reform the notoriously corrupt Los Angeles Police Department and institute newly vigorous, professionalized policing. The outcome of that effort was far more vigorous policing but largely against selectively targeted groups. Police had always taken a specific interest in the Mexican American community, disproportionately applying laws against drunkenness and vagrancy. But with Prohibition, police had a new means and rationale for targeting the city's most vulnerable residents. Fully two-thirds of arrests of Mexican ethnics in 1924 were for charges of liquor-law violations. Like their Virginia colleagues, Los Angeles police had incentives to maximize arrests. Fines and automobile seizures brought revenue to city coffers. The LAPD vice division collected $118,929 in fines for Prohibition violations in 1924 (over a million dollars today). In 1930, the Southern California district of the Prohibition Bureau collected $1,029,560 in fines. The Mexican ethnics arrested in Los Angeles for Volstead violations were usually penny-ante violators, found with small amounts of liquor. Of the 449 liquor cases before the Federal District Court in Southern California involving Mexican Americans during the war on alcohol, the vast majority of violators were charged with selling less than four pints.[46]

Mexican Americans no less than other marginalized groups saw opportunities as well as dangers in the illegal market. In contrast to their well-protected and fabulously wealthy bootlegging peers, however, small-scale Mexican American producers lacked the economic resources or networks to secure protection from officials. John Rodriguez and Pedro and Marie Sandoval, for example, along with another family member, smuggled four gallons and one quart of whiskey from Mexico. Stopped by enforcement officers, they were charged and sent to jail, unable to post the hefty bail. When their case was finally heard several months later, the judge convicted all three on importing charges and fined them $2,500, a sum greater than the combined annual income of three average Mexican laborers. Mexican immigrants also risked deportation. In 1922, the District Court in Southern California ordered the deportation of Leandro Leyvas, Antonio Nava, Manuel Hernández, Guadalupe Huerta, and Pedro Sánchez after they were each charged with smuggling less than one quart of liquor. For Mexican Americans, as for African-Americans, Prohibition marked an expansion and intensification of abuse by police authorities.[47]

White enforcement officials already associated ethnic and racial minorities with "criminality." While abuse of the law in policing minority and poor communities in the war against alcohol was so widespread as to be invisible, a few incidents drew media attention if only briefly. In Oklahoma City in 1931, sheriff's deputies shot and killed two Mexicans they said were "bandits" running contraband liquor. The victims turned out to be students, and one was a relative of future Mexican president Ortiz Rubio. The local deputies rapidly won an acquittal, but not before Mexico's acting consul in Illinois, H. Valdez, came to Oklahoma to oversee the investigation. He soon found himself caught in the net of antiliquor laws when police arrested him for violating the Volstead Act. They claimed to have found bootleg liquor in his car. Pressured by federal authorities and Mexican officials, an Oklahoma judge eventually dismissed and expunged the charges against Valdez. Such special handling was the exception to the rule of selective enforcement under Prohibition.[48]

In large East Coast and midwestern cities such as New York, Chicago, and Pittsburgh, ethnic working-class men and women bore the brunt of episodic crackdowns. In 1923, Chicago mayor William Dever announced a zero-tolerance policy that more than doubled the number of cases in district court from 3,642 in 1922 to 8,837 in 1924. As one study noted, it was primarily working-class homes that police burst into "in search for liquor, beer and the ubiquitous home still." In New

York, one review of voluminous federal cases found that enforcement "rarely strayed from the ethnic working-class." Most offenders charged for violations or possessing insignificant amounts of alcohol had names that could have come from the "entry records of Ellis Island."[49]

In the industrial behemoth of Pittsburgh, which vied with Chicago and New York for the title of wettest city in the nation, large-scale producers and suppliers operated with the tacit protection and collusion of public officials and police. Such tolerance was not extended to poor families and home producers who might threaten organized criminals' hold over the trade. For the mostly European-born industrial workers, Prohibition was yet another insult on top of company-controlled civic life and poor working conditions in the years prior to unionization. Their homes, clubs, ethnic halls, and bars faced a disproportionate number of raids. One Pittsburgh resident complained of uneven enforcement in a letter to the "Booze department," grousing that "Washington favored the rich." "Why is it that the poor man's club is raided while the rich man is left alone?" Bert Iacobucci, a Pittsburgh steelworker, recalled years after the war on alcohol ended that local police selectively enabled some community residents to sell moonshine while it targeted others: "[V]ery few Italians had a chance to make it." . . . One clique was making it, and these big shots had good connections to police. The little guy is the one that gets arrested. . . . If they see a little man, right away they turn him in." Among the unprotected, he recalled, the police came to private homes looking for moonshine "every day."[50]

To some steelworkers, the selective police tactics were part and parcel of Jones & Laughlin's authoritarian policies. Ormond Montini, an Italian-born steelworker, said, "[P]eople who were close to the company were able to sell moonshine . . . because the police department worked with Jones & Laughlin. They were together but if you weren't with them, they raided your place." Like many Italians during the nation's war on alcohol, Montini's father made wine every year for home consumption. His neighbors also made wine, digging large holes

in their gardens to store the five-gallon jugs. Police raided his neighbor's house with "sledge hammers and busted up his wine." Looking
back years later, Montini recalled, "they'd just come and break your
door down. They didn't need search [warrants]. . . . We didn't know
any better."[51]

Just outside of Pittsburgh, in the town of Aliquippa, many workers
said, quite accurately, that the police were in the hands of the "boss of
Aliquippa," Jones & Laughlin. Another steelworker, Lou Tadora,
recalled police raiding his family's home twice during the war on alcohol: "They come in to search for liquor." When Tadora's brother asked
about a search warrant, "they told him to keep his mouth shut." Police
had long kept an eye on gatherings of workingmen, and sometimes
broke them up; mill owners feared that such social occasions might
serve as places for union organization. The great steel strike of 1919
intensified such surveillance. Prohibition provided a blanket pretext to
invade workers' homes, clubs, gatherings, and boarding houses.[52]

. . .

THE dramatically rising numbers of single women in the country's
growing clerical industry was a celebrated social change in the years
after World War I. Prohibition opened up a less public but similarly
innovative survival strategy for working-class wives and mothers.
Working-class women had long taken in boarders to contribute to the
family economy without compromising household duties and child
rearing. Setting up a home brewing operation or making wine for the
family or for sale also provided a way to supplement incomes for poor
women willing to run the risk. Working-class women in Aliquippa
and Pittsburgh produced and sometimes sold alcohol with enthusiasm
and resolve. Bert Iacobucci's wife recalled her mother making wine at
home. Once, she sent her daughter to deliver a jug to an acquaintance.
When police spotted her carrying the wine, the patrol wagon picked
her up and took her to the station. She was "scared stiff" but was later
released to her parents when they paid a fine. In Arkansas, the deputy

administrator of Prohibition proclaimed that fully "75 percent of the liquor being sold" was handled by women, likely something of an overestimation.[53]

Newspapers circulated sensationalist stories about Gertrude Lythgoe, a native of Ohio and bootlegging "queen," who ran a large rumrunning operation out of the Caribbean, and Texas Guinan, New York's famous speakeasy queen. With glamorous heroines, such stories obscured the tawdry mainstream of this illicit economy. In Butte, Montana, wives and widows cooked liquor on kitchen stoves to make ends meet. Mrs. Michael Murray, with two children at home, served as the "cook," while her husband and a friend marketed the liquor she produced. A widow, Nora Gallagher, told police that she set up a still on her kitchen stove in order to outfit her five children for Easter. In New Orleans, 173 women appeared in federal court records on charges of selling. Most of these female bootleggers were widowed, divorced, or separated from husbands who worked as "stevedores, laborers or grocers." Many of the offenders had several children, others were single mothers. As with other socially marginal targets of enforcement agents, police typically arrested women with small quantities of alcohol. Ann Foster was arrested for the sale of a single pint of beer. Pauline Mistich sold two bottles of beer to one agent and spent sixty days in prison for it. In addition to their role as producers, women used their positions as soft-drink operators and street vendors to engage in the side business of liquor sales. Women who owned restaurants and grocery stores managed to retail liquor for larger wholesalers.[54]

Many female violators lacked the resources to get the kind of protection the well-organized contraband liquor business in New Orleans offered. Large operations had access to networks of graft and protection from police and judges, and major suppliers could even purchase insurance policies with local organized crime underwriters to cover the payments of bonds, court costs, and half of the fines should they be caught. The policies even provided financial aid to family members dependent on the lost income from jailed violators. But judging from the fact that the children of female violators not infrequently ended up in foster homes or charity institutions while they served out their sentences, they lacked access to such protection.[55]

Arrests and prosecutions of female bootleggers raised a distinct problem: dependent children. Female violators pleaded for leniency as "desperate mothers" and "dutiful wives" who sold liquor to support their children because of a sick, incapacitated, or absent husband, or simply to obey their spouse. In New Orleans, Mary Fatzer, whose daughter had left her in charge of her two children, was at first sentenced to ninety days for violating the Volstead Act in July 1930. When a judge learned of Fatzer's responsibility for her two grandchildren, he reduced her term to one month. The children were placed in the Waldo Burton Home for boys until she completed her term. In another New Orleans case, when Pauline Mistich was convicted, the Society for the Prevention of Cruelty to Children stepped in and offered to care for her children should she be jailed. While gender-based pleas and dependent children led judges to reduce sentences for first-time offenders, repeat offenders—even mothers or elderly women—expected scant mercy. Marie Tria, mother of six, was arrested in the Crescent City in 1932. The judge sentenced her, a repeat offender, to one year in federal prison and fined her $500. A third charge of selling intoxicating liquor led to a fifteen-month sentence for octogenarian Rose Fontana. In Butte, Montana, one judge who claimed that he "did not like to commit women to jail" locked up twice-caught Kate Farlan for six months.[56]

In Butte and New Orleans, female bootleggers were overwhelmingly white. One study of New Orleans court records found only six African-American women arrested in the trade. Racial and ethnic policing of violators—and patterns of racial and ethnic communities' inclusion in or exclusion from the trade—varied regionally. In contrast to Richmond, segregation in New Orleans seems to have provided a shield for African-Americans from enforcement surveillance. In the well-organized and infamously wet city, federal agents were left to do the lion's share of enforcement. Perhaps they did not target the city's creole community, or it may be that tightly controlled white criminal rings excluded African-Americans from the trade. In Arkansas, on the other hand, female African-Americans participated and faced arrest. Of one group of sixteen women arrested for participating in the trade, most of whom were mothers with children at home, half were African-American.[57]

In Chicago, too, women frequently ran small working-class retail "kitchen table" operations. Informers to Mayor Dever named women as the operators of small blind pigs "selling booze" out of family homes. One female writer, who signed herself the "dutiful wife of a violent drunkard," complained about an operation patronized by her husband: "He spends all his money there . . . and spends it for that moonshine." Another letter reported a kitchen-table establishment run by a woman. Her husband wasted his wages there, she complained, and the operator had rejected the wife's request not to serve him."[58]

So great was the number of women participating in the traffic that assistant attorney general Willebrandt pleaded with Congress for funds to build a new women's prison to handle the "crisis of numbers" of women arrested for Volstead Act as well as Harrison Narcotics Act violations. Congress heeded her plea, and the first federal prison for women was opened in Alderson, West Virginia, in 1929. Working-class women's participation on the supply side of the underground traffic and their novel rates of incarceration offered a grim counterpoint to popular narratives of youthful flappers and glamorous urban jazz clubs.[59]

·   ·   ·

POLICE blotters, court records, investigators' logs, and prison statistics from across the country testify to the real meaning of the nation's war on alcohol for poor Americans. Small mom-and-pop violators ended up in the hands of the law while large suppliers more often remained untouchable, even respectable. The arrest of small-time bootleggers and single mothers making kitchen brew had, of course, almost no

impact on the oceans of supply. Diverted industrial alcohol, liquor stolen from government-bonded warehouses, large smuggling operations,
and organized crime's breweries and distilleries had no difficulty sup-
plying the nation's fabulously profitable illegal market.

As a result of this continued easy availability, ardent drys clamored
for even stronger and stricter enforcement. While a few wet states, such
as New York, abandoned efforts to enforce the dry law when faced
with clogged court dockets and flagrant violations, many other states
amplified penalties for violators and broadened police powers in the
desperate hope of drying up the land. In 1925 Indiana passed the Wright
"bone dry" law, whose provisions called for removal from office of any
state, county, or municipal official who neglected to enforce Prohibition, provided rewards to prosecutors who won convictions, and stipulated stiffer fines and penalties for violators. Possession of a still merited
between two and five years jail time. In Virginia, the 1925 Layman's
Act enhanced rewards for local and state officials for arrests and prosecutions, raised fines and penalties for violators, and loosened search and
seizure restrictions. Michigan amended its laws no less than seven times
to strengthen enforcement and end the busy rum-running traffic along
the Detroit River. Ultimately the state made it a felony to manufacture,
sell, or even possess liquor. Search warrants could be issued on the "affi-
davit of any citizen" who had "good reason" to believe the law was
being violated.[60]

While draconian laws sometimes led to better enforcement outcomes, they could also have the opposite effect. In Texas, the 1919 Dean
Act was "too extreme by far," according to a government report, to
make enforcement effective. By setting penalties for possession of liquor
at one to five years in a state penitentiary, it led juries to return verdicts
of not guilty, "unwilling to stamp the brand of felon upon a fellow man
for possession of one quart of liquor." Even so, the Texas prison population swelled during the 1920s, with Prohibition offenders contributing
a large portion of those new prisoners. Evidently, Texas all-white juries

did not see all violators as "fellow men," convicting African-Americans disproportionately.[61]

At the federal level too, patent failures of enforcement also led to the adoption of stricter penalties for violators by the decade's end. Congress passed the Jones Act in 1929, upping maximum penalties for first offenses from six months in jail and $1,000 to five years and $10,000. By making first time violations felonies, the law also made consumers liable to felony charges, because according to the federal criminal code, a person who failed to report a felony had committed one. Those who purchased a bottle or patronized a speakeasy could now be prosecuted for a felony under federal law.

As a growing number of wet commentators predicted, Prohibition ultimately failed to stop the flagrant violation of the law. Outside of a few celebrated federal operations against criminal gangs in Detroit or the high-profile efforts to put "public enemies" like Al Capone behind bars, enforcement mostly captured and prosecuted small-scale violators marginal to the overall industry. Those of modest means, whether white, black, Latino, rural or urban, male or female, suffered not only from the high price of liquor, its poor and even poisonous quality, and the rise of gangland violence and vice in their neighborhoods, but also from the capricious and in some places terrorizing levels of enforcement.

While Prohibition was not necessarily the central concern of working-class men and women, selective enforcement added a significant new assault on their efforts to sustain an independent realm of leisure, culture, and community ritual. In 1929, President Hoover created the National Commission on Law Observance and Enforcement, or Wickersham Commission, to study enforcement patterns across the nation. The commission hired self-described teetotaler James Forrester to report on the attitudes of workers and organized labor toward the Eighteenth Amendment. Forrester, a diligent researcher, conducted a large set of interviews with national, state, and local labor leaders in Pennsylvania, New Jersey, and Indiana. He went into communities to speak with groups of rank-and-file workingmen in their homes, making it a point to speak not only to male breadwinners but to "wives, mothers and members of the family." He found "unanimous opposition to our existing federal Prohibition policy" and "intense . . . strong and bitter resentment." "Everywhere" he encountered "the same resentments and the same sentiments." Forrester, a total abstainer, was deeply disappointed by his findings. "These convictions," he lamented, "have been forced upon me, much against my will, by the things I learned, the things I saw, and the stories told me during this investigation." Forrester's exhaustive investigation led him to conclude that "wage-earners . . . were 99 out of 100 opposed to prohibition." His findings, he reported, were representative "of the situation in all parts of the country, particularly in all industrial centers."[62]

The reasons workers gave for their opposition to the ban on alcohol differed substantially from the arguments of elite opponents in the Association Against the Prohibition Amendment or the Women's Organization for National Prohibition Reform. It was not state's rights, the threat of the Eighteenth Amendment to property rights, or its potential to open the door to other forms of regulation that concerned them. Instead, they identified Prohibition as an attack on working-class men and women. As Forrester summarized their views, workers considered these laws "discriminatory against and unjust to them." Indeed, "a large majority, including the women members of the family, feel that the Prohibition laws . . . have only affected the working people and their family and social life. Many of them believe that the Prohibition amendment and its enforcing act was never seriously intended, even by its proponents, to be applied to any but the working man. . . . They complain that the wealthy and well to do can get all the liquor they want, therefore, the rich are not being deprived of anything . . . and that they can and do violate the Prohibition laws with impunity and without interference or censure. But that working people, because they have not the money with which to pay the high prices now charged . . . are deprived of it and must take the impure, dangerous, and poisonous

liquors locally manufactured, sold by the bootlegger and be content."
Speaking to the reality of selective enforcement, Forrester noted, they
"resented being classed as criminal" for violating the Prohibition laws.[63]

.   .   .

SELECTIVE enforcement failed to stem the flow of liquor or the wave
of crime that accompanied it. What enforcement efforts did accomplish
was the formation of a new and widely shared grievance among the
diverse communities that bore its brunt. The hostility of the heavily
immigrant working class to the law was reciprocated wholeheartedly
by their largely Protestant betters. "If it is true that foreign-born workers are rebellious against this country because of Prohibition," said the
Board of Temperance, Prohibition and Public Morals, "they should
remember that the country is not being run for their benefit." In their
complacency, the Board did not grasp that these workers were now
increasingly enfranchised and capable of steering "the country" in new
directions. A signal opportunity to do so, particularly for immigrant
industrial workers in large cities, but also for working-class African-
Americans, would come when New York governor Alfred E. Smith
ran for president in 1928. He voiced their grievances, brought new
groups into the Democratic Party, and began detaching African-
Americans from the Republican Party. This critical election marked
the entry of immigrant workers into the Democratic Party as a solid
and influential group of voters, even before 1932 and 1936, when
Franklin D. Roosevelt would solidify the New Deal political coalition
that endured for much of the twentieth century.[64]

4

GESTURES OF DARING,
SIGNS OF REVOLT

IN THE NOVEMBER 27, 1925, ISSUE OF *THE NEW YORKER*, THE new magazine of wit and urbanity, twenty-two-year-old socialite Ellin Mackay gleefully recounted the attractions of New York's vibrant nightlife scene. Nightclub excursions afforded affluent young club-goers "privacy"—presumably from the tight surveillance of their elders—and interaction with "people we find amusing." In the pre-Prohibition days cabaret entertainment had drawn such crowds and raised alarms about risqué behavior. Prohibition's saloon closures, however, turned these alcohol-laced outings into deeper expressions of cultural revolt, sites for the enactment of new identities of urban avant-garde modernity and more permissive social and sexual norms.[1]

The Eighteenth Amendment was, at its core, an effort to rid the nation of the saloon and protect vulnerable "others" from intoxicating liquor. The law's wide reach, however, transformed the leisure life of a much broader swath of Americans than the purported targets of saloon closures. Protected from the capricious arm of everyday dry-law enforcement, and better able to afford the high cost of illicit liquor, a subset of self-identified avant-garde urbanites flaunted their social drinking in defiance of the law. Prohibition fueled a zeitgeist of cultural experimentation among these affluent "children of the night" who threw off the weight of constricting social norms through their leisure practices. This semisecretive new world—outside the purview of state surveillance and controlled by organized criminals—was no longer guided by the rules of decorum that had just years earlier circumscribed elite social drinking.

Prohibition as a result sharpened the rift between a set of strict bourgeois norms—of thrift, discipline, and delayed gratification—associated with proprietary capitalism and the new, more permissive norms coincident with the rise of consumer capitalism. This transformation was at bottom the result of slow erosion, by the wave of long-term trends and global events: urbanization, secularization, the vast repercussions of World War I, along with mass consumption and mass culture. The more than decade-long storm of the Eighteenth Amendment, however, in a remarkably short period, reshaped the boundaries of day-to-day leisure and recreation for nearly all Americans. In the face of coercive law, there arose a self-conscious cultural rebellion among a pace-setting intelligentsia. One New Yorker went so far to declare that Prohibition fueled a cultural "state of civil war." The epicenter of the experimental, subculturally invigorated nightlife was New York City. But its reverberations could be felt in small cities and towns elsewhere. This new permissive world of mixed-sex nightlife recreation was but one unintended consequence of Prohibition, one so taken for granted today that its origins in the shocked aftermath of the Eighteenth Amendment have been occluded.[2]

. . .

THE social capital of the wealthy notwithstanding, Prohibition left only partially standing the institutions and older rituals of elite drinking. As it shut saloons, it also closed "respectable" venues where the well-to-do and middle class drank: plush hotel bars, fine restaurants, and "lobster" palaces. Many of these establishments, already under pressure from rising rents and tight office space, shut their doors rather than operate with reduced profit margins. Celebrated hotels from the Holland House to the Knickerbocker folded in the first year of Prohibition and were turned into office buildings. The Manhattan Hotel at Madison Avenue and Forty-Second Street closed in 1921. The Buckingham, immortalized in Edith Wharton's *Age of Innocence*, ended operations one year later. In 1925, the Savoy too closed. Famous restaurants went under as well: Delmonico's, patronized for generations by New York's wealthiest, shut its doors in 1924. One New York owner of an old-style lobster palace—part restaurant, part cabaret—explained his decision to close: "We can't go on at a profit on soft drinks. We obey the law and lose money and we can't afford that."[3]

The New York grand hotels that remained open provided their clients with liquor in a semisurreptitious manner to avoid fines and closure. Many likely followed the strategy of Boston's high-end Ritz-Carlton. Waiters there carried small, hidden pocket flasks, pouring the liquor when vetted customers ordered drinks and always on the lookout for investigators. Efforts to keep stock on hand to satisfy customers' thirst without risking fines or closure required careful maneuvering. A bootlegger provisioned the Ritz with four or five bottles of liquor at a time and made several trips a day. That way, he satisfied management's desire to ply guests with profitable liquor without the risk of keeping large stocks on hand. Some hotels kept their illegal supplies on the roof or in other out-of-the-way places. Others provided customers costly setups of corkscrews and ice, avoiding directly serving illegal liquor. Overnight guests at some hotels could expect the number of a local bootlegger from the concierge. Those who wanted liquor in their room had to order it themselves, however, at punishing prices. At the Ritz, a pint went for over $80 in inflation-adjusted dollars. Some hotels more openly served liquor: the Normandie operated a small speakeasy in the basement. It too, however, had shut its doors by 1927.[4]

Restaurants, too, served liquor stealthily. Frank Grisoli's in Brook-

lyn served liquor to "parties that were well known" but took care not
to serve strangers. Nick's in midtown escorted patrons who wanted a
drink through the basement and a narrow door to a small room. Patrolmen who turned a blind eye to violations were rewarded with cash
payoffs. Some eateries profited from loyal and influential customers:
Moskowitz & Lupowitz served "liquor and all kinds of wines." The
"politicians and police officers [who] visited the place" kept everything
"undercover." Elite and middle-class public recreational drinking may
have continued in a few of its usual venues, but under sharply constricted circumstances, particularly in the early years of Prohibition.[5]

The closure of older establishments and the timidity with which
"respectable" night spots served liquor created a tremendous market
opportunity for criminal entrepreneurs proferring alternative sources
of alcohol-laced entertainment. As out-of-business signs sprouted in
restaurant windows and lobster palaces, barrooms and night clubs
mushroomed in shadier back alleys. One New York police commission
estimated the number of speakeasies in Manhattan alone at 5,000 in
1927. A 1928 investigation of the city's speakeasies by the antivice organization the Committee of Fourteen found at least one per block.[6]

These night spots ran the gamut from high-end supper clubs such as
S&E's to sleazy gyp joints and Harlem buffet flats. One motor car salesman, L. R. Best, joined with his flatmates to run a small speakeasy out
of their "richly furnished" brownstone on West Seventy-Sixth Street.
Patronized by Assistant Attorney Joyce and Alderman Quinn, it was
well protected. When police paid a visit, tipped off by a neighbor's
noise complaint, Best told them that "nobody has to worry [about]
what is going on in here" since the influential officials who patronized
the place would "take care in case anything is wrong." A supper club
on West Fifty-Second Street too catered to a "very high class" of drinkers. It specialized in fine foods, its well-heeled patrons arriving in "evening clothes." With police providing protection, it managed to stay
open, though discreetly, to avoid the less easily managed federal offi-
cialdom. Local police posed few problems to operating illicit establish-

ments, especially well-protected venues, but these night spots still ran the risk of the sporadic crackdown by zealous federal officials, such as U.S. attorney Emory Buckner's padlocking campaign.[7]

As a result, a vibrant new growth of Manhattan's Prohibition-era nightlife thrived in its shaded spaces—in basements, back alleys, lofts, second-floor offices—and behind locked doors. Speakeasies, so called for their hushed, semisecretive character, evaded detection through multiple means. Some required patrons to carry cards to gain entry. Others had lookouts who vetted customers through a peephole before deciding whether or not to open the door. Speakeasy owners sometimes hired "steerers" to scout hotels for thirsty customers. Once satisfied a prospective patron was not an agent, they directed him to a club, providing a card for admittance. One investigator won entry to a speakeasy, a loft at Thirty-Fourth Street and Seventh Avenue, in just such a way. He described the precautions its owners used to evade detection: "A lookout questioned me, looked the card over, pressed a button, then asked me to follow him to a steel door . . . pressed another button, which was then unlocked by another man from the inside. The lookout then left me and I followed the other man downstairs to a door which was unlocked by him and I was admitted to a room where three young women were sitting at a table near the piano, singing and entertaining male patrons."[8]

These three hostesses were part of another innovation of Prohibition nightlife. Women participated in the world of leisure, pleasure, and entertainment on both the consumer and business side. Working-class men and women and small groups of pacesetting urbanites were already pioneering new forms of leisure earlier in the century, stepping out to dance halls, lobster palaces, and cabarets. But the saloon's disappearance severed the association of social drinking from boisterous working-class male drinking, and with it the accompanying taint of prostitution for women of any class who entered those venues. Ironically, by forcing alcohol-laced leisure underground and taming its bawdy public face, nightlife that included mixed company blossomed

among upper- and middle-class women, ushering in the world of leisure familiar to Americans ever since.[9]

To be sure, women's participation in the new world also built upon
longer-term trends such as increasing economic independence. Before
and during World War I, a new cohort of single women left their homes
for jobs. In the war's wake, they joined a new generation of independent female wage earners. Not surprisingly, some stepped out into the
illicit establishments. More than one vice investigator remarked on the
large numbers of "unaccompanied women" in Prohibition night spots.
The Phoenix restaurant drew a clientele of men and women of the
respectable and "better classes." In midtown and the Upper East Side,
women could be seen at Loloy's, Mike's Speakeasy, the Open Door, the
Atlantic Cabaret, and the Red Moon. One especially popular establishment refused to introduce single men to the women who patronized it,
likely increasing its popularity among women just seeking a fun night
out with female companions. Stanley Walker's chronicle of New York
nightlife cut to the heart of the gendered alterations of Prohibition
drinking: "Soon after 1920 great, raving hordes of women began to
discover what their less respectable sisters had known for years—that it
was a lot of fun, if you liked it, to get soused. All over New York these
up and coming females piled out of their hide-aways, rang the bells of
speakeasies, wheedled drugstores into selling them gin and rye, and
even in establishments of great decorum begged their escorts for a nip
from a hip flask."[10]

While many affluent women enthusiastically participated in the
new world of social drinking, patronizing illegal, subcultural night
spots, their less affluent sisters were just as likely to be present in the
new nightclubs as employees. Nightclub owners recruited young
women who were attracted by higher pay than might be earned in
office or factory work for jobs as hostesses, waitresses, and "cigarette
girls" in the thriving, unregulated, nightlife scene. Hostesses plied male
patrons with expensive drinks by providing entertainment and, sometimes, sexual favors. Like other celebrated moments of sexual libera-

tion, the liberation associated with the more permissive sexual norms in the world of drink applied better to the consumer side of the equation than to the supply side and far more to men than to women.[11]

The women who drank with gusto and in mixed company and worked in the subterranean New York night spots were often young. Into the heightened generational gulf that followed World War I, drinking under national Prohibition filled a vacuum for them, shaping a new identity in opposition to the stricter values they associated with their parents, whose crowning achievements ended with the global conflagration of World War I and Prohibition. By carrying a hip flask or frequenting a jazz club, young women and men identified themselves as part of a smart, modern, and sophisticated set. Drinking by women and youth became, as one observer remarked, "an adventure, a gesture of daring, a sign of revolt." Alcohol's forbidden status imbued it with deeper, more alluring meaning. As an anti-Prohibitionist writer incisively remarked, "There is just one thing that the 'reformers' overlooked. They forget, if they ever knew it, that the 'hunt,' the 'pursuit of the unattainable,' is the most fascinating game in the world." The risky adventure of illicit social drinking became a source of social status in urban youth culture and on college campuses.[12]

Stepping out required not only flouting the law, it meant entering sites controlled by criminal entrepreneurs, away from the watchful gaze of state surveillance—and of parents. Such rebellion encouraged cultural experimentation of all sorts. Social drinking excursions during Prohibition were alluring not least due to a new ethos of sexual permissiveness for young women. New York urban sophisticates who stepped out to Small's Paradise, La Fey, or the Red Moon might don new styles of flapper dress—skimpy, low-cut dresses ending above the knees—a symbol of their rejection of the strict sexual mores associated with the prohibitionists. Without curfews or chaperones, Prohibition-era nightlife adventurers sought out thrilling entertainment from swift music to gay revues. Formerly fringe entertainment forms took center stage in illicit Prohibition venues. Drag shows that once played only in working-class "vice districts" found glitzy new homes and mixed-class audiences around Times Square, courtesy of organized crime gangs. "Panzy" shows, queer reviews, and "beauty and masquerade balls" thrived in unregulated spaces freed from usual strictures of respectability. At the Tent, a "black and tan" or mixed-race venue in the back part of town in Atlantic City, young "colored fellows" in wigs masqueraded in women's clothes "striking in color and design" for adventurous mixed-class patrons. Affluent adventurers attending such shows affirmed their distance from the "puritanical" "social purity" forces associated with the antiliquor crusaders—and signaled their own tolerance and urbane sophistication.[13]

Those who stepped out flouted not only the law and gender norms but racial boundaries as well. The nightclubs of organized crime leaders clustered in sections of the city where the police permitted the illicit liquor traffic to thrive and neighbors lacked connections to complain or cause trouble. Harlem became a center for white leisure entertainment. White "slummers" who flocked to African-American neighborhoods could drink and dance to their hearts' content protected by the largely underground illicit markets that operated unhindered in these neighborhoods. Guidebooks and entertainment media like *Variety* provided novices' introductions to Harlem's night spots, popularizing them. Harlem, reported the antivice Committee of Fourteen, became a "slumming ground for certain classes of whites who are looking for picturesque thrills." In Chicago, too, organized crime rings based their nightclub entertainments in the majority–African-American South Side.[14]

While racial geographic boundaries were crossed, inside many clubs cultural boundaries between blacks and whites could be drawn, if anything more sharply. As the nightclub world moved into Harlem, its stakeholders created an essentially all-white leisure zone. African-Americans worked and entertained affluent white adventurers in Harlem's vibrant nightclubs but could rarely return as patrons. The Cotton Club and Connie's, for example, were owned by white organized criminals and operated as segregated establishments, like many of the other large upscale clubs. Organized-crime's networks also included many smaller establishments, the "black and tans" and off-the-beaten-track buffet flats, some of which proferred pornographic interracial performances catering to white male thrill seekers. One investigation of eighty-five nightspots in Harlem found that the vast majority, fully 90 percent, were white-owned. African-American–owned Small's Paradise was an exception, and Small, in contrast to many white owners, encouraged black patronage. So too, sometimes, did entrepreneurial white owners. Jae Faggen and Moe Gale capitalized on the potential market of African-American nighttime adventurers barred from downtown ballrooms by opening the unusual integrated Savoy in 1926 on 140th Street. There largely black night-goers packed in to dance to their hearts' content, pioneering innovative dance forms like the Lindy Hop.[15]

Despite the segregation policies of many clubs, including some of the upscale black and tans, African-Americans and whites did mix freely in many smaller, more marginal clubs, "rent parties," and Harlem's buffet flats. Those interactions were inevitably circumscribed by broader structures of discrimination. As a result, not all African-Americans welcomed such patronage. Jazz pianist Lil Hardin Armstrong felt uncomfortable under the gaze of white musicians. "We used to look out at you all and say, "What are they staring at? Why are they all here?" Armstrong suspected white musicians attended in part to appropriate African-American jazz styles for their higher-paid downtown gigs. The young Benny Goodman was but one of a generation of white musicians in Chicago captivated and inspired by the music of Bronzeville's jazz joints and later Harlem's vibrant music scene. He brilliantly capitalized on what he learned as the leader of the Big Band swing scene of the 1930s.[16]

Prohibition's cultural upheaval contributed to the widening popularity of jazz, the pioneering music birthed in the rich loam of African-American urban life left by the first wave of the Great Migration—over one million African-Americans migrated from the south to northern cities during World War I and through the 1920s. The new interracial mixing and freer social norms of Prohibition venues expanded the meaning of liberation far beyond the wet-dry debate sparked by the law. The increasing popularity of jazz brought new record deals for African-Americans with disks marketed as "race records." Jazz clubs flourished not just in New York but in metropolises like Chicago and in smaller cities—East St. Louis, Philadelphia, Pittsburgh, Cleveland, and Detroit—where migrants from the deep south had recently settled. Prohibition-era nightlife expanded the reach of African-American cultural innovations.[17]

Prohibition's reorganization of New York nightlife and the inter-racial mixing that took place in these venues helped lay the ground-work for the Harlem Renaissance. In their uptown excursions, New York socialites and literary elites expanded their circle of friends and acquaintances. Journalist and cultural critic Carl Van Vechten, publish-ers Alfred and Blanche Knopf, Wall Street bankers, and village artists regularly visited Harlem's black-and-tans. Van Vechten, the white patron most closely associated with the New Negro Renaissance, in turn invited prominent African-American cultural producers to house parties at his posh West Fifty-Fifth Street residence. Harlem rent par-ties hosted by business entrepreneur Madam C. J. Walker also fostered increased interracial socializing.[18]

Harlem's cultural intelligentsia leveraged the new friendships and connections sparked by Prohibition's social upheaval into new book deals and larger audiences for their creative work. Langston Hughes and Nella Larsen found new audiences for their work with Van Vech-ten's backing. Newly published African-American talent shaped the era's literary production and left a significant cultural legacy. The quest of affluent "moderns" for liberation from dominant constricting norms, and the night-club owners who catered to their tastes, celebrated Afri-can-American culture, and, especially, its presumed "spontaneity." The celebration, however, was imbued with heavy stereotypes of its own.

Carl Van Vechten's controversial 1926 best-selling novel *Nigger Heaven* introduced wider white audiences to Harlem's urban culture, rife with superficial, pejorative and one-dimensional typecasts of African-Americans. The black writer Claude McKay's novel *Home to Harlem* similarly painted a portrait of sexualized Harlem nightlife, drawing fire from luminary W.E.B. Dubois for catering to the prurient interests of white audiences.[19]

.   .   .

THE liberation experienced by young, affluent, "modern" adventurers—both white and black—has been well recounted in chronicles and literary productions of the period. The exploitive effects of the new illicit market on largely working-class residential communities, on the other hand, is less well known. Since working-class African-Americans rarely patronized posh nightclubs, they no doubt experienced "slumming" differently than the affluent whites who flocked uptown. Prohibition clubs provided welcome jobs for some, but the new opportunities came at great personal risk and significant costs for the surrounding homes. Influential African-Americans voiced sustained protests over the negative impact: the "city administration seems to have given over this section of the town for the exploitation of vicious practices," complained one Harlem newspaper, "without the slightest effort at restraint or concealment." Similar practices in Chicago's South Side led one African-American newspaper to denounce the conditions as "a direct slap in the face" of the black electorate. Throughout the 1920s, African-American newspapers protested the thriving illegal markets in liquor—as well as prostitution and gambling—dominated by white organized criminals. One 1928 New York editorial complained, "White New Yorkers . . . turned Harlem into a 'raging hell'" after dark. "Five out of every seven cigar stores, lunchrooms and beauty parlors in Harlem are 'speaks' selling gin . . . two and three to a block on every main road." Harlem "had been turned into a modern-day plantation for white thrill seekers."[20]

Harlem residents had little to no protection from the crime and violence that flourishes around illicit markets. At the height of the "negro vogue," Harlem's Thirty-Second Precinct recorded the second greatest total bookings for crime in New York history, despite the police concession that "serious offenses are relatively few among Negroes." Organized criminals also brought violence to poor neighborhoods. In lower Harlem, in an immigrant neighborhood on a warm July day in 1931, machine-gun fire led to the death of one child and the injury of four more who had been playing outside when one rival gang attacked another on East 107th Street during the Harlem-Bronx beer war. In Chicago, in turn, bombs ripped through the South Side Plantation Café in 1926, and one year later, a blast wrecked another South Side liquor establishment with such force that it broke windows within a several-block radius. To add insult to injury, while violence flourished unabated, when police did respond to pressure and crack down, they tended to target less-well-protected African-American establishments. Harlem's two largest news outlets criticized the police for unfairly targeting the Harlem community for enforcement.[21]

The shadow of Prohibition allowed another industry to take root in Harlem: the illicit drug trade. Federal efforts to eradicate liquor marched hand in hand with the government's widening campaign to ban illicit drugs, and gave birth to a similarly thriving and profitable black market. Gambling kingpin Arnold Rothstein, who built a formidable new empire in the illicit liquor traffic, diversified into narcotics to build a global drug business with headquarters in New York. The supply side of the trade penetrated into poor communities at the same time as the illicit drink trade. In New York a stretch of territory along Fifth Avenue between 132nd and 138th streets in the late 1920s became the center of the traffic in opium, marijuana, and cocaine. The wide availability of drugs in one Harlem neighborhood, reported one entertainment weekly, had earned it the dubious nickname of "coke village." The affluent whites filling Harlem's jazz clubs provided a steady supply of deep-pocketed consumers. During these same years, Chicago's South Side became the center for the thriving black market of illegal drugs in the windy city.[22]

The setting of the drug trade in Harlem and Chicago's African-American South Side followed the same logic as the black market in liquor. City authorities restricted "vice" traffic to areas of the city without weighty political protectors. Suppliers for illicit trades could operate more conspicuously in communities whose residents lacked political or economic resources. For much of the 1920s, African-American criticism of the thriving liquor, gambling, drug, and prostitution businesses in Harlem residential and commercial districts fell on the deaf ears of city officials. The flowering of the "negro vogue" allowed a rank undergrowth of crime and social decay to flourish unopposed.[23]

If the twenties "roared" for only a tiny subset of avant-garde affluent urbanites, the cultural innovations this new intelligentsia produced—their zeitgeist of cultural rebellion—had far wider reverberations. The excursions of thrill seekers, the jazz scene, the spirit of self-expression, excess, and permissive sexual norms found a wider audience outside metropolitan centers. New channels of mass popular culture, such as Hollywood movies, featured jazz clubs as thrilling backdrops, making far better known the music and dance styles nourished in the cities. Tabloid news stories serialized in lurid detail escapades of the denizens of this underworld. The era's literature took up the refrain, embodied best by F. Scott Fitzgerald, who chronicled the fast-paced, heavy-drinking lifestyle of his wealthy "smart set." Radio audiences within range of small stations in New York and Chicago might turn their dials to WMAQ to enjoy nightly Savoy performances by the Dickerson orchestra, featuring Louis Armstrong, or New York's WHW for the vibrant and swift sounds of Duke Ellington's "jungle music" performed at the Cotton Club. Soon, wider national audiences were able to do the same—thanks to the Columbia Broadcasting System.[24]

Thus, the cultural earthquake that upturned urban centers in places like New York and Chicago radiated, with perhaps even greater consequences in the cultural shallows of America's smaller towns and cities. In a superficial reading, such as often accorded to F. Scott Fitzgerald's *The Great Gatsby*, the Prohibition era might be caricatured as little more than a wild ride for an urban clique. To more careful readers of Fitzgerald and the times, Prohibition's vibrant subcultural rebellion could be seen as a cultural inflection point, a disruption and renegotiation of the parameters and norms of acceptable bourgeois propriety. Coming after the decades-long emergence of an urban industrial culture and the cataclysm of world war, the cultural storm of Prohibition swept the nation into an increasing embrace of ideals of self-fulfillment, pleasure, and liberation within the segmented realm of leisure—mores that meshed well with the new political economy of modern consumer capitalism. Prohibition, to the lament of the men and women who instituted the reform, proved a cultural accelerant.

Drinking excursions, for example, gained cachet among a far larger group of youth outside metropolitan centers as a means of identifying with this affluent modern and urbane world of sophistication. Drinking on college campuses among rising numbers of middle-class youth became a source of public hand-wringing over the unintended consequences of the war on alcohol. Samuel Harden Church, president of the Carnegie Institute of Technology, remarked in 1926, "In the olden times, when the boys and girls had parties and dances, nothing in the way of liquor drinking was noticeable at all. . . . Now it has become the fixed habit in the whole student body in Pittsburgh, or at least more or less so, to carry a hip flask and that which goes with it." The Wisconsin *Daily Cardinal* student paper quipped that "without a doubt, Prohibition has been an incentive for young folks to learn to drink."[25]

Among the growing number of college youths across the nation, drinking went hand in hand with new styles of dress and sexual norms associated with this new modern urban world of sophistication. By donning new attire, smoking a cigarette in public, and drinking, a young man or woman far from the centers of metropolitan nightlife might be embued with a felt essence of personal liberation. As one writer to a midwestern campus newspaper, the Ohio State *Lantern*, wrote: "We do all the things that our mothers, fathers, aunts and uncles do not sanction, and we do them knowingly. . . . We are 'playing the game' . . . smoking, dancing like Voodoo devotees, dressing décolleté, 'petting,' and drinking." The Ohio youth was flouting an older set of norms by adopting those of the trend-setting affluent young cultural moderns in places like New York.[26]

. . .

BY the tail end of the "noble experiment," even the staunchest advocates of Prohibition could see that their attempts to reform alcohol-laced leisure practices among the nation's "better citizens" had backfired. Their greatest achievement had become a tombstone marking the coffin of the forces of "social-purity" as the arbiters of respectable bourgeois public norms. Earlier moral projects of the social-purity reformers, such as the antivice campaigns and efforts to eradicate the "white slave traffic," had disciplined the leisure practices only of marginal "others." In a titanic overreach, Prohibition circumscribed elite leisure, though in a far less draconian manner than it assaulted the habits of poor men and women. In doing so, it sparked a cultural reaction among elite men and women that would permanently undermine the authority of the social-purity forces and redraw the boundaries of acceptable bourgeois recreation. Alcohol emerged from its decade in the shadows with a reinforced place within bourgeois leisure, literature, and institutions.

The Committee of Fourteen, New York's premier antivice organization, founded in 1905, had stood as the paragon of bourgeois norms of propriety. Its campaigns to clean up commercialized vice, crime, and "character-destroying" influences in the city had once met with wide approval. Top-ranking supporters included a cross section of New York's elite, from bankers, big business interests, lawyers, and doctors to settlement-house workers. In the 1920s it continued to investigate "crime breeding" speakeasies and publicized the dangers of a new "hostess traffic"—young women recruited from nearby factory towns for work in the illicit nightclub industry. Such exposés, however, were met with widespread hostility in the press and even among some of the city's women's clubs. Its campaign to eradicate "unwholesome influences for young people" in the "unregulated public dance halls, clandestine night clubs, and vice and crime-breeding speakeasies"—"nests and rendezvous for idlers and quasi-criminals"—sounded a sour note to the newly sophisticated urbane bourgeois men and women, and some of their hinterland movie-house patrons, enthralled by the new world of Prohibition leisure. By 1930, the Committee, faced with leadership defections and a budget crisis, began to focus on crime prevention, abandoning its earlier emphasis on "suppression." The taint of "repression," top staffers admitted in a confidential report, led to "a misunderstanding of the work of the Committee of Fourteen or else a lack of interest." The committee's last-ditch efforts to drum up financing failed. Closely associated with the tarnished repressive moral project of the antiliquor crusaders, it lost support among New York's elite and dissolved in 1932.[27]

At the national level too, strict moral norms were increasingly jettisoned in favor of a greater emphasis on personal rights by the end of the "noble experiment." The Supreme Court's 1930 reversal of the conviction of Mary Ware Dennett for sending a sex-education pamphlet through the mails under the Comstock Law—an 1873 act that made it illegal to distribute such materials through the mail—demonstrated the waning traction of such repressive strategies. The wider revolt against the coercive mores and values identified with Prohibition eventually dug the grave not just of the Committee of Fourteen or the Comstock Law but an earlier reform ethos. Progressive reformers had linked their call for reshaped economic arrangements with an emphasis on social cohesion and moral regulation. The newly chastised reform liberalism that emerged to take its place in the 1930s was somewhat more attentive to individual rights, tolerance, and pluralism.[28]

The cultural counterrebellion against Prohibition was part of a wider vigorous intellectual rebellion against the coercive projects of evangelical Protestantism. H. L. Mencken, the pioneering satiric journalist, bristled with contempt for the "boobus Americanus," the conformist, "moronic," "peasant," fundamentalist middle-class masses. Urbane intellectuals and writers from New York to Paris, angered first over wartime repression, then the Red Scare, and finally Prohibition, railed against posturing preachers, wartime repressers, and the inanities of the "noble experiment." [29]

The Prohibition era, as a result, congealed a more coherent idea of civil liberties. Concerns over individual rights and freedoms had risen in opposition to the Alien and Sedition Act in 1917 and the repression of free speech during the Red Scare. But in the 1920s a wider group of Americans expressed concerns over the dangers to civil liberties. The Bill of Rights, once an abstract set of principles, took on more substantive meaning. While elite men and women were for the most part protected from the draconian arm of the law, train-station searches of valises, intrusions into the homes and parties of the well-to-do, automobile searches to catch violators, and rife violations of Fourth- and Fifth-Amendment constitutional protections—along with government lawlessness—raised significant new concerns. These developments, and the wider effort of evangelical Protestants to impose their agenda through state legislative action, whether through requiring all children to attend public schools, imposing Bible reading, or barring the teaching of evolution, drove home a heightened concern for individual rights. A wider segment of intellectuals and reformers eventually joined well-known lawyers such as Clarence Darrow and prominent individuals such as Felix Frankfurter and Roger Baldwin in adopting the gospel of rights as a more central ethos. [30]

Baldwin, a wartime pacifist jailed for his beliefs, opened the offices of the American Civil Liberties Union in New York in 1920. In the decade that followed, the ACLU expanded its work from protecting political speech and dissent to protecting individual freedoms against Protestant evangelical efforts to affirm their beliefs through law. That effort culminated in the 1925 Scopes antievolution trial. The highly publicized courtroom battle did not rescind the Tennessee state law banning the teaching of evolution, but it did heighten awareness of the threat to individual freedoms by the staunchly religious men and women associated with the absolutist project of Prohibition. The intellectual revolt against coercive Protestant religiosity that radiated outward from metropolitan centers eventually broadened the definition of liberty for all Americans as the nation increasingly embraced a pluralist ethos and a new emphasis on personal rights and freedoms.[31]

If New York and Chicago among other urban centers led the nation out of the Prohibition era, the staunchest of its religious crusaders were not going to be swept away without a fight. For this group, William Jenning Bryan's plea for the firm guiding light of old-time religion and the Committee of Fourteen's pleas for rooting out "unwholesome influences" resonated perfectly with their swelling anxieties over the spirit of self-expression and excess, the lack of law observance, interracial mixing, and more permissive sexual norms. Not surprisingly, these zealous foot soldiers did not blame their bold and ambitious reform for these results. Instead, they pleaded for better, stricter enforcement and demanded punishment for violators. With public officials unable or unwilling to rein in violations, they mobilized an army of citizen enforcers to shore up the law themselves.

Women's prayer crusades spread outward from Hillsboro, Ohio, in 1873 and helped spark the formation of the Woman's Christian Temperance Union. *(Ohio State Library)*

Children play outside a Polish neighborhood saloon in Chicago in 1903. Saloons were often the lowest rung of local ward politics. Bosses built ethnic loyalties in exchange for services such as much-needed paved streets. *(Chicago History Museum)*

Annual convention of the Anti-Saloon League of Virginia, January 1914. Virginia was a stronghold of the "church in action" against the saloon. *(Library of Congress)*

Richmond P. Hobson, a "father of Prohibition," in 1914, the year he introduced the Prohibition amendment to the House.
(Library of Congress)

"The New Morality Play." A 1919 cartoon reveals the concern that Prohibition would bring rising drug use. Prohibition led to a symbiotic crackdown on narcotic drugs.
(Library of Congress)

Prohibition Bureau agents' enforcement efforts were aided by customs officials, the Coast Guard, and, after 1924, the Border Patrol. U.S. officials destroy liquor at the Brownsville Customs House, December 20, 1920. *(Courtesy of the Runyon Collection, Dolph Briscoe Center for American History, University of Texas Austin)*

Prohibition enforcement fell heavily on poor, marginal violators such as this family arrested in a raid on Mulberry Street, New York City. *(Getty Images)*

Captured stills in a working-class district in Chicago before they were destroyed. *(Chicago History Museum)*

"Welcome Home." An Oregon newspaper comments on the threat to bourgeois privacy posed by Prohibition after zealous state officials arrested a prominent Portland corporate manager for serving liquor at a New Year's Eve celebration in 1924. *(Morning Oregonian)*

The local liquor war in Williamson County, Illinois, led to close to twenty deaths. Ku Klux Klan supporters, pictured here at the funeral of S. Glenn Young in 1925, leveraged the war on alcohol to draw recruits and wage a wider war against "un-American" threats. *(Williamson County Historical Society)*

Alcohol-related gang violence, such as the St. Valentine's Day Massacre on February 14, 1929, sparked a nationwide obsession over rising crime. *(Library of Congress)*

Al Smith drew a warm welcome on the campaign trail from immigrant ethnic workers. The turnout at one such rally in Boston was vast. *(Boston Public Library, Leslie Jones Collection)*

Influential antiliquor crusaders such as Harry Anslinger found a new mission in the war against narcotic drugs. Herbert Hoover appointed Anslinger the nation's first antidrug czar in 1930. *(Library of Congress)*

Labor-union members march in opposition to Prohibition in Newark, New Jersey, on October 31, 1931. *(Library of Congress)*

"Mrs. Ella Boole vs. Miss Texas Guinan." In this 1933 drawing, printed in *Vanity Fair*, artist Miguel Covarrubias caricatures the WCTU president and the larger-than-life speakeasy owner, suggesting who was winning the culture war. Women participated in the new business of drink as consumers and suppliers. *(Vanity Fair)*

"Prohibition Blinders." Prohibition repeal and the Depression set the stage for Roosevelt's landslide. The Republican Party's "lily-white" strategy eroded the traditional loyalty of African-Americans to the party of Lincoln. Cartoonist Wilbert Hollaway comments. *(Pittsburgh Courier)*

5

CITIZEN WARRIORS

Back of the little army of men who have been charged
with the enforcement of the Prohibition laws there are
forming . . . determined citizens who are mobilizing in
answer to the clear call of conscience. The ranks of this
supporting army are swelling daily.

—Roy Haynes, National Prohibition Commissioner[1]

ON A COLD EVENING IN THE WINTER OF 1923, REVEREND
Philip R. Glotfelty and Williamson County Board of Supervisor chairman Sam Stearns met at the local Methodist church in the town of
Marion, Illinois. Rivers of "demon rum," they believed, flowed
through the coal-mining region, and the two men organized a group
of "better citizens" to stem the tide of bootleg liquor. The prohibitionists' great triumph had ended the legal liquor traffic and shut saloons,
only to see them rapidly replaced by poor-quality mule liquor sold at
higher prices in "soda parlors," ramshackle bars, and new roadhouses.
Jake's and Tono Moloni's were just two of the roadhouses where thirsty
imbibers could find a drink. Conveniently located along major road-
ways, they did brisk business, their parking lots filled, especially on
Friday and Saturday nights. In the outlying mining communities,
hardscrabble customers quenched their thirst with glasses of bootleg
liquor poured in the clapboard shacks that dotted the county, serving
liquor in open defiance of the law. Complaining that Williamson had

become a veritable Mecca for bootleggers and criminals of all sorts, these "better citizens" declared they wanted "the law enforced," and warned, "[I]f our officers are not doing their duty, we must resort to such measures as will accomplish the end we desire one way or another." Deeds followed words and they formed the Marion Law Enforcement League. Three years into national Prohibition, the Eighteenth Amendment had failed to end the "liquor evil." Now grassroots antiliquor warriors planned to take action into their own hands.[2]

Led by the league, hundreds of local men—including many of the region's Protestant ministers and small shopkeepers—laid plans for a large-scale raid. Federal Prohibition Bureau agents deputized the volunteer army, providing it legal authority. On the evening of December 22, 1923, the enforcers gathered at the Odd Fellows Hall in Carbondale, then fanned out across the county. That night they arrested more than one hundred bootleggers and moonshiners. In the following weeks, they carried out four more raids, each outdoing its predecessor in reckless ambition. In the final raid, a volunteer army of one thousand deputized citizens, largely members of the local Klan, spread out across the county. They raided roadhouses and private homes and set fire to some of them. In the violent battles that followed, more than a score of local residents were killed.[3]

Events in Williamson County—their scope, duration, and violence—were not typical of Prohibition enforcement efforts nationally, but they provide a dramatic example of developments mirrored elsewhere on smaller scales. Citizen-warriors in places from Denver, Colorado, to Fayetteville, Indiana, buttressed the state's Volstead army. Marching under the banner of "law and order," they backed local, state, and federal efforts to bring liquor violators to justice. Sometimes they acted as the eyes and ears of policing agents, but in many instances they supplied manpower for raids and arrests, blurring the lines between civil society and the state. This novel fusion of law and order with perceived threats to "100 percent Americanism" by immigrants, Catholics, religious modernists, "new women," and urban African-American communities produced a citizen's army—the first incarnation of the formidable twentieth-century grassroots religious right.

. . .

THE federal Prohibition Unit faced an almost impossible challenge. It rapidly expanded its ranks from its initial 1,550 agents, but the rising number of agents had a vast territory and over one hundred million Americans to police. Even with the backing of the Customs Bureau, the Coast Guard, state enforcement officials, local police, and, starting in 1924, the Border Patrol, the task was daunting. Prohibition enforcement officers knew that truly effective alcohol enforcement would require not only the cooperation of state and local law officers, but also of private "moral agencies" and the nation's citizens. Building on the earlier World War I government efforts to enlist citizen volunteers to police the home front, the government's Prohibition leaders now encouraged the idea that an active citizenry was an essential ingredient for success in the war on alcohol.[4]

Foremost among those leaders stood federal Prohibition commissioner Roy A. Haynes. Haynes hailed from Hillsboro, Ohio, the birthplace of the antisaloon prayer crusades that had sparked the formation of the Woman's Christian Temperance Union. Steeped in this antiliquor ethos, Haynes was a firm believer in the cause. Powerhouse Anti-Saloon League lobbyist Wayne Wheeler handpicked him for the top post in the new agency. Haynes pledged to "devote every ounce of his energy" to the cause and lived up to his promise. Speaking before audiences across the nation, he drove home the importance of a vigilant citizenry to Prohibition's success. "The individual citizen," he announced, "must become militant in its defense." Enforcement assistance was the citizen's "duty toward his country." Haynes proclaimed that citizens must guard and defend the law because so much was at stake. "Dry Rot," he blasted, threatened to crumple the nation. The tendency to "shrug at American traditions, American standards, laws and regulations . . . the teachings of religion disguised and nurtured under the cloak of 'modernism' "—all were "evil influences." They could be destroyed if "an alert citizenship will recognize them for what they are and tear them out." To fight these "perils to the heart of the Republic," the state required the mobilization of vigilant citizens. The Prohibition Bureau under Haynes, and even well after his departure in 1925, lauded the "active sympathy and support of citizens organized to enforce the law." Applauding the efforts of "local law enforcement committees" for their "fine public service," the Bureau encouraged local "mass meetings" to demand better enforcement.[5]

The volunteer enforcement militia that coalesced in answer to this call of duty was the militant core of a wider movement to shore up white Protestant nationalism. Moderate antiliquor crusaders essential to the law's original passage were conspicuously absent from this enforcement vanguard. Some retreated from public view content that their "work has been finished." Others, including Progressive luminary Jane Addams, used their public authority to counsel patience and education to win compliance: "Give Prohibition three generations and it will do away completely with drink," she optimistically averred. The National Federation of Settlements and the National Organization of Social Workers agreed with Addams's plea, recounting uplifting stories of family and neighborhood changes: "better food and clothing," "better homes," and "improved relations between husbands and wives."[6]

The militant core Prohibition army, however, mobilized under no such gradualist banner. They fought to bring "lawless elements" to justice immediately; the sanctity of the law was at stake. Anti-Saloon League leader Purley Baker declared liquor-law violators criminals who should "be arrested, fined, sent to prison, and justly punished." The general principle of law and order had wide support, even among many who had opposed the passage of the Eighteenth Amendment. Any other course of action threatened respect for law generally. Chief Justice William Howard Taft, who had strongly opposed the Eighteenth Amendment, called lack of compliance "unpatriotic." A Philadelphia lawmaker declared, "So long as any statute remains on the books but one course is open to the citizen, and that is respect for the law as law, and any other doctrine is subversive." Even liberal Harvard law professor Felix Frankfurter in 1923 called for "honest and effective enforcement."[7]

As flagrant violations continued unabated and president Warren Harding declared the lack of law observance a "national scandal," a powerful group of antiliquor crusaders feared a "vicious conspiracy" to "discredit and ultimately overthrow Prohibition by violation and non-enforcement." Millions of crusaders believed that it was their duty not only to comply with the law but to ensure that others did so as well: "Every Citizen an Enforcer" trumpeted one antiliquor crusader. The well-heeled and influential Prohibition organizations, the Woman's Christian Temperance Union and the Anti-Saloon League, pledged their organizational leadership and national membership to winning compliance with the law, becoming phalanxes of the powerful Volstead citizen army.[8]

• • • •

IN the 1920s, the Woman's Christian Temperance Union remained one of the largest women's organizations in the country. From its humble origins in Hillsboro, Ohio, in 1873, it had grown into a huge mass-membership organization with chapters in forty-four states. In its early years, the organization linked its antisaloon crusade to other campaigns for home protection. Members worked for child welfare, prison reform, and women's suffrage. But as the twentieth century unfolded, the war on alcohol became its major preoccupation, so that by 1924 the organization declared it "the central goal through all the years." The organization's membership experienced steady growth through the first two decades of the twentieth century. In the glow of the crusade's triumph, the WCTU won additional recruits, gaining 60,000 new members from 1919 to 1921 and another 25,000 in the following two years. Membership peaked at 355,000 in 1923. If youth auxiliaries were included, the organization boasted close to 500,000 members. Membership declined slowly in the 1930s as the luster of the great reform became deeply tarnished. Even then, WCTU leaders found renewed purpose and energy in expanding their mission beyond alcohol to wage war against other recreational narcotic substances—that is, drugs.[9]

The success of their "four decades of peaceful anti-alcohol warfare" imbued the organization with a new mission. Leaders campaigned to ensure the law's success at home. While some leaders followed the call of the *Union Signal*, the organization's flagship newspaper, to "speed up our work for world Prohibition," and others advocated for new campaigns for "peace" and "purity," president Anna Gordon, standing before members gathered at the 1921 convention, proclaimed law enforcement "our new crusade." "Our enemy is very much alive as a law breaker and a beer bolshevist," she warned. "An inescapable obligation rests upon every law-abiding citizen bravely to cooperate with federal and state officials. Let us display the maximum of Christian courage in fighting for law enforcement." The Union passed resolutions backing enforcement, and launched its own "law enforcement plans." It declared purchasers as well as sellers "law breakers," erasing the fine line that had been drawn by the Volstead Act to protect the buyer from criminal prosecution.[10]

The organization drove home its law-enforcement message at all levels. Its earlier motto "Education for Temperance" morphed into "Education for Enforcement." An extensive guide, "Understanding Law Enforcement," and pamphlets and posters such as "Rally to the Final Struggle" and "Law Enforcement the Battle Cry" galvanized its members to action. Even its repertoire of songs took up the law-enforcement battle cry. The Flint (Michigan) WCTU chapter was but one example of the penetration of the theme at the local level. Chapter members opened meetings with the inspirational song "Work for Enforcement Where You Are." Temperance plays written for schools and youth similarly taught the merits of enforcing national Prohibition.[11]

Petitions had earlier served as an important weapon in winning support for Prohibition. Now the organization launched new petition campaigns at the local level to end the "leprous" conditions in towns and communities. Chapters pressured public officials for better enforcement. Both leaders and rank-and-file members joined "law enforcement" mass meetings, backed "civic enforcement leagues," and lobbied for tough legislation at the state and national level. Their efforts to elect supporters of the antiliquor crusade to public office culminated in the abandonment of their nonpartisan stance to campaign for Republican Herbert Hoover in 1928.[12]

The organization did not limit itself to pressuring public officials and educating citizens. It directly worked with enforcement officers to prosecute violators. Government officials were eager for the support of "active citizens," and local chapters and state divisions built a close working relationship with professional law enforcement. Public officials spoke to chapters and statewide meetings to explain the different methods violators used to evade the law and the ways members "can help in enforcement." State officers told the crusaders to "watch" druggists and physicians and stores selling "flavoring extracts." The *Union Signal* published the speeches of government officials to encourage its members to aid in their duty to defend the law.[13]

The energetic grassroots membership of the WCTU wasted no time taking up this charge. Cook County Union president Iva Wooden, for example, mobilized even in the face of the violence and corruption of Capone territory working with federal officials to rein in violators. Members targeted roadhouses where "teenage girls" sold beer to "all sorts of men," touching on public anxieties over the new opportunities the unregulated traffic offered to young women. The Cook County president encouraged her members to step up, investigate, and report violations in their neighborhoods. The Oak Park-River Forest Union heeded her call, devoting their energies to shutting down one establishment. Flint WCTU members were equally vigilant, proudly reporting their role in dismantling two stills in 1926. Though exponentially outmatched, their actions did not go unnoticed. Illinois State WCTU president Helen Hood reportedly received a death threat by mail: "You are on our list to be murdered in the near future."[14]

WCTU leaders and local members alike reveled in their self-described militancy and courage. Anna Gordon, the WCTU president, championed the law enforcement efforts of her members and youth "legionnaires." The Union "army of Prohibition national guards," Gordon proudly proclaimed, "have . . . proven themselves to be valuable detectives . . . having aided in the capturing of stills and having shared the joys of destroying confiscated 'wet goods.'" Inez Deach, president of the West Side Union near Chicago, reported that she had "the joy of helping break up a boot-legging place." But despite these militant actions, members and chapters were not modern-day Carrie Nations. Unlike the hatchet-wielding, antisaloon crusader who made national headlines in the early twentieth century, the organization pointedly averred that it worked through properly constituted legislative, political, and enforcement channels.[15]

As the liquor-law enforcement crisis stretched over months and then years, the WCTU adopted a shriller tone toward those it held responsible for violations. At the start of the decade, the organization's "Americanization department" had displayed a "friendly" if paternalist posture towards immigrants. The *Union Signal* encouraged its members to "work among the foreign born" and "bring together native-born and foreign[-]born neighbors for a pleasant social hour," to read at least one book" about their neighbor's country, and to "go with [them] to the library." This gentle assimilationist approach faded as the nation's war on alcohol stalled and suffered reversals. In 1923, the WCTU backed legislation calling for the "deportation of aliens convicted of Prohibition violations." Outright coercion replaced moral suasion. Compliance among this "great problem" class required education—but now through disciplinary means: "Officers of the law" would act as "schoolmasters" to bring foreigners toward "American ideals." The prevalent association of "foreigners" with liquor-law violations in public discourse contributed to this sharpened coercive edge. The Indiana

WCTU claimed "seventy five percent of liquor law violators are foreigners." The increasingly defensive tone of the WCTU toward immigrants, many of them Catholic, stretched as the 1920s progressed to new endeavors as well. The WCTU joined the swelling fight for compulsory Bible reading in public schools. Its members were at the forefront of that struggle in the states considering such action, revealing an increasing embrace of militant Protestant religiosity during the 1920s.[16]

The WCTU formed but one phalanx of the Volstead army. While the WCTU had historically balanced the prominence of its antialcohol crusade with multifaceted reforms for "purity," the Anti-Saloon League's sole goal had always been the eradication of the drink traffic. The ASL was also no stranger to law-enforcement methods. Coercion always featured in its devotion to ending the liquor traffic through law. Enforcement was, indeed, one of the organization's four divisions—along with agitation, legislation, and fundraising. Still, key leaders had long emphasized educational work first and foremost. Ernest Cherrington, along lines Jane Addams would have agreed with, argued that "legislation and enforcement . . . cannot alone solve the beverage alcohol problem. . . . The ultimate realization of the temperance reform depends primarily not on legislation but education." The coalition building required to win the grand reform had papered over these differences in approach and tone. But the thin fabric of unity tore in the wake of widespread disregard for the law. Cherrington lost his battle for an emphasis on education after the law's enactment, and the organization's leadership pivoted strongly toward law and order, though at the cost of many earlier allies. Despite a drop in financing after the passage of the law, the militant core Protestant evangelical leadership of the Anti-Saloon League pursued alcohol law enforcement with all the energy they could muster from their loyal troops.[17]

"Singleness of purpose," declared Wayne Wheeler, chief ASL lobbyist, was essential to the success of the Eighteenth Amendment just as it had been to its passage—that sole purpose should now be "law enforcement." The goal was simple and direct but the strategy multipronged—

involving politics, legislation, and vigilant citizens. The Anti-Saloon League's *National Prohibition Enforcement Manual* advised supporters on how they might aid the cause. It drew up an organizing blueprint, calling for "civic leagues" to bolster law enforcement in each county of the land. These county leagues, in turn, worked to inspire smaller, local leagues to action. Civic leagues, sometimes also dubbed "law enforcement leagues," were often organized with the aid of local Protestant ministers. They taught citizens to grasp the problem of enforcement at the local level and function as the nemesis of the bootlegger to curb the widespread illegal traffic. The leagues worked to secure enforcement through local officials and campaigned for the election of dry candidates. If these methods proved insufficient, the ASL also called for "the full power of publicity to compel action."[18]

The Anti-Saloon League was well positioned to undertake the formation of enforcement bodies. State league leaders, district officers, and local-league-affiliated pastors, along with their millions of churchgoing Protestant congregants, provided a multileveled powerhouse that directed its energies to ensuring the law's success. State league leaders worked to cement relationships between the organization and law-enforcement agents and to oil the wheels of state and federal enforcement. In Texas, state superintendent Reverend Atticus W. Webb held law-enforcement "mass meetings" and claimed credit for forging a "working agreement" between federal officers and the Texas Rangers. "Close cooperation" between the two levels of enforcement, he declared, was the result of his efforts. The close working relationship between the Anti-Saloon League and government enforcers was built through league influence in personnel and hiring decisions of Prohibition agents. Critics complained of the blurred lines between government enforcers and the "Protestant church in action," calling attention to government officials who advised applicants to Prohibition field offices to seek endorsement from their district Anti-Saloon League.[19]

Porous enforcement boundaries stretched in other directions too. The Anti-Saloon League, like the WCTU, averred in 1920 that "law can best be enforced only through the regularly constituted authorities, and not by unofficial or private detective or private inspection agencies." Enforcement could best be secured by "aiding all public officials whose duties it is to enforce it." The national organization, in other words, disavowed vigilante activity. Antiliquor crusaders were not unified, however, on what constituted appropriate enforcement "aid." The lines between indirect support and active engagement were murky and frequently breached.[20]

Ohio league leaders, for one, encouraged active citizen engagement in enforcement efforts. League state superintendent James White went so far as to distribute blank search warrants to district workers, likely authorized by sympathetic justices of the peace, and directed them to the search-and-seizure provisions of the state enforcement law. He ended his instructions to the antiliquor crusaders by wishing them "all success in your task of law enforcement." With such encouragement, grassroots Prohibitionists did not shirk their duty to uphold the law. Local antiliquor crusaders in Mahoning County, Ohio, organized a "county dry league" in 1923. Violations were rife in the city of Youngstown, with its heavily industrial and working-class immigrant neighborhoods. In many dwellings, reported one newspaper, "it is possible to purchase drinks at any hour of the day or night." Such violations galvanized staunch Prohibitionists to action. Five hundred of them gathered at the Trinity Methodist Church to mobilize a crackdown. Following league guidelines, they first watched for violations and called on local police to act. When their efforts were rebuffed, the county dry league pursued alternative channels, linking up with "unofficial enforcement squads." The local league hired private detectives and led raids with citizen "volunteers" to arrest violators.[21]

Ohio law facilitated, even encouraged, such vigorous citizen enforcement. State law provided for special "liquor courts" in towns and villages. Local justices of the peace with countywide jurisdiction presided over these courts. The law provided financial incentives for strict enforcement, effectively creating an enforcement market. When they successfully prosecuted liquor-law violators, town judges earned extra income, paid out of the fees of those convicted of infractions. Large numbers of urban, ethnic, working-class immigrants from nearby cities were dragged before local town justices who imposed heavy fines. These liquor courts were known to impose absurdly lengthy sentences. In at least one case of possession for a minuscule quantity of liquor, a violator, according to one newspaper report, was sentenced to jail for eleven years. In dry towns neighboring heavily wet Cincinnati, fines paid by liquor-law violators contributed to funding cleanup squads. In North College Hill, a local ordinance stipulated that one half of the fees earned by the liquor courts would go to a "secret service fund" to secure further enforcement. The violent raids these self-sustaining squads conducted in Cincinnati and elsewhere targeted private dwellings in heavily immigrant districts. One editorial in the *Cleveland Plain Dealer* described the "reign of terror" and "deplorable perversion of justice" that resulted.[22]

Despite such energetic enforcement, violations continued unabated. And as enforcement failures multiplied, the ASL and WCTU leaders' commitment to working through "regularly constituted authority" eroded. With its secretive operations and anti-immigrant white supremacist Protestant agenda, the burgeoning Ku Klux Klan was perfectly suited to fill the ranks of "volunteer" liquor law enforcement squads. The hooded order forged the third and most powerful phalanx of the volunteer enforcement army. The growing local Anti-Saloon League's law enforcement leagues and Klan klaverns were not one and the same, but local league-affiliated ministers who established civic enforcement leagues frequently allied with the Ku Klux Klan. The league and the Klan shared key local leaders, personnel, and symbiotic goals.[23]

· · ·

THE Ku Klux Klan had flourished during the Reconstruction era in the nineteenth century; its white supremacist terrorism was memorialized in D. W. Griffith's film *Birth of a Nation*. In 1915, William Joseph Simmons, a one-time southern Methodist circuit rider turned Woodmen of the World fraternal organizer, revived the Klan in Atlanta to defend native-born white Protestant supremacy. Only a few thousand members joined its ranks until 1920. Then membership snowballed. Postwar social conflict, including a new militancy among organized labor and African-Americans, and more permissive sexual norms, fueled white Protestant nationalist anxieties and created a fecund climate for Klan mobilization. Savvy promoters contributed to mushrooming growth. In 1920 Joseph Simmons signed a contract with the publicists Elizabeth Tyler and Edward Young Clarke of the Southern Publicity Association. Their claim to fame rested in no small part on their successful fund-raising earlier for the Anti-Saloon League and the Salvation Army. Tyler and Clarke marketed the hooded order by creating a motivated "sales" force to peddle it. "Kleagles" pocketed a portion of the initiation fee when they "naturalized" a new member and attracted bumper crops of new recruits with promises of restoring patriarchal white Protestant cultural values in public life.[24]

Nothing, however, helped the Klan to turn itself into a dynamic social movement more than the new opportunity provided by the war on alcohol. The Klan leveraged the broad scope of the law to pursue its anti-Catholic, anti-immigrant, anti-Semitic, and white-supremacist agenda, winning two to five million Americans to its ranks by 1925. Already in 1920 Klan organizers broadcast a mission to "clean up" communities by putting bootleggers, moonshiners, and "vice operators" out of business. The Klan frequently gained a foothold in communities, and new recruits, by waving the flag of "unearthing the bootlegger." In Orange County, California, the Anaheim klavern attracted public attention when it warned a local hotel owner, J. H. Clark, accused of peddling bootleg liquor to his clientele, to "leave town in ten days or suffer the consequences." Soon afterwards, the Klan became a powerful force in the city as well as in the county. The southwestern Klan thrived by advocating "rigid economy" and "merciless law enforcement, particularly of Prohibition laws." In Fremont, Colorado, another Klan stronghold, a national Klan speaker championed similar themes: "Money and politics must cease to play a role in our courts . . . particularly in Prohibition enforcement." In Athens, Georgia, too, the local klavern gained early recruits by promising to clean up rife liquor-law violations.[25]

The Klan supplemented the militant temperance sentiment of the Anti-Saloon League and the Woman's Christian Temperance Union with promises of militant action, selling itself as an upholder of law and order. In Jackson City, Oregon, the local klavern promised to "aid the officers of the law." In Denver, Colorado, the kleagle lambasted the local "vice" and "crime" situation, proclaiming, "We . . . assist . . . at all times the authorities in every community in upholding law and order." Where local authorities failed to do their job, the Klan promised to step up to the plate. As one Denver Klan leader, a Methodist minister, railed: "If our officials cannot enforce the law, we should teach them how. . . . I have no respect for the official who winks at the law." Their activities provoked controversy, but also praise—sometimes in surprising places. One Chicago judge who presided over the trial of a liquor-law violator praised the Klan for "going in and handling a case when and where the police fail."[26]

In regions where sheriffs, local police, or state authorities resisted Klan activism—from Inglewood and Los Angeles, California, to Niles, Ohio—vigilantism turned into gunfights and, sometimes, open warfare. Such violent contests provoked controversy and, eventually, the erosion of support for Klan activity. But in many places, vigorous cleanup actions won the support of local and state enforcement agents under public pressure to shut down sources of liquor supply. From Jackson City, Oregon, to Birmingham, Alabama, the Klan worked closely with local police. Indeed, Klansmen and officials were not infrequently one and the same. In Anaheim, California, local police officers patrolled the streets in full regalia at the height of Klan power. In Birmingham, Alabama, Klan member and police chief J. J. Shirley advised a Nashville, Tennessee, colleague to organize his own klavern to assist police in law enforcement and the public safety commissioner welcomed Klan aid in antiliquor raids. Sheriffs, police, and justices of the peace in such regions deputized Klan members to win additional foot soldiers for vice cleanup. In Texas, Klan chapters claimed credit for citizen arrests, winning gratitude from law officers. In Ohio, Texas, Indiana, Colorado, and Oregon, Klansmen arrested thousands of liquor-law violators who were arraigned in court and frequently convicted.[27]

These cleanup raids characterized the Klan as militant Protestant warriors in the dry cause: an army upholding Anglo-Saxon white Protestant nationalism. Not surprisingly, the Klan targeted "foreign bootlegging" as the central problem in achieving compliance. The dry mission intersected perfectly with its anti-Catholic, anti-immigrant, anti-Semitic, and white-supremacist agenda. When the La Grande, Oregon, police cracked down on liquor-law violators, the Klan buttressed its forces, targeting Italian, African-American, and Mexican neighborhoods. In Denver's Little Italy, the Klan provided manpower for police raids—conducting door-to-door house searches in antiliquor raids that netted predominantly Italian Americans. In Inglewood, California, the local klavern raided the home of a ranching family of Mexican origin, a "suspected winery." The Klan aided local police in a series of antiliquor raids on "Chinese cafes" in Birmingham in 1924. Klansmen made up the volunteer squads of vigilante raiders who targeted ethnic working-class communities in the massive liquor raids and "reign of terror" in Youngstown and Niles, Ohio. In Madison, Wisconsin, the chief of police along with the Dane County federal Prohibition officer, to their credit, refused Klan offers to clean up liquor violations in "Little Sicily." The mayor, however, did not hesitate to deputize Klansmen in antiliquor raids conducted in 1925.[28]

When President Harding lambasted the "national scandal" of noncompliance in 1922, the Klan offered evangelical Protestants a solution. Aggrieved over widespread violations and affronted by the social change they associated with it, the Klan would serve as a citizen enforcement army. They would uphold the values of the militant anti-liquor crusaders and wage war for "100 Protestant Americanism." Prohibition effectively explains why the second incarnation of the Ku Klux Klan snowballed when it did. Widespread flouting of liquor laws crystallized in concrete form a wider host of dangers to the survival of white Protestant patriarchal nationalism—from shifting gender norms to the increased power of Catholic immigrants and religious modernism. The Eighteenth Amendment and the Volstead Act, and the many state enforcement laws, provided the hooded order, and white Protestant nationalists more generally, an unprecedented opportunity to wage a wider war to safeguard white Protestant native supremacy.

The millions of grassroots men and women who joined the Klan's ranks did not simply find it attractive because of its character as a "social and civic organization" much like others for white Protestant Americans—such as the Lion's Clubs or the national temperance organizations—as some interpretations of the order suggest. Members joined because the Klan promised more: it was willing to take action where the "official" temperance bodies and white Protestant civic organizations would not—to take violent vigilante action against the enemies of white Protestant nationalism. Controlling drink—when produced and consumed by deviant "others"—proved a powerful tool in the Klan's arsenal of weapons, and a mandate for its activities. *The Fiery Cross*, the Indiana Klan newspaper, articulated this mission: "The Klan is going to drive bootlegging forever out of this land. It is going to bring clean moving pictures to this country. It is going to bring clean literature to this country. It is going to break up the road side party, and see to it that the young man who induces a girl to get drunk is held accountable."[29]

The order's virulent anti-Semitism and anti-Catholicism gave a practical direction and focus to its dry mission. The old Right, within and outside of Klan ranks, identified Jews with a national slide into moral decay and linked that slide to flagrant liquor violations. As one anti-Semitic tract fulminated in 1922: "This idea of drink will be maintained by means of the Jewish stage, Jewish jazz and the Jewish comics until somebody comes down hard upon it as being incentive to treason to the Constitution." The use of sacramental wines for religious purposes by the "enemies" of white Protestant nationalism made them easy scapegoats as sources of bootleg liquor. Henry Ford, perhaps the best-known anti-Semite of his day, helped spread such ideas. His newspaper, the *Dearborn Independent*, went so far as to declare "bootlegging a 95 percent Jewish controlled industry." The *Colonel Mayfield Weekly*, a Dallas-based Klan paper, proclaimed, "My fight right now . . . is against the Homebrew and the Hebrew."[30]

The Klan's conspiratorial world view also targeted the Catholic Church as the "Antichrist." Once again, the Klan leveraged the war on alcohol to battle the threat. *The Dawn*, the Illinois Klan newspaper, in one issue alone printed four stories with these headlines: "Priest sent to jail for drunk driving," "Catholic Father held for liquor forgeries," and "Drunken priest kills pastor." The linkage led raiders to target not just Catholic immigrants but their parishes and religious symbols. In a series of antiliquor raids in 1923, a Catholic priest recalled raiders who ripped crucifixes from the walls of Catholic immigrant homes and stomped and spat on them. Klansmen targeted the priest's church too, smashing the parish's sacramental wine.[31]

Native Protestant trespassers of Klan "morality" were not exempt from Klan "justice." Protestants who strayed from its moral vision—through adultery, moonshining, or family desertion—faced Klan retribution. But the Klan's instrumentally applied cleanup agenda was more deeply concerned with the drinking of others than with its own. Stories abounded of raiders who confiscated liquor only to drink it themselves. One Colorado klavern was even run by a local "vice operator" who served liquor at local meetings. His Klan position likely bolstered the power he required to control supply and shut down competing sources. Despite their avowed mission, Klansmen were not total abstainers. The Klan secretary in Le Grande, Oregon, remarked that the knights at one social event forgot their "craving for moonshine" and devoured "hot dogs and Ku Klux Klan cake." When they spilled into public view, the drunken escapades of Klan leaders, from Grand Dragon D. C. Stephenson to publicists Tyler and Clark, eroded the membership and prestige of the hooded order.[32]

Such incidents do not signify that the Klan's antialcohol mission was mere window dressing for its goal of terrorizing immigrants, Catholics, and other minorities—though it served that purpose well. Many militant evangelical Protestant pastors throughout the midwest, south, and west who along with their flocks championed the order truly judged liquor an "evil" and the "Devil's drink." In Colorado, chapters worked to bar from membership "notorious moonshine drinkers." If they were going to succeed in upholding their white supremacist Protestant vision, however, reining in liquor-law violations by those deemed significant threats to Protestant nationalism was crucial—even if members of the righteous army sometimes lapsed into "sinful" behavior.[33]

In some states, Klan organizers astutely revived old laws still on the books as a legal tool to justify their enforcement activities. Indiana Grand Dragon Stephenson built a powerful Klan enforcement arm with a nineteenth-century regulation, the Horse Thieves Act, authorizing "citizens . . . not less than ten" to form into companies "for the purpose of detecting horse thief and other felons and for mutual protection." In 1924, about 22,000 of the 25,000 members of the Horse Thief Detective Association were Klansmen. With authorization from sympathetic county commissioners, the "detectives" carried weapons, made arrests, and, in the absence of warrants, held persons in custody. In one series of sensational raids in Indianapolis, the association arrested 125 persons on charges of operating speakeasies and gambling establishments and purchasing liquor—a crime by Indiana statute. The wholesale convictions that followed made plain the cooperation of judicial officials charged with upholding antiliquor laws. Klan leaders claimed credit for more than three thousand cases of Prohibition law violations brought to the Indiana courts from June 1922 through October 1923, largely through the efforts of the Horse Thief Detective Association.[34]

The Klan's organizational independence from its enforcement body in Indiana and its veiled public references to this role protected the order from the kind of official scrutiny that had earlier prompted a series of congressional investigations into Klan vigilantism. *The Fiery Cross* mentioned "some force at work for law enforcement" and "parties of citizens" assisting sheriffs in raids. Where the Klan flourished, whether raiders donned their white masks or not, Klan backers knew whom to thank, while opponents knew who was responsible.[35]

Vigilante enforcement raids were the radical edge of a broader dry mission that included political reform strategies. Wherever the Klan achieved a significant degree of political power, liquor-law observance was high on its agenda. When Klan members won four seats on the Anaheim, California, city council, they adopted a strict "law enforcement" ordinance. It provided for harsh punishment of liquor offenders, outlawed slot machines, and tightened traffic laws. In Colorado in 1924, Klan-backed candidates won the governorship, both senate seats, and the state attorney general's office on a platform of government efficiency, spending cuts, and better Prohibition enforcement. And that same year in Indiana, when the Klan-dominated Republican Party won control of the legislature, the pope and demon rum were its campaign's primary issues. The following year the legislature passed anti-Catholic measures and a new "bone-dry" bill to strengthen and codify state Prohibition legislation in one all-encompassing, draconian law. Drafted by Indiana Anti-Saloon League superintendent Reverend Shumaker, the act required jail time for first-time possession of even small quantities of alcohol.[36]

The Klan's war against alcohol provided it with powerful allies among the large and well-organized antiliquor crusade bodies—the Woman's Christian Temperance Union and the Anti-Saloon League. Together, these three organizations wove together an army of citizen enforcers, forging the first massive entry of the Christian Right of the twentieth century into public view and into national politics. As an intertwined social movement, the organizations had much in common.

All were evangelical Protestant efforts to shore up the United States as
a Christian nation, and all embraced coercive and disciplinary means to
do so. At the national level, the ASL and WCTU ignored the raging
controversy over the Klan's virulent intolerance and the violence of its
dry mission, but their silence spoke volumes about the complicity of
many members. State ASL and WCTU leaders teamed up with the
Klan in the midwest, south, and west. They did so most publicly on
political platforms, sharing the stump in their campaigns for white,
Protestant, and dry political candidates.[37]

These groups cooperated in other ways too. Women could not join
the hooded order, but many WCTU members found their way into the
Women of the Ku Klux Klan. In Indiana, prior activism in the antiliquor crusade proved the most common avenue into the WKKK. The
national WCTU ignored the controversy and criticism raging nationally over the racism and vigilantism of the Ku Klux Klan, but it quietly
publicized the efforts of local "citizens" who banded together to conduct investigations and were deputized to join in antiliquor raids. The
organization's members, in regions with supportive ideological waters,
skirted close to the Klan's strains of virulent racism, conspiratorial
vision, and vigilante action.[38]

Regional Anti-Saloon League leaders collaborated even more
closely with the "white knights." Indiana league superintendent E. F.
Shumaker told national leaders that the "Klan is doing many things we
would like to do." Hugh Pat Emmons, Klan Exalted Cyclops in Saint
Joseph County, claimed that Shumaker met with him to encourage
cooperation among the Klan, the Anti-Saloon League, and the Horse
Thief Detective Association. In some places, league leaders were prominent Klan leaders as well. South Carolina ASL superintendent E. M.
Lightfoot, a Baptist minister, was a Klan kleagle and actively recruited
for the order. In Alabama, J. L. Musgrove, a national chairman of the
Anti-Saloon League, was a proud member of the Klan and a substantial
financial backer to imperial headquarters. When liberal iconoclast
Clarence Darrow declared that "the father and mother of the Ku Klux

is the Anti-Saloon League," he was close to the mark. Washington-based league lobbyist Wayne Wheeler, concerned over the damage such affiliations might do to the league's national reputation and ability to fund-raise, sought to distance the organization from the Klan, but many state and local league affiliates worked hand in glove with the organization.[39]

Many of the grassroots men and women who had worked in the antiliquor crusade through the ASL or the WCTU found a new champion in the more militant Klan. Pietistic ministers, Methodists, Baptists, and Disciples of Christ who established law-enforcement leagues frequently backed the formation of Klan klaverns at the local level. Liquor-law enforcement provided them a concrete tool to defend militant Protestant Christianity from modernist and un-American threats. County "dry leagues" and local "civic leagues" often walked in lockstep with the Klan in the battle for a dry land.[40]

The nation's war on alcohol fueled a powerful citizens' army. The WCTU, the Anti-Saloon League, and the Ku Klux Klan knew that the success of the war hinged on citizen backing. This shadow enforcement force buttressed the better-known federal, state, and local enforcement apparatus of Prohibition agents, customs officials, the Coast Guard, and the Border Patrol with contributions of personnel and funding. Overwhelmed enforcement officials frequently welcomed the aid from this vibrant grassroots movement. Once in motion, however, the actions of the dry warriors proved difficult to control. Their activities sparked controversy, raised alarms, and catalyzed opposition. When they unleashed violent social conflict and brought national headlines, they raised to national level growing doubts about the merits of the war on alcohol.

Opponents had already argued that the legislation endangered personal liberty prior to the enactment of the Eighteenth Amendment. The actions of the citizen-warriors proved their case beyond their own worst expectations. By charting the rise and fall of citizen enforcement in one place, we can gain a better understanding of the logic of the citizen-warriors, the axis along which the war on alcohol turned on the ground level, and the controversies that ensued. Such a thick description reveals how and why the war on alcohol became an issue of pressing concern, particularly for the immigrants, Catholics, and minorities the enforcers so heavily targeted. It also reveals why the Klan's meteoric rise proved short-lived. The controversial citizens' army sparked a countermobilization that successfully reined in Klan power, eroding support for the hooded order.[41]

.   .   .

WILLIAMSON County, Illinois, is nestled in the southern portion of the state known as "Little Egypt." About an equivalent distance from the borders of Missouri, Indiana, and Kentucky, the region shared more with its rural southern neighbors than with cosmopolitan Chicago, three hundred miles to the north. Its largely old-stock population, made up of descendants of settlers from Kentucky, Virginia, and the Carolinas, was heavily churched, stamped by the influence of the Methodist and Baptist pastors who preached revivalist and fire-and-damnation sermons. Coal mining tipples dotted the landscape, bringing economic development to the region with its thick veins of bituminous coal. Herrin, a bustling community of about twelve thousand residents, was the economic center. Neighboring Marion, the county capital, boasted about the same population as Herrin, but was more sedate, with shaded, tree-lined streets and a central square. The brick buildings and paved streets in Herrin and Marion contrasted with the bleakness of life of many outlying mining communities, with their ramshackle shacks, unpaved streets, and grinding poverty.[42]

The southern Illinois miners were proud members of the United Mine Workers of America. Their families credited the union for ending the low wages and dangerous working conditions prevalent in non-union mines. Many of the local miners had won an element of security and a small stake in proprietary capitalism: over half of the county's thirteen thousand miners owned their homes. The largely native-born

Protestant miners' world view was militant but not radical. It drew deeply from a well of patriotism and religiosity. The miners' staunch localism brought district leaders into frequent conflict with the national union throughout the 1920s. The hold on the economic security they built was thin. Class tensions bubbled just below the surface. The 1920s heightened those challenges. The mining industry was increasingly undergoing mechanization, thinning out the availability of jobs. Along with agriculture and textiles, mining was one of the "sick" industries bypassed by the economic growth experienced by other industries during the 1920s.[43]

Abject poverty was still the norm in the nonunion coalfields, and Williamson's miners, as well as their families, were vigilant against any threats to their union and hard-won security. Just such a threat appeared when William J. Lester, the absentee owner of the Southern Illinois Coal Company, locked horns with the union in a battle to undermine its power during a strike at his strip mine in 1921. The company brought in strikebreakers from Chicago to load and ship coal. Lester's effort to break the union's power culminated a longer history of conflicts over the raw power of the mine company, and the unwieldy economic might it exerted over local resources. These conflicts raised the ire of a broad segment of the community when the company closed a main road running through mine property. Hostility deepened when the company's arrogant guards, flaunting their weapons, meted out abuse to those who used a detour skirting the mine property.[44]

Conflict between the Southern Illinois Coal Company and the miners in 1922 escalated into open warfare when mine guards armed with machine guns killed two union men who attempted to stop the mine from loading coal during the strike. A large group of UMWA men surrounded the mine and captured around fifty men, including mine managers, guards, and strikebreakers. Some of the captured nonunion workers and mine managers were killed on the spot; others fled, only to be hunted down. Six of the captured strikebreakers were roped together and brought to the local Herrin cemetery. There, a crowd, including miners' wives, mercilessly tortured and killed the guards and workers, and riddled their bodies with bullets.[45]

The "Herrin massacre" made national headlines. President Harding declared it "a shocking crime of barbarity, butchery and madness." But the local community rallied around the miners. Though a grand jury returned forty-four indictments for murder, declaring the actions "almost unbelievable" in their "relentless brutality," local jurors acquitted all five men charged with murder. The contest between the raw and unwieldy power of capital and local miners had escalated into seething, brutal class warfare. The killings and the escape of the perpetrators from justice, freed by a "jury of their peers," provoked anxiety among Herrin's "better citizens." County boosters decried the dark reputation Herrin's name won in the eyes of the world. The Herrin massacre unveiled deep class cleavages and grievances that structured life in southern Illinois.[46]

The miners' brutal actions revealed deep-seated fears Herrin County residents had about workers' tenuous hold on economic security. Local Protestant ministers who tended their flocks in the churches that dotted the landscape directed residents toward another danger that promised to undermine Herrin's way of life: the public vice operating in and around the town, with its saloons, gambling dens, and "corrupt" hotels that drew customers with "painted women." Herrin was steeped in deep traditions of evangelicalism, but many of its residents ignored the strictures of its preachers and found solace in the drink culture of its saloons. Illinois reformers had worked hard but had lost their battle for a state dry law. They won a district "local option" bill in 1905, but it lacked the teeth to rid the region of "vice." When the mines were working at full tilt, many of Herrin's working men found their reward imbibing at bars in the smaller towns and in Herrin itself.[47]

Pastors and reformers in Herrin, as in many other places, had high expectations that the Eighteenth Amendment and Volstead Act would put an end to the "drink evil," but liquor continued to flow. Bootleggers organized profitable supply rings. One minister, a member of the

Ministerial Association of Williamson County, later described the vice situation as "unbearable"—the local sheriff "allowed the bootleggers, the gamblers, and the houses of ill-fame to operate openly," and the state's attorney made little effort "to curb this wholesale law-breaking." County councilmen passed resolutions calling for "rigid enforcement" of state and national Prohibition laws. These laws, they declared, were being "continuously and persistently violated." One cleanup supporter warned that Herrin had become a veritable Mecca for bootleggers, with women as well as men engaged in the modern occupation of "mule" vending. The presence of infamous organized-crime entrepreneurs' bases of operations in the region—the county was home to bootleggers Charles Birger and the Shelton brothers—exacerbated an already bad situation.[48]

In the spring of 1922, shortly before the labor strife came to a head, businessmen and Protestant ministers joined together to forge a new law-and-order organization, the Marion Law Enforcement League. The cleanup effort revealed the malleability of class grievances. With a working class bifurcated along ethnic, racial, and religious lines, conflict in Herrin that only months earlier had been directed against the mine company in open class warfare pivoted toward the threat of immigrant "outsiders" to Herrin's way of life. By targeting "foreign" drink culture, Protestant evangelical ministers and Herrin's merchants, small shopowners, and county officials drew a segment of the largely white Protestant native union miners into the Klan's cleanup ranks.[49]

The Italian immigrants who had recently settled in Herrin provided a convenient scapegoat. The strong veins of soft coal and the promise of jobs had drawn many newcomers into southern Illinois in the early twentieth century. In 1920, the foreign-born population of Herrin along with their American-born offspring stood at 15 percent. In all of Williamson County they made up closer to 20 percent, and in neighboring Franklin County the number stood at around 35 percent. Immigrants broadened the region's largely evangelical Protestant religious environment, evidenced by the flourishing Catholic parish, the

Rome Club (an Italian fraternal organization) and plans for the construction of a second Catholic church. The small but visible and largely Catholic Italian immigrant community, composed mostly of unskilled laborers, including mine workers, divided the working-class community along ethnic and religious lines. With its culture of wine-drinking, it lay outside the moral influence of the Protestant pastors, who drew on these cleavages for their antiliquor crusade, etching them deeper into the social fabric in the process.[50]

The Enforcement League held its first meeting on January 16, 1923, at the First Methodist Church. Reverend Goff, pastor of the Presbyterian Church in Marion and vice-president of the league, presided. Reverend A. E. Prince of the First Baptist Church and Methodist Church minister Reverend Glotfelty—a "demon in human form" opined the local Catholic priest years later—served on the law enforcement committee. The Enforcement League found a powerful ally in the Ku Klux Klan. One local Herrin pastor and cleanup leader admitted that while he had "been accustomed to working through the Anti-Saloon League," now the hooded order provided a more militant vehicle. Another Herrin cleanup observer averred, "Effectively . . . the Ku Klux Klan superseded the League."[51]

In Illinois, the Klan established itself first in Chicago in 1921 under the name of the Southern Publicity Bureau, fruit of the efforts of Tyler and Clarke, the promoters and former ASL fundraisers. By the summer of 1922, klaverns blossomed in southern Illinois, and a year later the Klan was recruiting in droves. In May and June, Klan rallies blanketed the county, attesting to the order's escalating power. The large nighttime rally at a farm field outside the town of Carterville was but one of a number of such spectacular gatherings. Between four and five thousand masked klansmen took part in an initiation ceremony that June. Klansmen drove to the field, parking some eight hundred cars in a large circle. With car headlights illuminating the rituals taking place inside the circle, Klansmen sporting their white-robe regalia "naturalized" new members, introducing them to the organization's secret rules, symbols, and language. The masked men joined in a chorus of "Onward Christian Soldiers" as a large wooden cross was ignited, its flames visible far and wide. Over the next year, the Klan made significant inroads throughout Williamson County. On one occasion, a social picnic at the county fairgrounds brought whole families out to enjoy a day of races, contests, and a picnic dinner. These social familial occasions were one side of Klan activity. On the other side stood the cross burnings and vigilantism. Crosses illuminated the night on seventeen different occasions near Herrin's Catholic church during the Klan's reign, attested the local parish priest.[52]

The many Protestant ministers who enthusiastically embraced the Klan propelled its strength. At the First Christian Church in Marion on May 20, 1923, masked Klansmen stepped to the front of the church as "a hushed thrill of apprehension" stirred the crowd. They handed the visiting evangelist a token of their thanks for his "good efforts" for the community. The presiding minister, Reverend Laird, lauded the Klan, declaring the organization "stand[s] for something good." Some weeks later, Klansmen put in an appearance at another church, Reverend Glotfelty's Methodist church, offering a donation and declaring they stood for the "betterment of humanity."[53]

With the hooded order thriving, the moment seemed ripe to act upon the cleanup sentiment that had been building. The Marion Law Enforcement League, the Klan, and the local Protestant pastors joined forces in the summer of 1923 to mobilize public support for waging a local war on alcohol. On August 19, all the members of the local Ministerial Association preached to their flocks on "law enforcement." At the leading Protestant congregations in Marion and Herrin, ministers regaled their flocks with sermons on its importance. In nearby Carterville, Reverend Lyerla preached on enforcement as well. The Klan's best allies, these ministers offered the Klan warm words of support and rallied their congregations for a law-and-order mass meeting to be held the following day.[54]

Fifteen hundred residents responded to their pastors' calls to assemble in front of the Marion Courthouse. Local pastors, taking their turns on an improvised soapbox, called for county officials to "clean up or clean out," in the words of Reverend Glotfelty. "No matter where we go in Williamson County, the law is being flagrantly violated." With enforcement officials unwilling or unable to do their job, he declared in favor of citizen action: "We propose to do our duty . . . if we have to do it ourselves." The ministers targeted Catholics and immigrants as the source of the problem: "The fellows who are most to blame . . . are those imported from across the sea." Reverand Glotfelty went so far as to declare all of the members of the local Catholic parish "bootleggers," pledging they would all be in jail "before the foundations of the new church were built."[55]

This anti-immigrant and law-and-order mobilization provided one means for Protestant preachers and county boosters to attempt to bury Herrin's reputation for violent class hatred earned during the Herrin massacre. County council officials, not surprisingly, were some of the earliest and most prominent members of the cleanup crusade. It was time, they declared, to "rid Williamson County of its black name with the rest of the world." They hoped "to make a name of which the world will be proud." Law Enforcement League leaders sought to wrest action from lackadaisical state authorities. They traveled to Springfield, but their pleas to Illinois governor Len Small fell on deaf ears. A local committee, led by Sam Stearns, the chair of the Williamson County Board of Supervisors and a Klan Exalted Cyclops, then traveled to Washington, where they met with Prohibition commissioner Roy Haynes. After hearing about the conditions in Williamson, Haynes threw up his hands. He could clean up the county if he had an army, but he didn't. The men provided a solution: they had the foot soldiers; they just wanted authorization and support. Haynes agreed. If the men gathered the evidence, he would send in the federal agents needed to lead the raids and prepare prosecutions.[56]

The committee hired Seth Glenn Young, a native of the Kansas prairies, born in a sod house and raised in a middling merchant and farming family, to gather the evidence. His mother had made "a name for herself for Prohibition in Kansas," and by the time the twenty-eight-year-old Young came to Williamson, he had won regional fame as a "noted sleuth." When Prohibition passed, Young won a position unearthing bootleggers as a Prohibition agent for the Southern Illinois district. Young's pistol-happy methods led to trouble when he fatally shot unarmed Luke Vukovic in his home in East St. Louis during a liquor raid gone awry. Charges were dropped, but the incident led to Young's dismissal. Young was eager for a new mission and spent that fall gathering evidence at "soft drink parlors" and bars. Proof of law violations in hand, he traveled to Washington with the local committee and appealed to Haynes for the promised support. Haynes dispatched Gus Simons, divisional chief of general Prohibition agents from Pittsburgh, and Victor Armitage and J. F. Loeffler from Chicago.[57]

Buttressed by local armed raiders, overwhelmingly Klansmen, the agents met at the Odd Fellows Hall in the town of Carbondale, to the south and west of Herrin, on the night of December 22, 1923. The Prohibition agents deputized Young and five hundred other men. Agent Simons administered the federal oath, and called for men "not afraid to die." The men broke into small groups, armed with guns and warrants, and spread out over the county. They raided over one hundred places, and arrested more than seventy-five alleged Volstead violators, transporting them to Benton for arraignment. The first raid netted a large catch: Charles Birger—the leader of one of the region's largest bootlegging rings.[58]

Two weeks later, a second raid was led by Prohibition agent Armitage and Young, now federally deputized. The raiders targeted scores of private homes in Herrin's Italian community, a presumed source of bootleg liquor. Alex Ruggeri, an Italian-born baker, recalled the invasion of his family's home. A gang of Klansmen broke in, helped themselves to his cheese and wine, arrested him, and dragged him to jail. Besieged Italian Herrin residents turned to their consulate for help. Vice consul Giovanni Picco arrived from Springfield and took over one hundred affidavits from Herrin's Italian citizens, who described a veritable reign of terror: rough treatment, theft, and planted evidence. Picco protested the "terrororization of foreign residents of Herrin" to the State Department. National Guard troops were called in to quell the unrest. With no further raids taking place, the guardsmen declared conditions peaceable after a week and left Williamson County immigrant residents on their own to face down Klan terror.[59]

Still, the violence and chaos raiders unleashed, the National Guard troops, and foreign-government protests over the treatment of their citizens raised enough controversy to make the federal agents back off from their promise to clean up Herrin. Illinois federal Prohibition division chief William W. Anderson announced that "no further raids" would be undertaken "under present conditions." Federal authorization for the volunteer army in Williamson County was at an end. Any further raids under federal auspices would unfold, government officials averred, "without accepting reinforcements from the Ku Klux Klan or any other volunteer organization." But federal agents did continue to enlist such citizen support elsewhere, leading the Bureau to issue several directives to forbid it. The federal Prohibition Bureau found it necessary to remind all its employees repeatedly in 1927 and 1929: "There may be times of great emergency when it becomes necessary for a Federal Prohibition Agent to accept voluntary help," but "[n]o armed volunteer must ever accompany Federal Agents on a raid."[60]

However, in Williamson County, the army of dry enforcers once mobilized was not easily deterred by the abandonment of federal authorization. With warrants issued by a local justice of the peace for a third action, raids under Young's direction netted sixty-six prisoners on January 18, 1924. Sam Stearns, County Council chairman and Klan Cyclops, gleefully declared, "We've got the bootleggers on the run now, but we want to give them their hats, so they can keep on running." The Klansmen continued their raids—their biggest to come. Meeting on February 2 at Johnson City's Redmen Hall, in a town six miles north of Herrin, Young led over one thousand men in raids that

spanned from Johnston City across the smaller mining towns of Spill-
ertown and Carterville and into Herrin. Over 138 persons were
arrested, transported to Benton for arraignment, and marched through
town with streets lined with Klan supporters. Each raid grew more
reckless in its ambitions, with raiders crashing into private homes and
setting fire to some of them. Newspapers reported "fires of mysterious
origins" at the "homes of people alleged to be in the bootlegging business." Two "soft drink" parlors, Jake's and Tono Moloni's, were burnt
to the ground. This time, Italian citizens were not alone in demanding
redress. Johnson City's French citizens called on their consulate for aid.
The French government protested the reign of terror to Illinois officials, but the state attorney general claimed that "[i]t was a Prohibition
matter" and there was little he could do. The consul then complained
to Washington.[61]

With Klan opponents mobilizing, the raids contributed to all-out
warfare in Herrin's streets. Ora Thomas, a thirty-two-year-old miner
with flaming red hair who had been charged with bootlegging, and the
local sheriff were the most vocal Klan opponents. Thomas and E. E.
Bowan called on the local priest to join them in forging an anti-Klan
organization, the "Knights of the Flaming Circle." The priest demurred,
but he assented to the armed guard parishioners set up when rumors
spread that Klansmen planned to burn the church down. When stakeholders in the illicit trade bolstered anti-Klan forces with armed muscle, confrontations culminated in a riot and shootout at a local hospital.
With shattered glass littering hospital hallways, the chief administrator
decried an "insane mob" and called on Congress to investigate. Constituted authority broke down: Young threw the mayor and the sheriff
in jail and took over those roles himself. His Klan "deputies" patrolled
the streets with crudely cut badges.[62]

With Klan and anti-Klan forces battling, Governor Small placed
the county again under martial law and ordered five companies of the
Illinois National Guard to Herrin, where they reasserted public authority over the next weeks, released the mayor and sheriff from jail, and

proclaimed that only authorized officers could carry firearms. State officials held conferences with the local American Legion, the Rotary Club, and the Lion's Club, pleading for help in ending the orgy of violence. Governor Small called for a local "citizen's committee" to reestablish law and order. Young now also faced charges brought by the victims of the Klan raids for assault, battery, and theft.[63]

Battles between anti-Klan and Klan elements continued into the following year, but the large-scale raids ended. While the federal government and state authorities dropped support for the army of Williamson County's dry warriors, the violence between wet and dry forces took longer to subside. Williamson's Protestant ministers continued to laud Young as "a savior of mankind," but with the charges against him and the imposition of martial law, the local Klan ended payment for his services. Young moved to East St. Louis to organize for the Klan. He returned to Williamson later that year, locking horns with Knights of the Flaming Circle leader Ora Thomas. Young and Thomas were killed in a gun battle in January 1925. Thousands of Klansmen from many states poured into Herrin for Young's funeral, held at the large brick First Baptist Church.[64]

Young's death symbolically marked the eclipse of local Klan power. Even earlier, support had been declining. The Klan swept the springtime elections in 1924, but one year later the local Klan newspaper was bankrupt and the mayor, a former Klansman, came into office on an anti-Klan platform. Gun battles, over fourteen deaths, and martial law proved too high a cost to pay for the cleanup even for the violence-hardened citizens of Williamson County. The nightmare of massacres and gunfights between Klan and anti-Klan forces was over. The mayor discouraged local Klan parades and promised to heed Illinois's anti-Klan state law barring supporters from parading in masks.[65]

But before the collapse of its power, the local Klan succeeded, at least partially, in accomplishing its goal. The raids closed approximately fifty "soft drink parlors" for good. But more importantly, the reign of terror against Williamson's immigrants led many of them to heed the Klan's call to leave the county. The number of foreign-born and residents with foreign-born parents of Williamson County stood at 11,460 in 1920. Ten years later, it had been reduced to 8,174. Over three thousand immigrants and their children had been driven out. Williamson County's "better citizens" successfully mobilized the grievances of their less-well-heeled evangelical Protestant brethren, only recently expressed in class conflict, toward the shared agenda of white Protestant nationalism. This militant nationalism focused its resentment on the more vulnerable working-class men and women of a different ethnicity and religion.[66]

. . . .

THE conflict between wet and dry forces left deep scars in Herrin. By 1925, leading citizens sought to foster reconciliation within their community. Local newspaper editor Hal Trovillion and Herrin Presbyterian minister John Meeker, the one cleric who opposed the methods of the cleanup movement, drew upon the strong evangelical tendencies of the region to heal the town's wounds. Trovillion called in pastor Howard S. Williams to conduct revival meetings and encourage his fellow citizens to "drop . . . the gun for the Gospel." Shops shut their doors during the noonday meetings, bringing hundreds to the Herrin Annex Theater. Eventually, all the Protestant ministers in Herrin save one climbed onboard the revival bandwagon.[67]

The evangelist's crusade, a campaign backed by the county's militant Protestant ministers, now abandoned law enforcement as a solution for the liquor scourge. The charismatic preacher, fists flailing, challenged the logic of national Prohibition. "Reformation," he declared, "can never precede regeneration. There must be deeper motives to quit drinking booze than man's laws. If the United States government would spend ten percent of the money now engaged in chasing bootleggers to erect gospel tents and put evangelists in the field, they could settle this liquor problem within the next twelve months." The violence of the war on alcohol contributed to the erosion of support for "law enforcement" to combat the drink evil even in starkly Protestant subcultures.[68]

While Herrin may have been unusual in conflict ending in the arms of the church, similarly critical lessons about the reliance on law enforcement as a solution for the drink evil were mounting across the nation. National newspapers carried stories of events in "bloody Herrin" in vivid detail, charting the escalating violence, the murders, the racial and religious prejudice all in the service of the war on alcohol. The Association Against the Prohibition Amendment publicized the lawlessness of Prohibition officers, including Gus Simons, who had helped organize the Williamson raids. The collusion of federal officials, the reckless action of state Prohibition officers, and Klan violence contributed to growing cries against the lawlessness resulting from national Prohibition.

Williamson exemplified in magnified form the mobilization of the "citizen enforcement" shock troops Prohibition unleashed across the nation. As the New York Times declared, "What has happened there holds a moral for the rest of the country." For the growing legions of critics, the actions of the dry enforcers highlighted the grave threat the Eighteenth Amendment posed to personal liberty and constitutional safeguards. Clarence Darrow crystallized best the swelling critiques of that army. He condemned the "psychology of hate and bitterness . . . which makes any act of cruelty permissible. . . . Scarcely a week passes by that we do not witness some new evidence of the ferocity of these men and women who seem to be moved by a religious zeal to enforce Volsteadism." Attacking their "fanatical actions" and "obsession" with enforcement, he declared their actions amounted to "tyranny and despotism." This was no mere rhetoric. His words derived their power from the egregious scenes of violent vigilantism by the army of the religious right unleashed by Prohibition. Since poor immigrant ethnic and minority communities were most frequently the target of raids that gravely violated their constitutional rights, it was these men and women who mobilized vocally against Prohibition. They increasingly sought to make their voices heard in the political process to rid the nation of the "dry tyranny."[69]

6

NEW POLITICAL LOYALTIES

IN 1928, THE BATTLES OVER PROHIBITION IN FAR-FLUNG
places from Herrin, Illinois, to Richmond, Virginia, from Pittsburgh,
Pennsylvania, to Portland, Oregon, coalesced in the contest for the
presidency. In the late summer, with the election just a few months
away, Republican and Democratic party strategists sent out speakers to
mobilize support and drum up the votes needed to win the election.
The war on alcohol featured prominently in their efforts to bring voters
to the polls. On the Republican side, the dry champion was U.S. assistant attorney general Mabel Walker Willebrandt, whip-smart and such
an energetic enforcer that her critics dubbed her "Prohibition Portia."
In the attorney general's office, Willebrandt attacked alcohol supply
networks, despite the high-level government corruption that reached
all the way to her one-time boss, attorney general Harry Daugherty.
Willebrandt's prosecutorial vigor netted notorious bootleggers such as
Cincinnati's George Remus, but she complained frequently about the
uphill enforcement battle she faced with incompetent officials, public
indifference, and corruption. Though not without vocal critics, Will-

ebrandt's energy and resolve made her one of the best-known women of her day and immensely popular among antiliquor crusaders.[1]

The Republican Party National Committee Speaker's Bureau sent Willebrandt crisscrossing the nation to rally Prohibitionists for Hoover. On September 7, she stood before 2,500 Methodist ministers at their annual conference in Springfield, Ohio. That very day the clergymen had taken the unusual step of endorsing Hoover. With the "moral" issue of Prohibition at stake, they justified the direct entry of the church into partisan politics. After praising the Methodists for their contribution to winning passage of the Eighteenth Amendment, the assistant attorney general blasted the Democratic presidential candidate, Alfred E. Smith. As governor of New York, Smith had repealed the state's enforcement law. He had, she declared, effectively nullified the Constitution, pulling "down one of the 46 pillars the people had erected" to enforce the Eighteenth Amendment. She then trumpeted a call to battle: "There are 2,000 pastors here. You have in your churches more than 600,000 members of the Methodist church in Ohio alone. That is enough to swing the election. The 600,000 have friends in other states. . . . Every day and every ounce of your energy are needed to rouse the friends of Prohibition to register and vote."[2]

Willebrandt's direct appeal to the ranks of organized Protestantism was vetted and approved by top-ranking members of the Republican National Committee. They gambled that the voters it galvanized would be worth the inevitable backlash condemning Willebrandt's mixture of religion and politics. The controversy that swirled around the speech revealed not just the power of the war on alcohol as a mobilizing tool, but also how firmly rooted it was in religious, class, and cultural cleavages. That year, for the first time, those long-standing cleavages found expression along partisan lines. In the molten fires of the alcohol war, a wider set of conflicts crystallized, transforming political allegiances, and eventually the balance of the political party system.[3]

Despite the willingness of some party strategists to stoke the fires, the prominence of Prohibition as the burning question of the campaign dismayed influential leaders of both political parties. In earlier elections both had sidestepped the hot-button topic, aware of its divisive power in big-tent parties with wet and dry wings. In 1928, Franklin D. Roosevelt, who was running to replace Al Smith as governor of New York, backed Smith as the Democratic candidate but expressed his concern about the centrality of the liquor issue to a dry Democratic supporter: "Personally, I hope that this election is not going to turn fully on a Prohibition referendum." High-ranking Republican strategists also hoped to douse its inflammatory power. Early in the campaign, party chairman Hubert Work even declared, "Prohibition is not an issue . . . and will not be allowed to enter the campaign." Belying Work's determination, one Chicago ethnic newspaper proclaimed the central campaign question: "Prohibition or No Prohibition!"[4]

The controversy over the war on alcohol could not be suppressed. After almost a decade, the Eighteenth Amendment and the Volstead Act had touched every corner of the nation and aroused such passions for or against Prohibition that no one could keep it out of the campaign. Staunch antiliquor crusaders such as Massachusetts Anti-Saloon League leader Elizabeth Tilton stood steadfastly with the organized Protestant churches, particularly the evangelicals, in support of the law. To Tilton, the amendment was a pillar of the social and cultural dominance of the Anglo-Saxon elite and middle class, arbiters of virtue and public good against, in Tilton's words, "the foreign invasion" of "undeveloped races congested in Big Cities." Opposing Tilton's outlook was the ethnic working class, many of them recent immigrants. Crowded into neighborhoods like Polish Hill in Pittsburgh and the stockyards of Chicago, they denounced the Volstead Act as "the most vicious and tyrannical piece of legislation enacted anywhere in the world." In Al Smith, they found a champion. As governor of New York, Smith had expressed his disapproval of the war on alcohol and the intolerance of the wider world view it encapsulated. Working-class men and women had already voiced their opposition to the antiliquor crusade at the local level. In 1928, however, they were drawn into national politics, looking to Smith to change the law and defend their freedoms and communities.[5]

The war on alcohol was not the only or arguably even the most important grievance of a working class faced with job insecurity, seasonal layoffs, few workplace protections, and shallow welfare safety nets. In 1924, Robert La Follette had won support from heavily ethnic working-class wards in industrial cities and towns for the Progressive Party ticket championing a broad program of labor protection and opposition to Prohibition. The two major national parties, by contrast, did not offer sharp differences on policies that were directly relevant to working-class economic concerns. Under their consciously broad tents, they included well-heeled capital sectors with wide swaths of ordinary voters needed to win the popular vote. Working-class concerns received only muted attention lest business elites and agrarian interests defect to the rival party. Both parties spoke of advancing economic growth and prosperity in terms that could appeal to wide groups of voters; neither focused on the specific concerns of the largely immigrant industrial working class.[6]

Prohibition opposition became the cudgel that broke apart earlier loyalties and forged new ones. Unlike the 1924 campaign, in 1928 urban ethnic working-class opponents of the law were joined by a small group of wealthy capitalists who hoped to capture the Democratic Party to further their business and regulatory interests, above all their goal of stemming the growth of federal power. General Motors titan John J. Raskob, for example, saw the Eighteenth Amendment and the Volstead Act as the entering wedge for a federal leviathan. Spurred to action by Prohibition, they committed funds and credibility to the effort to rebuild the Democratic Party, which had not won a national presidential campaign since 1916, and to turn it into the new party of business. Little did this small group of corporate and financial moguls know that they were mobilizing a new core of urban working-class voters who drew the opposite lessons from Prohibition and would

strongly support energetic federal actions to protect them in the face of
the Great Depression.

. . .

BEFORE 1928, urban workers were not strongly identified with the
Democratic Party. Republicans, the majority party since the Civil War,
backed by large corporations and manufacturing interests, had appealed
widely to city voters and urban industrial workers as the party of industrial growth and economic nationalism. Between 1896 and 1932, the
United States was "normally" Republican. "Through the long, lean
decades Democrats could only be alert for dissension or corruption,"
one political scientist wrote, "and now and then enjoy an uneasy and
incomplete ascendancy for a presidential term or two." Indeed, even
northeastern industrial cities were considered safe Republican strongholds in presidential elections right up to 1928. The Democrats' axis of
power lay in the agricultural south and west. Since William Jennings
Bryan's campaign in 1896, the Democratic Party had a progressive
edge, favoring some regulation of business, but it still failed to appeal
strongly to urban ethnic workers.[7]

To be sure, some immigrant groups, especially the Irish, had forged
powerful Democratic organizations in cities like New York and Boston. Offsetting them, other immigrant groups, such as Germans, leaned
strongly to the Republican Party. Immigrant workers newly arrived
from southern and eastern Europe lacked firm partisan loyalties, their
allegiances brokered en masse through ethnic ward politicians and local
precinct captains of both parties. In cities with limited resources to
address widespread poverty, party precinct captains and ward leaders
provided much-needed neighborhood services and built strong clientelist loyalties that favored incumbent regimes.[8]

In the early 1900s, ethnic working-class voters' loyalty to one party
or another, especially for newer immigrants, depended on local circumstances. In Chicago, Germans as well as African-Americans provided the votes for the city's powerful Republican political organization

that elected William Hale Thompson mayor in 1915. Republicans kept a strong grip on Chicago and on Illinois politics for the next thirteen years. Chicago's Democratic Party had the loyalty of Irish and Czech voters, and Democrats controlled a host of city council seats and other offices. Polish voters were evenly split between the two parties. In New York and Boston, the Irish had built powerful Democratic organizations, while Italians favored Republicans. In Pittsburgh and Philadelphia, industrial workers—whether Slovakian, Czech, Russian, Italian, or Polish—overwhelmingly voted for the Republican Party. The Republican Party had such a stranglehold on politics in these cities that it mirrored the post-Reconstruction one-party rule of Democrats in the South.[9]

Republicans also dominated national politics. The coalition forged by Woodrow Wilson in 1912 temporarily broke the Republicans' hold as the majority party. Yet Wilson's success that year was due in large part to the split within the Republican Party between President Taft and Theodore Roosevelt, who headed the Progressive Party ticket. Wilson only narrowly won reelection in 1916 on a promise to keep the United States out of World War I. After World War I and Wilson's ill-fated campaign for the League of Nations, the Democratic Party was greatly weakened. By 1920, it no longer benefited from a split among Republicans and was even abandoned by those groups (such as the Germans) who had signed on to Wilson's coalition to keep the United States from entering the war. In 1920 Republican Warren Harding easily defeated his Democratic opponent, James Cox.[10]

For eight long years, the Democratic Party proved unable to distinguish itself from the Republican Party. Its earlier progressive impulses had been largely agrarian in orientation, expressed best by William Jennings Bryan's "prairie radicalism," but the Democratic platform of 1920 was barely more progressive than the Republican on the whole and in some important respects less so. While Democrats recognized the right of workers to "regulate hours and working-conditions" and to "just compensation," Republicans acknowledged labor's "right to collective bargaining." The Republican platform called for the government to facilitate arbitration in industrial disputes, favored labor laws to protect women, backed equal pay for equal work in government service, sought to bar convict labor products from interstate commerce, and called for congressional action to end lynching.[11]

Many reform leaders who favored a more equitable society just as easily found a home within Republican ranks as among Democrats. Jane Addams and Harold Ickes, among other reformers, were Republicans, even if they were not always comfortable there. Robert La Follette made his 1924 bid for president at the head of the Progressive Party, which had split from the Republicans, not from the Democrats. Influential members of Congress, such as Nebraska's Frank Norris, champion of public control over utilities, and Wisconsin's Robert La Follette Jr., champion of organized labor, were Republicans. It was far from preordained that the Democratic Party would become the home of urban ethnic working-class voters, and of a liberal–labor coalition.[12]

The election of 1928 marked a breakthrough moment. Urban ethnic workers shifted loyalties decisively to the Democratic Party, reshaping the political landscape for Franklin Roosevelt's 1932 victory four years later, when cities and the nation swung massively into the Democratic column. Though the 1932 landslide election is often identified as the moment of realignment, the movement of urban working-class voters to the Democrats happened earlier. The war on alcohol cemented a broader sense of shared identity among immigrant ethnic workers, sweeping away earlier inward-looking identities that had for decades fragmented urban, ethnic partisan loyalties, and forging the basis for new loyalties.[13]

Leading the charge against Prohibition in these urban, ethnic communities were elite opinion shapers who bristled with contempt for the law. These "better sorts"—ranging from local business leaders to the priests who presided over baptisms, communions, and marriages—brought significant resources to the campaign. Catholics, freethinking Czechs, and liberal Protestant German Lutherans all identified Prohibition as the quintessential symbol of elitist Protestant hostility toward immigrant communities. "It isn't foremost about thirst," explained one ethnic Chicago newspaper. "Prohibition's opponents do not have beer mugs emblazoned on their banners." It was a rejection of "morality through police handcuffs." Ending the war on alcohol promised to dethrone the Billy Sundays and "the dictatorship they seek to establish." Ethnic-language newspapers—Polish, Czech German, Italian among them—mobilized their communities and channeled their hostility to the law into the political process at the very time that the national Democratic Party was beginning to court these communities as a potential new base.[14]

.   .   .

CHICAGO'S storied melting pot provides a fruitful example of how ordinary men and women built new partisan loyalties. As we saw earlier, the city's ethnic communities had mobilized large parades to oppose the prohibitionist tide even before World War I. After the war, Anton Cermak, Chicago's Democratic boss, worked tirelessly to channel opposition to Prohibition more effectively into the political process. Cermak led a successful fight for a resolution by Cook County Democrats in 1920 calling for an amendment to allow the legal manufacture of light wines and beers. At the state level, Cermak unsuccessfully pressed the Democratic Party to back Volstead Act modification. Despite such setbacks, Cermak parlayed his position as leader of the city's wets to win the position of Cook County Commissioner in 1922. At the same time, he led a successful citywide ballot effort to amend the Volstead Act, which inspired new levels of electoral participation among Chicago's immigrant masses.[15]

Conveniently the alcohol war allowed Cermak and other urban bosses to turn persistent charges of corruption against their opponents. Cermak slammed the Eighteenth Amendment and the Volstead Act for creating widespread collusion among police, grafters and gangsters. He took no direct action to undercut those relationships in his county, which included Cicero, the base of Al Capone's operations in the late 1920s. Instead, he sought to undermine the power of organized crime by relegalizing drink. Thriving black markets, argued Cermak, were the inevitable result of antiliquor legislation. A portrait all too familiar to Chicagoans: stills in operation, speakeasies everywhere, and gang wars commonplace in the struggle for control, he blamed on the "folly" of Volsteadism. "Murder, death, destruction . . . and the need for more jails and penitentiaries" were the outcome. Chicago's Czech community and its liberals alike applauded Cermak's stand. He was a "champion of human rights" declared the news source for many of the city's Czechs. Chicago's best-known lawyer, Clarence Darrow, declared his support for Cermak in 1924: "I like Tony Cermak 'cause he's wet and 'cause he doesn't make excuses."[16]

In 1922 and 1926 Cermak used referendums to mobilize the widespread hostility to the war on alcohol at the local level. In both ballot initiatives, an overwhelming majority of voters voiced discontent with the Volstead Act. At first glance, the results seemed to lend support to the view that the antiliquor crusade ran along an urban-rural axis. A closer look at ward-level data, however, revealed that "the Protestants, the native whites of native parentage, the employed, the persons paying the highest rents, the home owner, the persons with superior educational attainments" tended to be the most supportive of the war on alcohol. Inversely, "the Catholics, the foreign born, the unemployed, the persons who pay the lowest rents, and the non-home owners" were the strongest opponents. Social class, closely linked to religious and ethnic identities, not urban and rural residence alone, was the strong predictor of the strength of Prohibition opposition or support.[17]

Many ethnic voters drawn to the voting booth in 1922 and 1926 returned to the polls in 1927 to dump Mayor Dever, elected four years earlier on promises to rein in corruption and enforce Prohibition. Dever's "worst offense," a *New Republic* article lamented, "was, apparently, the unnecessary zeal which he displayed in enforcing the dry law." His cleanup campaign never surmounted the judicial, official, and police collusion with organized gangs, and only fostered even more hostility toward the law among poor communities. Instead of looking inward, Dever's police cracked down most heavily on the marginal but numerous numbers of small-time liquor-law violators. Where Dever's campaign did manage to restrict the freedom of organized criminals, the result was even more violence in poor neighborhoods, as rival gangs competed for smaller markets. Taking advantage of dissatisfaction with Dever's policies, "Big Bill" Thompson, who had left the mayor's office amid graft and corruption scandals, returned to power in 1927, declaring himself "wetter than the Atlantic Ocean."[18]

A *New Republic* journalist chalked up Thompson's victory to "a class-conscious sub-community" in American cities that was just beginning to "find itself out." These voters compensated for their "privations and for their own hard, mechanical, monotonous work" by participating in "organized sport, relaxation, entertainment, [and] jollification." They "drink a lot" and "dance a lot." Hostility toward "the respectability, the alien conventions, the moral self-importance and the exclusiveness of the older Chicago," the journalist presciently reported, contributed to a "felt sense of group identity as a wider class and as Americans." As a result, "even once rival ethnic groups" were now collectively "reaching out for their social and economic places in the sun of American society." Forecasting precisely the developments of 1928, the journalist shrewdly predicted that the same people "who vote enthusiastically for a Thompson or a Hylan at one election may vote with even more rejoicing for Al Smith at the next."[19]

Chicago's ethnic voters had already been introduced to New York's governor in 1922 when Smith spoke at a massive Chicago rally organized by Anton Cermak in favor of the legalization of light wine and beer. Smith received an enthusiastic reception from the throngs of Chicagoans who had filled the streets when he took to the stage to support their effort. Like Cermak, Smith was opposed to the Eighteenth Amendment and the Volstead Act. He believed the law unworkable, hypocritical, and a tyrannical effort by a minority to control the habits of others. During his 1928 presidential run, Smith moderated his earlier outspoken hostility to Prohibition with more moderate demands, mindful of southern and western Democratic drys, but his reputation as a brazen opponent of the law was made.[20]

Cermak and Smith both represented a new breed of politicians whose careers were built on the growing importance of immigrant ethnic voters in the nation's industrial cities. Ambitious and savvy, both entered first ward politics and then city politics in the early twentieth century using politics as stepping-stones for upward mobility. Each climbed the ranks of urban politics, their careers built with the votes of the diverse, largely working-class immigrant populations of New York and Chicago. A year after Thompson's election, Smith's campaign drew these voters into national politics.[21]

Smith's career as a politician was buoyed by his affable personality and love of the stage and, not least, by his Irish Catholic roots in a world of Irish-dominated city politics; Cermak's Czech roots limited his ascent, thanks to Chicago's Irish-dominated Democratic political scene. In 1918 Smith won the governorship of New York. Although his inner circle had always included influential businessmen, he earned a reputation as a farsighted progressive. He backed legislation favorable to his working-class constituents, championed administrative reform, and included two well-known progressives, Belle Moskowitz and Frances Perkins, as close advisors. He won liberal support by backing public efforts to relieve the post–World War I housing shortage, calling for the public regulation of city utilities, and vetoing repressive state laws passed in the grip of the Red Scare. It was Smith's Prohibition opposition, however, that earned him national recognition. In 1923, he signed New York State's Mullan-Gage Act, rescinding the state's Prohibition enforcement code despite the warnings of advisors not to. This bold move earned him the undying hostility of the nation's antiliquor crusaders and catapulted him to the position of the nation's leading Prohibition opponent.[22]

By 1928, Smith was a seasoned politician battle-tested during his hard-fought 1924 primary campaign against William Gibbs McAdoo, the leader of the party's dry agrarian wing and darling of the Ku Klux Klan. At the 1924 Democratic National Convention held in New York, the epithet "rum and romanism" stuck to Smith and cost him the support of many southern and western Democrats. Delegates from Chicago and New York, on the other side, passionately backed Smith. They castigated Klan intolerance and fought a symbolic but fruitless battle to have the party condemn the hooded order. None other than William Jennings Bryan rose to squelch the proposed resolution, hoping to stave off party rupture.

Despite such moderating efforts, the 1924 Democratic National Convention turned into a bitter battleground, perhaps the most contentious in the party's history until the riotous Chicago convention of 1968. The journalist Arthur Krock summed it up as a "snarling, cursing, tedious, tenuous, suicidal, homicidal roughhouse." New York was home turf to vast numbers of immigrants, who packed the convention galleries to make their hostility to the Klan and to Prohibition known, and the proceedings proved raucous. Bryan sought to move the convention to another city: Washington, D.C., St. Louis—anywhere but New York. McAdoo and his supporters reacted to the crowd by, if anything, amplifying their antiurban rhetoric. The great metropolis was "reactionary, sinister, unscrupulous, wanting in national ideals . . . rooted in corruption, directed by greed and dominated by selfishness." Though McAdoo was no country rube but long a high-powered New York lawyer originally from the south, he grasped this antiurban rhetoric as a convenient handle for the deeper conflict between the world view and dominance of an older Protestant Anglo-Saxon elite and middle class against a rising immigrant working class and their pluralist allies.[23]

Anti-Catholicism would have inevitably played a motivating role in the opposition to Smith but it took on a shrill, panicked tenor due to Smith's Prohibition stand. The Methodist Board of Temperance, Prohibition and Public Morals declared that it would prefer Thomas Walsh, a Catholic from Montana who backed the Eighteenth Amendment, over Smith. With Walsh unable to generate any support in large industrial cities, antiliquor crusaders dropped any pretense of pluralism, demonizing Smith's Catholicism, Tammany political machine ties, and wet stand as a triple-headed monster.[24]

South Carolina senator Nathaniel B. Dial summed up the stakes: "The Democratic Party must declare whether it will serve high, straight outspoken American Democracy or some kind of shambling, bastard, shame-faced mixture of so-called Democracy and alien-conceived bolshevism or socialism or hell broth of all." After inconclusive balloting that stretched over long days, Smith proposed that both men should withdraw. Finally, on the 103rd ballot, the delegates nominated John W. Davis, of West Virginia. A distinguished lawyer, Davis declared himself in favor of Prohibition enforcement, but McAdoo denounced his lukewarm support and attacked him for favoring "personal liberty." In a small consolation, then, the Davis nomination was a quasi-Smith victory and the 1924 convention a prelude to Smith's nomination in Houston four year later.[25]

While the Democrats suffered a crushing defeat at the hands of incumbent president Calvin Coolidge, the bruising convention fight revealed the new strength of the party's urban ethnic wing and its heavily ethnic working-class base. Four years later, the party built on that strength to nominate Al Smith. Smith won the nomination handily, choosing Arkansas senator Joseph T. Robinson, a dry, as his running mate to mollify the party's southern and western wings. Prohibition opponents lost their bid for a plank calling for reform of the Volstead Act. The party instead asked simply for "honest enforcement" of the Eighteenth Amendment.

Once free of convention politics, Smith undercut the party's moderate position on Prohibition. He sent out a telegram to all delegates announcing his support for "fundamental changes" in the Volstead Act and declared his intention to lead the fight. It was "the "duty of the chosen leader of the people to point the way . . . to a sane, sensible solution of a condition which, I am convinced, is entirely unsatisfactory to the great mass of our people." Smith's stand was heartfelt. Four years earlier, he had written to Roosevelt declaring the Volstead Act "a complete failure. . . . It made us a nation of hypocrites, a by-word and a mockery to all the other nations of the world." He pledged that, if elected, "so far as my persuasive powers were effective that the matter should not escape Congress's immediate attention." But new to national politics in 1924, he was more cautious publicly, concerned that the climate was not yet ripe and fearful of the retribution of the party's antiliquor crusaders. In 1928, with the widening controversy over the Volstead Act and the bitter opposition to it among urban ethnic communities, Smith was bolder, making it the vital issue of the campaign. Smith's close friend John Raskob, the automobile executive, was just as passionately opposed to the Eighteenth Amendment and bolstered Smith's confidence and his campaign coffers to elevate the controversy to new prominence.[26]

Like Smith, Raskob was a bootstrapper and Catholic. He had risen into the nation's economic elite as a protégé of corporate mogul Pierre du Pont. Smith and Raskob met through friends and forged a lasting friendship. Both men believed the law unworkable, impractical, and a thinly veiled attack on Catholic immigrant culture. But Raskob's opposition was also fueled by his conviction that the Eighteenth Amendment threatened private property and economic liberty. These concerns were shared by a small but influential group of wealthy men and women that included Pierre and Irénée du Pont and lawyer and businessman William Stayton. In 1918 they had founded the Association Against the Prohibition Amendment to sound the alarm that the Eighteenth Amendment's dramatic expansion of government authority set a dangerous precedent that could lead to further erosions of economic liberty. Raskob joined the AAPA in 1922, and by 1928 he served on its board.[27]

Although Raskob was by habit and class a Republican, his business pursuits left little time for party politics. In 1928, because of his desire to pursue a new adventure and his alarm over Prohibition, he turned his business and financial skills to Democratic politics, backing Smith's primary campaign. In return, Smith granted his friend and backer the position he coveted, chairman of the Democratic National Committee, over the cries of advisors who felt Raskob's wetness, Catholicism, and above all inexperience made him unsuitable.[28]

Despite his inexperience, Raskob quickly established a commanding role within the Democratic Party, spearheading attacks on the anti-liquor law as a necessary first step to halting the growth of federal power. With Raskob at the helm, Smith's progressive tendencies faded from public view. Smith did revive his call for public control of utilities, a position that sharply contrasted with Hoover's, but for the most part the Democratic National Committee downplayed the party's reform ethos. Raskob reassured businessmen that they had nothing to fear from a Democratic victory. He declared Smith "a strong advocate of less government in business and of more business in government. . . . He believes in no disturbance of honest businessmen and his career demonstrates his fairness to labor." Socialist Party presidential candidate Norman Thomas declared, "The Democratic Party under the leadership of Governor Smith . . . has served notice that it is out to serve big business first and last." Smith and the DNC, he charged, sought to "catch the workers by dangling before them an elusive beer bottle while they deliver themselves over body and soul to the Raskobs of Wall Street."[29]

While financial titans such as Raskob hoped to make Democrats the party of business and small government, ordinary urban voters were drawn to the party for different reasons. Smith's New York constituents already knew his progressive record, and in industrial cities such as Chicago, Smith tailored his speeches to the "positive functions" of government and a forward-looking ethos: "We won't be of the past." "As far as I am concerned," he declared, "government should be constructive and not destructive; progressive and not reactionary. I am entirely unwilling to accept the old order of things as best unless and until I become convinced that it cannot be made better." Government, he averred, "should do things." Precisely what government should do he did not detail, except for amending the Volstead Act—an appeal that powerfully resonated both with his financial backers and urban working-class voters.[30]

Where Raskob and the AAPA feared the "tyranny of federal power," particularly its regulatory power over business and the economy, urban ethnic voters feared the cultural tyranny of the Anti-Saloon League and its hold on policy makers. In the face of the negative impact of the alcohol war in their communities, they sought to grasp the reins of federal power and orient it in new ways. When the Wickersham Commission asked John P. Frey, secretary treasurer of the AFL's Metal Trades Department, for labor's view of Prohibition, Frey responded: "[O]ne of the statements that I hear most frequently is that the Eighteenth Amendment and the Volstead Act were passed to permit the rich man to have anything he wanted, and directed wholly at the poor." Elite opponents picked up on this criticism. In a light vein, Raskob chided automobile magnates Alfred Sloan and Walter Chrysler for their hypocrisy in publically backing the Volstead Act while privately indulging in alcohol-laced leisure. Thanking Chrysler for vouching for him at a private club that served cocktails, he jested, "I am having a lot of fun taking a crack at you every now and then about denying the workingman his glass of beer, with your lockers filled with vintage champagnes, rare old wines, and selected brands of old whiskey." Such jesting belied the more serious impact of the war on alcohol on poor communities, but revealed the odd coalition Prohibition opposition brought together.[31]

Together, these bedfellows remade the Democratic Party. Raskob infused vast sums of capital into the party and helped it build a solid organizational footing. Frances Perkins, a vocal critic of Raskob, later conceded "This was the only time that I've ever known the Democratic Party when it seemed to have plenty of money." Raskob was personally responsible for raising $6 million, equal to about $80 million today. One recent biographer declared him "one of the greatest campaign fundraisers the Democratic Party had ever seen." With Raskob at the helm of the Democratic National Committee, the party focused on the antiliquor crusade in regions where hostility toward the war on alcohol ran strong, particularly in large urban centers. In the south and west, on the other hand, the Smith campaign focused on prosperity and farm relief. Efforts to hold the loyalty of traditional Democrats in these regions by downplaying Prohibition, however, ran up against Republican opponents who trumpeted Smith's Catholicism, his links to Tammany, and his hostility to the antiliquor crusade.[32]

The anti-Catholicism, Prohibition, and anti-immigrant sentiment that cost Smith the nomination in 1924 reared its head again during the general election in 1928. When Roosevelt wrote to Democratic workers asking for a report on regional conditions—and forging ties that would soon serve himself—southern Democrats reported anti-Catholicism as a significant impediment. One Savannah Democrat averred, "A good many of the country people really believe that a vote for Smith is a vote for the Pope." H. M. Anderson of West Virginia likewise declared, "Religious prejudice . . . will lose for us quite a number of Democratic votes, especially in the rural section and among the Methodist and Baptist denominations." The Methodists and Baptists were also the most ardent supporters of the antiliquor crusade. Some insisted that their objections to Smith lay with his anti-Prohibition stand, not his religion, but in the eyes of most of his opponents, "Rum and Romanism" were inextricably linked.[33]

The Protestant churches, especially the Methodists and Baptists, led the anti-Smith charge. Bishop James Cannon Jr. of the Methodist Episcopal Council, South, and Dr. Arthur J. Barton, chairman of the Committee on Social Service of the Southern Baptist Convention, powerful antiliquor crusaders, met in Asheville, North Carolina, to organize opposition. They launched devastating attacks throughout the south. The Moral Welfare Department of the Presbyterian Church in the U.S.A. joined the fray, passing a resolution that fall denouncing any candidate opposed to national Prohibition. Protestant ministers opposed Smith through the press and from the pulpit. Emma Guffey-Miller, a high-ranking Pennsylvania Democrat, blamed "the Protestant churches working not as religious bodies but as political organizations" for "carrying the country against the Democrats."[34]

The party faced major defections in usually solid Democratic territory. "Democrats for Hoover" clubs mushroomed in Democratic strongholds across the nation. Oklahoma Democratic committeeman Scott Ferris reported to Roosevelt the dire situation in the West: "25 years of Prohibition teaching by Dr. [William Jennings] Bryan, Prohibition in our Constitution, and . . . religion and Tammany" were, he warned, "whipping up a real Texas cyclone. . . . Every Protestant preacher in this state is not only a campaign manager for Hoover, but is a speaker therefor. Every member of the Ku Klux Klan, W.C.T.U, Ultra-prohibitionists, [and the] Anti-Saloon League are vigilantly going about, spreading vicious propaganda against us." But Ferris had a solution: "We must find out who is for us and who is against us and utilize the ones that are for us to bring those who are against us into the fold. If that can't be done, we must bring forward other first voters and the passive voters who have not heretofore voted at all to take their place. This can be done with intensive organization."[35]

Roosevelt was so impressed with Ferris's letter that he highlighted passages of the two-page analysis, penciled notes in the margins, and drew up a memo that included Ferris's diagnosis and proposed remedy for distribution to key Democratic leaders, including Raskob, Rhode Island senator Peter G. Gerry, and Eleanor Roosevelt. As the campaign unfolded, party officials adopted Ferris's proposal of "intensive organizing" to draw in new voters at the national, state, and local levels. Whether this strategy was a direct result of Ferris's analysis we cannot know, but Roosevelt's memo suggests that top party strategists were keenly taking notice of the importance of previously untapped reservoirs of "passive voters" to Democratic Party strength.[36]

In search of these passive voters, party officials targeted industrial cities like Chicago, where they organized intensively to bring new voters to the polls and win over others who had marked their ballots for Republican candidates in the past. In Chicago, congressman Adolph Sabath set up the "Al Smith for President Foreign Language Bureau" with the backing of the DNC. Independent Polish, Czech, Italian, and German groups mobilized for Smith. Party leaders made their pitch at the ward and precinct level and set up a hundred "mass meetings," urging voters to register in time for the election. In September, Democratic state and county leaders announced plans to bring in more party headliners to stump for Smith than Illinois had ever before seen.[37]

Chicago's multiple major ethnic newspapers lent support by providing Smith a great deal of favorable coverage. They announced Democratic meetings in advance and urged voters to register to vote. At stake, announced one popular Czech daily, was "Governor Al Smith or Prohibition." It covered Smith rallies from Boston to Baltimore and trumpeted the candidate's national appeal. The major Polish newspaper backed Smith as well, declaring the election one of the "most important . . . in the history of the country." The high stakes included "the victory of religious tolerance, the victory of personal freedom, and all the great principles which the Constitution of the United States guarantees."[38]

Chicago's largest German-language newspaper, the *Abendpost*, with a circulation of around fifty thousand endorsed Smith as well. The newspaper earlier leaned toward the progressive wing of the Republican Party. Now it identified Prohibition as the "most important" matter. "If a Republican wins," the editors predicted, "it will take years before there is another opportunity to . . . topple the dry tyranny of the ASL and its allies." The election of Al Smith would mean its "collapse." The daily newspaper published a long biographical portrait of the man from the "sidewalks of New York," announced campaign rallies, and called for volunteers from either party to join a "Germans for Al Smith Club." The goal quite simply was to "get rid of national Prohibition."[39]

The *Abendpost* pressed eligible nonvoters to register by Chicago's deadline: "Citizens who have passionately and energetically protested Prohibition, now is the time to voice that protest through the voting process. Those who fail to take up the opportunity . . . have no right to protest the Dry Tyranny in the future. . . . This goes for men and for women. And when it means missing a half-day of work, and even if one is sick and weak, you must register. . . . Who doesn't utilize their voting right, lets themselves be labeled a second class citizen." Such energetic efforts among the city's foreign-language and heavily working-class groups boosted Democratic strength.[40]

Another usually Republican Italian newspaper put the contest in the clearest terms: "Prohibition or No Prohibition!!" Reminding its largely working-class readership that a president alone could not change the Eighteenth Amendment, the editors urged voters to cast their ballots also for lesser candidates who favored repeal, including Anton Cermak. The paper's editor declared: "I like Hoover very much, but I will vote for Smith." "[I]ndependent Americans . . . would vote for Smith to show there was no religious bigotry in America." This editor, like editors of other Chicago foreign-language newspapers, championed opposition to Prohibition at the forefront of their Smith endorsements, linking it to pleas for religious tolerance.[41]

Smith had already won an enthusiastic reception in the windy city in August when he proposed to lead a nationwide fight to amend the Volstead Act. Such strong support among ethnic leaders, and vigorous party mobilization, translated into visible enthusiasm from ethnic voters throughout the fall campaign. During one October campaign rally, men and women in attendance toppled chairs and gave the pro-Smith speaker a standing ovation when he called for Volstead Act reform and denounced "intolerance and bigotry." They turned out en masse when Smith arrived on October 17; close to forty thousand gathered at Union Station. The next day, a crowd estimated at around one hundred thousand turned out to hear the "happy warrior" at the Coliseum, despite a downpour. Democratic workers set up radios in all wards so that those

without one in their home could hear the broadcast in their neighborhood. Religious tolerance and Prohibition opposition were the two
symbiotic themes that garnered the most enthusiasm among Smith supporters. When Smith declared in favor of amending the Volstead Act
during one speech, the crowd burst into wild cheering. He repeated
these successes from Boston to New York, Cincinnati, and Milwaukee.
Standing before audiences in the nation's great industrial centers sporting his brown derby, he spoke on modification of the Prohibition law,
"their favorite subject" according to one antiliquor crusader, and he
"aroused crowds to a fevered pitch."[42]

No city was more thoroughly Republican than Pittsburgh, the
nation's tenth largest city. Located at the intersection of the Ohio,
Monongahela, and Allegheny rivers, Pittsburgh was an industrial
behemoth attracting immigrants from the Balkans, Croatia, Slovakia,
and Poland. They packed into neighborhoods such as Polish Hill,
South Oakland, and the North Side, or lived in company housing
built outside Pittsburgh proper by steel manufacturer Jones & Laughlin, along the Ohio River. Each national group had its own churches,
saloons, and halls, and antagonisms among the diverse immigrant
groups flourished. Opposition to Prohibition helped overcome some
of the barriers separating the various ethnic groups, providing a common shared grievance as immigrants and heavily Catholic working-
class Americans. They began to view themselves in the context of
larger national politics, and by the 1930s forged a pervasive "ethnic
class consciousness."[43]

Pittsburgh politics was dominated by a powerful Republican orga-
nization. The tiny local Democratic Party was a hollow shell. No
Democratic presidential candidate had won Pittsburgh since 1856, and
Democrats had failed to elect a single city councilor or any other
municipal candidate since then. In Pittsburgh as in Philadelphia,
Republican ward politicians provided constituents services in exchange
for votes. These "exchanges" sometimes included direct vote buying.
The going rate in early twentieth-century Philadelphia was one dollar

per vote. To get their constituents to the polls, Republican Party leaders also sometimes paid the fifty-cent poll tax required of each voter. In
the community of Aliquippa, just outside of Pittsburgh proper, steel
manufacturer Jones & Laughlin used its power over its employees to
ensure the Republican hold on power. Voting Republican was, effectively, a condition for employment. Workers remembered being driven
in trucks from their jobs to polling places and told how to vote. One
worker later confessed, "You were Republican because they wanted
you to be—I vote, I wasn't even a citizen I vote. . . . Cause J&L wanted
you to . . . they tell you to go out there and vote." The solidly Republican hold on Pittsburgh and its environs, however, faced new challenges in the late 1920s and early 1930s.[44]

The 1928 presidential election gave Democrats an opportunity to
break ground and plant seeds for a more viable political presence in the
region. For the first time, Pittsburgh's ethnic industrial workers looked
to the Democratic Party to voice their interests. Democrats used the
springboard of the war on alcohol—and the ethnic, religious, and class
resentments it congealed—to build new party loyalties. By less than a
decade later, Pittsburgh had become a solidly Democratic stronghold.
The fledgling local Democratic Party even managed to recruit a few
bold men to challenge the Republican stranglehold in the autocratic
Jones & Laughlin plants in Aliquippa. New Democratic recruits sowed
the seeds for the vibrant Democratic organization that blossomed in the
1930s. Mike Zahorsky, who had worked for Jones & Laughlin since age
thirteen, joined the Democratic Party during the Smith campaign in
1928. He backed Smith because Smith was a fellow Catholic. Peter
Muselin, who later joined the Communist Party, was one among the
handful of workers who joined the Democrats in the 1920s. As he rec-
ollected years later, he signed on with the Democrats because he
believed in "political equality." Ormond Montini, who settled in
Aliquippa in 1918 to work for Jones & Laughlin, later acknowledged
the importance of the Smith campaign: "That's when . . . all of them
guys started. . . . That's when the Democratic party first started up on

that hill there. That's when they started signing up . . . when they started pushing the Democratic Party."[45]

In the company town of Aliquippa, the row proved hard to hoe. Working for Smith—or any opponent of the Republican Party—entailed risks. Montini recalled a worker who was fired after he hung a Smith campaign poster in his home. A Republican campaign worker saw the poster and apparently reported it to the company. The autocratic methods the company used to ensure political control meant that very few men and women dared to declare or shift their political loyalties. Only in 1936 did the stakes become high enough, and the countervailing forces powerful enough, for the town to tip toward the Democrats. By then, with FDR seeking a second term and New Deal politics in place even in Aliquippa, working-class men and women swung firmly into the Democratic column.[46]

Pittsburgh proper provided more maneuvering room for Democrats. Republicans controlled city politics to be sure, but their dominance was not maintained with the heavy-handed methods used in Aliquippa. Despite the heavily Republican bias of Pittsburgh's four main newspapers that covered Hoover rallies and Republican events in depth and reported on the Democratic campaign sporadically, Smith support swelled. As the election season unfolded, the city's main dailies could no longer ignore the ever-larger Democratic rallies, such as one "standing room only crowd" at the Carnegie Music Hall. On November 2, 1928, city news coverage revealed a deepening anxiety among local Republican ranks. A straw vote had shown the party in a precarious position, its usual easy dominance at risk. The "remarkable numbers of new eligible voters," the *Post-Gazette* remarked, posed a threat to usual Republican dominance.[47]

Working-class enthusiasm for Smith animated the Democratic Party in and around Pittsburgh. Seventeen Smith for President clubs formed in Allegheny County. Working-class Croatian, Italian, and Greek communities forged independent Smith outfits. Local Democratic leader David Lawrence boasted of "the most active Democratic

organization the party has had here in years." For the first time in
memory, the Party had enough eager volunteers "to enable the party to
have watchers in every one of the 1,400 districts in the county." Pennsylvania Democratic committeeman Joseph Guffey confidently, and
presciently, proclaimed that "Smith's anti-Prohibition position . . .
would swell the ranks of Republicans shifting their allegiance to the
Democratic nominee in those big cities by thousands." Raskob, too,
affirmed a "tidal wave of sentiment for the Governor in Philadelphia
and Pittsburgh." Smith's Prohibition position, reported the *New York
Times*, "has blurred the political dividing lines and brought thousands
of Republican recruits to the Smith banners."[48]

The coalition Smith built was not only multiethnic but multiracial.
"Never before in history," reported the *Pittsburgh Courier*, the largest
and most influential African-American newspaper in the nation, "have
negroes shown so friendly an interest in a Democratic Presidential candidate." Savvy Democrats worked to leverage such support to dent the
Republicans' hold on the African-American vote. Democrats formed a
"Smith for President Colored League" with an initial budget of
$125,000, more than $1.5 million dollars in current dollars. Over sixty-
nine prominent blacks joined, and state-wide leagues were organized
in Illinois, Texas, Missouri, California, Kansas, New Jersey, and Ohio.
The best-organized state was Missouri: African-Americans set up
twenty-nine local Smith for President clubs. J. Finley Wilson, Grand
Ruler of the black Elks, Bishops Reverdy Ransom and John Hurst of
the African Methodist Episcopal Church, and Neval H. Thomas,
NAACP branch leader in Washington, D.C., all backed Smith. So too
did the New Jersey Colored Republican State Committee. Robert L.
Vann, the *Pittsburgh Courier*'s editor, ensured a steady stream of favorable news articles and editorials for Smith.[49]

This reversal of racial politics in 1928, however partial, was a
remarkable development. The Democratic Party was seemingly irrevo-
cably tied to the politics of white supremacy in the south. Remaining
silent on the subject of lynch terror, it moreover separated the handful

of African-American delegates from white delegates with chicken wire during the 1928 Houston convention. That Smith could still manage to appeal to substantial numbers of African-American voters in northern communities demonstrated the depth of their anger over the Republican Party's "lily-white" strategy in the south and Klan influence within the party. As a candidate, Smith continued to ignore significant African-American grievances—from peonage to lynching—but he did denounce the Ku Klux Klan and championed a broad ethos of tolerance. Inspired by his more inclusive world view, some influential African-American leaders now argued that the debt African-Americans owed to the "party of Lincoln" had been paid in full.[50]

Pro-Smith sentiment percolated in northern urban African-American communities such as in Chicago's African-American South Side. The Smith for President Colored League set up headquarters at the Trentor Hotel and a Negro-Republican Al Smith Club was organized. The indefatigable Cermak campaigned on the South Side to win African-American votes for the Democratic Party, including for his own campaign for Senate. At one rally, a Universal Negro Improvement Association spokesman joined Cermak on the platform. These South Side rallies decried the Republican Party's ties to the Klan downstate, as well as its "lily white" strategy to gain the south from the Democrats. Cermak proclaimed his support for amending the Volstead Act, but cleverly made clear his opposition to the selective enforcement of some amendments (the Eighteenth) and not others. "[A]ll amendments, including the Fourteenth and the Fifteenth," he proclaimed, should be enforced. The *Chicago Tribune* reported that mention of Al Smith at one South Side rally brought enthusiasm "border[ing] on slight[ly] hysterical," accompanied by round after round of applause. The *Chicago Defender*, the city's African-American newspaper, lent support as well, reporting on the number of influential African-Americans who "vigorously supported Smith." "Al Smith Flays Ku Klux Klan in Talk" trumpeted one headline. Another article declared that Smith learned at his mother's knee that "the greatest thing about this country was that noble expression from the Declaration of Independence that all men were created equal."[51]

Al Smith signaled new winds of tolerance and a far more urban identity for the party identified historically with white supremacy and rural interests. He lambasted the Klan and the antiliquor crusade and in doing so converted the party's first substantial cohort of urban African-American voters who shared Smith's hostility to the Eighteenth Amendment. In Chicago, African-Americans were the social group "most desirous of repeal." Smith support ran strongest among poorer African-Americans, many of whom had moved north during and after World War I and had experienced the brunt of Volstead Act law enforcement. They also had long experience with arbitrary policing and the selective use of legal statutes to target, arrest, and imprison African-Americans for petty violations. Drinkers in African-American poor communities disproportionately suffered from poisoned liquor as well, unable to afford better-quality illegal liquor. The roughshod treatment of less powerful sections of the city by the illegal drink trade was just one more way the law adversely affected them. Affluent imbibers in search of thrills and entertainment "slummed" in the vice districts located in black neighborhoods, protected from the more draconian aspects of enforcement.

In Chicago's African-American South Side, as a result, Prohibition opponents were welcome speakers. When one Democratic speaker told a South Side audience that he backed repeal because "Prohibition is the most monumental fraud ever perpetrated on any people in any time in the world . . . [e]very time they try to enforce it they violate the rights guaranteed us in the Constitution," he won enthusiastic applause. Such sentiment alarmed National Women's Republican Study Club leader Jeanette Carter, who attributed Smith support to poor African-Americans switching political allegiance because "they want a drink." Carter's dismissal belies the complicated reasons some African-Americans looked to Smith in 1928, but it rightly links such support to working-class opposition to Prohibition.[52]

Marcus Garvey's pan-Africanist Universal Negro Improvement Association, with its massive working-class following, firmly backed Smith. The UNIA's endorsement was motivated first and foremost by Garvey's objection to Hoover's support for American corporate rubber interests in Liberia. Hoover, Garvey charged, headed a capitalistic group with "no soul in its dealing with the oppressed of the world." Smith, by contrast, was a man with "broad humanities, broad sympathies who loves mankind not because they are of any one skin color but because they are all children of God." The UNIA also backed Smith's anti-Prohibition stand: "Governor Smith says he wants to see the Prohibition law changed, and we are with him heart and soul." Harlem, New York, announced the *Negro World*, "like countless communities throughout this nation, is being prostituted by Prohibition. . . . Let any man rid the Commonwealth of this cancer and he will earn the undying gratitude of this and future generations." The UNIA worked to energize its voting base for Smith, with the *Negro World* announcing mass meetings of the Democratic Party and praising the "recent heavy registration . . . indicat[ing] that there are thousands of citizens who are preparing to use the franchise for the first time." The paper described the process and warned of the pitfalls for first-time voters, instructing readers on how to properly mark ballots. It urged, "To the Polls for Smith."[53]

Such enthusiastic Smith support convinced a significant number of African-American voters to vote for the Democratic Party candidate on November 6, denting African-Americans' historic Republican loyalty. Nationwide, African-Americans clung solidly to their traditional political home, but in northeastern industrial cities from Pittsburgh to New York tallies showed a marked shift to the Democrats. In Pittsburgh, in 1924, John Davis, who headed the Democratic ticket, won only 5 percent of the black vote in the overwhelmingly African-American fifth ward. In 1928, Smith garnered just under 40 percent of the African-American vote. In 1932, FDR built upon that defection, winning close to one-half of African-American votes. By 1936, a majority of African-Americans in Pittsburgh and other industrial cities stood with the Democrats. In New York, African-Americans voted 94 percent Republican in the 1920 presidential election, while only 3 percent voted Democratic. In 1928, divergent studies of voter returns show at the low end of results just under one-third of New York black voters for Smith and at the high end 41 percent. Roosevelt solidified that shift in 1932 garnering 58 percent of the African-Americans' vote. By 1936, African-Americans were solidly within the Democratic Party. In Chicago and Cleveland, the shift was smaller, but still notable. Smith won 27 percent of African-American votes. Within the African-American community, voters lower on the socioeconomic scale proved most likely to mark their ballots for Smith. After 1928, African-Americans in Chicago never again supported Republicans with the strength they had historically.[54]

While trends in African-American communities were just starting to shift, a far larger number of northern white urban ethnic working-class men and women voted for the Democrats in 1928. In Chicago turnout ran high, with 76 percent of eligible voters going to the polls, many of them voting Democratic. Voters occupying lower ranks on the socioeconomic scale, as elsewhere, were more likely to vote for Smith, a pattern that would hold steady for decades to come. Democratic gains in 1928, according to a detailed study of Chicago ward-level data, made 1928 the most "significant election in the period." Smith carried twenty-six of the city's fifty wards, some by "very handsome majorities." More recent immigrants—Italians, Poles, Slovaks, Czechs—who had arrived in the second wave of mass immigration and who held largely unskilled or semiskilled jobs, marked their ballots overwhelmingly for Smith. Prior to 1928, Chicago's Polish community had divided its vote fairly evenly between the Democratic and Republican presidential candidates. Four years afterward, nearly 80 percent of the city's Polish voters voted for Smith. Chicago's German community, with its traditional home in the Republican Party, lurched toward the Democratic Party in 1928, with 45 percent of German ethnic voters for

Smith. By 1932, a majority of them swung to the Democrats. Before the election of 1928, John Allswang found, "one could not generalize about an ethnic vote . . . [while] from this election forward the concept had real meaning."[55]

In 1928, Anton Cermak failed to win the Senate seat in the face of downstate Republican opposition; by 1930 Chicago was a Democratic stronghold and he won Chicago's mayoralty race with a sweeping majority. So, too, did a large slate of Democratic candidates. Emboldened by his strong victory, Cermak charted the party's course for future victories: "We are going to read out of the party any of our candidates who want to run as drys." To Cermak and his supporters, the war on alcohol proved a mobilizing tool they leveraged to build a powerful urban Democratic Party.[56]

Even in Pittsburgh, a fortress of once impregnable Republican rule, defections were growing. Hoover squeaked to victory by only eight thousand votes; Smith won a shocking 48 percent, the best Democratic result since 1856. Ethnic working-class wards strongly backed Smith. He won fourteen, including the Hill District populated by workers from southern and eastern Europe, the Polish neighborhoods of the sixth ward, the eastern European South Side, and German and Irish areas of the North Side. In Pittsburgh's heaviest "foreign born and low rent" neighborhoods, such as the heavily working-class industrial first and second wards, Smith won a stunning 77 and 75 percent of the vote. These neighborhoods later became the strongest Congress of Industrial Organizations (CIO) and politically "class conscious wards" in the nation. Smith also captured mining and industrial counties outside the city with heavily ethnic immigrant populations—Elk, Luzerne, and Lackawanna—that had not voted Democratic since the nineteenth century.[57]

A similar shift took place in Boston. Voters who had previously voted Republican in ethnic, immigrant working-class wards surged toward the Democratic Party. In 1924, ethnic Italian voters had split their vote fairly evenly between the Republican and Democratic presidential candidates. In 1928, however, Democrats won an overwhelming 95 percent of the Italian vote. New York witnessed similar patterns. Heavily Italian areas had given Republicans a slight edge in 1920. By 1928, those areas voted 77 percent for Smith, a move solidified in 1932 when Roosevelt won 79 percent of the Italian vote.[58]

Other industrial cities and towns across Massachusetts led this traditional Republican stronghold into the Democratic column in 1928, where it has remained ever since. The same regions that strongly backed Smith also supported a 1930 effort to end state enforcement of the Volstead Act. In New England, entire communities of French-Canadians or Italian-Americans swung out of the Republican Party. They remained there, providing the ethnic working-class base for the New Deal. Smith won a plurality of the vote in the nation's twelve largest cities; as a result, 1928 proved to be "a critical election."[59]

A solid stream of pro-Smith support came from ethnic voters who simply transferred their loyalty from the Republican Party. In Pittsburgh and Philadelphia, thousands of usually Republican voters mobilized "Republicans for Smith" clubs. New voters participating in a presidential contest for the first time provided another significant swell. The huge increase in Democratic votes in the period from 1928 to 1936 occurred without a commensurate decline in Republican votes, revealing the importance of first-time voters to Smith's tally. In the cities where Smith won the greatest support, not surprisingly, the pool of ethnic voters had increased markedly.[60]

Democratic committeeman Scott Ferris had pointed to this untapped reservoir of potential new voters. Encouraged by such savvy party strategists, ethnic newspapers, local politicians, and even the UNIA labored to bring these newcomers into the political process. In New York, the Board of Elections struggled under the press of nearly a half million new voters who registered there. In Chicago, too, registration leapt in record numbers, particularly in heavily ethnic wards. A startling 61 percent of those who marked their ballots for Smith had never before participated in a presidential contest. Waving the banner of Prohibition opposition, the Democratic Party mobilized previously uninvolved groups into the political process. With the coming of the Great Depression, those numbers would continue to swell, deepening further the alliance of working-class ethnic Americans to the Democratic Party and forging the social base for the New Deal.[61]

. . . .

DESPITE these tectonic shifts in the American electorate, Smith nonetheless suffered a crushing defeat in the national vote. Hoover won 58.2 percent of the popular vote to Smith's 40.8 percent. Smith carried only eight states. A large defection of traditional Democrats in the south and the west contributed to that upset. In the southern states of the former confederacy, Hoover won almost half the vote, a stunning counterweight to Smith's gains in Republican territory. In traditionally Democratic states outside of the deep south, including Oklahoma, Kentucky, and West Virginia, Hoover's gains were even greater. He won 60 percent, to the Democrats' 40 percent. These defections obscured the revitalization of the Democratic Party that was underway but not complete as the party's power base shifted from the south and west toward its new center of gravity—the nation's burgeoning urban centers.[62]

The election of 1928 closed one political era and opened another. The Democrats became the party newly epitomized by its urban ethnic working-class voting base. The adoption of new Democratic loyalties, however, was not a spontaneous process. Democratic leaders leveraged opposition to the war on alcohol to draw these men and women into the political process. Elite Prohibition opponents hoped to rescind the Eighteenth Amendment to reinforce the principle of "home rule." Ethnic working-class men and women joined them, but not because they were "duped" into supporting an agenda of Wall Street bankers. Prohibition was a real grievance in poor communities. By making the Democratic Party the vehicle to rescind it, Al Smith, John Raskob, and others were giving urban ethnic voters and their leaders one of their signal goals. But this was far from all they wanted. Until the New Deal, neither party addressed the specific concerns of working-class voters over economic security and labor rights. In 1928, opposition to Prohibition offered these voters a choice relevant to their lives, opening a new partisan channel for the class-oriented politics ahead. By 1932, with the national and global economic crisis, they would press claims to economic security and labor rights beyond what some of their party leaders were willing to address. Into that role Franklin D. Roosevelt stepped, bringing the burst of policy breakthroughs of the New Deal, and leaving behind John Raskob and his AAPA associates who helped forge the new coalition.[63]

The rift took place only in the wake of Roosevelt's election. After the 1928 debacle, Raskob prepared for the next election. He placed the party organization on a permanent footing, setting up a year-round office in Washington and a new publicity committee. The campaign also rallied a committed cadre of activists. One of them, Earl Purdy, wrote presciently to Roosevelt that Smith's "leadership has brought into our party a lot of good red blood, has revitalized the organization from top to bottom . . . our numbers have been considerably augmented with sincere men and women who will stay with us permanently. . . . With combined forces we will march on to victory four years hence."[64]

In Washington, Republican Herbert Hoover took the oath of office as the nation's chief executive in the midst of a vast crisis of crime and lawlessness. He set out to vigorously enforce the "noble experiment." The effort triggered renewed debate over the Eighteenth Amendment and helped turn the tide against national Prohibition, contributing to the Democratic victory in 1932 that Purdy had predicted four years earlier. The world may have looked with puzzlement over the continued American preoccupation with the controversy over the war on alcohol as the global economy careened toward disaster and the future of capitalism remained uncertain, but Prohibition remained a salient issue.

7

BUILDING THE PENAL STATE

HERBERT HOOVER WON THE ELECTION OF 1928 BY A LAND-slide. Al Smith had mobilized a new bloc of voters for the Democratic Party, but the overwhelming majority of the nation's electorate chose the "full dinner pail" over the man from the "sidewalks of New York." The problem of Prohibition survived the defeat of its first national opponent. The nation was awash in illegal liquor, the criminal justice system was overburdened, and flagrant violations raised the specter of an epidemic of lawlessness. During the campaign, discontented Republicans called on Hoover to address this, and he promised to take action. The urgency of the problem was driven home just three weeks before his inauguration. In what the media quickly dubbed the "St. Valentine's massacre," "Machine Gun" Jack McGurn's henchmen executed seven men in a Chicago garage. In a ploy almost as shocking as the body count, the murderers brazenly sported police uniforms and official badges.[1]

On March 4, 1929, Hoover stood at the Capitol before the great throng that had braved the cold, penetrating rain to celebrate his inauguration. Millions more, dry and snug in their homes, heard Hoover's address on their radios, an event broadcast live by the nation's fledgling networks. Hoover wasted no time in identifying the first critical business of the nation as "the Failure of our System of Criminal Justice." The most "malign danger" facing the nation, he averred, was "disregard and disobedience to law." This "alarming disobedience," the "growth of organized crime," and the "abuses in law enforcement"—all unforeseen consequences of Prohibition—were nothing less than challenges to the legitimacy of the American state. He called for an overhaul of the "entire federal machinery of justice" to "reestablish the vigor and effectiveness of law enforcement." To begin the process, Hoover called for a federal commission to study the system of criminal justice and propose remedies. "Reform, reorganization and strengthening of our whole judicial and enforcement system . . . have been advocated for years," the new president told national listeners, and the "first steps toward that end should no longer be delayed."[2]

The former engineer's opening salvo to build a "more effective organization" of criminal justice drew on his deep conviction that social-scientific expertise should guide government policy. In the spirit of Progressivism, as secretary of commerce in 1922 he had commissioned an unprecedented and ambitious series of studies on social trends in agriculture, industry, and society to provide a baseline of knowledge for national policy making. The fruit of that effort was a massive two-volume study, *Recent Social Trends* (1928). Thousands of pages detailed many aspects of social and economic life. Hoover's move to confront the simmering crisis of Prohibition enforcement was unsurprisingly a study commission. With his announcement, Congress withdrew a resolution starting its own commission and passed a generous appropriation bill for the president's initiative, the National Commission on Law Observance and Enforcement, commonly known as the Wickersham Commission after its chairman, George Wickersham.[3]

This less-well-recognized aspect of Hoover's speech was a watershed. Never before in United States history had the chief executive identified crime as a problem of national concern in an inaugural address. Until the 1920s, crime had been largely understood as a quintessentially local problem, a staple offering of community and state politics. The Enforcement Acts passed during Reconstruction to end the racial terrorism of the first Ku Klux Klan was the great exception to this approach, and that short-lived effort ended in failure. In 1925, Calvin Coolidge broke the federal taboo by establishing the first federal crime commission. The blue-ribbon group was largely a symbolic endeavor, with Coolidge declaring "religion the only remedy" to lawlessness. Hoover's more muscular and activist administration expanded the federal government's new role exponentially.[4]

Hoover told Americans that crime was the paramount threat faced by the nation, one whose depth and breadth had outstripped local and state capabilities and demanded vigorous federal attention. His first speech after his inaugural address kept up the anticrime drumbeat. With fists clenched, he declared fighting lawlessness "more vital to the preservation of American institutions than any other question." By framing crime as a problem of truly national scope, Hoover continued the progressive trend of envisioning a role for the federal government in tackling large social problems. Often caricatured as a staunch individualist tilting against the New Deal era's expansive embrace of federal power, Hoover was a pioneering architect of the modern federal penal state.[5]

The antiliquor war forged a neglected but critical chapter of American state development. In a period of otherwise conservative retrenchment, the Eighteenth Amendment and the Volstead Act dramatically expanded the scope of federal authority, opening the door for the revolutionizing of citizen–state relations that the New Deal institutionalized after 1932. The story of American state development is usually told by focusing on the expansion of the regulatory state during the Progressive Era and the New Deal, leapfrogging over the Prohibition years. That narrative misses the upsurge of federal and state coercive power from 1919 to 1933, an upsurge that resulted in the greatest expansion of state building, outside of wartime, since Reconstruction, helping to shape the New Deal order that rose after Prohibition's demise. Overshadowed by high-profile art, literature, and public works agencies, and social provisioning projects from social security to labor rights, the unprecedented development of the federal government's law enforcement and punitive capacities contributed to the bone and sinew of the twentieth-century American state. Nothing did more than the nation's Prohibition war to build this less-examined side of state building in the first half of the twentieth century. The radical federal endeavor to abolish the liquor traffic is the missing link between Progressive Era and World War I state building and the New Deal.[6]

For starters, Hoover called for a "searching" national investigation into the "whole structure of our Federal system of jurisprudence," including "the method of enforcement of the Eighteenth Amendment." Given the controversy over Prohibition, most observers assumed that the commission would have a narrow focus on Prohibition enforcement alone. Felix Frankfurter later contended that Americans had misidentified Hoover's emphasis on law enforcement as simply Prohibition enforcement. Most who acknowledged the broad charge Hoover gave to the commission dismissed it as a rhetorical tactic to deflect attention from the embarrassments of Prohibition enforcement. Pauline Sabin was so angered by the wider charge of the commission that she resigned from the Republican National Committee in protest: "I had thought . . . Mr. Hoover meant to concentrate on the results of the Prohibition law alone . . . I was fooled." Instead, Sabin established the Women's Organization for National Prohibition Reform as a direct effort to repeal the Eighteenth Amendment.[7]

In truth, Hoover's wide charge expressed his hope, shared by many antiliquor crusaders, that enforcement of the Eighteenth Amendment could be improved by more "effective organization of our agencies of investigation and prosecution." Undaunted in his support of the Eighteenth Amendment, Hoover also believed liquor law violations were "but a sector of the invasion of lawlessness" that made life and property in the United States "more unsafe than any other country in the world." The nation's crime problem, in his view, could not be reduced to the failure to enforce Prohibition at the federal, state, and local levels. Something deeper had gone wrong in American life. Hoover tapped into a deep and wide vein of public anxiety. Widespread concerns over criminality had first emerged on the national stage in the wake of World War I, a period rife with social conflict. From these first sparks, the public clamor for a war on crime had reached fever pitch, fanned not least by the flagrant violence and lawlessness of liquor scofflaws.[8]

Ironically, during Prohibition, from the ashes of the initial triumph over demon rum and the saloon rose a new specter of criminality. Many Americans believed that a crime spree of "dramatic proportions" was sweeping the nation. Solicitor general James M. Beck averred as early as 1921 that "the present wave of crime" had "no parallel since the eighteenth century." The nation's press through the whole period of national Prohibition was filled with articles on the subject. *McClure's* "America, Land of the Lawbreaker" was one of many articles sounding the alarm over "the greatest American crime wave. As evidence, they listed the military-grade weaponry adopted by police, including "tear gas, machine guns, and armored cars" used to fight it. Criminologist Harry Elmer Barnes wrote at mid-decade that "few subjects occupy more space in contemporary literature . . . than analyses of the crime wave, its extent, causes and possible remedies."[9]

In the immediate postwar years, Prohibition violations did not figure prominently in discussions of crime. Labor strikes, race riots, and anarchist bombings led to growing calls for law and order, predating the intensive enforcement of Prohibition and its alarming shortcomings. The increasing use of automobiles also played its part in public concerns over lawlessness. Automobile theft and motor vehicle violations became two new classes of crime. Armed "bandits," additionally, took advantage of cars to make rapid getaways, birthing innovative and sensationalist high-speed heists. In 1926 alone the *New York Times* reported on forty-three major bank robberies in five states in America's heartland: Oklahoma, Kansas, Arkansas, Missouri, and Indiana. A new breed of holdup bandits outpaced local law enforcement, quickly crossing state lines and escaping with their loot. The new tabloid papers eagerly pandered to the public appetite for the presumed "carnival" of crime. Episodes of local violence now made headlines from shore to shore, contributing to a wide public perception that the nation was engulfed by an orgy of crime. City tabloids printed gruesome pictures of the bloody corpses of criminals killed during battles over territory. The extravagant and colorful lifestyles of gangsters made good copy, too, with some seasoned city reporters even transitioning to screenwriting for a rash of Hollywood gangster films.[10]

While the news media's profit-seeking flogging of crime fanned public perceptions of a crime wave, murders by sawed-off shotguns and lavish gangster funerals were not the products of the tabloid imagination. A new class of criminals had welled up, feeding on the collateral violence and crime that resulted from the war on alcohol. While crime statistics were in their infancy in the 1920s, statistical evidence, even from the most cautious reports, points to a spike in the prosecutions of certain classes of crime, if not necessarily proving an actual rise in crime. Nationwide, violent crime showed evidence of increase over the decade. Murders and assaults prosecuted went from twelve per 100,000 in 1920 to sixteen per 100,000 in 1933. After Prohibition's end, they declined sharply to ten per 100,000. Yet measuring crime by prosecution or incarceration fails to capture the on-the-ground experience of rising violence resulting from the war on alcohol, not least because so many crimes went unpunished or even unreported. New York City, for example, witnessed 337 murders in 1928, but in 115 of these cases no arrests were made. Chicago's situation was worse. Chicago's infamous Beer Wars resulted in the doubling of the murder rate from 1918 to 1927. One study of homicide in Chicago and surrounding Cook County from 1926 to 1927 found that of 130 murders linked to gangs, only twenty-six went to court. Nonetheless, Chicago prosecutions of all kinds climbed precipitously during the war on alcohol, far outstripping population growth. The number of cases in municipal court tripled in the nine-year period from 1920 to 1930, spiking to 350,000 in 1929 from 100,000 in 1920. In Illinois more broadly, the number of felony convictions spiked from 12,000 in 1918 to just about double that number in 1927. But it was not just large cities that saw spikes in crime. In the midsize city of Richmond, for example, the murder rate tripled in the five years from 1920 to 1925. By 1935, it stood at 37, up from 8 in 1920.[11]

Like Chicago, Boston saw prosecutions for murder, manslaughter, and robbery climb, but prosecutions for breaking and entering, larceny, and assault declined. One Boston observer sought to diffuse the furor over crime by citing these countervailing trends. Rising rates of prosecution, the author pointed out, did not necessarily correlate to rising rates of crime across the board. Average citizens who opened their newspapers, however, remained alarmed by the quality and quantity of the stories of government-bonded warehouse thefts, bank holdups, and high-profile gangland killings combined with real increases in arrests and incarcerations.[12]

The nation's war on alcohol turned rising concern over urban crime into a national obsession. The Volstead Act created a broad new class of criminals and dramatically raised the number of crimes prosecuted. Arrests and prosecutions for crimes related to motor vehicle offenses also increased with the passage in 1919 of the Dyer Act making interstate trafficking in stolen vehicles a federal crime. Concomitant increases in the prosecution of drug users during the war on alcohol further stoked the public panic about crime. The primary engine of the spike in arrests in many cities and states, however, was the Volstead Act and its state equivalents. In Columbus, Ohio, there were just under two thousand arrests for violations of liquor laws in 1929 alone, which was ten times the number of auto thefts, twenty times the number of arrests for robbery. In Virginia, liquor-law felonies outstripped all other forms of felony. In 1917, Virginia had 1.8 felony prosecutions per 100,000 population; by 1928, that number had increased to 68.7 and Volstead violators made up just about one-fourth of all prisoner convictions.[13]

More disturbing than the numerical increase in crime was its changing nature. Organized crime was not new, but the war on alcohol turned an entire industry over to criminal entrepreneurs who not surprisingly thrived as never before. Already influential in urban centers through the control of gambling and sex trafficking, organized crime skyrocketed to entirely new levels of power, visibility, and influence on the windfall profits of black markets in drink. Crime kingpins used these riches to cultivate ever deeper relationships with politicians, urban judges, and police, compounding the public's loss of faith in the criminal justice system. "One of the serious factors" in the "alarming" increase of "serious crimes," warned the Missouri Crime Survey, "is the fact that there seems to be a larger amount of organized crime than ever before." Contemporary experts pointed to the primary role of the "noble experiment" in its rise. E. W. Burgess of the Illinois Crime Survey warned that the "overlords of vice . . . flourish in Prohibition's shadow." John Landesco, research director of the American Institute of Criminal Law and Criminology, agreed: "Prohibition has enormously increased the personnel and the power of organized crime." Critics of the Eighteenth Amendment blamed the "crime wave" as a whole, not just organized crime, on Prohibition: "Too much law by stupid legislation," wrote one *New York Times* letter writer contemptuously. "The adherents of Prohibition promised us a sort of millennium," the writer observed, "but . . . instead of a utopian Sahara we have a land where crimes and acts of violence fill the first page of every daily newspaper."[14]

While the correlation between the crime wave and the Volstead Act appeared evident to some, others pointed to rising prosecutions for crimes against property to argue that other factors were at play. Investigations got underway to understand and remedy the "crime problem." Large cities, including Boston, New York, Cleveland, Chicago, and Los Angeles, along with states such as New York, Missouri, and California, established crime commissions, with nine large-scale surveys published between 1919 and 1925. In the next five years, the pace of investigation increased, with twenty-six more reports going to press. Concerned private citizens and businessmen bankrolled some of these studies, state legislatures funded others, and all drew on long-standing networks of "good government" reformers—from civic-oriented businessmen, judges, and lawyers to policy-oriented social scientists.[15]

Despite pretenses of scientific objectivity, a number of these studies, and even more so the legislative outcomes, were clearly shaped by the clamor for a crackdown on crime that emphasized swift punishment and a more efficient criminal justice system to deter crime. New York State's infamous Baumes Law ignored the more nuanced findings of its Crime Commission, taking instead a "tough on crime" approach, establishing mandatory life sentences for offenders convicted of a fourth felony, retrenchment of procedural protections for the accused, and abolition of the "good-time system" that offered reduced sentences for good behavior while in prison. Other states followed New York's lead in adopting, in the words of one penologist, an "orgy of drastic penal legislation." Liquor-law violators and, increasingly, drug violators suffered the consequences as desperate drys imposed ever stiffer penalties throughout the decade. Not to be outdone, Congress passed the Jones Act of 1929 that made a first violation of the Volstead Act a felony and raised maximum penalties to five years in prison and a $10,000 fine.[16]

This "tough on crime" approach was but one facet, albeit common, of 1920s efforts to remedy the crime problem. Progressive reformers true to form emphasized the social causes of crime and sought to reform the inefficiency and injustice of the penal system. And many of the social scientists identified as a precondition of effective reform new forms of knowledge for a problem of such scope. In a rehearsal of the New Deal's institutional and administrative reforms, what concrete solutions they advanced called for more professionalized administration, better knowledge of criminal patterns through systematic crime statistics, and court administrative reform. Two members of Roosevelt's future brain trust, Harvard law professor Felix Frankfurter and Columbia University professor Raymond Moley, cut their policy teeth in municipal and state crime studies of the 1920s and early 1930s. The Harvard Law School's Boston Crime Survey called attention to the embryonic state of knowledge about crime and the consequent difficulty of measuring its scope and variability, including the correlation between crimes against property and employment fluctuations. The reports called above all for the need to reform the entire structure of the justice system.[17]

Just as the forces of Prohibition had gravitated to a national solution to the saloon problem, local and state crime surveys were soon followed by national efforts to study and turn back the rising tide, first with Calvin Coolidge's slapdash and symbolic effort and more energetically with Herbert Hoover's Wickersham Commission. The National Commission on Law Observance and Enforcement drew some of the best minds in the social sciences and jurisprudence to study the problem of enforcing Prohibition and reforming criminal justice. Roscoe Pound was the most eminent legal scholar on the commission, and he was central to drafting many sections of its reports. Felix Frankfurter, Pound's colleague and rival at Harvard, drew on his own experience with municipal surveys and helped draft the initial blueprint for the commission's work. He traveled to Washington to share his expertise with members, and provided detailed advice to two commission members throughout. The commission took as a given that crime could not remain the purview of foundations, settlement houses, municipalities, or states alone. It was a leading example of a recently born engine of public-policy formulation with Washington officials relying on social science experts in the nation's leading universities and nonprofit foundations, a network that would take more permanent form during the New Deal.[18]

The commission's eleven members, mostly men in the legal profession, many with earlier experience in local and state crime surveys, with a prominent university leader as well, met over a period of two years and produced tens of thousands of pages of documents. The commissioners brought on board experts in the areas to be covered to direct the reports, along with a staff of twenty-five additional researchers. Though rife with internal factionalism and unable to smooth out some significant contradictions in its Prohibition report, the commission's work was, nonetheless, monumental and historic. It published fourteen reports totaling well over three thousand pages and another five volumes of records. The reports represent an unprecedented moment of self-scrutiny under government auspices. Despite its conservative sponsors, the reports' findings included powerful indictments of American society, many at odds with the policies and world view of the Hoover administration. Over and over again, seeds planted by the authors of these studies would germinate and flower in the New Deal period. The commission's work points to important continuities between Hoover's initiatives and later expansions of federal capacity, albeit for now limited to the quasi-military sphere of "crime control."

The National Commission on Law Observance and Enforcement was just one of the ways the Eighteenth Amendment drove forward the effort to retool the criminal justice system. The public clamor over crime provided the opportunity to centralize criminal knowledge in Washington and develop new surveillance techniques. In collaboration with the International Association of Police Chiefs, a centralized Bureau of Identification began collecting criminal fingerprints in Washington in 1924. This system of "scientific" identification and classification of criminals triumphed over other forms of identification, such as the Bertillon system of anthropometric measurement. Additionally, Prohibition police eagerly embraced wiretapping to catch large and elusive violators. Agents listened in on the phone conversations of bootleggers who had escaped detection because of the collusion of local and state authorities. Wiretapping enabled them to snag violators at the site of major deliveries and to gain actionable evidence of illegal cash transactions otherwise hard to trace. This surveillance, which marked an expansion from earlier mail-censorship programs, played a role in the capture of some large bootleggers, including Dutch Schultz in New York, Al Capone in Chicago, and Roy Olmstead in Seattle. The Supreme Court gave the program a green light in its 1927 *Olmstead v. United States* decision, which allowed the admission of government evidence gained through wiretapping.[19]

The Wickersham Commission set the stage for systematizing federal crime reporting. "The outstanding fact is the absence of facts," the commission declared, "in terms of national knowledge about actual crime, its rise and fluctuations." Exactly how national crime statistics should be gathered was a topic of heated debate. Commission researcher Sam B. Warner, a respected expert on crime statistics, pointed out that relying on police reporting, as the Bureau of Investigation had been doing, entailed multiple problems. Many crimes went unreported, and police arrests and reports were not necessarily accurate or impartial. He argued for starting with victims of crime, to be identified by Census Bureau enumerators. Police lacked sophisticated reporting structures, their statistics were open to manipulation, and police gathering would likely lead to the underreporting of certain kinds of crime. To delegate control of national criminal statistics to policing agents would prioritize social knowledge of certain forms of crime and erase others. Statistics based on victim reporting might better capture classes of crime underrepresented in police statistics, including instances of police brutality. Commission members Max Lowenthal and George Wickersham were convinced by his arguments and also favored data collection by the Census Bureau.[20]

On the other side, August Vollmer, head of the International Association of Police Chiefs, and a commission consultant, favored centralized gathering of criminal statistics based on police reporting. With the strong backing of the International Association of Police Chiefs and the Bureau of Investigation, which desired to keep its control over crime statistics, the decision was made to utilize police data. The resulting *Uniform Crime Reports*, published since 1930 by the Bureau of Investigation (renamed the FBI in 1935), became the primary index of American criminality. The heated contest for control of national crime statistics revealed the stakes involved in a seemingly mundane task. Police agents and social scientists understood that how these statistics were gathered and by whom would shape first knowledge and later policy about crime. This otherwise obscure decision on sources of data made during the war on alcohol has shaped the national understanding of crime ever since.[21]

On a more concrete level, record keeping was growing more urgent because of the headlong growth of the numbers of prisoners housed in the nation's increasingly overcrowded penitentiaries and jails. Before Prohibition, the federal government had been only a negligible player in the administration of criminal justice. In 1890 there were fewer than two thousand nonmilitary federal prisoners. In 1915, there were still only three thousand. By 1930, the number had increased fourfold. Prison numbers dramatically escalated in the 1920s because of new classes of crime, especially liquor-law violations. That population equaled 3,720 in 1920; by 1933, upon repeal, it had more than tripled, reaching 13,352. Volstead Act violators constituted the highest class of long-term violators in the penitentiaries by 1930. Liquor-law violators made up one-third of all long-term violators in the five leading federal facilities that year. Overcrowding led to the use of military installations to temporarily house prisoners. Volstead violators, reported Major Joel E. Moore, charged with overseeing the camps, were responsible for "a large measure" of prison congestion. Drug offenders offered stiff competition. Together the two classes made up more than 50 percent of all of those incarcerated in federal prisons by 1930.[22]

Overcrowding in federal and state prisons alike reached crisis proportions by the turn of the decade. Three federal prisons had been constructed between 1891 and 1907—Fort Leavenworth, Kansas; the Atlanta penitentiary; and McNeil Island in Puget Sound, but the wave of Prohibition violators along with newly punished drug violators quickly overflowed these institutions. McNeill Island had a cell capac-

ity of 3,738; in 1928, 7,598 inmates were housed there. Fort Leavenworth, designed to hold approximately 2,000 prisoners, housed 3,770
in 1929, and riots over bad food and harsh discipline were the result. In
1929 a full-scale riot led to major property destruction, the death of one
inmate, and the injury of many others. Two years later, in yet another
uprising, prisoners threatened guards with guns, sticks, and dynamite.
A group of men escaped, kidnapped the warden, and commandeered
two cars. A widely publicized manhunt followed, ending with capture
of three escapees and the death of four others.[23]

State prisons were also bursting at the seams. In Pennsylvania's Eastern Penitentiary in 1922, 1,700 prisoners were crammed three and four
to a cell designed for a single inmate. "There is less room per prisoner
in some of the cells than a dead man has in his coffin," reported one
observer. Overcrowded conditions led to widely publicized riots in
New York State's Dannemora and Auburn prisons. In Texas, Volstead
Act enforcement contributed to prison overcrowding so severe during
the 1920s that the State Prison Board simply refused to take in any new
inmates in order to pressure the state legislature for prison reform. Virginia's penal population doubled between 1923 and 1931. In Georgia
felony and misdemeanor prisoners filled the state penitentiary to capacity by 1921, while the county chain gangs were overcrowded. Especially noteworthy was the large increase in the number of white
prisoners. The Prohibition-era punishment wave led to the tripling of
North Carolina's imprisonment rate. In California, San Quentin, the
largest prison in the nation, housed 6,062 inmates by 1933, nearly twice
its capacity. A member of the California parole board reported in 1929
that prisoners were "jammed into every attic, basement, and cell."[24]

At the federal level, deplorable conditions, overcrowding, and tensions inside the facilities led to a rapid increase in prison construction at
the end of the 1920s and into the New Deal period. Hoover pressed
Congress for prison construction, declaring that "our Federal penal
institutions are overcrowded, and this condition is daily becoming

worse." Overcrowding, he warned, was a "direct cause of outbreaks and trouble." He sent Congress plans for prison construction over a five-year period at a cost of $6.5 million (over $92 million in inflation-adjusted dollars). To meet the problem of overcrowding and to avoid disorder while construction was underway, he arranged to house more than 1,650 prisoners at Alcatraz, Blackwell's Island, and the Fort Leavenworth army installation. In 1932, a new penitentiary in Lewisberg, Pennsylvania, opened. Alcatraz, formerly utilized to house military prisoners, was revamped as a maximum-security prison island for hardened inmates. When it reopened in 1934, it welcomed none other than Prohibition kingpin Al Capone, whom Hoover had doggedly worked to convict. New federal prisons were built in Chillicothe, Illinois; El Reno, Oklahoma; and Milan, Michigan; federal prisons specifically designed to hold pretrial defendants were constructed in New Orleans and El Paso, Texas. Most new facilities were designed to house male inmates, but some federal prison construction included facilities for women, such as the Federal Industrial Institution for Women that opened in 1927 in Alderson, West Virginia. By the end of 1930 the number of federal prison facilities had risen to fourteen; ten years later the number of federal prisons and jails reached twenty-four.[25]

In 1930, President Hoover also pressed Congress to fund an expansion and elevation of federal prison administration, birthing the new Federal Bureau of Prisons, a subdivision of the Justice Department, led by penologist Sanford Bates, former director of the California prison system. With this reorganization, prison management became a formal policy function equal in stature to the FBI. New forms of record keeping were also established during national Prohibition to track the rising number of prisoners. The Census Bureau since the nineteenth century had enumerated the number of prisoners in federal and state prisons. During the 1920s, the developing federal penal state systematized its reporting. A yearly report, *Prisoners in State and Federal Prisons and Reformatories*, was first published in 1926. Initially primitive in its statistical analysis, it developed into permanent and increasingly sophisticated yearly reporting and was eventually taken over by the newly established Federal Bureau of Prisons.[26]

The end of Prohibition in December 1933 did not lead to an immediate decline in incarceration. The numbers of Americans behind bars ticked upward for the whole period from 1920 to 1940. From 1920 to 1930 the average population in federal prisons tripled, leaping from 3,720 to 11,400. From 1930 to 1940 it continued to climb, nearly doubling again. Those serving out sentences for Volstead Act violations, new liquor convictions for failure to pay the reestablished federal liquor tax, prosecutions for drug users, and crimes against property correlating with skyrocketing rates of unemployment kept those numbers climbing. Large state-prison populations in Texas and California, already overcrowded in the 1920s, kept climbing through the 1930s. Taken together, at the federal and state levels prison populations nearly doubled from the 1920s to the 1940s. By way of contrast, the start of World War II and the next thirty years witnessed close to no growth in the federal prison population. Relative to booming population growth during these same years, the rate of incarcerated Americans then not only held flat but declined sharply from its Prohibition-era spike. Similarly, the spike in state prison populations from 1920 to 1940 was also followed by decreased rates of incarceration. State prison population numbers fluctuated over this period, but states such as Illinois, Indiana, Ohio, Kentucky, and Tennessee, among others—states that witnessed sharp increases in Prohibition-related crime or where there was strong dry sentiment—saw declines in their prison populations after 1940. As a result, while there were 125 prisoners per 100,000 population in state and federal prisons in 1940, in 1970 that number stood at 98. Declining rates of incarceration reversed sharply in the last third of the twentieth century with a second phase of systematic state-prison growth beginning in the 1970s followed by a leap in federal incarceration levels after 1980, correlating with the second war on drugs.[27]

The expanded and newly organized federal prison system was but one enduring legacy of Prohibition. The demands of Prohibition enforcement fostered novel alternatives to incarceration as well, chief among them parole. First established in the late nineteenth century, by 1925 all but two states had parole laws. To critics who decried parole for coddling the criminal, reformers replied, in one Pennsylvania report, "Parole is not leniency . . . on the contrary, parole really increases the state's period of control." Prisoners who once left the jails unsupervised faced periods of supervision and restriction on their mobility after their release. The federal government also expanded its parole system, pressed by the glut of prisoners. Hoover established a Federal Board of Parole in 1930. He also increased the number of federal probation officers ten-fold to supervise convicted violators rather than sending them to over-crowded prisons. As a result, 12,300 convicted violators were placed on probation between 1930 and 1931, and another 15,700 in 1932.[28]

Prohibition also gave new urgency to long-standing efforts to reshape another central institution of American criminal justice: the courts. Prohibition highlighted deep inefficiencies in the nation's courts and reinforced calls for administrative reorganization. Federal courts, Assistant Attorney General Willebrandt reported in 1924, were strained to the breaking point by huge backlogs: fully 22,000 cases were pending at the end of that year. Courts, to their credit, had processed large numbers of Prohibition violators, convicting many. In 1928, for the fiscal year ending June 30, federal court judges convicted 44,022 liquor-law violators. This caseload shock provided ammunition for court reform. Former president William Howard Taft had called for a centrally coordinated judiciary as early as 1914, but Congress had resisted. Pressed by the mounting backlog of Prohibition cases, Congress enacted federal court procedural reform in 1922, granting the chief justice new authority to assign judges to any district court in the nation as needed and to create a judicial council to centralize and reform court procedures. An annual judicial conference of senior circuit-court judges was tasked with gathering statistics and improving court efficiency by crafting new rules. Earlier court reformers' efforts had focused first on the

municipal level, then the state level. Now the crisis of Prohibition
enforcement contributed to a managerial revolution at all levels, including the federal judicial administration.[29]

.   .   .

THE nation's liquor war transformed national criminal law doctrine as
well. While plea bargaining had become a common practice in lower
state and local courts by the turn of the century, overloaded federal
courts quickly adopted the practice. The overwhelming number of
cases led to mass sentence discounting, such as the infamous court
"bargain days," with violators on designated days crowding court-
rooms and pleading guilty in exchange for light fines and penalties.
Raymond Moley lamented the "Vanishing Jury" with plea bargaining
overrunning the nation's courts, driving the point home with the striking fact that of 13,117 felony prosecutions begun in Chicago in 1926,
only 209 ended in convictions by jury. The press of liquor cases and
rising criminal prosecutions forced the acceptance of new norms more
widely within the federal criminal justice system. National Prohibition
also firmed up entrapment doctrine. Courts saw an explosion of entrapment cases and Fourth Amendment defenses under the Volstead Act.
Even with Supreme Court decisions upholding enforcement tactics and
poking holes in established constitutional protections against unwarranted search and seizure, legal defenses citing entrapment now became
a standard weapon of the American defense bar. The years of constitutional Prohibition, in short, introduced some of the salient aspects of
modern criminal law and procedure at the federal level.[30]

During Taft's tenure as chief justice from 1921 to 1930, the Supreme
Court widened the scope of federal police power with decisions backing aggressive enforcement. A surprising coalition of justices such as
Chief Justice Taft and liberal associate justice Louis Brandeis found
common ground in a series of decisions upholding that unprecedented
power. In *United States v. Lanza* in 1922 the court effectively backed
the conscription of state resources to shore up the Eighteenth Amend-

ment, interpreting the amendment's "concurrent enforcement" clause to mean that states along with the federal government had a duty to enforce the law. The justices forged a novel doctrine of "dual sovereignty" as an exception to constitutional protections against "double jeopardy," which sought to ensure that criminal defendants would not be charged and punished for the same crime at both the state and the federal levels. The Taft Court expanded federal surveillance power with the *Olmstead v United States* decision on wiretapping in 1928. These decisions eroded constitutional protections and challenged traditional jurisprudence on local self-government. "Some decisions," legal scholar Robert Post has written, as a result "read strikingly like post–New Deal decisions ceding to Congress virtually unfettered authority."[31]

Despite the hostility of a majority of justices on this court to later New Deal legislation on economic regulation and planning, in the realm of criminal justice the Taft Court's decisions during Prohibition sharply expanded federal government power. With Prohibition seemingly a permanent part of the Constitution, the justices were forced to accept at some level the administrative state and reconstruct their judicial philosophies accordingly. Out of Prohibition, thus, was born a new doctrine of judicial neoconservatism. Conservative judicial philosophy had traditionally sided with limited federal power, states' rights, and local custom. Now justices like Taft, anxious to uphold the rule of law itself, consistently decided in favor of the expansion of federal power. With the repeal of the Eighteenth Amendment and its corrosive effects on the rule of law, the neoconservative fusion disappeared from conservative judicial philosophy only to reappear decades later when chief justice William Rehnquist's court upheld federal powers and legal positivism for conservative ends. Prohibition, by applying such extreme stress to institutions of law and order, gave birth to a brief flowering of a judicial perspective that would only more fully flourish in the late twentieth century.[32]

Unfettered by the Taft Court's backing of the federal government's role in policing, Congress opened the public purse to finance expansive new powers. Though enforcement spending in no way matched the law's grand ambitions, Congress made an exception for federal policing powers from the decade's otherwise thoroughgoing agenda of Republican retrenchment. While President Harding had drastically scaled back spending in his quest for a "return to normalcy," Congress failed to return federal spending to prewar levels, largely because spending on law enforcement rose close to 20 percent annually during the decade. The Prohibition Bureau alone had at its disposal an appropriation of over $15 million in 1929, triple the sum allocated nine years earlier, and equivalent to over $200 million today. And this was just one facet of law-enforcement expenditures, which were almost five times as great in 1930 as in 1920.[33]

This spending created the country's first significant national police force. The Prohibition enforcement apparatus was more than four times the size of J. Edgar Hoover's Bureau of Investigation, precursor to the Federal Bureau of Investigation. When Hoover took over the Bureau in 1924, he had a staff of fewer than 450 special agents. The newly established Border Patrol also had only 450 agents to police both the Mexican and Canadian borders with a total length of nearly 7,500 miles. The Prohibition Bureau, in contrast, employed 2,278 agents and a support staff of nearly 2,000 by 1930.[34]

From the start, the newly born Prohibition Unit encountered problems proportionate to its elephantine size. Inexperienced and untrained, the force was particularly open to pulls of bribe, graft, and corruption, fueled by the vast profits of black market liquor. As a result, between 1921 and 1928 nearly one-tenth of the service was dismissed for cause—including bribery, extortion, theft, and falsification of records, among other offenses. Only 41 percent of agents passed a new civil service test introduced in 1927, gutting the bureau at one stroke. New agents who could pass the exam but lacked practical experience were brought on board to replace the dropouts.[35]

The war on alcohol put these inexperienced federal officials—

customs officers, Border Patrol agents, Prohibition Bureau officers—in frequent and often violent confrontations with civilians. Poorly trained Prohibition Bureau officials were, according to federal admissions, responsible for approximately 260 deaths in enforcement of the law. The *Washington Herald* put the number killed at over one thousand, more likely, though not fully accounting for the dry army as a whole. Tellingly, for example, one Border Patrol agent, reputed to be a "stone cold killer," estimated that between 1924 and 1934 patrol agents alone had killed close to five hundred "contrabandistas," cross-border liquor smugglers of Mexican origin. Battling liquor violators was not the fledgling patrol's primary charge, but it nonetheless became centrally involved in its enforcement. El Paso squads secreted themselves at night along the Rio Grande, waiting to ambush smugglers loaded down with large cans of alcohol or bottled liquor. One former agent recalled a gunfight every seventeen days in his subdistrict. Along the border, the war on alcohol provided an opportunity for some of its more notorious gunfighters to engage in the "sport," as one former agent recalled, of hunting people. Not surprisingly, rife government lawlessness was one of the topics Hoover raised in his inaugural address and a subject investigated by the Wickersham Commission. Killings by Prohibition Bureau agents, compounded by a pattern of acquittal, provided ammunition to the law's opponents. President Hoover, however, blamed not the law, but its administration: citizens would obey the law if and when the government established more efficient and professional policing.[36]

The Federal Bureau of Investigation under the nation's other Hoover was perfectly positioned to profit from the president's call for more efficient and professional policing and public clamor over crime by building a smaller but more disciplined and respected force than the Prohibition Bureau. J. Edgar Hoover parlayed the public obsession over crime and the all-too-evident problems with the Prohibition Bureau into a brief for his nominally more professional federal anticrime arm. Despite lower funding and congressional attention, Hoover labored throughout the decade to build a law-enforcement agency untainted by the problems that had engulfed the federal Prohibition Bureau. He held his agents to high professional standards, rotating personnel assignments to keep agents from developing corrupting intimacy with local and state politicians. Hoover openly measured the Bureau of Investigation's professionalism against that of the Prohibition Bureau, and as that agency collapsed his was well placed to fill the void. By 1940, the FBI had doubled in size.[37]

While J. Edgar Hoover laid the foundation for a more professional, bureaucratic national crime-fighting apparatus, Herbert Hoover did not wait to restart a national effort to clamp down on the growing power of organized crime. Frustrated by the thriving liquor traffic, Hoover asked his attorney general, William Mitchell, if he had the authority to call out the military to crack down on rum-running and the violent fights over territory between rival gangs along the Detroit River. The president took a direct role in the effort to capture "Public Enemy No. 1"—Al Capone—soon to be the most famous resident of the federal prison on Alcatraz Island. Hoover charged his attorney general and secretary of the treasury Andrew Mellon with securing Capone's conviction. Backed by the highest levels of government, the team concocted an unusual strategy. Ignoring the murders committed by his henchmen, for which local and state police failed to prosecute him, it used federal power to convict him of income-tax violations on the unreported profits he made through his illegal businesses. Upon Capone's conviction, Frank Loesch, the Chicago Crime Commissioner, who also served on the Wickersham Commission, thanked the president for his behind-the-scenes efforts: "I hope that some day you will allow me to tell the public how much you had to do with it and how much impetus was personally given by you."[38]

President Hoover's reputation as an individualist belied his use of federal power in the war against crime. He built a more muscular federal prison system. He backed the expansion of the FBI's purview to include kidnapping in the wake of the Lindbergh baby murder; he called on Congress to widen federal authority to act against criminal gangs engaged in deadly warfare in New York, and he worked to unify, professionalize and expand the Border Patrol, which doubled in size in its first five years of existence. He also bolstered the federal government's deportation authority "to more fully rid ourselves of criminal aliens." He won some of that authority when the 1931 Alien Act provided for the deportation of noncitizens convicted of violating antinarcotics law. Hoover's antidrug chief at the newly born Federal Bureau of Narcotics aided the cause, testifying that "aliens were at the root of the narcotics problem."[39]

.   .   .   .

THIS development points to an underappreciated aspect of the war on alcohol—namely its symbiosis with its less-known twin: the federal campaign for narcotic-drug eradication. The challenge of alcohol Prohibition drew federal officials into more aggressive narcotics enforcement of all kinds, often encouraged by the same reformers behind the Eighteenth Amendment. The nation's nascent antinarcotics regime was in important ways the stepchild of alcohol Prohibition. It drew upon the dry campaign's assumptions, logic, infrastructure, and some of its principal actors. There were, however, important differences. Without a tightly organized grassroots movement, the antinarcotics movement was chiefly backed by state agents, moral entrepreneurs, and a small number of influential and well-heeled private contributors such as pharmaceutical companies.

What it lacked in the intense grassroots mobilization for alcohol Prohibition, it gained in the widespread assumption that suppression of recreational drug use constituted a positive public good. Recreational narcotic use was far less popular, identified more centrally as a threat to youth, and its usage was more closely associated than alcohol with marginal, "deviant" groups. As a result, drug prohibition proved less controversial and far outlasted the alcohol Prohibition regime, remaining one of the most significant legacies of the era.

Narcotics prohibition also depended, in a way the war on liquor had

not, on international agreements for the suppression of global drug trafficking. The Prohibition Unit's Division of Foreign Control had successfully negotiated some international agreements to suppress liquor
smuggling, but the nation's nascent antinarcotics regime involved even
more centrally a two-pronged strategy of international as well as
domestic drug control. While supporters of the 1914 Harrison Narcotics Act had hoped from the beginning to utilize the law as a mechanism
to prohibit narcotics use and traffic, the measure passed in the guise of
a revenue act, merely requiring anyone dispensing cocaine, opium, and
morphine to register, pay a tax, and display a stamp. It did not specifically criminalize nonmedical users of narcotics. Until 1919, the courts
refused to go along with federal efforts to use the law to prosecute drug
users, interpreting such criminalization as beyond the original intent of
Congress. After the ratification of the Eighteenth Amendment in January 1919, however, courts increasingly sided with the prohibitionist
goals of narcotics officials. In *Webb et al. v. U.S.* in 1919, for example,
the Supreme Court forbade nonmedical addiction maintenance, a once
common practice. Men and women addicted to drugs—previously
thought of as morally weak and more pathetic than dangerous—were
increasingly classed as criminals.[40]

   The logic of alcohol Prohibition, an effort to eradicate the traffic
and use of one mind-altering, physically damaging recreational sub-
stance, hardened public opinion toward substances widely judged to be
more addictive and harmful than liquor. The passage of the Eighteenth
Amendment also sparked new fears that the nation's tipplers might turn
to even more dangerous narcotics. Opponents of the war on alcohol
had made that very argument, but once alcohol prohibition became
law, that worry led inevitably to a parallel crackdown on narcotic drug
use. New York's special deputy police commissioner in 1920 declared
that drugs, not alcohol, were at the heart of the "crime wave," Prohibition having "driven criminals from whisky to narcotics." The nation's
fledgling drug-enforcement bureaucracy, created after passage of the
Harrison Act, gained significant new power with the coming of alco-

hol Prohibition, doubling the number of narcotics-enforcement allocations between 1919 and 1920. Antinarcotics enforcement now became
a semiautonomous division within the national Prohibition Unit in the
Treasury Department, and piggybacked to prominence on the new
alcohol enforcement infrastructure.[41]

Congress did its part by passing more expansive drug prohibition
legislation, and drug users and traffickers were increasingly put behind
bars. Congress established the Federal Narcotics Control Board via the
Jones-Miller Act in 1922, outlawing the import and export of opium
and other narcotic drugs such as heroin. Heroin had come into circulation to fill a void in the market after the Harrison Act and Jones Miller
Act dried up domestic sources of cocaine and opium. Ironically, heroin
trafficking increased in no small part due to the suppression of less
harmful narcotic substances. The commodity won a favored place in
the illicit trade, since it was more potent than opium, with a higher
value per weight, and legal manufacture in other countries made supplies plentiful. It also lacked the strong odor of opium and therefore was
less likely to be detected by enforcement agents. The shift of the new
illicit traffic toward more potent, dangerous, and thus profitable substances paralleled the illegal liquor market's turn from beer to harder,
more potent liquors that were easier to transport.[42]

Chief among the professional crusaders who had championed liquor
Prohibition and now fought a wider "world war" against the narcotics
evil was Richmond Hobson. This "father of Prohibition," once the
highest-paid lecturer of the Anti-Saloon League, emerged quickly as
the leader of the new antidrug moral entrepreneurs. In 1920, Hobson
produced a twenty-five-page "textbook" for school distribution on the
perils of narcotic drugs. In 1923 he founded the International Narcotics
Education Association (INEA), a nonprofit organization that sought to
educate the "human race in the truth about alcohol, opium, morphine,
heroin, cocaine and to eradicate their traffic and use." Hobson's antidrug organization sponsored a large conference bankrolled by Congress in 1926. Foreign and domestic experts, representatives of the

American Chemical Society, the American Legion, the American Academy of Political and Social Science, and large numbers of physicians came together to discuss the drug problem. Hobson's address characteristically exaggerated its scope. He claimed that over one million Americans were addicted to drugs: federal narcotic officials put the number of addicts at around 130,000.[43]

Well versed in the alarmism he had deployed to galvanize support for the Eighteenth Amendment and the Volstead Act, Hobson refurbished and redeployed the same tropes to a new end: "The race must either find a remedy, must know the truth, and break the shackles, or take the road toward extinction." Paralleling earlier prohibitionist claims that alcohol use was responsible for crime and poverty, he declared that "most of the daylight robberies, daring hold ups, cruel murders, and similar crimes of violence are known to be committed chiefly by drug addicts, who constitute the primary cause of our alarming crime wave." Over the course of the 1920s, the frenetic energy Hobson earlier devoted to the antiliquor crusade now flowed into the antidrug campaign. He did not abandon support for the liquor crusade. His continued high regard in prohibitionist circles led the Prohibition Party to seek his nomination for president in 1936. But as alcohol Prohibition lost its luster, eradication of the drug problem became Hobson's new mission, just as it did for other antiliquor crusaders. The WCTU actively supported the new "war against narcotic drugs," especially in the 1930s once the war against liquor had been lost.[44]

For all of his manic energy and alarmism, Hobson was no Don Quixote. He was one of a dedicated group of antidrug moral-policy entrepreneurs who worked with U.S. state builders to forge an international drug prohibition regime. His work was preceded by missionary Charles Brent's efforts to win opium prohibition in the new U.S. Pacific territories; and medical-doctor-turned-diplomat Hamilton Wright, who helped win antiopium agreements at The Hague prior to World War I. Hobson's efforts now secured the backing of influential citizens and intersected with a wider congressional campaign. Josiah Lilly, head of the Eli Lilly Company, was a staunch supporter of the International Narcotics Education Association and made regular financial contributions. Irénée du Pont and Alfred I. du Pont abandoned their qualms about the expansion of federal power to become respectively a contributing member of Hobson's World Narcotic Defense Association and a founding member. Herbert Hoover strongly backed the effort to "destroy [narcotics'] fearful menace."[45]

Despite friction between the different arms of the antinarcotics effort, high-ranking government officials worked with Hobson to win international agreements and domestic legislation. After Hoover left office, Hobson won the support of Franklin D. Roosevelt's attorney general, Homer Cummings, for his antidrug crusade. Hobson drafted Cummings's speech on the drug "menace" for a series of radio broadcasts in 1935. The speech was infused with characteristic alarms blaming the "narcotics evil" for "most of our crime." WCTU president Ida Wise was also a featured speaker. The antidrug crusade enlisted influential new allies, such as the nation's fledgling pharmaceutical companies, but drew upon a well of support from antiliquor crusaders and their still-active organizations.[46]

For Hobson and his fellow crusaders, shutting down international sources of supply was the keystone for eradicating illicit drug trafficking. In 1927, Hobson founded the World Narcotic Defense Association to work for suppression of the global drug trade. With headquarters in New York, it built an international branch to sway foreign diplomats and international reformers to take up the cause. In the 1920s, the League of Nations was a hotbed of international negotiations on drug trafficking. While the United States was not a league member, its leadership in international antidrug efforts won it an unofficial seat at the table for league drug conferences. Herbert Hoover sent an American delegation to the league's conferences in 1931, led by the chief of the newly established Bureau of Narcotics, Harry Anslinger. Despite their unofficial status, the United States delegation exerted strong influence in the talks. For their part, league officials hoped cooperation over the drug question would bind the United States closer to the fledgling organization.[47]

Hobson now established an organization, Le Centre de l'Association Internationale de Défense Contre les Stupéfeciants, in Geneva to bolster U.S. efforts with the league. A direct offshoot of the World Narcotic Defense Association, the organization brought in international representatives to lobby for the controls and curbs sought by the American delegation. It won its goals with the league's agreement to form a central control board with authority to limit the crops and the number of refineries in each nation. By 1934, forty-one nations had signed on to the Geneva limitations. The basic edifice of a remarkably resilient global drug control regime was set in place between 1931 and 1934, led by the United States. It has provided the principal pillars of international drug-Prohibition agreements ever since. Franklin Roosevelt telegraphed Hobson words of congratulation. International agreements in turn put pressure on the United States to pass stricter domestic legislation for compliance. After the Senate ratified the Geneva treaty in 1932, Narcotics chief Harry Anslinger, Hobson, Attorney General Cummings, and Roosevelt argued in favor of the adoption of the Uniform State Drug Control Law, not least to bolster the credibility of the United States "in its efforts to . . . further combat this evil abroad."[48]

During the alcohol Prohibition war, the antinarcotics infrastructure won new authority and independent stature as well. Herbert Hoover established the Federal Narcotics Bureau in 1930. This newly muscular agency was independent of the fast-sinking Prohibition Bureau, whose narcotics division had been rocked by scandal. The son and son-in-law of division chief Levi Nutt, it was uncovered, had been on the payroll of recently murdered crime kingpin Arnold Rothstein, serving as his lawyers in a tax evasion case brought by the Treasury Department. The more muscular—and now scandal-free—Narcotics Bureau quickly established to the American public and also the wider world the nation's commitment to crack down on the illicit traffic in drugs at home and globally. Congress generously appropriated $1.7 million (about $23 million in inflation-adjusted dollars) for its first year of operation, a hefty commitment at a time of worldwide depression.[49]

Hoover named Harry Anslinger, the well-known former assistant commissioner of the Prohibition Bureau, to lead the new Narcotics Bureau. A stalwart supporter of the antiliquor crusade, Anslinger brought its moral fervor and Manichaean outlook to his new mission. Versed in global affairs, he had worked in the State Department lobbying foreign governments to stem the profitable liquor-smuggling traffic, especially through the Bahamas, on British ships. Anslinger not only won cooperation from a reluctant Britain, he reached similar agreements with Canada, France, and Cuba. His remarkable successes in liquor diplomacy during the 1920s earned him the position of Chief of Foreign Control in the Prohibition Bureau, where he emphasized the imperative of strict enforcement to root out violations.[50]

For effective Volstead enforcement, Anslinger called for the criminalization of purchase, proposing fines of no less than $1,000 and six months in jail for a first purchase and no less than two years in prison for second-time liquor purchasers. His appeal for draconian liquor-law penalties made little headway, but at the helm of the new Federal Bureau of Narcotics Anslinger applied this same harsh treatment to drug violators more successfully, urging judges to "jail offenders, then throw away the keys." He lobbied hard for the Uniform State Narcotic Drug Law, developed under his guidance and adopted by the National Conference of Commissioners on Uniform Laws in 1932. After its adoption, he pressed states to adopt the uniform antidrug law in order to outlaw new classes of drugs, standardize drug prohibition legislation across the states, and coordinate enforcement between the federal government and the states. Roosevelt threw his support behind the uniform act in 1935.[51]

The Uniform State Narcotic Drug Law illustrates how the alcohol and drug prohibition movements had converged in driving figures such as Richmond Hobson and Harry Anslinger. By the time of Hoover's presidency, it was clear to astute observers that the "noble experiment" had failed and that the ban on liquor would be lifted. True believers like Anslinger and Hobson learned from the errors of the war on alcohol, carrying these lessons to the first American war on drugs. In marked contrast to the Eighteenth Amendment and the Volstead Act, the Uniform State Drug Law prioritized the role of the states in the drug fight. The Federal Bureau of Narcotics laid out the standards and schedules for narcotics prohibition, but then pressed each state legislature to take action: the "Federal Government alone," declared Roosevelt's Attorney General Cummings, "cannot reach this menace, uniform legislation is vitally necessary." By 1939, all but nine states had adopted uniform antinarcotics legislation backed by the Federal Bureau of Narcotics, and more were on the way.[52]

The alcohol-prohibitionist-turned-antinarcotics leader, Harry Anslinger, also sought to heighten public awareness of a new menace. Some states in the southwest, beginning with California in 1913, had passed antimarijuana laws in the 1920s. Outside the southwest, where it was associated by policy officials with Mexican Americans, marijuana was of little public concern. It was not in wide use nor understood as habit-forming or dangerous like cocaine or heroin. Anslinger initially dismissed it as a minor threat. Under pressure from public officials in the southwest, Anslinger eventually came to support legislation to criminalize the drug. Not coincidentally, the antimarijuana drive coincided with heightened hostility toward Mexican Americans during the unemployment crisis of the Great Depression and a massive effort under Herbert Hoover to deport "foreign" Mexican ethnics to relieve unemployment, resulting in over five hundred thousand deportations through pressure, scare tactics, and federally sponsored police raids.[53]

Anslinger adopted some of the same tropes of the earlier antiliquor and drug crusaders: "A significant majority of rape, assault, and murder cases," he claimed, "were directly associated with the use of marijuana." Ignoring the counterarguments of critics, he seconded one congressman's declaration that marijuana "was about as hellish as heroin." This linkage, based on scant scientific evidence, nonetheless led the federal government to group marijuana with heroin and cocaine in its schedule of illicit substances. Anslinger won passage of the Marijuana Tax Act of 1937, which imposed a prohibitive tax on importers, sellers, dealers, and anyone else handling the drug. In the wake of the legislation, many states followed the federal government's lead and legislated fines for marijuana violators identical to those for heroin users.[54]

During the Cold War, United States concern over drug trafficking ebbed and flowed. Anslinger's bureau played a bit part in the wider United States effort to exert power as the leader of world capitalism. The nation's antinarcotics chief allied the bureau's efforts to control drug trafficking with covert operations to stop groups deemed a threat to United States interests. His agency could be found involved wherever the United States encountered the threat of Communism. Federal Narcotics Bureau allocations declined sharply through the 1930s as the Depression ground on, and prosecution of drug violators declined during the nation's postwar boom as well. But Prohibition had forged the bureaucratic structures, assumptions, and logics that paved a firm foundation for the second and vastly more ambitious drug-prohibition effort launched in the 1970s.[55]

* * *

THE repeal of Prohibition did not signal an end to the expansion of the federal government's role in crime control that began in 1919. The increase in state power continued and the changes were permanent. With the coming of the New Deal, with an administration even less ambivalent about the expansion of federal power, it expanded further. Nine major crime bills sailed through Congress in 1934. Attorney General Cummings announced, "We are now engaged in a war that threatens the safety of our country . . . a war with the organized forces of crime." Roosevelt's New Deal war on crime grew out of the nation's Prohibition wars. Similar to other early New Deal legislation, these measures drew upon Hoover's efforts and expanded them in new directions, increasing federal authority further. Roosevelt's omnibus crime control package broadened federal government jurisdiction over crime. It expanded the jurisdiction of the Bureau of Investigation, now renamed the Federal Bureau of Investigation, granting it new authority over kidnappings, bank robberies, and extortion, and it empowered federal agents to make arrests and carry weapons. It also pioneered the first federal gun-control legislation because of the grave concerns over rampant gun violence. Jane Addams spoke out in 1929 in favor of "disarmament" of Prohibition: "If this necessitates Federal control of the sale of firearms so much the better." Such legislation was forthcoming with the National Firearms Act of 1934. The original bill's call for prohibitive taxes on all private ownership, and the creation of a national gun registry was scaled back as a result of National Rifle Association opposition. But the NRA did not oppose all legislation. It supported a prohibitive transfer tax, and thus virtual ban, on sawed-off shotguns, machine guns, and silencers, and restrictions on imports.[56]

The reputation of federal officers had been badly tarnished by the corruption and dismal performance of the Prohibition era. The Roosevelt administration sought to repair the damage, launching a media campaign to remake the image of the federal enforcement arm, and to counter a popular romance with criminals. Crime figures such as Al Capone and John Dillinger had built populist, and seemingly popular, reputations in the interwar years. Capone opened a large soup kitchen in Cicero to feed the growing army of the unemployed, and gained wide media attention with it. Dillinger sought to manufacture an image as a modern-day Robin Hood. He only robbed banks, he said, and these institutions had deeply damaged reputations in the 1930s. At the suggestion of conservative Fulton Oursler, future editor of Reader's Digest, Attorney General Cummings launched a campaign to "publicize and make the G-men heroes." The campaign was headed by a Washington-based newspaper correspondent charged with embellishing the FBI's image through media stunts. This campaign widely publicized the violence and exploits of criminal bands and above all their pursuit and capture by federal agents. The favorable publicity legitimized anticrime legislation and erased the public association of federal agents with criminality and the abuse of rights that had flourished during national Prohibition.[57]

The years of alcohol Prohibition from 1919 to 1933 left a powerful imprint on the federal state, tilting it toward policing, surveillance, and punishment. Historians, political scientists, and other scholars have long noted the peculiar evolution of the modern American state, especially compared to modern western European states. The United States government is heavy on coercion, light on welfare. The American national state is both unique and contradictory—at once weak but interventionist, underdeveloped yet coercive. Not surprisingly, those paradoxical strains contributed to the oft-remarked love-hate relationship so many Americans have with their national government—at once proudly patriotic and fearful of Washington. These characteristics owe as much to the 1920s, a decade shrouded in "normalcy," as to the explicitly and better-known state-building Progressive and New Deal eras.

During the war on alcohol, the adolescent federal state bulked up its coercive and surveillance powers—not only through the creation of the Prohibition Bureau, but also through the expansion of the federal prison system, the Border Patrol, the Federal Bureau of Investigation, and the federal narcotics regime infrastructure. Along with these steps toward enforcement and punishment came the application of social-science expertise to understand crime at the state and national levels and the first systematic attempts to gather national crime and prison statistics, among other initiatives. The growth of the federal state in pursuit of Prohibition enforcement is, in other words, a classic case of the aggregation of knowledge and power—the attempt to understand human behavior in order to control it. Prohibition constituted the formative years of the federal penal state and shaped the assumptions and logic still driving this nation's domestic and global war on drugs.

. . . :

AT the same time, Hoover's press for federal criminal knowledge and the study of the criminal justice system provided space for an extraordinary moment of state self-evaluation. Hoover's admiration for social-science expertise opened a door, much to his later irritation, for a far-reaching survey, the National Commission on Law Observance and Enforcement—and an indictment—of the making of the coercive state underway. Some of the commission's most damning and incisive findings were swept under the rug or remained tantalizing paths not taken in penal reform, but some others did contribute to modernizing, systematizing, and retooling criminal justice.

The National Commission on Law Observance and Enforcement opened up an opportunity to examine the surveillance state in the making. It was, according to some influential legal scholars who worked with the commission, a historic opportunity. Through it they hoped to reframe the nation's attitudes toward crime and criminal justice. George Wickersham, the commission's director, according to Felix Frankfurter, saw his leadership of the commission as "the most important work of his life." Louis Brandeis and staff researcher Mary Van Kleek viewed the commission's work as "epochal." Felix Frankfurter declared the commission's work "tremendously important." While Frankfurter had extremely low regard for Hoover's knowledge of crime and criminal justice, and was not an official commission member, he saw the commission as a great opportunity to shift the "mental climate of America on crime and criminal justice." He compared its work with the great reform studies of the English Royal Commission during the nineteenth century.[58]

Frankfurter was instrumental to the commission's work. Roscoe Pound, the commission's heavyweight, was on vacation when work got under way and, according to George Wickersham, was in a state of exhaustion. Wickersham turned to Frankfurter for advice. Frankfurter traveled to Wickersham's Long Island home and then on to Washington for the commission's first meeting, hammering out the blueprint for its work and advising on the best researchers for the job. It was of the utmost importance, Frankfurter told two close friends on the commission, to secure the commission's emancipation from the "tyranny," and the "tutelage, and direction of the President." He drove home the importance of "independent and imaginative thinking—the power of cutting below the surface and illuminating hitherto dark places." A research staff with "creative faculties for investigation and rather capacious powers of interpretation" must be brought on board, he said.[59]

The emancipation Frankfurter hoped for would prove difficult for the Prohibition reports—a deeply irritated Hoover sought revisions to what he judged the overwhelmingly wet findings of the commission. But its funding and broad charge allowed wide leeway for research into other areas: crime causation, statistics, police, prosecution, courts, penal institutions, probation and parole, juvenile delinquency, criminal justice and the foreign born, lawlessness by government law-enforcing officers, and the cost of crime. The commission ignored Hoover's original call for attention to the growth of organized crime, and only one subcommittee was devoted to the Eighteenth Amendment. In the end, the commission's separate reports also covered several arenas not originally identified, such as police brutality and enforcement of the deportation laws, with their conclusions deeply at odds with the commission's creator. Indeed, they shared more with the social justice ethos that would find a place in Washington during the New Deal.[60]

The sharp tone of the commission's report on crime causation revealed that this was no ordinary government report. "There was," it announced, "something fundamentally wrong in the very heart of . . . government and social policy in America." The commission's reports unpacked the injustices of the coercive nation-state: overzealous agents, corruption, and "lawlessness" from the Prohibition Bureau to the Immigration and Naturalization Service. It denounced the repercussions for the Mexican American population of the deportation laws characterized by methods it deemed frequently "unconstitutional, tyrannic and oppressive." The large *Report on Lawlessness in Law Enforcement* took on abuses of state policing power at all levels. Government officials, it announced, "should always remember that there is no more sinister sophism than that the end justifies the employment of illegal means to bring offenders to justice." The report shed light on the widespread illegal police tactic known in the early twentieth century as the "third degree"—a shorthand term for the use of physical force and psychological brutality to extract confessions and information from suspects. It detailed methods that included "beatings to harsher forms of torture" such as floggings with rubber hoses, sleep and food deprivation, the "water cure," threats with weapons, whippings, the threat of mobs, and other "threats of bodily injury or death." These "species of torture," it said, were "well known to the bench and bar of the country." It condemned their use and called such police practice "shocking in its character and extent."[61]

The report on *Penal Institutions, Probation and Parole,* released in June 1931, was similarly harsh. It condemned the "present prison system" as "antiquated and inefficient. It does not reform the criminal. It fails to protect society. There is reason to believe that it contributes to the increase of crime by hardening the prisoner." Staff researchers visited European correctional institutions, part of a much wider transatlantic exchange of reform ideas, and concluded that "a new type of penal institution must be developed, one that is new in spirit, in method and in objective." The authors called for legislative reform of the prison labor system, including the payment of wages to the prisoner for his labor, "not merely as an incentive to good work, but as a means of maintaining his dependents and promoting his self-respect."[62]

Sanford Bates, the eminent penologist appointed by Hoover as the superintendent of the new Federal Bureau of Prisons, drew on the Wickersham Commission's harsh findings to win support for his effort to reform prisons. Citing the commission's findings in an article entitled "Have Our Prisons Failed Us?" he answered with an indubitable "yes." "Punishment, gloomy dark prisons of ages past," argued Bates, did not resolve crime. Bates's goal was to turn "criminals into "good citizens" by instituting new carceral methods. His plans for prison reform to build "the prison of the future" came to fruition under the New Deal. His new federal practices of prisoner classification, systematization of carceral procedures, record keeping, and discipline were replicated in several state prison systems. Prisons, however, never achieved the "model" ideals their advocates hoped for—extremely harsh conditions, corporal punishment, isolation, and draconian discipline remained the norm, especially on the state and local level. Bates's "enlightened" ideals of reforming the nation's "failed" prisons into institutions devoted to turning "criminals" into "good citizens" failed as well, dying on the shoals of the more fundamental mission of prisons as instruments of social control.[63]

Other reports did not contribute so directly to shaping public policy, but their findings dismantled some of the central assumptions of the Hoover administration that so closely linked "aliens with criminality." The exhaustive report *Crime and the Foreign Born*, led by Edith Abbott, dean of the School of Social Service Administration of the University of Chicago, exploded the widespread stereotypes of foreigners as criminals, declaring in no uncertain terms that such associations had no basis in fact. The foreign-born, the extensive and well-documented report found, were underrepresented in the ranks of those charged with crimes. The findings undermined the nativist discourses so prevalent during the alcohol-prohibition war and contributed to widening currents of liberal pluralism.[64]

Other studies, such as the *Report on the Cost of Crime*, criticized the use of criminal law to reform moral behavior. The study enumerated numerous ways to reduce crime costs, including "limiting the extent to which social control by means of criminal law is attempted." With obvious reference to alcohol prohibition, the authors concluded, "[W]e think that the cost of enforcing the criminal law would be less if it did not attempt to forbid and punish acts participated in by large number of otherwise law-abiding citizens who do not regard such prohibited acts as 'criminal' except in a technical sense." The commission's *Report on the Enforcement of the Prohibition Laws of the United States* was not quite as bold, but as commission member Monte Lemann later wrote, "not-withstanding a concession or reservation here and there," it was "pre-dominantly wet in tone." Hoover's "face fell" when he was presented with the findings, remembered one commission member. Privately, Hoover declared the report "rotten." He handed it to Congress with a brief comment, registering his disagreement with the proposed revi-sion of the Eighteenth Amendment should "further trial fail," and declared it, instead, his duty "to enforce the law with all the means at our disposal without equivocation or reservation." While Hoover damned the Prohibition report with faint praise, he simply abandoned the other reports. They were released for publication in 1931 with no comment from the embattled chief executive, despite conclusions at odds with his administration's policies and findings powerfully critiqu-ing official practices of the nation.[65]

The most disruptive commission findings dealt with crime causa-tion. While one inquiry focused on psychological factors contributing to crime, echoing earlier discourses that subordinated the environment to "mental deficiencies," the other inquiries linked crime to structural problems and pointed the way toward social solutions to remedy it. Researcher Mary Van Kleek's studies on the relationship of work to crime among prisoners in Sing Sing found unemployment to be an important causative factor in "crimes against property." Another study on employment statistics and crime in Massachusetts forcefully averred that "the conclusion seems inescapable that the assurance of economic security might be expected to bring with it an appreciable reduction in the volume of crime." Similarly, an examination of crime in New York State led Van Kleek to emphasize that the first step toward better "law observance and enforcement," is "*security of employment.*" These findings foreshadowed the public-policy solutions America would embrace dur-ing the New Deal through social provisioning and job creation.[66]

One section of the report on crime causation—an inquiry on the "special problem of the Negro as related to work and to crime" by Ira D. Reid—was particularly damning. Pointing to the disproportionate numbers of African-Americans prosecuted for crime and incarcerated relative to their numbers in the population overall, the inquiry focused on a wide set of causative factors. It pointed out that as a "disadvantaged group he shares with the poor of all races any handicap imposed upon the poor by the administration of justice." But additionally, he faced the "possibility of race prejudice in all the steps of enforcement of law and punishment by the courts." To remedy the possibility of discrimination in law enforcement, the report called for "the employment of negro police" and "the use of negro jurymen" so that African-Americans could be tried by juries of their peers. Its findings pointed to the problem of extremely low wages, economic insecurity, and high unemployment among African-Americans. Looking at black prisoners in Sing Sing, it found that "unemployment, with all that it implies of insecurity in standards of living is the environment of the majority" and concluded that "being out of work is undoubtedly a very direct and common cause for crime."[67]

But the inquiry also turned the usual discussion about crime on its head, shifting the angle of vision away from common definitions of crime to identify, instead, another long list of crimes: "conscious and unconscious crimes against the negro." This record included the prevalence of peonage systems; the "use of Negro prisoners on chain gangs;" race riots; the "denial of citizenship; . . . restricted residential areas, denial of the right to work, denial of the right to vote, as well as inferior social and educational facilities." Of all the crimes committed "with impunity," the inquiry found the terror of lynching the most egregious, with "3,533 negro lives . . . lost." Legislation, it argued, was necessary to combat the scourge.[68]

Much of the work of the Wickersham Commission, as Ira De A. Reid's discussion of African-Americans' work and "law observance" most pointedly revealed, evinced the courageous frankness and capacious thinking Felix Frankfurter had called for. Newspapers like the *New York Times* publicized the findings of the commission with banner headlines such as "Wickersham Commission lays crime rise to unemployment," "U.S. oppresses aliens," "Deporting Methods Called Tyrannic," and "Wickersham Commission Hits Third Degree and Brutal Police." Such hard-hitting findings from a government body put the Hoover administration on the defensive. The reports reveal a groundswell of social criticism that contributed to the liberal turn of the New Deal.[69]

Still, Felix Frankfurter's high hopes that the commission might serve to change the "mental climate" in regard to crime and criminal justice were dashed. While the reports heralded new ideas for social reform, some of which would blossom during the New Deal, the wider findings received nowhere near the attention given to the Prohibition report, and the "war on crime" continued apace. One *New York Times* editorial remarked that while Prohibition's "position in the wide scope of the commission is subordinate and subsidiary, to the majority of the people it is first and most momentous." Another editorial echoed those sentiments, "To the public, however, illogically, logically or unreasonably, this subject . . . is of keener and more passionate interest than any other within the scope of the commission's purpose." The commission's Prohibition findings delivered a devastating blow to the "noble experiment" in which the state was overextended and at odds with majority behavior and mores. Other revelations about the brutal practices and "lawlessness" of government authorities from immigration officials to local police, as well as the crimes against African-Americans, bounced harmlessly off a thick armor of indifference among political commentators preoccupied with the burr of Prohibition and the economic crisis.[70]

The U.S. war on alcohol built the foundations of the twentieth-century federal penal state. At the same time, the widened scope of federal power and the state administrative apparatus over a fourteen-year period oriented Americans ever more toward the nation-state for the resolution of social problems, while inspiring paradoxical disquiet over that very expansion of the government's sphere of action. The Eighteenth Amendment and the Volstead Act helped pave the way for the burst of policy innovation during the New Deal. The intense attention to the social behavior of criminality during Prohibition's war on alcohol also opened up space at the national level for fresh, penetrating critiques of the coercive state and crime control. The Wickersham Commission reports sounded alarm bells about the relationship of structural inequality and unemployment to crime, and their pleas for "limiting the extent to which social control by means of criminal law is attempted" ring as urgently today as they did almost a century ago.[71]

8

REPEAL

ON JUNE 19, 1932, AT THE HEIGHT OF GLOBAL ECONOMIC catastrophe, the *Richmond Times-Dispatch* published a cartoon: "What Will History Say About Us?" A wizened "old man history" held over a warring globe a heavy book, *The Postwar Generation*. The men on the globe's surface raised clouds of dust, their fists and legs flailing, battling one another. But it was not the spectacular bank failures, the unemployment crisis, the breadlines, or the rise of fascism in Europe over which they fought: "In spite of all the momentous problems of our day crying for solution . . . the one question we talk about, argue about, rave about, think about, and dream about is PROHIBITION!" The cartoon was timely, printed on the eve of the Democratic National Convention in Chicago, where debate over the Eighteenth Amendment occupied center stage. Despite attempts by some Democrats to turn attention away from liquor with the slogan "Bread Not Booze," calls for bold economic reform were subordinated to the Prohibition controversy. When Nebraska senator Gilbert M. Hitchcock read the platform plank pledging the party to repeal, the convention hall exploded with nearly a half hour of cheering, parading, and applause.[1]

Despite three years of economic turmoil and widening immiseriza-tion, Prohibition continued to preoccupy public debate from the end of the 1920s well into the first years of the Great Depression. From the vaunted chambers of the Supreme Court to the ethnic fraternal halls of ordinary workingmen, Prohibition provoked passion. As Chief Justice Taft wrote to his son, "[I]t would seem as if more feeling could be engendered over the Prohibition Act than almost any other subject that we have in the Court." One traveling salesman from Erie, Pennsylva-nia, confessed to using the controversy to break the ice with prospec-tive clients and "immediately gain[ed]" their "undivided attention." Public opinion, he averred, "is more interested in Prohibition than in any or in all public questions of today. . . . Prohibition is a national word—known in every hamlet and city in this country and affecting— as nothing else does—every individual in this country every day they live." Leaders as diverse as Wickersham Commission member Judge Kenneth Mackintosh, Nicholas Murray Butler, the president of Colum-bia University, and Louise Gross, charter member of New York's Molly Pitcher Club and later the head of another anti-Prohibition organiza-tion, echoed Mackintosh's description of Prohibition as "one of the most outstanding economic and social problems since the question of slavery."[2]

Such grossly overblown rhetoric comparing the war on alcohol with the conflict over slavery points to the heat of this debate among contemporaries by the turn of the decade. Despite the oceanic popular bitterness charted in earlier chapters, elite public sentiment in the law's first years had stood firmly on the side of ensuring its success. Even influential opponents of the amendment prior to its ratification, such as Chief Justice Taft, backed it once it became law. Liberal academics too, such as Harvard professor Felix Frankfurter, free of constitutional duties to uphold the law of the land, opined the experiment "ought to be given a fair trial." Louise Gross remembered that those few women

REPEAL   233

in its early years "who had the courage to oppose Prohibition in public were branded almost as anarchist." Tellingly, until 1928, even the well-heeled Association Against the Prohibition Amendment remained largely a paper organization. With the amendment ensconced in the Constitution, opponents as well as supporters had good reason to believe that repeal would be all but impossible. No amendment had, after all, ever been rescinded. Many opponents worked, instead, to amend the Volstead Act. Such widespread sentiments led New York dry supporter George K. Statham to declare confidently in October 1928 that "the repeal of the Eighteenth Amendment "is about as likely as the repeal of the Thirteenth Amendment, the return of dueling, or gladiatorial combats. . . . The world moves, and it has never as yet taken a great moral or social step forward and afterwards retraced its step." Five years later, the Twenty-First Amendment broke the Eighteenth Amendment's record speed for ratification, bringing the war on alcohol to an end.[3]

A combination of forces powered the sharp reversal. Widespread disrespect for law, controversial actions of the Volstead vigilante enforcers, ever more draconian enforcement legislation, and the siren song of nightlife cultural experimentation led former supporters to conclude that the law was doing more harm than good. The growing wet bloc within the Democratic Party, in addition, pressed the issue into national politics, providing repeal with a new institutional ally. The economic crisis of the Great Depression tipped the scales already trending in favor of the wets.

Despite his defeat, Al Smith's presidential campaign did perhaps most to disrupt elite consensus over the Eighteenth Amendment. New York's Louise Gross remarked that Smith's "fearless discussion roused the entire nation." Governor Smith, she observed, "put the match to the dynamite and bl[e]w up the works so to speak. . . . Those earlier tongue-tied on the subject . . . will talk or write about . . . its crime, political graft, hypocrisy and scandal. . . ." Smith's election run broke "the dam of discussion" within the political parties as well. Prohibition allowed Smith to channel for the first time the concerns of a rising bloc of immigrant ethnic voters, and in so doing cemented their allegiance to the national Democratic Party. While unable to carry Smith to Washington, four years later this bloc led the fight over Prohibition and eventually became the bulwark for FDR's emerging New Deal economic policies.[4]

Smith's triumphant opponent, Herbert Hoover, only fanned the flames of opposition when he moved with characteristic efficiency to bolster enforcement and rein in rampant lawlessness. Not surprisingly, draconian new fines and penalties provoked even more opposition. The Wickersham Commission's Roscoe Pound gloated in 1930 that the drys "were running things with such a high hand" that "a good deal of climbing on the wet band wagon" would surely follow. Indeed, the passage of the 1929 Jones Act brought public disavowals from former Prohibition proponents. William Randolph Hearst, who had once declared the amendment "heaven sent," now blasted the Volstead Act for hindering temperance, contributing to rising crime, and over-crowding prisons. The Jones Act, he proclaimed, is "the most menac-ing piece of repressive legislation that has stained the statute books of this republic since the Alien and Sedition laws." Hearst subjected the Volstead Act to a barrage of negative reporting and held a prize contest for the best proposal on alternatives to the law. The Hearst offices were deluged with 71,248 proposals for alternative forms of liquor control, a collection at one estimate equivalent to a library of twenty thousand volumes each containing fifty thousand words. By 1929, popular resent-ment toward the "Volstead Army" had spread beyond the immigrant ethnic working class and their allies to the largely Protestant middle classes as well. At a movie showing in Erie, Pennsylvania, for example, the largely upscale audience burst into applause at a news clip of Senator David Walsh lambasting federal agents for killing three rum smugglers off the coast of Massachusetts.[5]

Even Hoover's own hand-picked Wickersham Commission, set up to evaluate the Prohibition effort and the criminal justice system,

fanned the flames of opposition. Roscoe Pound drafted the body of the
Prohibition report, buttressed by thousands of pages of records on the
conditions in each individual state. The report laid out the multiple
"bad features of the present situation," the law's "invitation to hypocrisy," "corruption," "strain on courts . . . and penal institutions." The
law, in short, was unenforceable. Influenced by Hoover's pressure, the
report's recommendations straddled the line. Two commissioners called
for immediate revision; others recommended a finite "period of further
trial," and revision only should such trial fail. The press sharply criticized such dual thinking and the impenetrable wet-damp-dry recommendations. Prohibition's opponents denounced the report for failing
to provide a reasonable unified solution to the widely acknowledged
crisis and, to Hoover's great lament, made effective use of the body of
the report to buttress arguments against the war on alcohol. The Voluntary Committee of Lawyers proclaimed that the report "constitutes
the strongest argument that has yet been made for the repeal of the
Eighteenth Amendment." Senator Robert Wagner triumphantly
announced that the report marked "the beginning of the end." Hoover
privately damned the report and predicted that it "would split the
Republican Party from top to bottom."[6]

Nonetheless, Hoover held fast to Bishop Cannon and the platform
of the Anti-Saloon League. He not only rejected the call of some commissioners for immediate revision, but also rejected the moderate rec-
ommendation for revision if "further trial" should fail. By abandoning
his own commissioners' findings, he cemented the public's perception
of him as dogged, stubborn, and tone-deaf, compounding his spiraling
unpopularity because of the economic crisis. The unlucky coincidence
of a material crisis with a wildly unpopular social law sealed Hoover's
political fate and that of the war on alcohol as well. Into this yawning
gap leapt an invigorated Democratic Party carrying Franklin D. Roosevelt to the White House in the historic landslide that had eluded
Smith.

Just as World War I provided a fertile climate of martial self-sacrifice

for the Eighteenth Amendment's enactment, the sobering exigencies of
the Great Depression transformed that climate sharply in favor of
repeal. By 1932, the United States had entered its third year of economic contraction. Farm prices were severely depressed, over five
thousand banks had failed, and many factories in towns and cities
throughout the country had shut their doors. The country staggered
under massive unemployment—one in four workers was without a job.
In industrial cities such as Chicago, Pittsburgh, and Cincinnati rates of
joblessness were higher; Chicago alone teemed with six hundred thousand men in search of work. Local, state, and charity relief organizations, as a result, could not keep pace with the vastly increased demand,
and municipalities ran out of money. In Chicago, city employees went
without pay for months. Anton Cermak, who had been catapulted to
mayor as an anti-Prohibitionist standard bearer in 1930, pleaded with
the federal government for unemployment relief. Washington, he
warned, "should send $150 million now or prepare to send federal
troops later." With Communists organizing demonstrations of the
unemployed, and the Bonus Expeditionary Force camped out on the
Washington Mall, fears of social unrest mushroomed.[7]

The economic crisis, and the seeming collapse of public and community institutions in its wake, shifted the terrain of debate over the
alcohol war. Organized-labor spokesmen who had long opposed the
Volstead Act now warned that the law was "saddling the government
with a stress that it could not stand without possibly wrecking it."
Under the cloud of mass unemployment, pronouncements that the law
sparked a "decided resentment among millions . . . against an unjust
and unfair law" found a new hearing among civic leaders. Matthew
Woll, vice president of the AFL, declared that workers "were losing
faith in the government's willingness to help them," with the economic
crisis compounding a "bitterness" toward the government already
imbued in them by Prohibition. Even among those opposed to economic reform, there was a recognition of the need to do something to
raise workers' morale and demonstrate government responsiveness to

the crisis. They found an answer in repeal: providing workers "their glass of beer" offered a means of alleviating one grievance rankling the immigrant working-class communities if leaving untouched the deeper roots of the crisis.[8]

Lifting the liquor ban promised not only a "decidedly soothing tendency on the present attitude of the workingmen," but also provided a small step toward ameliorating unemployment without additional government spending. An end to the alcohol war promised new jobs from a revitalized liquor industry and an improved market for farmers' grain. A legal liquor trade would also bring in much needed government revenue through the return of federal liquor taxes. Finally, along with these economic rationales, men like John Raskob hoped that repeal would buttress conservative pieties of "home rule" against the calls of reformers and radicals for increased centralized action to secure against the ravages of unemployment and to regulate business.[9]

The American Association Against the Prohibition Amendment had long warned that the Eighteenth Amendment centralized too much power in Washington and promised to open the door to other forms of regulation. Those fears now appeared prescient. By lining up in favor of repeal, opponents of reform saw a chance to turn back the clock. In this climate, repeal mobilization snowballed. By 1930, the AAPA had been joined by a host of other elite-led groups such as the Women's Organization for National Prohibition Reform, the Women's Committee for the Repeal of the 18th Amendment, the Crusaders, and the Volunteer Committee of Laymen. By the summer of 1932, 2,500,000 wets united in the United Repeal Council with none other than Pierre du Pont as chairman.[10]

. . .

UNDER this dark cloud, the Republican convention opened on June 14, 1932. The Prohibition controversy dominated convention debate thanks largely to powerful new converts to the wet Republican bloc. Foremost among them stood John D. Rockefeller Jr. who, along with his father, was the most prominent financial backer of the Anti-Saloon League. Rockefeller's bombshell recantation stunned liquor crusaders. Repeal, he now declared, was essential to "restore public respect for law" and the "distribution of powers between the states and the nation as originally established by the Constitution." Hoover did his best to mollify these influential Republicans without alienating the large group of Republican antiliquor crusaders, but in the end he satisfied neither. The party adopted a muddled plank—an "unintelligible straddle," blasted one commentator. Satirist H. L Mencken declared the plank's only virtue that it was difficult for "simple folk" to decipher. The lengthy plank, more of a treatise, declared in favor of "enforcement." It announced that "members of the Republican Party hold different opinions with respect to it and no public official or member of the party should be . . . forced to choose between his party affiliations and his honest convictions upon this question." The plank then called for "retain[ing] in the Federal Government the power to preserve the gains made," but also for an amendment to be submitted to state conventions not "limited to retention or repeal . . . for the American people . . . has never gone backward." Mencken felt the wet-dry plank was emblematic of the whole convention. "I have seen many conventions," he reported. "It is both the stupidest and the most dishonest." "So deep was the gloom of the departing Republican delegates over the straddle plank," another conference observer reported, "that most of them with whom I talked were predicting without reservation that the Democrats would win the election on the liquor issue if nothing else." From this moment, repeal was fated to be a purely partisan issue in the looming election.[11]

The Republican Party equivocated over the war on alcohol, but it unwaveringly championed the war on crime Hoover had declared in 1928. It lauded Hoover's "intensive and effective drive" against "public enemies" and pledged unquestioned support for further efforts. It promised as well to "continue the present relentless warfare against illicit narcotics," praising the administration for "greatly strengthening our power to deal with the traffic." These crime-and-narcotics planks following upon Hoover's earlier law-and-order state-building initiatives summarized his commitment to a federal penal and disciplinary state.[12]

The war on crime and drugs would continue during the New Deal, and indeed in many aspects never slackened, but the war on alcohol was nearing its end. Largely because of Hoover's awkward attempt to straddle the issue, the Democratic Party was the chief beneficiary of the widening public hostility toward the alcohol war. Much had changed since Hoover's landslide win four years earlier, and the Democrats were well positioned not least because Hoover had presided over three years of economic crisis. The "name and record of Herbert Hoover," one Republican convention observer remarked, hung around the necks of delegates "like a political mill stone." The party platform defended Hoover's past record, commended the president's "great leadership," and pledged to "break the back of the Depression and restore the economic life of the nation." It called for expanded support for agricultural credits and marketing, and loans for business, banking, and homeowners.[13]

The platform, along with Hoover's wider response to the economic crisis, evinced a willingness to exercise federal power to grapple with the crisis. Hoover favored loans and credit for businessmen and bankers through such innovative agencies as the Reconstruction Finance Corporation, and he backed public spending projects for western development projects, prominent among them the Hoover Dam. These, however, were by no means populist proposals. While the Republican Party platform acknowledged "the "great human suffering" resulting from the emergency, it proclaimed that "the people themselves by their own patient and resolute effort in their adjustment of their own affairs can and will work out the cure." Hoover's federal activism foreshadowed a strand of neoliberalism that would take firm roots in the later twentieth century, a kind of conservatism comfortable with a more expansive state devoted primarily to conservative policy ends. The Republican platform, and Hoover's cold refusal to signal any relief for the millions of jobless while the government spent large sums of money to enforce a much-hated law, gave the Democrats an easy opening to appeal to the "common man" by declaring in favor of "repeal and prosperity" and an end to "extravagant" Republican spending.[14]

Two weeks after the Republican Convention met, the Democrats gathered in Chicago in a far more optimistic mood. Democratic National Committee chairman John Raskob, who called the convention to order, urged delegates to pass a plank pledging all Democratic candidates to repeal. Raskob had placed the party on a firm organizational footing after Smith's 1928 presidential campaign, establishing a permanent headquarters and a new publicity machine. Now he sought to make repeal the party's trump card. In keeping the war on alcohol front and center, Raskob hoped to hold the loyalties of the working-class and immigrant industrial voting base that Smith had drawn to the party in droves, affirm the party's commitment to "home rule," and keep talk of more divisive economic reform policies in the background.[15]

Primary candidates Al Smith, John Nance Garner, Newton D. Baker, Albert C. Ritchie, and Franklin D. Roosevelt faced off. Smith and Ritchie came out strongly for repeal. Roosevelt, on the other hand, feared a repeat of the battles that rocked the party in 1924 and 1928. Pennsylvania's Democratic state chairman Joseph Guffey sought to convince Roosevelt that the "South was veering away from its extremely dry attitude." Guffey was right, but Roosevelt hoped to run a campaign uniting the urban industrial north with the south by focusing on Hoover's handling of the Depression, and, if anything, sidelining Prohibition. In contrast to Smith, much of Roosevelt's delegate strength coming into the convention lay in the south and west. Faced with a passionate wave of repeal sentiment within the rising urban ethnic bloc, however, Roosevelt soon abandoned hopes of eliding the Prohibition controversy.[16]

Anton Cermak, champion of the urban ethnic bloc, came to the convention girded for battle over repeal. In a tumultuous four-hour session, delegates debated the party's position. When one Idaho delegate read the merely damp minority report, the packed galleries of Chicago's ethnic Democratic rank and file booed from the galleries. The war on alcohol colored everything. These urban Democratic supporters wanted relief from the dire economic crisis, but clamored loudly for an end to the war on alcohol. At least one of them wrote to Roosevelt prior to the convention to determine where he stood on the issue. A self-described "ordinary workingman" from Chicago's stockyards district, J. A Huyge let Roosevelt know that he was "hostile, and bitterly so" to the "deplorable conditions" under Prohibition. He, like other voters from heavily working-class ethnic enclaves in the industrial northeast and midwest, voted Republican in 1924, but marked his ballot for Al Smith in 1928. Now he had but one question for Roosevelt: where did he stand on the Eighteenth Amendment? Roosevelt, by now seeing clearly the political traction he would win by coming out firmly in opposition, declared the "present state of affairs . . . absolutely disastrous."[17]

The strength of ethnic rank-and-file passions, the din of their raucous galleries, all coalesced in a tumultuous five-hour floor debate. At its close, none could mistake that the tide had turned in favor of the wets. Despite his wide popularity, Roosevelt saw how equivocation on repeal might undermine his chances to lead the ticket. If delegates pledged to other primary hopefuls combined behind a single "stop-Roosevelt" repeal candidate, FDR's path to the nomination might be derailed. The debate also brought clues that southern and western states were softening in their support for the Prohibition crusade. Alabama, Arkansas, Georgia, Kansas, Mississippi, North Carolina, and Oklahoma favored the minority straddle plank, but other southern and western states, including Texas, Kentucky, and South Carolina, now backed repeal. With the writing on the wall, Roosevelt freed his delegates to vote in favor of the plank. Repeal overwhelmingly won the day with a vote tally of 934 to 213. Every candidate on the Democratic ticket was subsequently pledged to the repeal of the Eighteenth Amendment.[18]

In Boston, antialcohol crusader Elizabeth Tilton tuned into the convention by radio from her home. Contemptuous of the overwhelming repeal sentiment, she lambasted "Democratic half-breeds" and conservative businessmen: "If the capitalists have, as is said, beaten this up for purposes of keeping the mind off economic issues, they have done a good job." Raskob may have hoped to do just that, but the ethnic men and women Tilton pejoratively dismissed supported repeal for their own reasons. The Volstead Act had brought ever more powerful gangs and criminal violence to their neighborhoods, unleashed a scare of quasi-official intimidation by the vigilante Volstead army, and gave even legitimate law enforcement unprecedented access to their homes. By 1931 even the Wickersham Commission acknowledged the "resentment" due to "incidents of enforcement . . . and searches of homes" that "necessarily seemed to bear more upon people of moderate means than upon those of wealth or influence." With a fresh sense of power in a newly urban Democratic Party, emboldened by the severity of the national economic crisis, ethnic rank-and-file party loyalists seized their chance to make the party into a vehicle to redress many of the core concerns of their communities.[19]

By releasing his delegates for repeal, Roosevelt lifted the major objection anti-Prohibitionists had to his nomination and scuttled Al Smith's hopes of a second run. With the repeal plank settled, Roosevelt quickly became the front-runner, winning a majority of delegates in early balloting. Winning the necessary two-thirds required for the nomination, however, proved harder. Several rounds of inconclusive balloting stretched late into the night. During the following day, the Texas delegation released their delegates for Roosevelt when he named John Garner as his vice-presidential choice. In the wake of Texas lining up for Roosevelt, William McAdoo swung California for the New York governor, cinching the needed two-thirds. Roosevelt supporters leapt from their seats, cheering, waving, and roaring their approval. All major candidates now released their delegates for Roosevelt. Smith was the exception, too bitter at having lost the nomination he felt that he deserved. Roosevelt and Garner now headed the Democratic ticket on a repeal plank. Tilton was devastated: "So crumbles the work of 20 years of my life." She shut off her radio, turned off her bedroom light, and buried her woes in sleep: "Dear, Dear Diary, we are beaten."[20]

. . . .

FOR his acceptance speech, Roosevelt crystallized the swirling calls for action and rolling party ethos. Flying to Chicago to address the convention in person, FDR broke with party tradition and demonstrated that he refused to be bound by the past. He declared the Democratic Party the "party of liberal thought and of planned action, of enlightened international outlook and the greatest good to the greatest number." He condemned the Republican Party's concern with the good of the few at the expense of the many. On the alcohol war he declared, "this convention wants repeal. Your candidate wants repeal. And I am confident that the United States of America wants repeal." In summary, he declared boldly a "New Deal for the American people."[21]

After winning the nomination, Roosevelt built an energetic campaign. He wrote to thousands of local party organizers requesting their opinion on the most important concerns in their regions. In industrial sections, even in communities reeling under massive unemployment, local organizers mentioned Prohibition over and again in tandem with bread-and-butter unemployment. In Centralia, Illinois, a local party activist declared, "something must be done and done quickly for permanent relief of unemployment or a revolution is certain." But another group of precinct captains from a Chicago industrial neighborhood called out the rampant "bootlegging," the "tremendous amount of money being spent . . . to enforce this legislation," along with "lack of employment," not to mention Hoover's handling of the veteran's bonus. From Plymouth, Massachusetts, and industrial sections of Pennsylvania as well, Democratic workers trumpeted "unemployment and Prohibition" at the core of their constituents' concerns.[22]

Accordingly, Roosevelt ran as a friend of the "common man" but kept the New Deal policy prescriptions calculatedly vague: As one voter put it to the future president, "[T]he people like your stand on Prohibition and farm relief, but they are asking the question over and over again 'what for reform measures can we expect from him?' " Roosevelt shrewdly alternated between calls for public works to promote jobs and relief and scolding Republican "extravagance" and lack of "economy in government." Soon the motto of "repeal and prosperity" emerged as a banner under which he could appeal to ethnic working-class men and women in the industrial northeast and midwest who were hostile to the alcohol war and suffering from unemployment, without alienating orthodox party elites. One campaign pamphlet, "Why wage earners want Roosevelt and Garner," tellingly fore-grounded repeal to promote recovery and generate jobs. Repeal as one solution to the crisis of unemployment was tailor made to win the loyalty of ethnic urban workers.[23]

Industrial workers, once heavily Republican, had come to the polls for Smith first in 1928 in places from Pittsburgh to Chicago. Pittsburgh's stalwart Democratic organizer David Lawrence had been instrumental in mobilizing local support for Smith in 1928. He now enjoyed close relationships with all of the ethnic neighborhoods. In Polish Hill he saw to it that every one of the sixteen Democratic committee persons was of Polish background. Polish and Croatian fraternal associations and several small labor locals provided campaign workers and distributed literature among their membership. In the working-class Italian neighborhoods of Bloomfield and Liberty, former Smith strongholds, the party cemented its bonds with new constituencies too. An Italian Democratic Committee was forged, with branches in Italian neighborhoods. In those wards, Catholic clergy even campaigned from their pulpits and fraternal organizations became meeting places for spreading what was rapidly becoming a Roosevelt movement.[24]

Emboldened by this grassroots enthusiasm, Lawrence wrote to Roosevelt, urging him to campaign in Pittsburgh. Roosevelt toured a dozen of the city's ethnic communities, bringing thousands out into the streets. On October 19, fifty thousand Pittsburghers jammed Forbes Field to welcome him. Lawrence warmed up the crowds with music from ethnic fraternal organizations. Attuned to his audience, Roosevelt pledged to legalize beer to bring "new revenues of several hundred millions of dollars a year"—and to balance the budget. He chided Hoover's "radical" and unorthodox economic theories and Republican extravagance, but reassured his listeners that protecting citizens from "starvation" and "dire need" was an essential expenditure that would not be spared. With this appeal, the Democratic Party continued on its upswing in the city's heavily ethnic working-class wards. Now, for the first time since 1856, the Democrats carried Pittsburgh, by twenty-seven thousand votes. From then, for the rest of the century, Pittsburgh became hardcore bedrock of the Democratic Party.[25]

In his landslide victory in 1932, Roosevelt consolidated a new Democratic majority, one he solidified in 1936. He won 57.3 percent of the popular vote to Hoover's 39.6 percent, a complete reversal of Hoover's lopsided win against Smith four years earlier. While industrial and ethnic workers only deepened their loyalty to their new party, middle-class Republicans brought to Roosevelt because of discontent with Hoover's handling of the Depression and the war on alcohol, abandoned him and returned to the Republican Party in 1936.[26]

If Elizabeth Tilton had been upset by the Democratic convention's enthusiasm for repeal, the election results cut her to the core. "Let me die a thousand deaths," she scrawled melodramatically in her diary, "civilization is undone." In fact, however, a new civilization was in the making—one more self-consciously pluralist and attentive to the grievances of those Tilton maligned as "half-breeds." A new urban, ethnic Democratic Party coalition was warmed in its infancy by passionate opposition to the nation's war on alcohol. After this more pluralist, urban-oriented Democratic Party felt its potential strength during the doomed Smith campaign, it matured quickly, aided by expert Democratic politicking and Republican missteps—not to mention the Great Depression—into a reliable voting block behind reforms of Roosevelt's New Deal.[27]

Roosevelt made good on the debt he owed to anti-Prohibition sentiment shortly after his inauguration. In his energetic first week in office, he rescued banks and restored confidence in the economic system. After a day of proposing new legislation, he declared, "I think it's time the country did something about beer," sitting down to draft the call to Congress to amend the Volstead Act, pending repeal. When the proposal was read on March 14—one of the first New Deal measures—cheering and applause broke from the galleries. By December 1933, the states had ratified the Twenty-First Amendment, officially ending constitutional Prohibition of alcohol.[28]

.   .   .

THE war on alcohol was over. The expansion of state authority that the war had engendered, however, did not disappear; it merely lurched forward in new directions. The Eighteenth Amendment in a period of otherwise conservative retrenchment had kept federal power at the forefront of public view. In so doing, just as Raskob and William Stayton, chairman of the Association Against the Prohibition Amendment, had feared, it fostered new appetites for the possible uses of such power. Despite the patent loathsomeness of the alcohol enforcement effort, faced with the Great Depression many recalled that muscular activism and sought to apply it to urgent social problems. One Illinois Democrat made the connection explicit. In 1932 C. O. Jaynes called on Roosevelt to back a four-day workweek "at a six-day-week wage." The "Eighteenth Amendment made it possible for the Federal Government to take over the enforcement of Prohibition. . . . Surely, capable and courageous leaders . . . could soon get another amendment to the Constitution which would empower Congress to shorten the workday for all labor throughout the nation."[29]

Such expansive expectations about the scope and efficacy of federal power had become widespread. World War I, the ensuing war on alcohol, and finally the economic crisis fostered broader acceptance for the long reach of federal power. The debate over what new form of liquor control would replace Prohibition also deepened national consciousness about the promises and perils of federal regulatory power. Many Prohibition opponents favored a central role for the federal government in control of the trade in any postrepeal world to come. Already in 1926, one highly publicized ballot of Yale students revealed that of the overwhelming number who opposed the Volstead Act (four-fifths), almost one-half favored the Quebec plan, the Canadian provincial model of government monopoly of the alcohol industry. Another staunch opponent, Maryland senator William Bruce, urged the passage of an amendment authorizing the federal government to take over "the entire management and control of the liquor traffic . . . to the exclusion of all private interests . . . for the benefit of the government." Hoover's National Commission on Law Observance and Enforcement also favored a significant role for the federal government in liquor control: in any new system the "federal government must be authorized to do a large part in the program and to do it efficiently." Six of the eleven commissioners favored some kind of "Gothenburg system" where the federal government retained significant responsibility for regulating and controlling the national sale of alcohol. The report called for a "National Commission on Liquor Control" with the power to "regulate and control the traffic like ICC power over railroads." These alternative solutions to liquor control suggest that the alcohol Prohibition years—while fanning fears over abuses of government power—ironically also contributed to broadening the range of solutions Americans could embrace during the Great Depression. Out of these contrary currents of thought FDR plotted the signature political style of the New Deal: regulatory approaches finely tuned to the problems of ambitious overreach.[30]

In the wake of repeal, the government did not depart the battleground of alcohol control, much to the dismay of the men of the AAPA. Even as repeal was speeding to ratification, policy makers forged a new system of regulation. In October 1933, Roosevelt brought together an Interdepartmental Committee, including key policy advisors Rexford Tugwell, Henry Wallace, and Harold Ickes. Out of their discussions, the Federal Alcohol Control Administration was born. The relegalized national liquor trade was to be subject to the National Recovery Administration's codes of fair competition regulating everything from labeling, advertising, and production to pricing. Under the codes, businesses could obtain licenses to engage in the trade by complying with the new regulations, but unlike many other industries whose rules were set largely by businessmen themselves, the liquor codes broke tradition, with no input from industry stakeholders. Such an unprecedented approach to a major American industry so alarmed the conservative men of the AAPA that rather than disbanding they renamed themselves the American Liberty League and pledged a rearguard action against the New Deal's rapid expansion of government power.[31]

Only when the Supreme Court took the side of these conservatives and declared the National Recovery Administration unconstitutional did government liquor control finally revert to the states. Postrepeal state liquor control, however, had little in common with the jumble of local ordinances that once structured the industry. New state liquor authorities systematized liquor control. Whether through monopoly control over sale or the licensing of private dealers, states established detailed requirements of how the trade should operate, with hours of sale, location with respect to school and churches, advertising, the character of retail outlets, the degree of visibility of the interior from the street, whether customers may sit at a bar or at tables, the ratio of chairs to bar seating, all subject to regulation.[32]

Implicit in these postrepeal alcohol control laws were the more permissive norms of a business and professional middle class who sought self-fulfillment and liberation within the new world of mixed-sex, semipublic, alcohol-laced leisure that blossomed under Prohibition. New liquor authorities established the appropriate parameters of relegalized recreational liquor use with their own moralistic assumptions. With the aid of police, they reined in the transgressive, experimental, and unregulated world of Prohibition-era nightlife. The largely evangelical and proprietary capitalist idea of alcoholic imbibing as an "evil," however, continued to fade, until only regional pockets of dry enthusiasm remained. Mississippi kept its liquor-prohibition laws on the books until 1966. As late as 1973, 545 United States counties banned liquor sales and 672 banned liquor sales for consumption on premises. In Oklahoma, drink by the glass was only legalized in 1986.[33]

Postrepeal drinking was integrated into new patterns of middle-class recreational leisure, and increasingly done at home. Before 1920 most beer and liquor was packaged in barrels and kegs. Improvements in bottling technology during Prohibition and the widespread introduction of home refrigerators after the 1940s made it possible to store beer at home. By 1942, consumption in off-site premises accounted for the majority of alcohol sales. But whether at home or in taverns or lounges, alcohol, despite its widely acknowledged addictive properties, health risks, and social costs, emerged from the crusade with, if anything, a more secure place in recreational leisure, and its harshest critics chastised.

. . .

THE formal end of Prohibition did not check the federal government's expansion into crime control. Americans now accepted its ultimate responsibility for reining in crime, a critical backstop to local law enforcement. Federal policing agents leveraged rising anxieties over Prohibition-era violence and rising crime to win new authority and muscle to wage war against it, expanding prisons and reorganizing national agencies. State and local penal administration and policing also professionalized and bureaucratized their structures, following the federal playbook, not least to rebuild public trust lost in the rampant corruption of the nation's war on alcohol. Studies of crime at all levels, backed by social-scientific experts, began a meteoric change in volume and impact.

From the promontory of today's colossal penal state, the most consequential harvest of the war on alcohol was the uniquely American cross-breeding of prohibitionary and punitive approaches toward illicit recreational narcotic substances, in which the central government was to play a leading role domestically and internationally. The war against drugs was a smaller but longer-lived effort birthed simultaneously. It was founded on the same logic as the alcohol Prohibition regime, drew upon its core assumptions, infrastructure, and moral entrepreneurs. Some of its best recruits were found in the Prohibition agencies. When that campaign lost luster and then was suddenly idled, the powerful moral entrepreneurs of the war on alcohol, their influential allies, government bureaucrats, and enforcement officers welcomed new campaigns on less hotly contested terrain.

Popular understandings of the Prohibition era have tended toward a view of the fourteen-year war on alcohol as an aberrant moment in the nation's history, wrongheaded social policy waged by puritanical zealots of a bygone Victorian era, with few lasting consequences. Whiggish notions of progress—and contemporaries' tendency toward a myopic view of the past—have obscured the important continuities and enduring legacies of that war. Despite a wide consensus that Prohibition of the liquor traffic was a fundamentally flawed crusade with devastating consequences, its spiritual and policy twin—the war on drugs—has gone largely unchallenged. Policy makers, educators, and a broad swath of the public take for granted that the dangers inherent in the evils of narcotic drugs requires a war for their eradication and the heavy penalization of drug users.

The nation's sharpest campaigns against narcotics, the first against alcohol and a second on drugs begun in the 1970s, were separated by forty years. Depression, World War II, increasingly permissive social norms, and national attention to fighting communism sidelined concerns over recreational narcotics traffic during those years. The social upheaval of the 1960s, and the concomitant celebration of drug use by middle-class youth, along with anxieties over rising crime, driven by black revolts that rocked the nation's inner cities, sparked the second moral panic of the century.

In 1971, Richard Nixon shrilly warned that drug abuse was a "national emergency" and "public enemy number one." Fourteen years later, Ronald Reagan exponentially widened the war with military analogies reminiscent of that energetic alcohol and drug warrior Richmond Hobson. "Americans swung into action" during World War II, Reagan proclaimed. Now citizens must wage a new war against the drug "horror," a cancer "killing America and terrorizing it with slow but sure chemical destruction." Putting an end to the "human wreckage" resulting from drug use would require a massive "crusade." Reagan promised to devote significant financial resources and institute tough drug policies with "zero tolerance for users" to win the battle. Between 1980 and 1997, the number of men and women serving sentences in the nation's increasingly crowded prisons for nonviolent drug offenses skyrocketed from fifty thousand to four hundred thousand.[34]

The parallels between these two wars—one in the early twentieth century, the second launched in the latter half and still raging in the new millennium—are unmistakable. Both were large-scale national efforts that targeted real social problems. Many educators, health-policy officials, scientists, social workers, and progressive reformers backed these efforts, witness to the ravages these substances posed to vulnerable and, in particular, poor populations. Their prohibitionist solutions to these real social problems, however, far overshot the ills they proposed to remedy. Launched with an ostensible logic of protecting vulnerable populations from harmful "horrors," these wars morphed in their fervor into state-sanctioned targeting of those same groups for extraordinarily harsh and socially devastating forms of social control.[35]

The selective enforcement that marked the nation's fourteen dry years has been replicated even more dramatically in the second war on drugs. Large and powerful cartels of drug suppliers operate with impunity, exerting intense pressure on governments at all levels through outright violence and pervasive webs of corruption. Small-scale users and street-level traffickers, on the other hand, languish in overcrowded prisons. Approximately one-fifth of inmates in state prisons are serving sentences for drug offenses. The number is closer to 50 percent in federal prisons, just as liquor-law violators once overwhelmed jails more than three-quarters of a century ago. In both state and federal prisons, in recent years, they have made up the largest single class of violators. The global scope of the drug war has also spiked incarceration rates and gang violence from Venezuela to Santo Domingo, Saõ Paolo to Lima. In Peru, a sharp rise in female prisoners was the tragic outcome of poor women's efforts to eke income from the drug trade as small-scale traffickers, just as female moonshine operators did in the 1920s.[36]

Middle-class drug consumers, in parallel with the nation's better-heeled liquor-law violators, remain largely immune from legal harassment or prosecution. The illicit trades wreaked their greatest havoc on large swaths of poor neighborhoods, with gangland warfare and struggles over territories—first close to one hundred years ago in Chicago, and more recently in Medellín, Cuernavaca, and East Los Angeles—on an exponentially greater scale. Government crackdowns bring some to violent ends but barely dent the supply or the public demand for illicit substances. Enforcement has varied widely between local and state police agencies and often devolved into highly local assaults on social groups identified in public discourse as social breeders of criminality.

In the more recent drug war, race has played an even more central role in sentencing and selective enforcement. As civil rights rendered explicit racial control laws illegal, the drug war provided seemingly racially neutral means for authorities to control racial minorities. The use of narcotics law as social control had its roots in the nation's war on alcohol, but has reached unprecedented levels. The uneven racial application of drug laws and discriminatory drug sentencing in some states of the union has been so blatant that one human rights organization has reported Georgia in violation of international agreements against racial discrimination for its discriminatory narcotics enforcement.[37]

Despite important parallels, key differences between these two wars account for the larger scope, duration, and resilience of the second narcotics war. Alcohol was far more widespread in its recreational use across social classes, and the effort to eradicate it was more controversial and unpopular from the beginning. Other narcotic drugs were more stigmatized, and more closely associated with minority populations—Chinese in the west, African-Americans in the south, Mexicans in the southwest—making a broad consensus for their criminalization and eradication easier to maintain. Another important difference was the alternative uses of some of these narcotics. Alcohol had few medicinal properties. The campaign for its eradication was launched, at its core, by religious crusaders and state builders anxious over the consequences of its recreational use. The story for other recreational narcotic substances was different. Narcotics such as morphine, opium, and even "coca" had medicinal properties. Such properties meant that important stakeholders, particularly fledgling pharmaceutical companies, had an interest in tight control over supply. They emerged as powerful allies for moral entrepreneurs and state bureaucrats fanning the flames of public moral panics. At the same time, the global location of production sites automatically entailed international agreements and alliances, the exclusive turf of the federal government. Just as local enforcement crossed over into social control, United States government officials combined drug interdiction with larger campaigns to influence the internal politics of foreign countries in their orbit.[38]

During the nation's war on alcohol, the markedly weaker state meant enforcement often took on a vigilante cast. The mobilization of the citizens' Volstead army wreaked havoc and generated tremendous controversy. A far more powerful, professionalized, and bureaucratized surveillance state is at the heart of the second narcotics war. A consolidated federal drug infrastructure is backed by a vast criminal-justice infrastructure at the state level and politically organized and deep-pocketed private contractors. For those who do not directly suffer its excesses, this much larger, more competent, and more lucrative prison industrial complex is, ironically, less not more controversial. Almost invisibly to many Americans, hundreds of thousands languish in prison for nonviolent drug offenses domestically, and drug violence rages internationally.

Transcending these similarities and differences, however, is a shared ethos—a consensus of "respectable" opinion behind prohibitionary and punitive approaches toward narcotics. During the 1920s, the anti-Prohibition crusader Louise Gross remarked that in the first years of the "noble experiment" those few women "who had the courage to oppose Prohibition in public were branded almost as anarchist." Even as late as 1930, a progressive like Eleanor Roosevelt could aver, "I believe in Prohibition," despite its devastating social consequences, although she admitted "some difficulties about enforcement." Since then, the taboo on alcohol has been replaced by an even more forcefully embedded consensus on the dangers of illicit narcotic drugs. The undisputed ravages that result from their abuse, however, have obscured, until recently, fundamental debates on the harm caused by criminalizing drug addiction, unfairly targeting minority users, and utilizing law for purposes of social control. The drug wars have also ravaged Latin American nations, with hundreds of thousands of lives lost from Cuernavaca, Mexico, to Lima, Peru. Nations on the supply side of the illicit narcotics economy have begun to tear the veil of consensus with their very survival at stake, calling upon the United Nations to consider alternatives to the global drug-prohibition regime.[39]

The war on alcohol was brought to an end by a powerful combination of mass hostility to the law, elite opinion makers who dared challenge the consensus, and politicians who saw repeal as the road to the White House and even party realignment. The ongoing United States drug war at the state, national, and international levels has also had disastrous human costs—but on an exponentially greater scale. Over three-quarters of a century ago, the men and women who studied and adapted their institutions to eradicate the liquor trade eventually opposed the heavily penal approach to the dangerous narcotic evil of their day. They embraced, instead, the New Deal's budding emphasis on economic equity and social provisioning. While no simple repeal will be enough to light the way out of our current quagmire in the war against narcotic drugs and the crisis of imprisonment ongoing today, a renewed challenge to the punitive ethos animating all of America's narcotic wars will be an important battleground.

ACKNOWLEDGMENTS

IT TAKES A VILLAGE. THIS BOOK COULD NOT HAVE BEEN written without the efforts of many individuals and institutions. I have been lucky to benefit from the help of an excellent group of student research assistants. Amy Friedman, Jane Wang, and Emmet von Stackelberg provided especially valuable assistance both as junior research partners during my time as a Radcliffe Fellow and later upon my return to teaching at Harvard. Special thanks goes to Rachel Stevens, whose sleuthing skills and diligence are unmatched. I am grateful to these assistants for tracking down elusive sources, reading reams of microfilm, and making uncountable trips to Harvard's many libraries. At the early stages of the project, Monica Mercado provided valuable support in Chicago.

Dozens of librarians and archivists around the country facilitated research visits, making my time in the archives more productive. My research trips made me all too aware of the threat posed to original scholarship by budget cuts and reduced hours and personnel at some of these repositories. This book could not have been written without the access to the collections and the talented expertise of librarians and archivists at the Chicago History Museum, the Franklin D. Roosevelt Presidential Library, the Harvard Law School Library, the Library of Congress, the National Archives and Records Administration, the Library of Virginia, the New York Public Library, the Pennsylvania Archives Center, and the Schlesinger Library, along with numerous other repositories. I am also grateful to the librarians at the Virginia Room of the Newport News Public Library, who perused local city directories in their holdings.

The generous support of the American Council of Learned Societies provided a much-needed year away from teaching. The Radcliffe Institute for Advanced Study provided the optimal setting for writing. I am indebted to all the fellows I shared a remarkable year with—for collegiality and inspiration. I presented early versions of this book in talks at the University of Bern, Switzerland, the Society of British Historians of the Twentieth-Century United States, as well as at a public talk at the Radcliffe Institute for Advanced Study; thanks to the audiences in attendance for their suggestions.

Numerous individuals took time from their own work to read chapter drafts, and offered invaluable suggestions. Cyrus Veeser generously read several draft chapters. Eric Foner and Michael Kazin read the manuscript in its entirety. Charles Forcey, who wields a pen like a magic wand, read draft chapters carefully. I am thankful to him for his friendship and his sharp editorial eye. Lilian Bobea supplied intellectual camaraderie, but more importantly conversations that pushed my thinking on the intersection of alcohol and drug policy. Susan Hewitt provided support and much-needed distraction. Franz Brüggemeier stepped up to the plate at a critical moment. Steve Forman ushered the book from the initial proposal to production with aplomb, patience, and an incisive editorial eye. It has been a pleasure to work with him and Travis Carr. I also wish to thank my terrific agent, Sandy Dijkstra.

To my sons, Noah and Pascal, thanks for reminding me that there is more to life than history and for, nonetheless, putting up with many conversations on the topic. This book has taken shape in a household of two historians and two book projects. I am grateful to Sven Beckert for the uncountable intellectual exchanges, along with the many adventures, distractions, and support over the years on this project, and beyond it.

ABBREVIATIONS USED
IN NOTES

Archives, Manuscripts, Government Records

BVLHC   Beaver Valley Labor History Collection, Archives Service Center, University of Pittsburgh Special Collections

CCAR   Chicago Commons Association Records, Chicago History Museum

COFR   Committee of Fourteen Records, New York Historical Society

CFLPSR   Chicago Foreign Language Press Survey Records, University of Chicago

DNC   Democratic National Committee Papers, 1932–1948, Franklin D. Roosevelt Library, Hyde Park, New York

EGP   Emma Guffey Papers, Schlesinger Library, Radcliffe Institute for Advanced Study

ETP   Elizabeth Tilton Papers, Schlesinger Library, Radcliffe Institute for Advanced Study

FFP   Felix Frankfurter Papers, Harvard Law School

FDR   Franklin D. Roosevelt Papers, Roosevelt Library, Hyde Park, New York

RHP   Richmond P. Hobson Papers, Library of Congress

LGP   Louise Gross Papers, New York Public Library

LDT   Lea Demarest Taylor Papers, Chicago History Museum

MWW   Mabel Walker Willebrandt Papers

NEWWS   New England Watch and Ward Society Records, 1918-1957, Harvard Law School

NCLOE   National Commission on Law Observance and Enforcement

PAC   Paul Angle Collection, Chicago History Museum

VPC   Virginia Prohibition Commission, Library of Virginia

TPP   Temperance and Prohibition Papers [microform]: Michigan Historical

Collections, the Ohio Historical Society, Woman's Christian Temperance Union, and the Westerville Public Library
VHS   Virginia Historical Society
WCR   Wickersham Commission Records, Harvard Law School

Newspapers and Journals

AC   *Atlanta Constitution*
AHR   *American Historical Review*
APSR   *American Political Science Review*
BDG   *Boston Daily Globe*
CDT   *Chicago Daily Tribune*
CR   *Congressional Record*
CTS   *Cincinnati Times Star*
HC   *Hartford Courant*
JAH   *Journal of American History*
JISHS   *Journal of the Illinois State Historical Society*
JSH   *Journal of Social History*
JUH   *Journal of Urban History*
LAT   *Los Angeles Times*
MR   *Marion Republican*
NAR   *North American Review*
NYHT   *New York Herald Tribune*
NYT   *New York Times*
PC   *Pittsburgh Courier*
RTD   *Richmond Times-Dispatch*
SSH   *Social Science History*
SLPD   *Saint Louis Post-Dispatch*
TPP   *Temperance and Prohibition Papers*
US   *Union Signal*
VQR   *Virginia Quarterly Review*
WP   *Washington Post*
WMLR   *William and Mary Law Review*

NOTES

Preface

1. "Roosevelt Beer Message" *NYT*, Mar. 29, 1933, 1; "House Votes on Beer Bill," *NYHT*, Mar. 14, 1933, 1.
2. "Roosevelt Gets Cases of Capital's 3.2 Beer," *NYT*, Apr. 7, 1933, 1; Capital Celebrates Beer's Return," *WP*, Apr. 7, 1933, 1.
3. "Prohibition Repeal . . . New York Celebrates with Quiet Restraint," *NYT*, Dec. 5, 1933; see, for example, David Kennedy, *Freedom From Fear: The American People in Depression and War, 1929–1945* (New York, 2005); Anthony Badger, *The New Deal: The Depression Years, 1933–1940* (New York, 1989). These books devote mere paragraphs to Prohibition. James Marone is one of the few scholars to acknowledge the importance of Prohibition as a significant chapter of American state development. See James Marone, *Hellfire Nation: The Politics of Sin in American History* (New Haven, 2003), 318–49.
4. Henry Bourne Joy quoted in David Kyvig, *Repealing National Prohibition* (1979; Kent, OH, 2000), 74.
5. Diana Louise Linden, "The New Deal Murals of Ben Shahn: The Intersection of Jewish Identity, Social Reform and Government Patronage" (PhD diss., CUNY, 1997), 21–45; see also Howard Greenfeld, *Ben Shahn: An Artist's Life* (New York, 1998), 100–111; Francis Kathryn Pohl, *Ben Shahn* (New York, 1994), 50–54.
6. Richard Hofstadter, *The Age of Reform* (New York, 1955), 292, 299; Andrew Sinclair, *Prohibition: The Era of Excess* (Boston, 1962), 182.
7. See, for example, Thomas Pegram, *Battling Demon Rum: The Struggle for a Dry America, 1800–1933* (Chicago, 1988); Jack S. Blocker, *American Temperance Movements: Cycles of Reform* (Boston, 1989); James H. Timberlake, *Prohibition and the*

Progressive Movement, 1900–1920 (1963; New York, 1970); Norman Clark, *Deliver Us from Evil: An Interpretation of American Prohibition* (New York, 1976); John J. Rumbarger, *Profits, Power, and Prohibition: American Alcohol Reform and the Industrializing of America, 1800–1930* (Albany, 1989); Richard Hamm, *Shaping the Eighteenth Amendment: Temperance Reform, Legal Culture, and the Polity, 1880–1920* (Chapel Hill, NC, 1995); Ann-Marie Szymankski, *Pathways to Prohibition: Radicals, Moderates and Social Movement Outcomes* (Durham, NC, 2003). On the symbolic nature of the crusade, see Joseph R. Gusfield, *Symbolic Crusade: Status Politics and the American Temperance Movement* (1963; Urbana, IL, 1986). See also Kyvig, *Repealing National Prohibition*; Michael Lerner, *Dry Manhattan: Prohibition in New York City* (New York, 2007). A notable exception to the dearth of attention to the national Prohibition years is Daniel Okrent, *Last Call: The Rise and Fall of Prohibition* (New York, 2010).

8. See, for example, John Kobler, *Ardent Spirits: The Rise and Fall of Prohibition* (New York, 1973), 221; Herbert Asbury, *The Gangs of Chicago: An Informal History of the Chicago Underworld* (New York, 1940); Gus Russo, *The Outfit: The Role of Chicago's Underworld in the Shaping of Modern America* (New York, 2001); Edward Behr, *Prohibition: Thirteen Years that Changed America* (New York, 1996); Donald L. Miller, *Supreme City: How Jazz Age Manhattan Gave Birth to Modern America* (New York, 2014).

9. Historians have noted the importance of Prohibition to Klan recruitment: see, especially, Leonard J. Moore, *Citizen Klansman: The Ku Klux Klan in Indiana, 1921–1928* (Chapel Hill, NC, 1991); Kathleen Blee, *Women of the Ku Klux Klan: Racism and Gender in the 1920s* (Berkeley, 1991); Nancy McLean, *Behind the Mask of Chivalry: The Making of the Second Ku Klux Klan* (New York, 1994). They have, however, neglected the Klan's instrumental use of the law in Klan vigilantism.

10. Robert Post, "Federalism, Positivism, and the Emergence of the American Administrative State: Prohibition and the Taft Court Era," *WMLR* 48 (2006), discusses this neglect. Studies of administrative state building include Stephen Skowronek, *Building a New American State: The Expansion of National Administrative Capacities, 1877–1920* (New York, 1982); Theda Skocpol, *Protecting Soldiers and Mothers: The Political Origins of Social Policy in the United States* (Cambridge, MA, 1992). Legal scholars have paid more attention to penality. See, for example, Lawrence Friedman, *Crime and Punishment in American History* (New York, 1993). See also Rebecca McLennan, *The Crisis of Imprisonment: Protest Politics and the Making of the American Penal State, 1776–1941* (New York, 2008). McLennan's otherwise excellent study leapfrogs over Prohibition. William J. Novak has called attention to the need for historians to chart the particular configuration of American state authority and abandon myths of the "weak" American state. See Novak, "The Myth of the 'Weak' American State," *AHR* 113 (June 2008), 752–72. This examination of the formation of the twentieth-century penal state seeks to contribute to the effort to provide new angles of vision on American state development.

11. David Kennedy draws connections between the Hoover administration and the New Deal but ignores the penal side of state building. See Kennedy, *Freedom from Fear*, esp. 1–217. Others have looked at the New Deal war on crime but have not traced its origins back to the war on alcohol. Claire Potter is an exception, see Potter, *War on Crime: Bandits, G-Men, and the Politics of Mass Culture* (New Brunswick, NJ, 1998).

1. The Making of a Radical Reform

1. ASL president quoted in "Ask U.S. to Forbid Liquor," *CDT*, Dec. 11, 1913, 5; see also "Unite to Fight Liquor," *WP*, Dec. 10, 1913, 2–3; "Nationwide Prohibition," *American Issue* (Nov. 1913): 1, 21, Reel 5, TPP; "Men First to Hobson," *LAT*, Dec. 10, 1913, 11; "Urge on Liquor War" *WP*, Dec. 8, 1913, 14 (Armor quotation).

2. T. Jason Soderstrum, "Richmond Pearson Hobson," *Alcohol and Drugs in North America: A Historical Encyclopedia*, ed. David M. Fahey and Jon S. Miller (Santa Barbara, CA, 2013), 1: 328; Harvey Rosenfeld, *Richmond Pearson Hobson, Naval Hero of Magnolia Grove* (New Mexico, 2000), 81–96; see also "Men First to Hobson," *LAT*, Dec. 10, 1913, 11. Hobson quoted in "Address before the Great Joint Committee" and "War on the Liquor Traffic, Address by Captain Richmond P. Hobson M.C. at a Reformers Conclave," Box 36, RHP.

3. Rosenfeld, *Richmond Pearson Hobson*, 35–64; Walter E. Pittman, Jr. "The Noble Crusade of Richmond P. Hobson and the Struggle to Limit the International Narcotics Trade, 1920–1925," *Alabama Historical Quarterly* 34 (Fall/Winter 1972): 181–93. For the making of the twentieth-century drug-control regime, see William B. McAllister, *Drug Diplomacy in the Twentieth Century* (London, 2000); Walter Earl Pittman, "Richmond P. Hobson, Crusader" (PhD diss., Univ. of Georgia, 1969), 162–64; Anne L. Foster, "Prohibiting Opium in the Philippines and the United States: The Creation of an Interventionist State," in *Colonial Crucible: Empire in the Making of the Modern American State*, ed. Alfred W. McCoy and Francisco A. Scarano (Madison, WI, 2009), 95–105.

4. *Intoxicating Liquors: Hearings Before the Committee on the Judiciary, House of Representatives*, Sixty-Third Congress, Second Session, Dec. 10, 1913, Apr. 15, 1914 (Washington, 1914), 3; "'Dry' Legions to Storm Capitol," *AC*, Dec. 10, 1913, 7.

5. On nascent antinarcotics efforts, see David F. Musto, *American Disease: Origins of Narcotic Control* (New Haven, 1973); Peter Andreas, *Smuggler Nation: How Illicit Trade Made America* (New York, 2013); McAllister, *Drug Diplomacy in the Twentieth Century*; Jeffrey Clayton Foster, "The Rocky Road to a 'Drug Free Tennessee': A History of the Early Regulation of Cocaine and the Opiates, 1897–1913," *JSH* (Spring 1996): 547–64.

6. Judith McArthur, "Demon Rum on the Boards: Temperance Melodrama and the Tradition of Antebellum Reform," *Journal of the Early Republic* 9 (Winter 1989): 527 (Mather quotation); Jack S. Blocker, *American Temperance Movements: Cycles of Reform* (Boston, 1989), 3. See also Norman Clark, *Deliver Us from Evil: An Interpretation of American Prohibition* (New York: 1976), 14–15; W. J. Rorabaugh, *The Alcoholic Republic* (New York, 1979).

7. Rorabaugh, *The Alcoholic Republic*, 3, 15.

8. Rorabaugh, *The Alcoholic Republic*, 237. The literature on Protestant religiosity is far too voluminous to cite here. On evangelicalism in the twentieth century, see George Marsden, *Fundamentalism and American Culture: The Shaping of Twentieth Century Evangelicalism, 1870–1925* (1982; New York, 2006). On the importance of religious currents to governmental authority, see John Compton, *The Evangelical Origins of the Living Constitution* (Cambridge, MA, 2014). On the importance of morality as a touchstone of American politics, see James Marone, *Hellfire Nation: The Politics of Sin in American History* (New Haven, 2003).

9. For one example of the tracts, see Robert G. Ingersoll, "Denunciation of Alco-

hol," in *Selected Articles on Prohibition of the Liquor Traffic*, comp. Lamar T. Beman (New York, 1915), 32–33; Judith McArthur, "Demon Rum on the Boards: Temperance Melodrama and the Tradition of Antebellum Reform," *Journal of the Early Republic* 9 (Winter 1989): 517–40.

10. Neal Dow, *The Reminiscences of Neal Dow: Recollections of Eighty Years* (Portland, ME, 1898), 331; Clark, *Deliver Us from Evil*, 48.

11. "Powderly's Temperance Views," *CDT*, Aug. 31, 1895, 12; see also Terence Powderly, *Thirty Years of Labor, 1859–1889* (1889), 594–95; Michael Kazin, *American Dreamers: How the Left Changed a Nation* (New York, 2013), 90–91 (quotation).

12. Janet Zollinger Giele, *Two Paths to Women's Equality: Temperance, Suffrage and the Origins of Modern Feminism* (New York, 1995); Ruth Bordin, *Woman and Temperance: The Quest for Power and Liberty, 1873–1990* (Philadelphia, 1981); Alison Parker, *Purifying America: Women, Cultural Reform and Pro-Censorship Activism* (Urbana, IL, 1997); Joseph Gusfield, *Symbolic Crusade: Status Politics and the American Temperance Movement* (Urbana, IL, 1963), 162.

13. On the vulnerability of poor women, see Linda Gordon, *Heroes of their Own Lives: The Politics and History of Family Violence* (New York, 1988). On immigrant womens' lives, see Donna Gabaccia, *From the Other Side: Women, Gender, and Immigrant Life in the U.S. 1820–1990* (Bloomington, IN, 1994). On elite women's approach toward working-class women for an earlier period, see Christine Stansell, *City of Women: Sex and Class in New York, 1789–1860* (Urbana, IL, 1986). On the WCTU, see Giele, *Two Paths to Women's Equality*, 63.

14. William H. Anderson, *Church in Action Against the Saloon* (Westerville, OH, 1906). For a discussion of the league, see Andrew Sinclair, *Prohibition: The Era of Excess* (Boston, 1962), 65; Peter Odegard, *Pressure Politics: The Story of the Anti-Saloon League* (New York, 1928); see also Austin Kerr, *Organized For Prohibition: A New History of the Anti-Saloon League* (New Haven, 1986), 80–81.

15. On Wheeler, see Daniel Okrent, *Last Call: The Rise and Fall of Prohibition* (New York, 2010), 39–41, 59–61, 131–33, 229–30, 301.

16. John Marshall Barker, *The Saloon Problem and Social Reform* (Boston, 1905), 2.

17. Michael Kazin, *The Populist Persuasion* (1995; New York, 1998), 90 (quotation). On the Volstead Act, see Okrent, *Last Call*, 109–12.

18. John Marshall Barker, *The Saloon Problem and Social Reform*, 66–67.

19. Address by Richmond P. Hobson, "Destroying the Destroyer," Dec. 1913, Box 37, 1, RHP; Kazin, *The Populist Persuasion*, 90–100; Kazin, *American Dreamers*, 90–91. The prohibitionist mobilization evinced elements of what some sociologists describe as "moral panic." See Erich Goode and Nachman Ben-Yehuda, "Moral Panics: Culture, Politics, and Social Construction," *Annual Review of Sociology* 20 (1994): 149–71.

20. Mae Ngai, *Impossible Subjects: Illegal Aliens and the Making of Modern America* (Princeton, 2004), 1–20; Matthew Frye Jacobson, *Barbarian Virtues: The United States Encounters Foreign Peoples At Home and Abroad, 1876–1917* (New York, 2000), 59–104; Nancy Foner, "How exceptional is New York? Migration and multiculturalism in the Empire City," *Ethnic and Racial Studies* 30 (Nov. 2007): 1001; Foner, "New York City: America's Classic Immigrant Gateway," in *Migrants to the Metropolis: Rise of Immigrant Gateway Cities*, ed. Marie Price and Lisa Benton-Short (New York, 2008), 51; Charles Merriam, *Chicago: A More Intimate View of Urban Politics* (Chicago, 1929), 134.

21. Charles Merz, *The Dry Decade* (New York, 1931), 12; Sinclair, *Prohibition*, 26; Perry Duis, *The Saloon: Public Drinking in Chicago and Boston, 1880–1920* (Urbana, IL, 1983), 145–71.

22. Harry G. Levine and Craig Reinarman, "From Prohibition to Regulation: Lessons from Alcohol Policy for Drug Policy," *The Milbank Quarterly* 69 (1991): 468; Clark Warburton, *Economic Results of Prohibition* (New York, 1932); Ilkka Henrik Makinen and Therese C. Reitan, "Continuity and Change in Russian Alcohol Consumption from the Tsars to Transition," *Social History* 31 (May, 2006): 171; "Alcohol Consumption United Kingdom," in *Alcohol and Temperance in Modern History: A Global Encyclopedia*, ed. Jack S. Blocker, Jr., Ian M. Tyrell, and David M. Fahrey (Santa Barbara, CA, 2003), 17. On 1910 per capita consumption in comparative perspective, see Jock Phillips, "Alcohol-Prohibition movement, 1880–1919," *Te Ara- The Encyclopedia of New Zealand*, http://www.TeAra.govt.nz/en/graph/40733/alcohol-consumption-in-new-zealand-and-other-countries-1910, accessed Mar. 5, 2014.

23. Clark, *Deliver Us from Evil*, 53; Barker, *The Saloon Problem and Social Reform*, 66–67. On the linkage of saloons and sex trafficking, see Jennifer Fronc, *New York Undercover: Private Surveillance in the Progressive Era* (Chicago, 2009), 66; Jane Addams, "A New Conscience and an Ancient Evil," *McClure's Magazine*, Mar. 1912, 593; Ella Boole on Addams in *Intoxicating Liquors: Hearings Before the Committee on the Judiciary*, Sixty-Third Congress, Dec. 11, 1913, Apr. 15, 1914, (Washington, DC, 1914), 3, 18. See also Sinclair, *Prohibition*, 59.

24. "Old Tim Socialist's Soap Box Really a Beer Box," *The Milwaukee Journal*, Feb. 7, 1971; Jon C. Teaford, *Cities of the Heartland: The Rise and Fall of the Industrial Midwest* (New York, 1995); *Germany and the Americas: Culture, Politics and History*, ed. Thomas Adam (Santa Barbara, CA, 2005), 3: 758.

25. Harold Gosnell, *Machine Politics: Chicago Model* (1937; Chicago, 1968); Alex Gottfried, *Boss Cermak of Chicago: A Study of Political Leadership* (Seattle, 1962); J. T. Salter, *Boss Rule: Portraits in City Politics* (New York, 1935); see also M. Craig Brown and Charles N. Halaby, "Machine Politics in America, 1870–1945," *Journal of Interdisciplinary History* 17 (Winter 1987); Bruce M. Stave, ed., *Urban Bosses, Machines, and Progressive Reformers* (Lexington, MA, 1972); John Allswang, *Bosses, Machines, and Urban Voters* (Baltimore, 1977); David Harold Kurtzman, *Methods of Controlling Votes in Philadelphia* (Philadelphia, 1935), 102–9; On other countries, see, for example, Martin Shefter, *Patronage and its Opponents: A Theory and Some European Cases* (Ithaca, NY, 1977).

26. On the Progressive reform era, see, for example, Daniel Rodgers, *Atlantic Crossings: Social Politics in a Progressive Age* (Cambridge, MA, 1998); Samuel P. Hays, "The Politics of Reform in Municipal Government in the Progressive Era," *Pacific Northwest Quarterly* 55 (Oct. 1964): 157–69;

27. "The Race Problem," *The Voice*, Oct. 28, 1890, 8 (Willard quotation); see Richmond P. Hobson, "The Truth About Alcohol," in *Selected Articles on Prohibition*, 41.

28. "Mighty Wave of Reform Sweeps the Entire South," *NYT*, June 2, 1907, SM 6. Gregory Mixon, "Good Negro-Bad Negro: The Dynamics of Race and Class in Atlanta during the Era of the 1906 Riot," *Georgia Historical Quarterly* 81 (Fall 1997): 599 ("veritable centers of vice"); John E. White, "Prohibition: The New Task and Opportunity of the South," *South Atlantic Quarterly* 7 (Jan.–Oct. 1908), 136 ("saloon was the ravager").

29. Thomas R. Pegram, "Temperance Politics and Regional Political Culture: The Anti-Saloon League in Maryland and the South, 1907–1915, *JSH* 63 (Feb. 1997): 75; see also "Mighty Wave," *NYT*, June 2, 1907, SM 6; White, "Prohibition: The New Task," 135–37 (quotations).

30. David T. Courtwright, "The Hidden Epidemic: Opiate Addiction and Cocaine Use in the South, 1860–1920," *JSH* (Feb. 1983): 69; see also Pittman, "Richmond P. Hobson, Crusader," 163–82.

31. *Some Scientific Conclusions Concerning the Alcohol Problem and its Practical Relations to Life*, papers read at the Semi-annual Meeting of the American Society for the Study of Alcohol and Other Drug Narcotics, Mar. 17–19 (Washington, DC, 1909) 19 ("Alcohol is a narcotic"); 87–90; 122 ("in the list of dangerous drugs"); 132 ("poisonous"); Richmond P. Hobson, *Alcohol and the Human Race* (Chicago, 1915). See also Sinclair, *Prohibition*, 61–62;.

32. Mary Hunt, *A History of the First Decade of the Department of Scientific Temperance Instruction in Schools and Colleges* (Boston, 1892); Elizabeth Tilton, *Retake the Heights*, 97–102, ETP; see also Tilton, "Turning off the Spigot," and *The Survey* Mar. 21, 1914; James H. Timberlake, *Prohibition and the Progressive Movement, 1900–1920* (1963; New York, 1970), 64–65.

33. *Proceedings of the 43rd National Conference of Charities and Corrections*, Indianapolis, May 10–17, 1916 (Chicago, 1916), 115.

34. Sinclair, *Prohibition*, 113; *Intoxicating Liquors*, 22 (Hobson quotation); *Some Scientific Conclusions*, 19; E. W. Davis to Hobson, July 17, 1915, Box 36, 1, RHP.

35. George Pell, *Revisals of North Carolina, Public and State Statutes*, 1 (Charleston, SC, 1908), 2058a, 2061; Ernest Cherringon, *The Evolution of Prohibition in the United States of America: A Chronological History . . .* (Westerville, OH, 1920); White, "Prohibition," 135; Charles Stelzle, *Why Prohibition?* (New York, 1918), 20.

36. Ernest Cherrington, *A New Plan of Campaign in the Interest of National Prohibition* (Westerville, OH, 1913), 5, 16–19; see also Charles Merriam and Harold F. Gosnell, *Non-Voting: Causes and Methods of Control* (Chicago, 1924).

37. On progressive reforms, see Rodgers, *Atlantic Crossings*; Musto, *American Disease*, 54–68.

38. *Intoxicating Liquors*, 41 (Wheeler quotation); "Georgia Prohis Showed in Front," *AC*, Dec. 11, 1913, 3 ("The government that wisely counts"); *Intoxicating Liquors*, 21 ("moment the federal government").

39. John R. Vile, *A Companion to the United States Constitution and Its Amendments* (Westport, CT, 2006), 202–9; *Intoxicating Liquors*, 21, 27, 31; see also Kerr, *Organized for Prohibition*, 150–51; Okrent, *Last Call*, 54–59 (quotation on 54).

40. For one example of those who wrote to thank Hobson, see Mary E. Dobbs to Richmond P. Hobson, Mar. 12, 1913, Box 38, 6, RHP. On Morris Sheppard, see Escal Franklin Duke, "The Political Career of Morris Sheppard, 1875–1941" (PhD diss., Univ. of Texas, 1958), 317–32; see also Lewis L. Gould, *Progressives and Prohibitionists: Texas Democrats in the Wilson Era* (Austin, TX, 1973).

41. "National Campaign," *American Issue*, Dec. 1913, 1 (quotations from *Portland Telegram* and *Nashville Banner*), TPP.

42. George Kibbe Turner, "The City of Chicago," *McClure's Magazine* 28 (Apr. 1907): 578–80; Robert A. Woods, "Winning the Other Half: National Prohibition: A Leading Social Issue," *The Survey*, Dec. 30, 1916.

43. Charles Eliot to Richmond P. Hobson, Sept. 16, 1914, Box 35, 1, RHP; William Howard Taft to Elizabeth Tilton, reprinted in *NYT*, Jan. 24, 1915.

44. Sinclair, *Prohibition*, 96.
45. Tilton, *Retake the Heights*, 14, 40–41, 77–96, 53; Elizabeth Hewes Tilton, biographical and genealogical material, Boxes 1–3, ETP. See also Tilton diaries, July 14, 1918, Nov. 16, 1920, Dec. 12, 1920, Jan. 24, 1923, Reel 993, ETP.
46. Tilton, *Retake the Heights*, 89–92; 96–101, 121. On Laidlaw's Prohibition views, see Harriet Burton Laidlaw to Dr. Henry Goddard Leach, Nov. 27, 1933, Harriett Burton Laidlaw Papers, and additional material related to her work on Prohibition, Reel 7, Women's Studies Manuscript Collections, Schlesinger Library, Radcliffe Institute for Advanced Study.
47. Tilton, *Retake the Heights*, 89–92.
48. Tilton, *Retake the Heights*, 89–92; 96–101, 121; see also biographical and genealogical material, Boxes 1–3.
49. Tilton, *Retake the Heights*, 97–101, 121.
50. Michael Kazin, *A Godly Hero: The Life of Williams Jennings Bryan* (New York, 2007), xiv, 172–79, 209; William Jennings Bryan "Why I am for Prohibition," *The Independent* 87 (July 17, 1916): 89 ("will bring the highest good"); Lawrence Levine, *Defender of the Faith: William Jennings Bryan, The Last Decade, 1915–1925* (New York, 1965), 106 ("impoverish the poor").
51. Sinclair, *Prohibition*, 100; L. Ames Brown, "National Prohibition," *Atlantic Monthly* 115 (1915): 473 (Theiss quotation). See also John J. Rumbarger, *Profits, Power and Prohibition: American Alcohol Reform and the Industrializing of America, 1800–1930* (Albany, 1989).
52. Tilton, *Retake the Heights*, 99; "Summary of Investigations Conducted by the Committee of Fifty, 1893–1903," 50–53, in *Selected Articles on Prohibition*, 118–19.
53. *Alcohol and Temperance in Modern History*, xii; Brown, "National Prohibition," 735; Mark Schrad, *Vodka Politics: Alcohol, Autocracy and the Secret History of the Russian State* (New York, 2014), esp. 127–85; Laura L. Phillips, *Bolsheviks and the Bottle: Drink and Work Culture in St. Petersburg, 1900–1920* (Dekalb, IL, 2000); see also "Suppression of Vodka," *British Medical Journal* (Jan. 23, 1915): 171–72; Helgi Gunnlaugsson and John F. Galliher, *Wayward Icelanders: Punishment, Boundary Maintenance and the Creation of Crime* (Madison, WI, 2000), 29–47; Else Osterberg, "Finland" in *Alcohol and Temperance in Modern History*, 240–43; Sturla Nordlund, "Norway" in *Alcohol and Temperance in Modern History*, 458–63; John H. Wuorinen, *Prohibition Experiment in Finland* (New York, 1931).
54. Pittman, "Richmond P. Hobson, Crusader," 147, 151; Philip P. Campbell, "The Hobson Amendment," *CR* 52 (Dec. 22 1914), in *Selected Articles on Prohibition*, 24–25. See also Ernest Cherrington, *Prohibition Textbook: Facts and Figures Dealing with the Liquor Traffic* (Westerville, OH, 1915), 6; Okrent, *Last Call*, 395; Robert Woods, "Winning the Other Half: National Prohibition: A Leading Social Issue," *The Survey* (Dec. 30, 1916): 350; Julius Liebmann and response by Elizabeth Tilton, *The Survey* (Feb. 20 1915): 566.
55. *Alcohol and Temperance in Modern History*, xii; see also "Prohibition Wave Sweeping Britain," *NYT*, Dec. 31, 1916, 3; Brown, "National Prohibition," 735; Campbell, "The Hobson Amendment," 24–25; Robert Woods, "Winning the Other Half: National Prohibition: A Leading Social Issue," *The Survey*, (Dec. 30, 1916): 350; Liebmann and Tilton, *The Survey* (Feb. 20, 1915): 566.
56. W. G. Nice to Richmond Hobson, Jan. 26, 1915; E. W. Davis to Hobson, July 17, 1915, Box 36, RHP; Merz, *The Dry Decade*, 25–50.
57. Sinclair, *Prohibition*, 117; Fronc, *New York Undercover*, 149–52.

58. *Hearings Before a Subcommittee of the Senate Committee of the Judiciary*, 65th Congress, 2nd session, S3529, 309 as in Sinclair, *Prohibition*, 121.

59. C. Child, "The German American in Politics, 1914–1917" (PhD diss., Univ. of Wisconsin, 1939) 111 as in Sinclair, *Prohibition*, 120. See also Okrent, *Last Call*, 83–84, 99; Clark, *Deliver Us from Evil*, 14–15.

60. Merz, *The Dry Decade*, 26–27.

61. Merz, *The Dry Decade*, 25–50; Tilton, Diary, Apr. 2, 1918, Reel 993; see also Tilton, *Retake the Heights*, 161.

62. Tilton, *Retake the Heights*, 97; Kazin, *Populist Persuasion*, 101.

63. "Enforcement Bill Passed," *Christian Science Monitor*, July 23, 1919, 1; "Senate Passes Dry Law," *NYHT*, Sept. 6, 1919; "Enforcement Bill Passed," *AC*, Sept. 6, 1919, 1; see also Okrent, *Last Call*, 108–12.

64. "Meeting Minutes," Jan. 17, 1920, WCTU Flint, Michigan, chapter, Minute Book 11, Reel 48, TPP; "John Barleycorn burned in Effigy" *AC*, Jan. 16, 1920, 1–2; "Reformers of Nation Join in Watch Meeting to Usher in New Law," *Denver Post*, Jan. 17, 1920; John Kobler, *Ardent Spirits: The Rise and Fall of Prohibition* (New York, 1973), 12 (Sunday quotation); Anna Gordon, Presidential Address, *Report of the Forty-Eighth Annual Convention of the National Woman's Christian Temperance Union*, 1922, 60, reel 9 TPP ("declaration of independence").

2. Bootleg, Moonshine, and Home Brew

1. "Prohibition Protested by 50,000 on Common," *BDG*, Apr. 7, 1919, 1.

2. "25,000 'Wets' Parade Today," *Baltimore Sun*, June 3, 1919; "25,000 Parade for Wets," *NYT*, June 3, 1919, 12. The newspaper mention of the "anti-Prohibition League" likely referred to the American Association Against the Prohibition Amendment (AAPA).

3. "Prohibition Protested," *BDG*, Apr. 1, 1919; see also "Labor Unites in Wet Protest," *CDT*, June 14, 1919, 1.

4. "'Wets' Mobilize at Capitol to Protest Dry Law," *CDT*, June 15, 1919, 5; James H. Timberlake, *Progressives and Prohibition* (New York, 1970), 95; "Move to Save Wine and Beer Lost in House," *NYT*, Jun. 18, 1919, 4; "Mild Beer Demanded by Labor," *Cincinnati Enquirer*, Jun. 15, 1919, 1 (Gompers quotation).

5. Central Federated Union leader Ernest Bohm claimed that 500,000 rank-and-file unionists endorsed the campaign: see "Beer Strike Gains Support," *NYT*, Mar. 8, 1919, 4; "No Beer–No Work Strikes are Voted," *BDG*, Feb. 22, 1919, 1; "No Beer, No Work Strike Referendum is Started," *NYHT*, Feb. 12, 1919, 1; see also Nuala McGann Drescher, "The Opposition to Prohibition, 1900–1919: A Social and Institutional Study" (PhD diss., Univ. of Delaware, 1963), 297–301; Tilton diaries, March–April 1919, Reel 993, ETP.

6. "Fewer than 20,000," *NYT*, July 5, 1921, 1 (quotation). On working-class Americanism in later context, see Gary Gerstle, *Working-Class Americanism: The Politics of Labor in a Textile City, 1914–1960* (1989; Princeton, 2002). Liz Cohen's work on 1920s' Chicago contends that ethnic industrial workers embraced wider, less insular, and more national working-class identities. She focuses on the importance of mass culture, mass consumption, and welfare capitalism to this development, less centrally on Prohibition; see Lizabeth Cohen, *Making a New Deal: Industrial Workers in Chicago, 1919–1939* (1990; New York, 2008).

7. Charles Merriam, *Chicago: A More Intimate View of Urban Politics* (New York, 1929), 12. For an overview of distinct ethnic communities, see *Ethnic Chicago*, ed. Melvin G. Holli and Peter d'A Jones (1977; Grand Rapids, MI, 1984); "Greek Wets Flay Prohibition," *Saloniki,* June 28, 1919, Box 20, 181, CFLPSR.

8. Charles Joseph Bushnell, *The Social Problem and the Chicago Stockyards* (Chicago, 1902), 44, 76–78; Breckinridge and Abbott, "University of Chicago Settlement Report" (1908) as in Norman Sylvester Hayner, "The Effect of Prohibition in Packingtown" (PhD diss., Univ. of Chicago, 1921), 13 ("most hospitable place"). See also "The Social Function of the Saloon," (July–Sept. 1898), Box 23, 2, CCAR. Chicago Commons Settlement House director Lea Taylor remarked that "our neighborhood saloons . . . never were markedly disorderly and vicious." See "Prohibition Survey of the Stockyards Community," Box 8, 5, LDT; Perry Duis, *The Saloon: Public Drinking in Chicago and Boston, 1880–1920* (Urbana, IL, 1983); Madelon Powers, *Faces along the Bar: Lore and Order in the Workingman's Saloon, 1870–1920* (Chicago, 1998).

9. "Auf Zum Protest," *AP,* May 23, 1906, 4; "Das Volk Stand Auf!" *AP,* May 28, 1906, 5; see also "US Flay Blue Laws," *CDT,* March 26, 1906; Maureen Flanagan, "Ethnic Entry into Chicago Politics: United Societies for Local Self-Government and the Reform Charter of 1907," in *JISHS* (Spring 1982): 5, 8, 44–45; Alex Gottfried, *Boss Cermak of Chicago: A Study of Political Leadership* (Seattle, 1962), 44; Michael Willrich, *City of Courts: Socializing Justice in Progressive Era Chicago* (Chicago, 2003), 44–45.

10. Gottfried, *Boss Cermak of Chicago,* 84; "44,155 Wets in Parade," *CDT,* Nov. 8, 1915, 1.

11. "Parade of Degenerates," *CDT,* Nov. 8, 1915, 3; Harold Gosnell, *Machine Politics: Chicago Model* (1937; Chicago, 1968): 145–46; see also "Chicago Wet By a Majority of 247,228," *CDT,* Apr. 2, 1919, 3; "Register Protest Against Prohibition," *AP,* Mar. 4, 1919; "Grave of Liberty," *AP,* Oct. 10, 1919, Box 13, 2, CFLPSR.

12. For a discussion of the strike, see Cohen, *Making a New Deal,* 1–52; nationally, see David Brody, *Labor in Crisis: The Steel Strike of 1919* (Urbana, IL, 1965).

13. For scientific management efforts to alter the workplace, see David Montgomery, *Workers' Control in America: Studies in the History of Work, Technology, and Labor Struggles* (New York, 1980), 32–40, 91–133.

14. "Prohibition Survey of the Stockyards Community," Box 8, 5, LDT; William E. McLennan, "Prohibition in Settlement Neighborhoods," 9, Box 1, 4, LDT. On Boston, see Alice Garnett, "Synopsis of Opinion on Law Enforcement in Congested Neighborhoods," in *Neighborhood* 4, 3 (Mar. 1930), 32–37.

15. Duis, *The Saloon,* 274–300; Roy Rosensweig, *Eight Hours for What We Will: Workers and Leisure in an Industrial City, 1870–1920* (New York, 1985), esp. 191–221. While the saloon was weakened by competition from new forms of mass culture, it was the Volstead Act that dug its grave. A case that saloon culture would have continued, even if in modernized form, can be made if one looks comparatively at the experience of Britain with its lively pub culture into the twenty-first century.

16. *CDT,* Feb. 1, 1920; see also, for example, "Hinky Dink Puts the Tubs Away for All Time," *CDT,* Feb. 2, 1920, 16.

17. McLennan, "Prohibition in Settlement Neighborhoods," Box 1, 4, LDT ("stranglehold"); Martha Benley Bruere, *Does Prohibition Work: A Study of the Operation*

of the Eighteenth Amendment Made by the National Federation of Settlements (New York, 1927), 186 ("drinkery not a political center"). See also "Study of Prohibition" Box 24, CCAR. For a positive assessment of Prohibition's results, see Harry S. Warner, "Prohibition: A Step in a Process," in American Academy of Political and Social Science, *Prohibition: A National Experiment* 163 (Philadelphia, 1932), 158.

18. Hayner, "The Effect of Prohibition," 37 (McDowell quotation); McLennan, "Prohibition in Settlement Neighborhoods," Box 1, 4, LDT (Boston reformer quotation); Bruere, *Does Prohibition Work*, 18; Warner, "Prohibition: A Step in a Process," 156–58 (Wald quotation). See also Ernest B. Gordon, *The Wrecking of the Eighteenth Amendment* (New York, 1943), 73.

19. On Whiskey Row, see Hayner, "The Effect of Prohibition," 39–49. On Central District survey, see Marian Winthrop Taylor, "The Social Results of Prohibition: A Study Made in the Central District of the United Charities" (PhD diss., Univ. of Chicago, 1923), 6; "Study of Prohibition," Box 24, 2, CCAR ("flourishing saloons"); Bruere, *Does Prohibition Work*, 4 (Charles Cooper quotation).

20. "Hinky Dink Puts Tubs Away for All Time," 16; Hayner, "The Effect of Prohibition," 44–46; Marian Winthrop Taylor, "The Social Results of Prohibition," 6; "March 1928 Bulletin: Prohibition Committee," Box 1, 6, LDT ("unwashed windows").

21. Frederic Milton Thrasher, *The Gang: A Study of 1,313 Gangs in Chicago* (1927; Chicago, 1960), 447–54; "Investigative Reports," Boxes 36–55, COFR; Thomas Pegram, "Brewing Trouble: Federal, State, and Private Authority in Pennsylvania Prohibition Enforcement under Gifford Pinchot, 1923–1927," *Pennsylvania Magazine of History and Biography* (Apr. 2014), 163–91. On Peak's Philadelphia saloon, see "Dry Agents Fight with 200 Men," *BDG*, Jan. 7, 1923.

22. See Thrasher, *The Gang*, 438–42, 447–54.

23. For beer prices prior to Prohibition, see, for example, "Now Higher Cost of Living May Extend to Price of Beer," *Detroit Free Press*, Apr. 8, 1911, 3; "Plans of Tribune Readers," *CDT*, Dec. 8, 1912, F 6; "Prohibition: Survey of the Stockyards Community." Prior to Prohibition, a bucket of beer could be had in the city's stockyards for as low as five cents. By 1930 the price rose to between 25 cents to 50 cents a glass; see Clark Warburton, *Economic Results of Prohibition* (New York, 1932), 155. In Chicago, whiskey once 15 cents a glass went for about 75 cents per glass for moonshine of very cheap quality. Hayner, "Effect of Prohibition," 20 ("Stuff is too high"). For workers' complaints on budgets, see interviews, 40–48, Carton 1, Western Electric Company, Hawthorne Studies Collection, 1924–1961, Baker Library, Harvard Business School.

24. Warburton, *Economic Results of Prohibition*, 233–39; 262–63; Investigation, by Stanley Root, Box 1, WCR (quotation); Norman Clark, *Deliver Us from Evil: An Interpretation of National Prohibition* (New York, 1976), 146; David Kyvig, *Repealing National Prohibition* (1979; Kent, OH, 2000), 31.

25. On sources of supply, see "Prohibition: Survey of the Stock Yards Community," Box 8, 5, LDT; Hayner, "The Effect of Prohibition," 47–48 (quotation on 47).

26. Hayner, "The Effect of Prohibition," 16–26 (quotation); "'I will' is Chicago Motto," Box 24, 4, CCAR ("the great baking companies").

27. Hayner, "The Effect of Prohibition," 48, 31; McLennan, "Prohibition in Settlement Neighborhoods," 8, Box 1, 4, LDT.

28. "Prohibition Survey of the Stock Yards Community," 7, Box 8, 5, LDT; McLennan, "Prohibition in Settlement Neighborhoods," 8, Box 1, 4, LDT.
29. For evidence for women's role in Chicago's trade see, for example, Michael Willrich, "'Close that Place of Hell': Poor Women and the Cultural Politics of Prohibition," *JUH* 29 (2003), 553–59; 568. Although Willrich points to poor women's efforts to have these places shut down, his evidence simultaneously reveals women's role in the trade. In contrast to Willrich, I have found extensive evidence of poor women's opposition to the law. Settlement house neighborhood women of various nationalities voiced "unanimous opinion" that conditions were worse under Prohibition. One organized group of Polish mothers not only called for amending the act, but for the return of the saloon: see "Neighborhood Interviews and Opinions," Box 24, 4, CCAR. See also "Prohibition Survey of Stockyard Community," Box 8, 5; McLennan, "Prohibition in Settlement Neighborhoods," Box 1, 4, LDT.
30. Addams observations reported in "'I will' is Chicago Motto"; Herbert Asbury, *The Great Illusion: An Informal History of Prohibition* (New York, 1950), 227.
31. "'I will' is Chicago Motto," Box 24, 2, 4, CCAR (quotation).
32. On the history of earlier violence, see Jeffrey S. Adler, *First in Violence, Deepest in Dirt: Homicide in Chicago, 1875–1920* (Cambridge, MA, 2006). For crime in Chicago from the Progressive Era through the 1920s, see Willrich, *City of Courts,* esp. 281–312; Herbert Asbury, *Gem of the Prairie: An Informal History of the Chicago Underworld* (1940; DeKalb, IL, 1986); John Landesco, *Organized Crime in Chicago* (Chicago, 1929); Humbert S. Nelli, *The Business of Crime: Italians and Syndicate Crime in the United States* (New York, 1976); Howard Abadinsky, *Organized Crime: An Examination of the Function, Structure, and Historical Background of United States Criminal Organizations from the late 19th Century to the Present* (Chicago, 1985), esp. 130–52.
33. Robin Einhorn, "Political Culture," in *The Encyclopedia of Chicago*, ed. James R. Grossman et al. (Chicago, 2004); "Vice Kings and Police," *CDT*, July 24, 1914, 3; "Neighborhood Interviews," Box 24, 4, 2, CCAR ("tremendous amount of graft") "Thompson," *CDT*, Apr. 19, 1931, 14 ("international reputation").
34. "Chicago Gangland Killings Show Close Alliance with Chicago Politicians," *CDT*, Mar. 31, 1929, G1 ("not ashamed"; "He drank with them").
35. National Federation of Settlements "Prohibition Committee," Mar. 1928, Box 1, 6, LDT; Thrasher, *The Gang*, 481; "Neighborhood Interviews," Box 24, 4, CCAR.
36. "Neighborhood Interviews"; Gottfried, *Boss Cermak of Chicago*, 141.
37. Thrasher: *The Gang:* 468, 480; see also Herbert Asbury, *The Gangs of Chicago: An Informal History of the Chicago Underworld* (New York, 1940); John Kobler, *The Life and World of Al Capone* (New York, 1971); Gottfried, *Boss Cermak*, 210–15.
38. Thrasher: *The Gang:* 468, 480.
39. "'I will' is Chicago Motto," Box 24, 4, CCAR.
40. McLennan, "Prohibition in Settlement Neighborhoods"; see also "'I will' is Chicago Motto"; Federal Council of Churches report quoted in Herbert Asbury, *The Great Illusion,* 227–28; McLennan, "Prohibition in Settlement Neighborhoods" (Polish banker quotation).
41. NCLOE, *Report on Crime and the Foreign Born* (Washington, DC, 1931); "'I will' is Chicago Motto."
42. See Asbury, *The Great Illusion*, 228.

43. *Danish Times*, Oct. 30, 1931, Box 9, 181, CFLPSR; Asbury, *The Great Illusion*, 287.

44. Asbury, *The Great Illusion*, 287; John P. Morgan, "Jamaica Ginger Paralysis," *JAMA* 248 (Oct. 15, 1982): 1864–7; see also L. A. Turley, H. A. Shoemaker, and D. T. Bowden, *Jake Paralysis* (Norman, OK, 1931); "The Public Health Service and Jamaica Ginger Paralysis in the 1930s," *Public Health Service Chronicles* 110 (May–June 1995): 363; John P. Morgan and Thomas C. Tulloss, "The Jake Walk Blues: A Toxicologic Tragedy mirrored in American Popular Music," *Annals of Internal Medicine* 85 (1976): 804–8.

45. Hayner, "The Effect of Prohibition," 20; "Neighborhood Interviews," Box 24, 4, CCAR (Italian doctor quotation); see also Marian Winthrop Taylor, "The Social Results of Prohibition."

46. Constantine Panunzio, "The Foreign Born and Prohjbition," in Annals of the American Academy of Political and Social Sciences, *Prohibition: A National Experiment* (Philadelphia, 1928), 49 (quotation); Hayner, "The Effect of Prohibition," 42 (quotation); crowd action identified as a "news item," no date, in Thrasher, *The Gang*, 261. Such resistance occurred in other industrial cities. In Pittsburgh a raid of nine saloons attracted a large crowd. In one raid, the wife of the owner of one establishment brandished a chair and threatened raiding agents. In a raid on the Foyzey and Lutz saloon, a "group of foreigners" formed a human barricade; see "Nine Saloons on Northside Raided," *Pittsburgh Post-Gazette*, Oct. 24, 1920, 2.

47. Hayner, "The Effect of Prohibition," 24–25, 42; "Neighborhood Interviews," Box 24, 4, CCAR; see also National Federation of Settlements, "Prohibition Committee," Mar. 1928, Box 1, 6, LDT; Thrasher, *The Gang*, 468.

48. See "Neighborhood Interviews," Box 24, 4, CCAR.

49. *Danish Times*, Oct. 30, 1931.

50. Robert Stanley, *Dimensions of Law in the Service of Order: The Origins of the Federal Income Tax 1861–1913* (New York, 1993); Stephen Skowronek, *Building a New American State: The Expansion of National Administrative Capacities, 1877–1920* (New York, 1982); see also Brian Balogh, *A Government Out of Sight: The Mystery of National Authority in Nineteenth-Century America* (New York, 2009), esp. 379–400.

51. Gottfried, *Boss Cermak of Chicago*, 15–16, 18, 22.

52. "In Behalf of Personal Freedom," *Denni Hlasatel*, Mar. 20, 1922, Box 1, 182, CFLPSR (Cermak quotation); see also Gottfried, *Boss Cermak of Chicago*, 115.

53. Gottfried, *Boss Cermak of Chicago*, 111–117; "Cermak's Stand," *CDT*, Oct. 16, 1922.

54. "Cermak's Stand," *CDT*, Oct. 16, 1922; Gottlieb, *Boss Cermak of Chicago*, 11–117.

55. Gottfried, *Boss Cermak of Chicago*, 11–117; "Brittens Biervorlag," *AP*, Nov. 1, 1922; "*Nass oder Trocken?*" and "Die Prohibitionsfrage am 7 November," *AP*, Oct 25, 1922; "This is our Fight," Oct. 17, 1922, 1–6, *Denni Hlasatel*, Box 1, 182, CFLPSR.

56. "Czechoslovaks Protest Against Prohibition," Oct. 4, 1922, Oct. 6, 1922, *Denni Hlasatel*.

57. "Czechoslovaks Protest Against Prohibition," Oct. 4, 1922, Oct. 6, 1922 *Denni Hlasatel*, Box 1, 182, CFLPSR; "This is Our Fight," Oct. 27, 1922, *Denni Hlasatel*, Box 1, 183, CFLPSR; John Allswang, *A House for All Peoples: Ethnic Politics in Chicago, 1890–1936* (Lexington, KY, 1971), 11, 121–23; Gosnell, *Machine Politics*, 145.

58. On increased immigrant voting, see Cohen, *Making a New Deal*, especially 210–

11; see also Kristi Anderson, The *Creation of a Democratic Majority* (Chicago, 1979), 9, 32; Allswang, *A House for All Peoples;* Charles Merriam and Harold F. Gosnell, *Non-Voting: Causes and Methods of Control* (Chicago, 1924).

3. Selective Enforcement

1. "Izzy Einstein's 'Revenuer's Blues' is Grand Slam," *WP*, Mar. 9, 1922, 1.
2. "Izzy and Moe Trap 48" *NYT*, May 8, 1922, 5 (quotations); "Izzy and Moe," *BDG*, Nov. 22, 1925, A24; "Two Barkeeps Faint," *NYT*, July 17, 1922, 6; "Izzy and Moe put on Blackface," *NYT*, Mar. 3, 1922, 6; see also Herbert Asbury, "The Noble Experiment of Izzie and Moe," in *Aspirin Age, 1919–1941,* ed. Isabel Leighton (New York, 1949), 34–50; Isidor Einstein, *Prohibition Agent No. 1* (New York, 1932).
3. "Izzy and Moe," *BDG*, Nov. 22, 1925, A24 (quotations). John Kobler labeled them the "most honest and effective agents: see Kobler, *Ardent Spirits: The Rise and Fall of Prohibition*, 294–95 (New York, 1973); Andrew Sinclair called them the "heroes of the enforcement service," Sinclair, *Prohibition: The Era of Excess* (New York, 1962), 184, 314. Daniel Okrent reports Einstein's claim of having arrested close to 5,000 violators; see Okrent, *Last Call: The Rise and Fall of Prohibition* (New York, 2010), 136, 188–89, 258–63, 295–98, 355. See also Charles Merz, *The Dry Decade* (New York, 1931), 135; Michael Lerner, *Dry Manhattan: Prohibition in New York City* (New York, 2007), 114; David Kyvig, *Repealing National Prohibition* (1979; Kent, OH, 2000), 27; Lawrence Friedman, *Crime and Punishment in American History* (New York, 1993), 266 ("Prohibition is often described").
4. "List of persons killed or fatally injured by officers of the Bureau of Prohibition," 15, Circular 55, Nov. 2, 1929, Box 13, 5, WCR.
5. Merz, *The Dry Decade*, 68; Athan Theoharis, *The FBI: A Comprehensive Reference Guide* (Phoenix, AZ, 1999); Kobler, *Ardent Spirits*, 221 (Kramer quotation). The first budget appropriation for the Prohibition Bureau in 1920 was $5 million; by 1930 it was close to $15 million. Enforcement spending overall was, however, larger since the Coast Guard was mandated to enforce the law. About half its expenditures during Prohibition went toward liquor law enforcement, estimated at another $13 million. By way of comparison, the initial budget for the newly renamed FBI in 1936 was $800,000. See Merz, *The Dry Decade*, 110; Clark Warburton, *Economic Results of Prohibition* (New York, 1932), 245–46; Sinclair, *Prohibition*, 184. See also Claire Potter, *War on Crime: Bandits, G-Men and the Politics of Mass Culture* (New Brunswick, NJ, 1998), 196.
6. William G. Brown, "State Cooperation in Enforcement," American Academy of Political and Social Science, *Prohibition: A National Experiment* 163 (Philadelphia, 1932), 30–38.
7. NCLOE, Enforcement of the Prohibition Laws. *Official Records of the National Commission on Law Observance and Enforcement*, 4 (Washington, 1931), 1082; 59, 68–69, 74; Okrent, *Last Call*, 145; see also Thomas Pegram, "Brewing Trouble: Federal State and Private Authority in Pennsylvania Prohibition Enforcement under Gifford Pinchot, 1923–27," *Pennsylvania Magazine of History and Biography* (Apr. 2014): 148; 153–56, 163–91.
8. William G. Brown, "State Cooperation in Enforcement," 32; U.S. Department of Commerce, Bureau of the Census, *Religious Tables*, Denominations, K–Z, statistics, history, doctrine, and work, 1936 (Washington, DC, 1941).

9. On Cannon and Prohibition in Virginia, see Robert A. Hohner, *Prohibition and Politics: The Life of Bishop Cannon* (Columbia, SC, 1999); Hohner, "Prohibition Comes to Virginia: The Referendum of 1914," *Virginia Magazine of History and Biography* 75 (Oct. 1967): 473–88; Mark Benbow, "The Old Dominion Goes Dry: Prohibition in Virginia," *Brewery History* 138 (Winter 2010): 20–53.

10. Hugh Harrington Frasier, "J. Sidney Peters and Virginia Prohibition 1916–1920," (master's thesis, Univ. of Richmond, 1971), 19–20; Hohner, "Prohibition Comes to Virginia," 473–88; Benbow, "The Old Dominion Goes Dry," 20–58. For a wider discussion of Virginia's extremely narrow electoral participation, see J. Morgan Kousser, *The Shaping of Southern Politics: Suffrage Restriction and the Establishment of the One-Party South, 1880–1910* (New Haven, 1974); see also Alexander Keyssar: *The Right to Vote: The Contested History of American Democracy* (New York, 2000), esp., 117–71.

11. Rev. John E. White, "Prohibition: The New Task and Opportunity of the South," *South Atlantic Quarterly* 7 (Jan.–Oct. 1908): 135–41 (quotations); see also William Henry Gravely, "Can the Water be made fine? An essay on Southern Politics, Primaries, Prohibition, Labor, the Negro Question" (1921), Box 3, Virginia ASL Collection, McConnell Library Archives, Radford University, Radford, VA.

12. Carl V. Harris, "Reforms in Government Control of Negroes in Birmingham, Alabama, 1890–1914," in *JSH* 38 (Nov. 1973): 576 (quotation); "Mighty Wave of Reform Sweeps the Entire South," *NYT*, SM, June 2, 1907; White, "Prohibition," The New Task," 140–47; Thomas Pegram, "Temperance Politics and Regional Political Culture: The Anti-Saloon League in Maryland and the South, 1907–1915," *JSH* (Feb. 1997): 75.

13. Hugh Frasier, "J. Sidney Peters: The First Commissioner of Prohibition, *Virginia Cavalcade* 22 (1987): 28–35; J. A. Knowles to J. Sidney Peters, n.d., and J. H. Bray to J. Sidney Peters, May 8, 1916; H. H. Sherman to J. Sydney Peters, April 13, 1916; J. Sydney Peters to C. T. Jordon, June 10, 1916, Box 6A, VPC.

14. Frasier, "J. Sidney Peters" 19–20, 28–35, 30–48; *Official Records of the NCLOE* 4, 1059.

15. "Dry Law Fees will be Reduced," *RTD*, Feb. 1, 1926, 1; see also "Dangerous Police Fees," editorial, *RTD*, Feb. 14, 1926, 6; "Seventeen Years in the Desert," *RTD*, Nov. 20, 1933, 2.

16. Wilbur R. Miller, *Revenuers and Moonshiners: Enforcing Federal Liquor Law in the Mountain South, 1865–1900* (Chapel Hill, NC, 1991); *Official Records of the NCLOE* 4, 1075; anonymous letter, Galax, VA, Apr. 9, 1927, provided by Frank E. Dobson to John R. Saunders, Box 29, 10, and E. Frank Dobson to John R. Saunders, Jan. 22, 1927, Box 8, 26, VPC.

17. John R. Saunders to Frank Dobson, n.d., Box 29, 10; H. B. Smith to E. Frank Dobson, Nov. 14, 1923, Box 29, 10, VPC.

18. Department of Prohibition, *Report to the Governor and General Assembly*, Eleventh Report, 1928 (Richmond, VA, 1929).

19. Department of Prohibition, *Report to the Governor and General Assembly* 6, 1922–1923 (Richmond, VA, 1924); Department of Prohibition, *Report to the Governor and General Assembly*, Eleventh Report, 1928. For arrests overall, see "Seventeen Years in the Desert," *RTD*, Nov. 16, 1933, 4; Nov. 9, 1933, 6.

20. Virginia, State Board of Charities and Corrections, *Annual Report of the State Board of Charities and Corrections to the Governor of Virginia for the Year ending Septem-*

ber 30, 1921, (Richmond, VA, 1922), 16–23; Arthur A. James, *The State Becomes a Social Worker: An Administrative Interpretation* (Richmond, VA, 1944), 64–125, esp. 124–25.

21. *Official Records of the NCLOE* 4, 1048, 1060. Virginia reporting statistics are remarkably incomplete. Many entries fail to list where the sentence was served. For those violators in a one-year period for whom a "remark" was made (3,105 of the 7,274 liquor-law violators prosecuted), 1,327 served on the roads. Department of Prohibition, *Report to the Governor and General Assembly, Sixth Report of the Department of Prohibition, 1922–1923* (Richmond, VA, 1924). See also United States, Prison Industries Reorganization Administration, *The Prison Problem in Virginia: A Survey* (Washington, DC, 1939). In 1946 a blanket prohibition was passed on "whipping, flogging or administration of any similar corporal punishment of any prisoner" on the road force and in the prisons. By this time there was a shift from punishment to rehabilitation. Previously, Virginia prisons operated on a purely punitive philosophy; see *A Report on an Administrative Survey of the Virginia Convict Road Force* (Charlottesville, VA, 1955).

22. J. T. Crute to H. B. Smith, Nov. 15, 1921, Box 54, 6; K. T. Crawley to John R. Saunders, Mar. 16, 1922, Box 54, 6; "Daily Report Records," Box 56, 7, VPC.

23. J. T. Crute to H. B. Smith, Box 54, 6; Crute, "Daily Report," Box 56, 7; "Daily Report," Feb. 12, 1923, Box 56, 7, VPC.

24. J. T. Crute, "Daily Report"s for May 30, 1922–Feb. 29, 1923 show a majority of those he arrested as thirty-nine "black" or "colored" to thirty-four whites; see Crute, "Inspectors Daily Reports," Box 54, Folder 6; Box 56, Folder 7, VPC; *Official Records of the NCLOE* 4 (Washington 1931), 1068.

25. "List of Persons Killed or Wounded by Bureau of Prohibition Agents," Circular 55, Nov. 2, 1929, Box 13, 5; WCR, 1928–1931; *PC*, Mar. 23, 1929.

26. *Official Records of the NCLOE* 4, 1068.

27. *RTD*, Mar. 17, 1925; "Law Seeking White Power," *PC*, Mar. 23, 1929.

28. See W. B. Turner arrest report and J. T. Crute to H. B. Smith, Dec. 21, 1921, Box 54, 6, VPC.

29. Records for arrests made by Chase for violation of the prohibition laws between June 1924 and January 1925 show fifty-nine "colored" or "black," forty-five whites and one person listed as "mixed race." Raids often netted more than one arrest. See A. S. Chase, "Inspectors Reports," June 1924–Jan. 1925, Box 61, 11; "Daily Report," arrest of Arthur Faulkner, Box 61, 11, VPC. Income statistics drawn from "Wages and Hours of Labor in Virginia, 1928," *Monthly Labor Review*, 31 (July 1930), 165.

30. Crute, "Daily Report," Jan. 11, 1923, Box 56, 7, VPC; "Dry Agents Kill Negro," *WP*, June 29, 192, 3.

31. Crute, "Daily Report," Nov. 18, 1922, Box 56, F. 7 VPC; Crute, "Daily Report," Dec. 14, 1922, Box 56, 7, VPC.

32. Frasier, "J. Sidney Peters," 19–20 ("apologists for lawbreakers"); "Mrs. Willebrandt says Law Can be Enforced" *NYHT*, April 20, 1926 (Cannon and Willebrandt quotations); Mabel Walker Willebrandt, *Inside Prohibition* (Indianapolis, 1929), 122; see also "Dry Agents, Facing Guns, Sometimes Must Shoot," *LAT*, Aug. 8, 1929; American Association Against the Prohibition Amendment, "Reforming America With a Shot Gun: A Study of Prohibition Killings" (Washington, DC, 1929).

33. Joseph Era, "Prohibition in Richmond" (master's thesis, Univ. of Richmond,

1996), 77, 91; *Official Records of the NCLOE* 4, 1071. Roanoke showed similar disproportionate rates of arrest: see *Official Records of the NCLOE* 4, 1071–74. The numbers are part of a far longer history of the disproportionate incarceration by race, a legacy of slavery. See, for example, State Board of Charities and Corrections, *Annual Report of the State Board of Charities and Corrections to the Governor* (Richmond, VA, 1912), 51–93. Statewide Prohibition reports show somewhat more even proportions of African-Americans to white violators. The disparity suggests that while African-Americans were more prone to targeting than whites in some cities, in other geographic areas segregation may have veiled them from prying federal and state policing eyes. Tanya Marie Sanchez makes this argument for New Orleans, where prosecutions for bootlegging fell heavily upon ethnic whites. See Tanya Marie Sanchez, "The Feminine Side of Bootlegging," *Louisiana History* 41 (Autumn 2000): 403–33. In areas of tightly organized supply chains, the risks of participating in the trade may have been too high for African-Americans. More research needs to be done on different geographic regions to come to definitive conclusions about the effects of segregation on the wider dynamics of selective enforcement.

34. "Report of arrests, search warrants executed, and seizures made under the Prohibition Law," Apr. 1923, Richmond Police Department, Box 38, 33; "Report of arrests, search warrants executed, and seizures made under the Prohibition law," Feb. 1925, Box 38, 34, VPC. The addresses of those arrested show a pattern of targeting poor, working-class, and African-American neighborhoods; see also Era, "Prohibition in Richmond," 53; *RTD,* Jan. 25, 1925, 12 ("whirlwind crusade").

35. "Smash Doors in Raid," *RTD,* Jan. 28, 1925, 3; *Official Records of the NCLOE* 4, 1064; "Report of arrests," Feb. 1925, Apr. 1923. Names of individuals were tracked in *Richmond Virginia City Directory Hill Directory, 1921–1925,* Richmond Historical Society.

36. *Richmond Police Department: A Legacy of Excellence* (Dallas, 2001), 23, 28–29, VHS. For the expansion of state penal powers resulting from the war on alcohol, see ch. seven. See also Erik Monkonnen, "History of Urban Police," *Crime and Justice* 15 (1992): 547; Nathan Douthit, "Police Professionalization and the War Against Crime in the United States, 1920–1930s," in *Police Forces in History,* ed. George L. Mosse (Beverly Hills, 1975); William Thomas Allison, "The Militarization of American Policing: Enduring Metaphor for a Shifting Context," in *Uniform Behavior: Police Localism and National Politics* ed. Stacy McGoldrick and Andrea McArdle (New York, 2006), 15–16; *RTD,* Jan. 25, 1925, 12; "Smash Doors in Raid," *RTD,* Jan. 28, 1925, 3. On police reform more broadly, see Nathan Douthit, "August Vollmer, Berkeley's First Chief of Police, and the Emergence of Police Professionalism," *California Historical Quarterly* 54 (Summer, 1975): 101–24; see also Gene E. Carte and Elaine H. Carte, eds., *Police Reform in the United States: The Era of August Vollmer, 1905–1932* (Berkeley, 1976).

37. In Newport News, a sample of arrest records for a three-month period in 1921 reveals disproportionate convictions of African-Americans charged with "possession, manufacture, storing and transport." In cases where racial identification was available, about half of arrested African-American were convicted; among whites, the vast majority of charges were dropped. The fines meted out for those convicted ranged between $60 and $120 (in contemporary dollars, between $800 and

$1,610) and from one to two months in jail. Newport News, "Report of Prohibition Cases Handled by the division of Police," City of Newport News, Virginia, Box 38, 29, VPC. Names of those arrested were tracked through local city directories for occupation and race; see City of Newport News, City Directory, 1920, 1923, Virginia Room, Newport News Public Library.

38. "Mob Storms Jail, Lynches Man," *RTD*, Mar. 21, 1925; "Klansmen Flog Negro in Northern Neck,' *RTD*, Apr. 10, 1926, 10.
39. *Official Records of the NCLOE* 4, 45; *Richmond Planet*, Jan. 17, 1920, 4.
40. Edward B. Rembert to Herbert Hoover, May 20, 1930; "George Hughes lynching in Sherman . . . ," May 1930, Department of Justice Classified Subject Files on Civil Rights, 1914–1949, National Archives, College Park, MD, Record Group 60, ProQuest History, Folder 101767-016-0217.
41. "New Bill Hits Illegal Search by Dry Agents," *PC*, Jan. 11, 1930, 20.
42. *The Oregonian*, Jan. 5, 1924; Feb. 5, 1924; April 6, 1924. See also Kenneth D. Rose, "The Labbe Affair and Prohibition Enforcement in Portland," *Pacific Northwest Quarterly* 77 (April 1986): 42–51.
43. "Profits of Vice," *PC*, Jan. 11, 1930, 10.
44. Booker T. Washington to Mr. W. H. Morgan, April 29, 1912, Box 35, 3, RHP. Earlier, Washington had publicly supported state prohibition in Georgia. These sentiments may have expressed a change of view or opposition to a federal approach rather than to all restrictive liquor legislation. For Washington's earlier views, see "Prohibition and the Negro," *Outlook*, Mar. 14, 1908; "Dry of Booze, Wet with Tears, *PC*, Dec. 6, 1924; *Richmond Planet*, Mar. 6, 1920, Jan. 3, 1920, Jan. 17, 1920; *PC*, Apr. 13, 1929; Lerner, *Dry Manhattan* (New York, 2007), 201, 223–25.
45. W. James, *The State Becomes a Social Worker,* 152–54; see, for example, Harris, "Reforms in Government Control of Negroes," 594.
46. Nicholas Bravo, "Spinning the Bottle: Ethnic Mexicans and Alcohol in Prohibition Greater Los Angeles " (PhD diss., Univ. of California-Irvine, 2011), 95–96, 100–101, 120. On Vollmer and the LAPD, see Douthit, "August Vollmer, Berkeley's First Chief of Police," 101–24.
47. Bravo, "Spinning the Bottle, 9, 98–99, 108, 116.
48. Bravo, "Spinning the Bottle," 75.
49. Douglas Bukowski,"William Dever and the Mayoral Elections of 1923 and 1927, *Chicago History* (Spring 1978): 109; Willrich, *City of Courts: Socializing Justice in Progressive Era Chicago* (Chicago, 2003). 561; Lerner, *Dry Manhattan,* 116.
50. Julien Comte, "Let the Federal Men Raid: Bootlegging and Prohibition in Pittsburgh," *Pennsylvania History* (Spring 2010): 77, 172; Bert Iacobucci interview transcript, Oct. 23, 1979, BVLHC.
51. Ormond Montini, interview transcript, Aug. 2, 1978, BVLHC.
52. Lou Tadora, interview transcript, Oct. 30, 1979, BVLHC.
53. See, for example, "Bootleg Queen, Cultured and Exotic," *New Orleans Times Picayune*, Oct. 22, 1925, in Sanchez, "The Feminine Side of Bootlegging," 404; Lerner, *Dry Manhattan*, 157; Bert Iacobucci interview transcript; "Women Bootleggers," *PC*, Nov. 23, 1929, 3 ("75 percent").
54. Mary Murphy, "Bootlegging Mothers and Drinking Daughters: Gender and Prohibition in Butte, Montana," *American Quarterly* 46 (June 1994): 185; Sanchez, "The Feminine Side of Bootlegging," 403–33, esp., 415–19.
55. Sanchez, "The Feminine Side of Bootlegging," 411–20.

56. Sanchez, "The Feminine Side of Bootlegging," 408, 420.
57. "Women Bootleggers," *PC*, Nov. 23, 1929, 3.
58. Willrich,"'Close that Place of Hell': Poor Women and the Cultural Politics of Prohibition," *JUH* 29 (July 2003): 558, 568.
59. Dorothy Marie Brown, *Setting a Course: American Women in the 1920s* (New York, 1987), 54–56, 154; Sanchez, "The Feminine Side of Bootlegging," 415.
60. *Official Records of the NCLOE* 4, 426, 68, 575.
61. *Official Records of the NCLOE* 4, 926. African-Americans constituted 40 percent of Texas prisoners during the Moody administration but less than one-fourth of the state's population. Prohibition violators "formed a large portion of the convict population." See Paul M. Lucko, "A Missed Opportunity: Texas Prison Reform during the Dan Moody Administration, 1927–1931," *Southwestern Historical Quarterly* 96 (July 1992): 36–46.
62. "Report of James J. Forrester and Interviews with Labor Representatives in Indianapolis, Lafayette and Vicinity," July 16, 1930, 1, 5, 6, 12 (quotations), Circular 291, Box 19, 2, WCR.
63. "Report of James J. Forrester," 5.
64. Lerner, *Dry Manhattan*, 117.

4. Gestures of Daring, Signs of Revolt

1. Lewis A. Erenberg, *Steppin' Out: New York Nightlife and the Transformation of American Culture, 1890–1930* (Chicago, 1981), 244; "Why We Go to Cabarets," *New Yorker*, Nov. 27, 1925, 7.
2. "Minutes, Fourth Annual Report of the Women's Committee for Repeal of 18th Amendment," 3, Jan. 24, 1930, Box 1, LGP.
3. Herbert Asbury, *The Great Illusion: An Informal History of Prohibition* (New York, 1950), 195–97; Erenberg, *Steppin' Out,* 238 (quotation). Other accounts of New York nightlife transformation include Donald Miller, *Supreme City: How Jazz Age Manhattan Gave Birth to Modern America* (New York, 2014); Michael Lerner, *Dry Manhattan: Prohibition in New York City* (Cambridge, MA, 2007), 199–226; Chad Heap, *Slumming: Sexual and Racial Encounters in American Nightlife, 1885–1940* (Chicago, 2009), 189–276.
4. "Ritz case" and "Report by Raymond Perry," Feb. 1, 1928, Box 10, 13, NEWWS; see also Asbury, *The Great Illusion*, 196; Investigation Report, 1920, Box 34; Investigation, "speakeasies," Box 37, COFR; Miller, *Supreme City*, 115.
5. Investigation Report, 1920, Box 34; Investigation, "speakeasies," Box 37; Moskowitz & Lupowitz restaurant, Investigation Report, Aug. 17, 1920, Box 34, COFR.
6. Miller, *Supreme City*, 124; Investigation Report, "Nightclubs, Speakeasies," 1928, Box 37, COFR.
7. Investigation Report, 1920, Dec. 8, 1920, Box 34; Investigation Report, 1920, Dec. 1928, Box 34, Investigation Report; "Speakeasies not included in nightclub list investigated, 1928," Box 37, COFR; Lerner, *Dry Manhattan*, 155–60.
8. Kevin Mumford, *Interzones: Black/White Sex Districts in Chicago and New York in the Early Twentieth Century* (New York, 1997), 144; Investigation Report, 1920, June 15, 1920, Box 34; Investigation Report, Dec. 8, 1920, Box 34, Investigation Report, June 25, 1924; Investigation of Vice Conditions during the Democratic Convention, 1924, Box 35, COFR.

9. Heap, *Slumming*, 17–153.

10. For a discussion of shifts in women's work during the war and postwar years, see, for example, Alice Kessler-Harris, *Out to Work: The History of Wage-Earning Women in the United States* (1982; New York, 2003), 217–49; see also Investigation Report, "Speakeasies, not included in nightclub list investigated, 1928", Box 37, COFR; Stanley Walker, *The Nightclub Era* (New York, 1933), 30–31.

11. Investigation Report, "Speakeasies not included in nightclub list investigated, 1928," Box 37, COFR.

12. Martha Benley Bruere, *Does Prohibition Work: A Study of the Operation of the Eighteenth Amendment Made by the National Federation of Settlements* (New York, 1927), 282; David Augustine Murphy, *The Eighteenth Amendment* (NY, 1923), 1.

13. *Pittsburgh Courier*, Sept. 4, 1924, 2. On the "panzy craze" and Prohibition-era newly transgressive nightlife scene, see George Chauncey, *Gay New York: Gender, Urban Culture, and the Making of the Gay Male World, 1890–1940* (New York, 1994), 327–35.

14. Heap, *Slumming*, 160; Mumford, *Interzones*, 15, 131, 150 (quotation); see also Elizabeth Schroeder Schlabach, *Along the Streets of Bronzeville: Black Chicago's Literary Landscape* (Urbana, IL, 2013), 10–15. Devarian Baldwin notes the geographic segregation of vice in Chicago's African-American South Side by 1910: see Deverian L. Baldwin, *Chicago's New Negroes: Modernity, the Great Migration and Black Urban Life* (Chapel Hill, NC, 2007), 24–26; Khalil Gibran Muhammad, *The Condemnation of Blackness: Race, Crime and the Making of Modern Urban America* (Cambridge, MA, 2010), 88–145.

15. Mumford, *Interzones*, 15, 131; Schlabach, *Along the Streets of Bronzeville*, 10–15; Lerner, *Dry Manhattan*, 220; Heap, *Slumming*, 202; Baldwin, *Chicago's New Negros*, esp. 21–51. On the Savoy, see Karen Hubbard and Terry Monaghan, "Negotiating Compromise on a Burnished Wood Floor: Social Dancing at the Savoy," in *Ballroom, Boogie, Shimmy Sham, Shake: A Social and Popular Dance Reader*, ed. Julie Malnig (Champaign, IL, 2009); Joel Dinnerstein, *Swinging the Machine: Modernity, Technology and African-American Culture Between the World Wars* (Amherst, MA, 2002); Jervis Anderson, *This Was Harlem* (New York, 1981), 312–13.

16. Heap, *Slumming*, 213 (Lil Hardin Armstrong quotation); Jay D. Smith, *Jack Teagarden: Story of a Jazz Maverick* (New York, 1960), 69–70; Nicholas M. Evans, *Writing Jazz: Race, Nationalism, and Modern Culture in the 1920s* (New York, 2000); William Howland Kenney, *Chicago Jazz: A Cultural History, 1904–1930* (New York, 1993); Geoffrey C. Ward, *Jazz: A History of America's Music* (New York, 2000).

17. David Levering Lewis, *When Harlem Was in Vogue* (New York, 1997); Baldwin, *Chicago's New Negroes*. Baldwin argues that the music clubs and nightlife of the South Side "stroll" provided the structural foundation for black intellectual life. See also Schlabach, *Along the Streets of Bronzeville*; Heap, *Slumming*; Nathan Irvin Huggins, *Harlem Renaissance* (New York, 1971); George Hutchinson, *Harlem Renaissance in Black and White* (Cambridge, MA, 1995); Ann Douglas, *Terrible Honesty: Mongrel Manhattan in the 1920s* (New York, 1995).

18. Heap, *Slumming*, 190, 215–16.

19. *Carl Van Vechten and the Harlem Renaissance: A Portrait in Black and White* (New Haven, 2012); Leon Coleman, *Carl Van Vechten and the Harlem Renaissance: A Critical Assessment* (New York, 1998); Van Vechten, *Nigger Heaven* (New York, 1926). See also Robert F. Worth, "Nigger Heaven and the Harlem Renaissance," *African American Review* 29 (Autumn 1995): 461–73; John Lowney, "Haiti and

Black Transnationalism: Remapping the Migrant Geography of Home to Harlem," *African American Review* 34 (2000): 413.

20. Heap, *Slumming*, 206 ("city administration"); Kathleen Morgan Drowne, *Spirits of Defiance: National Prohibition and Jazz Age Literature, 1920-1933* (Columbus, OH, 2005), 109 ("White New Yorkers"); Lerner, *Dry Manhattan* (New York, 2007), 200 ("modern-day plantation").

21. Allon Schoener, ed., *Harlem on My Mind: Cultural Capital of Black America (1900– 1968* (New York, 1968), 80; Clyde Vernon Kiser, *Sea Island to the City: A Study of St. Helena Islanders in Harlem and Other Urban Centers* (New York, 1932), 4 ("serious offenses"); "Child Slain, 4 shot as Gangsters Fire on Beer War Rival," *NYT*, July 29, 1931, 1; "Gang Murder of Boy Stirs Public Anger," *NYT*, July 30, 1931; Schlabach, *Along the Streets of Bronzeville*, 1–15; "Bomb damages Southside Café and Shoe Shop," *CDT*, July 10, 1926; Lerner, *Dry Manhattan*, 225; Heap, *Slumming*, 225; see also Winthrop D. Lane, "Ambushed in the City: The Grim Side of Harlem," *The Survey* 54 (March 1925): 692–94.

22. Howard Abadinsky, *Organized Crime: An Examination of the Function, Structure, and Historical Background of United States Criminal Organizations from the late 19th Century to the Present* (Chicago, 1985), esp. 98–99. Rothstein got his start in the gambling business and expanded into bootlegging during Prohibition and then used his whiskey ships to build an international drug-smuggling network. See also Jenna Weissman Joselit, *Our Gang: Jewish Crime and the New York Jewish Community, 1900–1940* (Bloomington, IN, 1983); Humbert S. Nelli, *Italians and Syndicate Crime in the United States* (Chicago, 1976); Heap, *Slumming*, 77; Joseph Spillane, "The Making of an Underground Market: Drug Selling in Chicago, 1900–1940," *JSH* 32, no. 1 (Autumn, 1998): 27–48; "Bystander is Shot . . . Bullets Fly in the Street," *NYT*, May 18, 1934, 32.

23. Spillane, "The Making of an Underground Market," 27–48, esp. 38–39.

24. Heap, *Slumming*, 124, 194; Schlabach, *Along the Streets of Bronzeville*, 24.

25. "The National Prohibition Law, Hearings before the Subcommittee of the Committee on the Judiciary," Sixty-Sixth Congress, April 5–24, 1926, 1: 600; Drowne, *Spirits of Defiance*, 74.

26. *Ohio State Lantern*, Jan. 9, 1922, quoted in Paula Fass, *The Damned and the Beautiful: American Youth in the 1920s* (New York, 1997), 307; Nancy Cott, *Grounding of Modern Feminism* (New Haven, 1987), 150.

27. On the committee's early composition, see Jennifer Fronc, *New York Undercover: Private Surveillance in the Progressive Era* (Chicago, 2009), 2, 36–38, 66–69. Though the committee took a different approach than the ASL to rooting out vice, it was closely linked in the public eye with the strict morality of the liquor crusaders. On the campaign and response, see "City Vice Conditions Worst in Twenty Years Survey Declares," *NYT*, June 9, 1928, 1; "Warren Denies Vice as Bad as Reported by Reform Leaders," *NYT*, July 10, 1928; "Women's Clubs Act to End Vice Spies," *NYT*, Feb. 7, 1931, 16; William F. Fuerst, Secretary, New York Foundation, Oct. 1, 1931; William Fuerst to William Baldwin, Jan. 1931, Box 8; Confidential Bulletin, April 30, 1930; "Broadening the Committee's Work" and "Plans for Slightly Enlarging the Committee's Work," Box 38, COFR.

28. Fred Siegal, *Revolt Against the Masses: How Liberalism Undermined the Middle Class* (New York, 2013), 41.

29. Eric Foner, *The Story of American Freedom* (New York, 1998), 185–87.

30. Foner, *The Story of American Freedom*, 197; Ken Kersch, *Constructing Civil Liberties:*

Discontinuities in the Development of American Constitutional Law (New York, 2004), especially 66–88.

31. For a discussion of the importance of civil liberties during the 1920s, see Foner, *The Story of American Freedom*, esp. 163–94; see also Fred Siegel, *The Revolt Against the Masses*. Though I am not convinced of the overall thrust of his argument, Siegel also emphasizes the 1920s as a key moment in crystallizing the ideas of modern liberalism. See also Ken Kersch, *Constructing Civil Liberties*, esp. 66–88.

5. Citizen Warriors

1. Roy Haynes, *Prohibition Inside Out* (New York, 1923), 225.

2. For a description of these conditions, see S. Glenn Young, *Life and Exploits of S. Glenn Young: World Famous Law Enforcement Officer* (Herrin, IL, 1938), 92–94, 112; "New League for Law Enforcement," *MR*, June 22, 1922. For a detailed account of events in Williamson, see Paul Angle, *Bloody Williamson: A Chapter in American Lawlessness* (New York, 1952), 117–205; "Form League for Law Enforcement," *MR*, June 21, 1922; "New League for Law Enforcement," *MR*, June 22, 1922.

3. Arlie Boswell, a Marion Klan leader, later admitted that all the liquor raiders belonged to the Klan. Masatomo Ayabe, "Ku Kluxers in a Coal Mining Community: The Ku Klux Klan Movement in Williamson County, Illinois, 1923–1926," *JISHS* 102 (Spring 2009): 75.

4. On the mobilization of citizen volunteers, see Chris Capozzola, *Uncle Sam Wants You: World War I and the Making of the Modern American Citizen* (New York, 2008), esp. 83–143; Charles Merz, *The Dry Decade* (New York, 1931), 88–110.

5. *Enforcement: An Address by Roy A. Haynes, Issued by the Sub-Committee on Temperance with the Approval of the Friends General Conference* (Philadelphia, 1922), 3; Haynes, *Prohibition Inside Out*, 303–5; Bureau of Prohibition, *Public Cooperation in Prohibition Law Enforcement* (Washington, 1930), 47–53.

6. *US*, Aug. 5, 1920; Addams quoted in "What American Women Think about Prohibition," May 31, 1927, untitled news clipping, and *Oakland Post-Enquirer*, Sept. 17, 1928; "Effects of Prohibition Fairly Tested," *CDT*, July 19, 1924; Reel 19, Jane Addams Papers (UMI Microfilm, Ann Arbor, 1985).

7. Baker quoted in "Report of Purley Baker to the Executive Committee" July 14, 1921, Anti-Saloon League Records, in Kerr, *Organized for Prohibition: A New History of the Anti-Saloon League* (New Haven, 1986), 216; Taft quoted in *Law vs. Lawlessness: Addresses delivered at the Citizenship Conference*, ed. Fred B. Smith, Washington, DC, Oct. 13–15, 1923 (New York, 1924), 20; Law Enforcement League, *Address by Honorary Joseph Buffington, Fourth Anniversary Banquet, Law Enforcement League of Philadelphia,* Mar. 11, 1926 (Philadelphia, 1926), 6; Felix Frankfurter, "National Policy for the Enforcement of Prohibition," *Annals of the American Academy of Political and Social Science* 109 (Sept. 1923): 193–95.

8. Warren G. Harding, State of the Union Address, Dec. 8, 1922, American Presidency Project, University of California Santa Barbara, http://www.presidency.ucsb.edu; Robert Post, "Federalism, Positive Law and the Emergence of the American Administrative State: Prohibition and the Taft Court Era," *WMLR* 48 (2006): 7; L. T. Frazier, "Every Citizen an Enforcer," in *Law Observance: Shall the People of the United States Uphold the Constitution*, ed. W. C. Durant (New York, 1929), 252.

9. "Legislative Program," *Report of the Crusade Anniversary Convention of the National*

Woman's Christian Temperance Union, 1923, Reel 9, TPP. On early membership, see Janet Zollinger Giele, *Two Paths to Women's Equality: Temperance, Suffrage and the Origins of Modern Feminism* (New York, 1995), 63–65, 112. For WCTU membership statistics from 1920 to 1930, see Joseph Gusfield, *Symbolic Crusade: Status Politics and the American Temperance Movement* (Urbana, IL, 1963), 162; Ines Haynes Irwin, *Angels and Amazons: A Hundred Years of American Women* (New York, 1934); "Report of the Forty-Sixth Annual Convention of the National Woman's Christian Temperance Union," 1919, esp. 71–79, Reel 9, TPP; Elizabeth Putnam, *Women Torch-Bearers: The Story of the Woman's Christian Temperance Union* (Evanston, IL, 1924); see also Alison Parker, *Purifying America: Women, Cultural Reform and Pro-Censorship Activism, 1873–1933* (Urbana, IL, 1997), 29.

10. Ian Tyrell, *Woman's World: Woman's Empire: The Woman's Christian Temperance Union in International Perspective, 1880–1990* (Chapel Hill, NC, 1991). On "peace" and purity," *US*, May 20, 1920; see also Alison M. Parker, *Purifying America: Women, Cultural Reform and Pro-Censorship Activism, 1873–1993* (Urbana, IL, 1997), 134–94; Anna Gordon, Presidential Address, *Report of the Forty-eighth Annual Convention of the National Woman's Christian Temperance Union*, 1921, 60–61 (quotations); "Resolutions," *Report of the Forty-Ninth Annual Convention of the National Woman's Christian Temperance Union*, 1922, 33, 42–44, Reel 9, TPP.

11. "Resolutions," *Report of the Forty-Eighth Annual Convention* 33. For a sample listing of the posters and pamphlets, see "Posters are Always Useful," *US*, Apr. 1, 1920, and "Material for Study," *US*, Nov. 14, 1925, 13; Minute Book, Apr. 24, 1922, Woman's Christian Temperance Union, Flint, Michigan, chapter, Reel 48, TPP; see also "The Time to Educate for Law Enforcement is Now" and "Is the Work of the Temperance Forces Finished?" *US*, Mar. 11, 1920. On plays, see *US*, Apr. 1, 1920.

12. Meeting Minutes, Nov. 28, 1926, Flint, Michigan, chapter, Reel 48, TPP; *Report of the Forty Annual Convention of the National Woman's Christian Temperance Union*, 1921, 33, 42–44, Reel 9, TPP; see also "Law Enforcement Plans," *US*, June 6, 1925; *US*, Mar. 24, 1928, 7.

13. Fannie L. Taylor, "Missouri Mid-Year Executive Stirs Women on Law Enforcement," *US*, July 8–15, 1920.

14. Cook County WCTU Minute Book, Dec. 1, 1925, in Rachel Bohlmann, "Drunken Husbands, Drunken State: Woman's Christian Temperance Union's Challenge to American Families and Public Communities in Chicago, 1874–1920, (PhD diss., Univ. of Iowa, 2001), 363; Meeting Minutes, Apr. 24, 1922, Annual Report of Flint Central, Flint, Michigan, chapter, Reel 48, TPP; Bohlmann, "Drunken Husbands," 364 (quotation).

15. On Carrie Nation see Fran Grace, *Carry A. Nation: Retelling the Life* (Bloomington, IN, 2001); Anna Gordon, Presidential Address, *Report of the Forty-Eighth Annual Convention*, 1921, 60–70 Reel 9, TPP; Cook County WCTU Minute Book, Dec. 1, 1925, in Bohlmann, "Drunken Husbands," 363–65.

16. "WCTU Points of Excellence," *US*, June 24, 1920, 7; "Legislative Program," *Report of the Crusade Anniversary Convention of the National Woman's Christian Temperance Union*, 1923, 137 ("officers of the law"); see also "Legislative Program," *Report of the Golden Jubilee Convention*, 1924, 72–75, Reel 9, TPP; Bohlman, "Drunken Husbands," 366; Leonard J. Moore, *Citizen Klansmen: The Ku Klux Klan in Indiana, 1921–1928* (Chapel Hill, NC, 1991), 34. On members' work for compulsory legislation for Bible reading, see "The Bible in the Public Schools," *Report of the Crusade Anniversary Convention*, 1923, 202–4, Reel 9, TPP.

17. The WCTU reported the resolve of local citizens to "hunt for and secure evidence" of liquor violations and to request the sheriff to "deputize reliable men in each neighborhood," *US*, Dec. 14, 1922, 3. For an account of the league's struggles, see K. Austin Kerr, *Organized for Prohibition: A New History of the Anti-Saloon League* (New Haven, 1985), 211–54 (Ernest Cherrington quotation, 219–21).

18. Kerr, *Organized for Prohibition*, 221; *National Prohibition Enforcement Manual* (Westerville, OH, 1921), 31, Reel 6, TPP; *National Prohibition Law Enforcement Manual*, Reel 6, TPP; These efforts are detailed in the campaign of the Ohio League for "Dry Enforcement Leagues." The Ohio League appointed a county organization for law enforcement and organized meetings at the county and local level. See, for example, letters from T. M. Ware, Oct. 22, 1922, June 13, 1923, Mar. 31, 1923, Reel 1, TPP.

19. See James H. Madison, *Indiana Through Tradition and Change: A History of the Hoosier State and its People, 1920–1945* (Indianapolis, 1982), 40–41, 301–2; Peter Odegard, *Pressure Politics: The Story of the Anti-Saloon League* (New York, 1928), 1–35. On Webb's activities, see W. J. Millburn to Purley, July 8, 1921, Reel 83, TPP; Atticus Webb, *Dry America: A Study for the Use of Churches, Sunday Schools, Young People's Societies, Women's Organizations, etc.* (Nashville, TN, 1931); United States Senate, *Hearings before the Subcommittee of the Judiciary, Apr. 5–26, 1926*, 1 (Washington, DC, 1926), 3889; "Wet Amendments Buried in the House," *NYT*, Dec. 9, 1922, 4.

20. See "resolutions adopted," in Minutes of the Meeting of the Executive Committee of the ASL, Jan. 15–16, 1920, Reel 83, TPP; see also Kerr, *Organized for Prohibition*, 220, 230–33; Robert Smith Bader, *Prohibition in Kansas: A History* (Lawrence, KS, 1986), 209; Thomas Pegram, "Hoodwinked: The Anti-Saloon League and the Ku Klux Klan in 1920s Prohibition Enforcement," *Journal of the Gilded Age and the Progressive Era* 7, no. 1 (January 2008): 89–119.

21. James White, Ohio League Superintendent, Nov. 20, 1920; see also White, Nov. 2, 1920, Nov. 4, 1920, Nov. 22, 1920, Reel 1, TPP. See also William D. Jenkins, *Steel Valley Klan* (Kent, OH, 1990), 25; "Restaurant is Raided Again," *Youngstown Vindicator*, July 27, 1923, 15; Jenkins, *Steel Valley Klan*, 29, 34–35.

22. "Dry League's Pet Measure in Ohio faces Disaster," *CDT*, Oct. 17, 1927, 4; Editorial, "Outrageous," *Cleveland Plain Dealer*, Nov. 8, 1926, 10, in Robert Post, "federalism, Positive Law, and the Emergence of the American Administrative State: Prohibition and the Taft Court Era," *William and Mary Quarterly Review* 48 (2006): 114.

23. Jenkins, *Steel Valley Klan*, 29, 34–35.

24. Nancy McLean, *Behind the Mask of Chivalry: The Making of the Second Klan* (New York, 1994), 5; David Chalmers, *Hooded Americanism: The History of the Ku Klux Klan* (Durham, NC, 1987), esp. 32–37; see also Thomas Pegram, *One Hundred Percent American: The Rebirth and Decline of the Ku Klux Klan in the 1920s* (Lanham, MD, 2011), 16.

25. John Moffatt Mecklin, *The Ku Klux Klan: A Study of the American Mind* (New York, 1924), 24–25, 27; Christopher Cocoltchos, "The Invisible Government and the Viable Community: The Ku Klux Klan in Orange County California during the 1920s," (PhD diss., UCLA, 1979), 1, 120; Shawn Lay, "Imperial Outpost on the Border: El Paso's Frontier Klan No. 100," in *The Invisible Empire in the West: Toward a New Historical Appraisal of the Ku Klux Klan in the 1920s*, ed. Shawn Lay (Urbana, IL, 1994), 76; Charles C. Alexander, *The Ku Klux Klan in the Southwest*

(Louisville, KY, 1965), 30–32; Goldberg, *Hooded Empire*, 27 ("money and politics"); Stanley Coben, *Rebellion Against Victorianism: The Impetus for Cultural Change in 1920s America* (New York, 1991), 139; Leonard J. Moore, *Citizen Klansmen: The Ku Klux Klan in Indiana, 1921–1928* (Chapel Hill, NC, 1998), 32–33, 78–79, 138–139; McLean, *Behind the Mask of Chivalry*, 107–11.

26. David Horowitz, "Order, Solidarity, and Vigilance: The Ku Klux Klan in La Grande, Oregon," in *The Invisible Empire in the West*, 205 ("aid the officers"); Robert A. Goldberg, "Denver: Queen City of the Colorado Realm," in *Invisible Empire in the West*, 41 (we . . . assist"); Goldberg, *Hooded Empire: The Ku Klux Klan in Colorado* (Urbana, IL, 1981), 62–63 ("If our officials"); *CDT*, Feb. 18, 1923, cited in *Fiery Cross*, Feb. 23, 1923 ("going in and handling").

27. *The Inglewood Raiders: Story of the Celebrated Ku Klux case at Los Angeles, and speeches to the Jury* (Los Angeles, 1923); Glenn Feldman, *Politics, Society, and the Klan in Alabama, 1915–1949* (Tuscaloosa, AL, 1999), 46; Jenkins, *Steel Valley Klan*, 65–69.

28. Goldberg, "Denver, Queen City," 48; Horowitz, "Order, Solidarity, and Vigilance," 205; *The Inglewood Raiders*; Jenkins, *Steel Valley Klan*, 117–52; Glenn Feldman, *Politics, Society, and the Klan in Alabama, 1915–1949* (Birmingham, AL, 2015), 29–30; William Snell, "The Ku Klux Klan in Jefferson County, Alabama, 1916–1930" (master's thesis, Stamford University, 1967), 63–67; Chalmers, *Hooded Americanism*, 86, 29; Norman Weaver, "The Knights of the Ku Klux Klan in Wisconsin, Indiana, Ohio and Michigan," (PhD diss., Univ. of Wisconsin, 1954), 139–41.

29. Moore, *Citizen Klansmen*, and Kathleen Blee, *Women of the Klan: Racism and Gender in the 1920s* (1991; Berkeley, 2008), emphasize the social attractions of the Klan; Nancy McLean pays closer attention to Klan vigilantism, see McLean, *Behind the Mask of Chivalry*, esp., 149–73; Richard Tucker, *The Dragon and the Cross: The Rise and Fall of the Ku Klux Klan in Middle America* (Hamden, CT. 1991), 8 (*Fiery Cross* quotation).

30. James Martin Miller, *The Amazing Story of Henry Ford: The Ideal American and the World's Most Private Citizen* (Chicago, 1922), 175 ("idea of drink"); "The Jewish Element in Bootlegging Evil," *Dearborn Independent*, Dec. 31, 1921 ("bootlegging"). See "How Jews Gained American Liquor Control," *Dearborn Independent*, Dec. 17, 1921; "Gigantic Jewish Liquor Trust and its Career," *Dearborn Independent*, Dec. 24, 1921; *Colonel Mayfield's Weekly*, Feb. 4, 1922, 238, as in Marni Davis, *Jews and Booze: Becoming American in the Age of Prohibition* (New York, 2012), 160 ("My fight").

31. *The Dawn*, Apr. 21, 1922; Alex Ruggeri interview by Paul Angle, July 30, 1951, Box 1, 2a, PAC; *MR*, Jan. 11, 1924; Father E. Senese interview by Paul Angle, Sept. 5, 1951, PAC.

32. Goldberg, *Hooded Empire*, 152; Horowitz, "Order, Solidarity, and Vigilance," in Lay, ed., *The Invisible Empire in the West*, 189.

33. Horowitz, "Order, Solidarity, and Vigilance," 189.

34. Max Bentley, "The Ku Klux Klan in Indiana," *McClure's Magazine* 57 (May 1924); Tucker, *The Dragon and the Cross*, 83; Madison, *Indiana Through Tradition and Change*, 49. Leonard Moore acknowledges that some klansmen operated under the Horse Thief Detective Association, but does not address their raiding activities, Moore, *Citizen Klansmen*, 123.

35. This congressional investigation focused attention on Klan's vigilante activity; see United States, House of Representatives, *The Ku Klux Klan, Hearings before the*

Committee on Rules, (Washington, DC, 1921). See, for example, "Raids in Mitchell," *Fiery Cross,* Mar. 16, 1923.

36. Cocoltchos, "The Invisible Government and the Viable Community," 179; see also Madison, *Indiana Through Tradition and Change,* 42.

37. Bohlman, "Drunken Husbands," 366; Moore, *Citizen Klansmen,* 34.

38. Blee, *Women of the Ku Klux Klan,* 110–11. On the WCTU, see, for example, "Citizens Committees Help in Law Enforcement," which reported the resolve of local citizens to "hunt for and secure evidence" of liquor violations and to request the sheriff to "deputize reliable men in each neighborhood," *US,* Dec. 14, 1922, 3.

39. Shumaker quoted in "Gillom's Case Against the Indiana Klan," in Tucker, *Dragon and Cross,* 112; James Benson Sellers, *The Prohibition Movement in Alabama, 1702–1945* (Chapel Hill, NC, 1943), 83,194–95; Feldman, *Politics, Society and the Klan,* 65; Snell, "The Ku Klux Klan in Jefferson County, Alabama," 124; Pegram, "Hoodwinked," 89–119 (Darrow quotation on 91); Odegard, *Pressure Politics,* 29; Kerr, *Organized for Prohibition,* 230–32.

40. Odegard, *Pressure Politics,* 1–35. Numerous studies at the local level bear out the important role of pietistic pastors as Klan leaders and backers. See Snell, "The Ku Klux Klan in Jefferson County, Alabama," 50–58; Cocoltchos, "The Invisible Government and the Viable Community," 136, 189; McLean, *Behind the Mask of Chivalry,* 91–95; Goldberg, *Hooded Empire,* 64, 187–88; Jenkins, *Steel Valley Klan,* 16–38.

41. For earlier precedents, see Chris Capozzola, *Uncle Sam Wants You: World War I and the Making of the Modern American Citizen* (New York, 2008).

42. Carroll Binder, "Herrin: Murder Trial or Holy Cause," *The Nation,* Oct. 11, 1922, 357–58; Irving Bernstein, *The Lean Worker: A History of the American Worker, 1920–1933* (New York, 1960), 367–77; McAlister Coleman, *Men of Coal* (New York; 1969); see also Angle, *Bloody Williamson,* 117–40.

43. McAlister Coleman, "The Herrin Trial and Its Background," *Call Magazine,* Nov. 26, 1922, 1–2; Binder, "Herrin: Murder Trial or Holy Cause," 357–58; Bernstein, *The Lean Worker* (New York, 1960), 367–77; John Stewart, [Jury] Foreman, "Complete Text: Grand Jury Report," Sept. 23, 1922, transcribed, PAC.

44. Coleman, "The Herrin Trial and Its Background," 1–2; Stewart, "Complete Text: Grand Jury Report," PAC.

45. Stewart, "Complete Text: Grand Jury Report," PAC.

46. "Successful Massacre," *The Outlook,* Aug. 9, 1922, 591; Illinois Mine Massacre, *Literary Digest,* July 8, 1922, 591. For a summary of the findings of the grand jury, see Stewart, "Complete Text: Grand Jury Report," PAC. The best narrative account of the violence in Herrin from the late nineteenth century through the 1930s is Paul Angle's *Bloody Williamson.* I am indebted to Angle for the rich research materials he deposited at the Chicago History Museum, upon which I have drawn for my own account. Another detailed account is provided by Masatomo Ayabe. Researchers should approach this study with caution. Ayabe takes at face value Klan assertions that the antiliquor campaign was not anti-immigrant. He claims that some Klansmen "began behaving more like unruly bullies than reform minded vigilantes," as if a qualitative difference can be made, and declares that Italian immigrants were "a threat to the healthy order of the local community." Ayabe, Ku Klux Klan Movement in Williamson County, Illinois (PhD diss., Univ. of Illinois, Champaign, 2005), 70, 264, 284, 315.

47. Rudolph Lasker, *Bloody Herrin* (Washington DC, n.d); *Life and Exploits of S. Glenn*

Young, 92–94; NCLOE, Enforcement of the Prohibition Laws, *Official Records of the National Commission on Law Observance and Enforcement* 4 (Washington, DC, 1931), 206–7.

48. *Life and Exploits of S. Glenn Young,* 117; "County Wants Liquor Banned," *Marion Republican,* June 12, 1923; *Chicago Daily Tribune,* Feb. 10, 1924.

49. "New Law and Order Organization," June 27, 1922, *MR;* "Form League for Law Enforcement," *MR,* June 21, 1922. Miners, who were on both sides of the wet and dry forces, stood as the largest occupational group by far in Williamson County. The Klan attracted a significant number of native white Protestant miners to their ranks and proved even more attractive to owners of small businesses, who were overrepresented in the ranks of suspected Klansmen relative to their numbers in the population. Leaders tended to be men of the "better sorts," including merchants, shop-owners, wholesale grocers, and county officials. Still, union-miner membership in the Klan caused conflict with the United Mine Workers, leading the national organization to bar members of the Klan from their ranks in 1924. The concern about Klan influence in the union was so great that four thousand union miners in Illinois threatened to strike until "all members of the Ku Klux Klan are thrown out of union ranks"; see *MR,* Feb. 1, 1924; *CDT,* Feb. 11, 1924. On the membership of the Klan in Williamson County, see Ayabe, "Ku Kluxers in a Coal Mining Community," 73–100.

50. See *Official Records of the NCLOE* 4 (Washington DC, 1931), 216–20; see also United States, *1920 Census of the Population, Williamson County,* www.ancestry .com. The hostility toward Italian immigrants led to the lynching of one Italian miner in Johnston City in 1915: see Ayabe, "The Ku Klux Klan Movement in Williamson County," 67–100."

51. *MR,* Jan. 16, 1923; interview with Father E. Senese by Paul Angle, Sept. 5, 1951, Box 1, 2a, PAC. See also *National Prohibition Enforcement Manual* (Westerville, OH, 1921), 31, Reel 1, TPP; William Chenery, "Why Men Murder in Herrin," Century Magazine (Dec. 1924), 187–94.

52. *MR,* May 26, 1923; June 27, 1923; see also *MR,* Aug. 24, 1924; Senese interview, *PAC.*

53. *MR,* May 21, 1923; "KKK visits Herrin Church," *MR,* June 25, 1923.

54. "Law and Order meeting held on public square," *MR,* Aug. 20, 1923; see also George Galligan, "My Four Year War with the Klan," *SLPD,* Jan. 27, 1927.

55. Glotfely quoted in *MR,* Aug. 20, 1923; see also *MR,* Aug. 30, 1923, and *MR,* Sept. 8, 1923, for anti-immigrant sentiments; Glotfelty quoted in *MR,* Jan. 12, 1924.

56. *MR,* Sept. 8, 1923 (quotation); *MR,* Jan. 12, 1924; interview with John Smith by Paul Angle, July 30, 1951, Box 1, Folder 2a, *PAC;* Angle, *Bloody Williamson,* 140–50. For another account, see Ayabe, "The Ku Klux Klan Movement in Williamson County," 25–100.

57. G. B. Young to Paul Angle, July 31, 1950; Irvin Young to Paul Angle, Sept. 7, 1950, Box 1, PAC; Angle, *Bloody Williamson,* 142–45; *MR,* Dec. 24, 1923, Dec. 26, 1924; *CDT,* Dec. 25, 1923, Jan. 10, 1924.

58. *MR,* Dec. 24, 1923, Dec. 26, 1923; Jan. 9, 1924; *CDT,* Dec. 25, 1923; see also Angle, *Bloody Williamson,* 141–45. One Marion Klan leader admitted that all the liquor raiders were Klansmen: Ayabe, "Ku Kluxers in a Coal Mining Community," 75.

59. Ruggeri interview, PAC; *MR,* Jan. 11, 1924; Senese interview, PAC; *MR,* Jan. 9, 1924, Jan. 11, 1924, Jan. 15, 1924; *CDT,* Jan. 11, 1924.

60. *MR*, Jan. 10, 1924, Feb. 4, 1924; *CDT*, Jan. 12, 1924; Prohibition Bureau Office Order 131, July 18, 1929, Circular, Box 1, 4, WCR.
61. "More raids made in county by Glenn Young," *MR*, Jan. 20, 1924, Jan. 25, 1923 (Stearns quotation), Feb. 6, 1924; *SLPD*, Jan. 30, 1927; *CDT*, Feb. 14, 1924 (state attorney general quotation); see also *CDT*, Mar. 14, 1924.
62. Senese interview, PAC; *CDT*, Feb. 10, 1924; Feb. 14, 1924; Angle, *Bloody Williamson*, 151–56.
63. *CDT*, Feb. 10, 1924; *SLPD*, Feb. 13, 1924, Feb. 14, 1924; *MR*, Feb. 13, 1924; *NYT*, Feb. 11, 1924.
64. The *St. Louis Post-Dispatch* ran a multipart series on events in Williamson; see *SLPD*, Jan. 30, 1927, Feb. 6, 1927, Feb. 13, 1927, Feb. 20, 1927, Feb. 27, 1927; see also Angle, *Bloody Williamson*, 165–68.
65. See "KKK Experiment in Journalism," Box 2, 6, *PAC*; "Factions Meet with Governor Small," Feb. 5, 1925; *SLPD*, Feb. 8, 1925; see also "Klan cannot Parade Masked," *MR*, Sept. 18, 1925.
66. *MR*, Jan. 25, 1923; *SLPD*, Feb. 8, 1925. Williamson County bled population during the 1920s and, no doubt, the sick coal industry played its part. Population stood at 61,012 in 1920 and 53,880 ten years later. The striking disparity between who left and who stayed reinforces the role of the Klan in driving out immigrants as well as African-Americans. Less than one-thirteenth of those who left were native-born whites of native-born parentage. By way of contrast, over one-third of immigrants and their children departed, as did between one-quarter and one-third of the small population of African-Americans. The Klan, in other words, starkly reshaped the demography of the county. United States, *Census of the Population*, 1920, and United States, *Census of the Population*, 1930. Historical Census Browser, University of Virginia Geospatial and Statistical Data Center, http://mapserver.lib.virginia.edu.
67. For an account of the revival meeting, see Hal Trovillion, *Persuading God Back to Herrin* (Herrin, IL, 1925), 18–25; see also Angle, *Bloody Williamson*, 220–25; "Religion and Social Service: the Reformation of Herrin," *Literary Digest*, Aug. 1, 1925, 28–29.
68. "Religion and Social Service," 28–29.
69. *NYT*, June 22, 1924; "Herrin—The "sore spot" of the Nation," Nation, Sept. 14, 1924; Clarence Darrow, "Name Your Poison," *Plain Talk* 1 (Oct. 1927), 3, 8.

6. New Political Loyalties

1. Dorothy Brown, *Mabel Walker Willebrandt: A Study of Power, Loyalty, and Law* (Knoxville, TN, 1984), 49–80; Claire Potter, *War On Crime: Bandits, G-Men and the Politics of Mass Culture* (New York, 1998), 16; Mabel Walker Willebrandt to parents, May 11, 1924, May 23, 1924, June 2, 1924, June 30, 1924, June 2, 1925, Boxes 3–4, MWW.
2. Speech before the Ohio Conference of Methodist Ministers, Sept. 7, 1928, 12, Box 4, MWW; *NYT*, Sept. 8, 1928, 1; Sept. 24, 1928, 1; Brown, *Mabel Walker Willebrandt*, 159–62.
3. Brown, *Mabel Walker Willebrandt*, 159–62; Mabel Walker Willebrandt, *The Inside of Prohibition* (Indianapolis, 1929), 303–17.
4. Franklin Delano Roosevelt to Willmoore Kendall, Aug. 20, 1928, Box 13, Campaign of 1928 Papers, FDR; Roy Peel and Thomas Donnelly, *The 1928 Campaign:*

An Analysis (New York, 1931), 58 (Work quotation); Brown, *Mabel Walker Willebrandt*, 163–64; *Tribuna Italiana Trans-Atlantica*, July 7, 1928, July 14, 1928, July 1, 1928, in John Allswang, "Portrait of a Campaign: Alfred E. Smith and the People of Chicago" (master's thesis, Univ. of Iowa, 1960), 53, 63–69.

5. Elizabeth Tilton diaries, June 26, 1928, June 28, 1928, Reel 993, ETP; *Danish Times*, Dec. 30, 1931, CFLPSR. My argument intersects with Lizabeth Cohen's on the breakdown of insular ethnic identities among Chicago workers during the 1920s. Cohen does not extensively treat Prohibition, however, and places more weight on the Depression as a critical moment in workers' shift in political loyalties. See Lizabeth Cohen, *Making a New Deal: Industrial Workers in Chicago, 1919–1939* (1990; New York, 2008).

6. Carl N. Degler, "American Political Parties and the Rise of the City: An Interpretation," *JAH* (June 1964): 41–59; David Burner, *The Politics of Provincialism: The Democratic Party in Transition, 1918–1932* (New York, 1968).

7. Burner, *The Politics of Provincialism*, 18; V. O. Key, "The Future of the Democratic Party, *VQR* (Spring 1952): 195, 163 (quotation); see also Walter Dean Burnham, *Critical Elections and the Mainsprings of American Politics* (New York, 1970).

8. Harold Gosnell, *Machine Politics: Chicago Model* (1937; Chicago, 1968); Alex Gottfried, *Boss Cermak of Chicago: A Study of Political Leadership* (Seattle, 1962); J. T. Salter, *Boss Rule: Portraits in City Politics* (New York, 1935); *Urban Bosses, Machines, and Progressive Reformers*, ed. Bruce Stave (Lexington, MA, 1972) ; John Allswang, *Bosses, Machines, and Urban Voters* (Baltimore, 1977); Martin Shefter, "Party and Patronage: Germany, England, and Italy," *Politics and Society* 7 (1977): 403–651.

9. George Schottenhamel, "How Big Bill Thomson Won Control of Chicago," *JISHS* 45 (Spring 1952): 30–49, esp. 35; John M. Allswang, "The Chicago Negro Voter and the Democratic Consensus: A Case Study, 1918–1936," *JISHS* 60 (Summer 1967): 145–75; Edward R. Kantowicz, *Polish-American Politics in Chicago, 1888–1940* (Chicago, 1975), 122–26; Eric Leif Davin, *Crucible of Freedom: Workers' Democracy in the Industrial Heartland, 1914–1960* (Lanham, MD, 2010), 19–21; David Harold Kurtzman, *Methods of Controlling Votes in Philadelphia* (Philadelphia, 1935); see also Walter Dean Burnham, *Critical Elections and the Mainsprings of American Politics* (New York, 1970), 50–51.

10. See V. O. Key, "The Future of the Democratic Party," *VQR* 28 (Spring 1952): 195; see also Burner, *The Politics of Provincialism*, 15–27; Degler, "American Political Parties and the Rise of the City," 41–59.

11. Republican Party Platform and Democratic Party platform of 1920, University of California Santa Barbara, Presidency Project, www.presidency.ucsb.edu.

12. On La Follette and Progressive Republicans, see David P. Thelen, *Robert M. La Follette and the Insurgent Spirit* (Madison, WI, 1976); Brett Flehinger, *Public Interest: Robert M. La Follette and the Economics of Democratic Progressivism* (Cambridge, MA, 1997). Harold Ickes wavered between the two parties and supported Al Smith in 1928. In an exchange with Jane Addams, he argued for backing Smith. For Addams's Prohibition views, see "What American Women Think about Prohibition," May 31, 1927, untitled news clipping, and *Oakland Post-Enquirer*, Sept. 17, 1928; "Effects of Prohibition Fairly Tested," *CDT*, July 19, 1924 all in, Reel 19, Jane Addams Papers (UMI microfilm, Ann Arbor, 1985).

13. John Allswang, *A House for All Peoples: Ethnic Politics in Chicago, 1890–1936*, (Lexington, KY, 1971), 111. Political scientists and historians have long debated the

significance of the elections between 1928 and 1936 in a literature too extensive
to cite here. I argue for 1928 as the election that brought immigrant ethnic
working-class voters as a bloc to the party for the first time, laying the foundations for the New Deal coalition. See also Burner, *The Politics of Provincialism*, 236;
Alan Lichtman, *Prejudice and the Old Politics: The Presidential Election of 1928* (Chapel Hill, NC, 1979), esp. 107–21; Gerald H. Gamm, *The Making of the New Deal
Democrats: Voting Behavior and Realignment in Boston, 1920–1940* (Chicago, 1989);
Samuel Lubell, *The Future of American Politics* (New York, 1952); V. O. Key, "A
Theory of Critical Election, " *Journal of Politics* 17 (Feb. 1955): 3–18; Cohen, *Making a New Deal*; Kristi Anderson, The *Creation of a Democratic Majority* (Chicago,
1979); James E. Campbell, "Sources of the New Deal Realignment: The Contribution of Conversion and Mobilization," *Western Political Quarterly* 38 (Sept.
1985): 357–76; James L. Sundquist, *Dynamics of the Party System: Alignment and
Realignment of Political Parties* (Washington, DC, 1983), 191–211

14. "Die Deutsche Füren," *AP*, Sept. 25, 1928.
15. Alex Gottfried, *Boss Cermak of Chicago: A Study of Political Leadership* (Seattle,
    1962), 142; "Volstead Law Expands Jails," Sept. 16, 1927, *CDT*, 10 ("rumrun-
    ning"); *Dennie Hlasatel*, Oct. 6, 1922 ("champion"); "Darrow Tilts with Dever,"
    Oct. 22, 1924, *CDT* (Darrow quotation).
16. Czech groups, Irish American Society of Cook County, and the Polish Fellow-
    ship League of Illinois, including nearly every Polish organization in the state,
    pledged "whole hearted support" for Cermak and the referendum. Cermak's wet
    position had more support than Cermak himself: Cermak won by a rather narrow
    margin of 20,000 votes. Gottlieb, *Boss Cermak*, 136.
17. Arthur W. Thurner, "Impact of Ethnic Groups on the Democratic Party in Chi-
    cago, 1920–1928" (PhD diss., Univ. of Chicago, 1966), 96; Allswang, *A House for
    All Peoples*, 11, 121–23; Gosnell, *Machine Politics: Chicago Model* (1937; Chicago,
    1968), 149 (quotations).
18. "Why Chicago Did It," *New Republic*, Apr. 20, 1927, 234–35; Ralph A. Stone,
    "Prosperity, Depression and War, 1920–1945," in John Hoffman, ed., *Guide to the
    History of Illinois* (Westport, CT, 1991), 95.
19. "Why Chicago Did It," 234–36.
20. Gottfried, *Boss Cermak*, 11–117; "Britten's Biervorlage" *AP*, Nov. 1, 1922; "Nass
    oder Trocken" and "Die Prohibitionfrage am 7 November," *AP*, Oct. 25, 1922;
    "Czechoslovaks Protest," Oct. 4, 1922, Oct. 6, 1922, "This is Our Fight," Oct. 17,
    1922, Aug. 27, 1922, in *Denni Hlasatel*, Box 1, 1–6, 182, CFLPSR.
21. Burner, *The Politics of Provincialism*, 77; see also David Farber, *Everybody Ought to
    be Rich: The Life and Times of John J. Raskob, Capitalist* (New York, 2013); Robert
    A. Slayton, *Empire Statesman: The Rise and Redemption of Al Smith* (New York,
    2001); Oscar Handlin, *Al Smith and His America* (1958; Boston, 1987), Christopher
    M. Finan, *Alfred E. Smith: The Happy Warrior* (New York, 2002).
22. Farber, *Everybody Ought to be Rich*, 182–87.
23. Burner, *The Politics of Provincialism*, 114–15.
24. Burner, *The Politics of Provincialism*, 117–28.
25. Jan. 4, 1925, 18, as in Burner, *Politics of Provincialism*, 165 (Dial quotation).
26. Burner, *The Politics of Provincialism*, 200; Roy Peel and Thomas Donnelly, *The
    1928 Campaign: An Analysis* (New York, 1931), 34; Al Smith to Roosevelt, n.d.,
    "Prohibition Issue," Box 15, Campaign of 1924 Papers, FDR.

27. Farber, *Everybody Ought to be Rich*, 225, 229–33.

28. Farber, Everybody Ought to be Rich, 233.

29. Farber, *Everybody Ought to be Rich*, 236 ("storage advocate"); 237 (Thomas quotations). David Kyvig, *Repealing National Prohibition*, (1979; Kent, OH, 2000), 40–79, 236, 238.

30. Allswang, *A House for All Peoples*, 19; Alfred E. Smith , *Campaign Addresses of Governor Alfred E. Smith, Democratic Candidate for President 1928* (Washington, D.C.; 1929), 202.

31. "Conference between Representatives of Organized Labor and members of the subcommittee on Prohibition," May 22, 1930, 17, Box 10, 3, WCR; Farber, *Everybody Ought to be Rich*, 250 ("taking a crack"); Kyvig, *Repealing National Prohibition*, 143.

32. Farber, *Everybody Ought to be Rich*, 250, 253 (quotations); "Hears Smith Gains in Pennsylvania, *NYT*, Aug. 25, 1928, 6.

33. William Ogburn and Nell Talbot concluded that Prohibition was the more influential of the two issues. Ogburn and Talbot, "A Measurement of the Factors in the Presidential Election of 1928" *Social Forces* 8 (Dec. 1929): 175–83; Burner, *The Politics of Provincialism*, 175–83; see also Sam Adams to Roosevelt, Aug. 8, 1928, Box 2; H. M. Anderson to Roosevelt, Oct. 17, 1928, Box 14; Willmoore Kendall to Roosevelt, Aug. 20, 1928, Box 13, Campaign of 1928 Papers, FDR.

34. On the Asheville declaration and Cannon's leadership of the anti-Smith drive, see Robert A. Hohner, *Prohibition and Politics: The Life of Bishop James Cannon, Jr.* (Columbia, SC, 1999), 221–34; Emma Guffy-Miller, Nov. 14, 1928 (quotation); Ellis Ellsworth to Emma Guffey Miller, item 39, Reel 6, EGP.

35. Farber, *Everybody Ought to be Rich*, 248; See also Hohner, *Prohibition and Politics*, 221–34; "Confidential Inter-Office Memorandum," Aug. 10, 1928, Roosevelt to Chairman Raskob and Senator Gerry; Scott Ferris, Democratic National Committee, Oklahoma City, to Roosevelt, Aug. 7, 1928, Campaign of 1928 Papers, Box 13, FDR.

36. "Confidential Inter-Office Memorandum," Roosevelt to Raskob and Sen. Gerry, Aug. 10, 1928; Scott Ferris to Roosevelt, Aug. 7, 1928, Box 13, Campaign of 1928 Papers, FDR.

37. During the campaign, Democrats advertised in almost every foreign-language publication. For a detailed analysis, see Allswang, "Portrait of a Campaign," 53, 63, 201; see also "Deutsches Al Smith-Bureau eröffnet," *AP*, Sept. 25, 1928; "Der Letzte Registrierungstag," *AP*, Sept. 26, 1928; "Democrats Aim Biggest Guns in Illinois," *CDT*, Sept. 26, 1928.

38. *Denni Hlasatel*, Aug. 23, 1928; Oct. 27, 1928; *Dziennik Zwiazkowy*, July 2, 1928, 4; Nov. 2, 1928, 14; *Polonia*, July 5, 1928 and Sept. 27, 1928, in Edward Kantowicz, *Polish-American Politics in Chicago, 1888–1940* (Chicago, 1975), 127–29. Thirty-five hundred Polish-American businessmen sponsored a dinner for Al Smith in September 1928; see also *CDT*, Sept. 16, 1928, 2, as in Allswang, "Portrait of a Campaign," 73.

39. "Die Deutschen Füren," *AP*, Sept. 25, 1928; "Deutsches Al Smith-Bureau eröffnet," Sept. 26, 1928; see also "Der Letzte Registrierungsstag," *AP*, Oct. 8, 1928; "Reifenbeteiligung bei der National-Wahl," *AP*, Oct. 19, 1928.

40. "Der Letze Registrierungstag," *AP*, Sept. 25, 1928. On registration, see also "Reifenbeteiligung bei der National-Wahl," *AP*, Oct. 8, 1928.

41. *La Tribuna Italiana Trans-Atlantica*, July 1, 7, 14, 21, 28, 1928, as in Allswang, "Portrait of a Campaign," 68–70.
42. For a detailed study of the campaign, see Allswang, "Portrait of a Campaign," 53, 63, 201. During Smith's mid-October Chicago visit, he received seventeen delegations of ethnic groups headed by Congressman Sabbath; *Chicago Daily News*, Oct. 19, 1928, in Thurner, "Impact of Ethnic Groups," 319. On the enthusiastic reception, *CDT*, Oct. 20, 1928, 1, 4 and Oct. 17, 1928; "Smith spricht am 16 Oktober im Coliseum," *AP*, Sept. 25, 1928; "Gov. A. E. Smith wird Heute Abend in Chicago sein," *AP*, Oct. 17, 1928; "Demokratische Wardorganisationen" and "Chicago bietet Al Smith sturmisches Willkömmen," *AP*, Oct. 18, 1928. For religious tolerance and Prohibition as central issues, see *CDT*, Oct. 20, 1928, 1, 4; Mississippi WCTU report, 1928, 12–14, Nellie Somerville Papers, Schlesinger Library, Radcliffe Institute for Advanced Study (quotations).
43. On "ethnic class consciousness," see Davin, *Crucible of Freedom*, 20–21. Davin notes the importance of the Smith campaign but says little about Prohibition. See also John Bodnar, *The Transplanted: A History of Immigrants in Urban America* (Bloomington, IN, 1985); Philip Klein, *A Social Study of Pittsburgh: Community Problems and Social Services in Allegheny County* (New York, 1938); Richard Polenberg, *One Nation Divisible: Class, Race, and Ethnicity in the United States Since 1938* (New York, 1980), 36.
44. Davin, *Crucible of Freedom*, 20–21; David Harold Kurtzman, *Methods of Controlling Votes in Philadelphia*; Bruce M. Stave, *The New Deal and the Last Hurrah: Pittsburgh Machine Politics* (Pittsburgh, 1970), 1–66. Former workers attested repeatedly that voting Republican was effectively a condition of employment. See, for example, Bert Iacobucci interview, Dec. 5, 1979, 7, 29–33, Box 2, 49, BVLHC.
45. Eric Leif Davin, "Blue-Collar Democracy: Ethnic Workers and Class Politics in Pittsburgh's Steel Community, 1914–1948" (PhD diss., Univ. of Pittsburgh, 1999) 39 (Zahorsky quotation); John Bodner, *Worker's World: Kinship, Community and Protest in an Industrial Society, 1900–1940* (Baltimore, 1982), 122. See also Bud Schultz and Ruth Schultz, *It Did Happen Here: Recollections of Political Repression in America* (Berkeley, 1989), 70–71; Ormond Montini interview, Aug. 2, 1975, transcript, Box 2, 30, Beaver Valley Historical Society, University of Pittsburgh, Archive Service Center.
46. Ormond Montini interview, Aug. 2, 1975, 30–31; Davin, *Crucible of Freedom*.
47. Stave, *The New Deal and the Last Hurrah*, 66; see also Michael P. Weber, *Don't Call Me Boss: David L. Lawrence, Pittsburgh's Renaissance Mayor* (Pittsburgh, 1988), 19; *Pittsburgh Post-Gazette*, Nov. 2, 1928; "Hears Smith Gains in Pennsylvania," *NYT*, Aug. 25, 1928, 6.
48. *Pittsburgh Post-Gazette*, Aug. 10, 1928, 2; Oct. 16, 1928, 17; Oct. 11, 1928, 13; Sept. 25, 1928, 4; Nov. 2, 1928, 4; Oct. 28, 1928, Despite the volunteer poll watchers, Lawrence still worried about Republican vote fraud. He hired a detective agency as well as a lawyer to watch out for it. Michael Weber, *Don't Call Me Boss: David L. Lawrence, Pittsburgh's Renaissance Major* (Pittsburgh, 1988), 35–36.
49. "All for Al," *Pittsburgh Courier*, Nov. 3, 1928; *Chicago Defender*, Oct. 20, 1928; Allswang, "Portrait of a Campaign," 95; Samuel O'Dell, "Blacks, the Democratic Party, and the Presidential Election of 1928: A Mild Rejoinder," in *Phylon: Atlanta University Review of Race and Culture* (Spring 1987): 5–8. See also *Pittsburgh Courier*, Oct. 27, 1928. One supporter from West Virginia in October 1928 noted the shift

of African-Americans writing to Roosevelt: the "colored people are forming more Democratic clubs than ever before, and seem very determined in their utterances," H. M. Anderson to Roosevelt, Oct. 17, 1928, Box 24, Campaign of 1928 Papers, FDR.

50. Nancy Weiss, *Farewell to the Party of Lincoln: Black Politics in the Age of FDR* (Princeton, 1983), 8; Allswang, "The Chicago Negro Voter," 160.

51. Allswang, "Portrait of a Campaign," 95; *Chicago Defender*, Oct. 20, 1928, Nov. 3, 1928; *CDT*, Nov. 3, 1928; Allswang, "The Chicago Negro Voter," 161; *Chicago Defender*, Oct. 27, 1928.

52. Allswang, "The Chicago Negro Voter," 160; "Negroes Cheer as Democrats attack Hoover," *CDT*, Oct. 4, 1928; *Chicago Defender*, Oct. 20, 1928. See also Lisa Materson, *For the Freedom of Her Race: Black Women and Electoral Politics in Illinois, 1877–1932* (Chapel Hill, NC, 2009), 151–68.

53. *Negro World*, Oct. 10, 1928 ("no soul"; "broad humanities"); July 7, 1928 ("we are with him"; "prostituted"); Nov. 3, 1928 ("recent heavy"; "To the Polls").

54. In Pittsburgh's overwhelmingly black fifth ward, the Democratic candidate won only 5 percent of the black vote in 1924. In 1928, Smith garnered 38.4 percent. FDR gained another 8.2 percent in 1932 to win 46.6 percent of the African-American vote. In 1936 a majority of African-Americans swung to the Democrats. See Bruce Stave, *The New Deal and the Last Hurrah: Pittsburgh Machine Politics* (Pittsburgh, 1970), 34. David Burner's study of New York sanitary districts with overwhelming numbers of black residents' returns finds 41 percent of the black vote for Smith; see Burner, *The Politics of Provincialism*, 237. Nancy Weiss's study, on the other hand, cites a lower number in her study of the New York returns but does not seek to reconcile her findings with Burner's: see Weiss, *Farewell to the Party of Lincoln*, 8. Samuel O'Dell points to the significance of this break, even though small: see O'Dell, "Blacks, the Democratic Party," 1–11. See also Allswang, "Portrait of a Campaign," 163, and "The Chicago Negro Voters," 145–75.

55. John Allswang, *The Political Behavior of Chicago's Ethnic Groups, 1918–1932* (New York, 1980), 38, 57–59, 127, 183–190, 209 (quotation on 38).

56. *CDT*, May 19, 1930; Thurner, "Impact of Ethnic Groups on the Democratic Party," 268, 329, 368.

57. Weber, *Don't Call Me Boss*, 35–36; Stave, *The New Deal and the Last Hurrah*, 37, 40–41; Davin, "Blue Collar Democracy," 110; Lubell, *The Future of American Politics*, 39–40, 56.

58. On Boston's Italian voters see Key, "The Future of the Democratic Party," 161–75; Gerald H. Gamm, *The Making of the New Deal Democrats* (Chicago, 1989), 85–89. On New York, see Burner, *The Politics of Provincialism*, 236; Lubell, *The Future of American Politics*, 28–57.

59. V. O. Key, "A Theory of Critical Elections," *Journal of Politics* (Feb. 1955): 4, 8; Lubell, *The Future of American Politics*, 28–41; Burner, *The Politics of Provincialism*, 13; see also Burnham, *Critical Elections and the Mainsprings of American Politics*.

60. One "Republicans for Smith" ward chairman wrote Roosevelt declaring the intention of the "thousands of Al Smith Republicans" in Philadelphia planning to switch registration to vote for FDR; see Michael J. Colby to Roosevelt, Nov. 3, 1931, Guffey folder, correspondence, Papers as Governor, *FDR*; Degler, "American Political Parties and the Rise of the City," *JAH* (June 1964): 56. While between 1920 and 1936 the actual electorate grew between 50 and 100 percent, in

nineteen cities with over 50 percent immigrant stock the Democratic vote sky-rocketed, increasing an average of 205 percent; Anderson, *The Creation of a Democratic Majority*, 9, 32.

61. Lerner, *Dry Manhattan*, 251. Thurner found large increases in voter registration in Chicago, especially in the heavily ethnic wards: Ward 19 jumped from 29,264 in 1920 to 49, 463 by 1930; Ward 15 leapt from 29,472 to 45,820 during the same period: Thurner, "Impact of Ethnic Groups," 368–71.

62. See Key, "A Theory of Critical Elections," 3–18; see also Key, "The Future of the Democratic Party," 161, 163.

63. See Key, "A Theory of Critical Elections," 3–18; see also Key, "The Future of the Democratic Party," 161, 163; Lubell, *The Future of American Politics*, 39–41; Anderson, *The Making of a Democratic Majority*; Allswang, *A House for All People*; Kyvig, *Repealing National Prohibition*, 155; Richard Oestreicher, "Urban Working-Class Political Behavior and Theories of Electoral Politics, 1870–1940," *JAH* 77 (March 1988): 1275, 1281. While Prohibition is typically viewed as the archetypal example of ethnocultural politics, it subsumed latent class resentments, presaging the future New Deal alignment.

64. See Thomas S. Carla, "Publicity Division of the Democratic Party, 1929–1930," *APSR* (Feb. 1931): 68–72; Earl Purdy to Roosevelt, Nov. 10, 1928, Campaign of 1928 Papers, Box 6, FDR.

7. Building the Penal State

1. "Gang Massacre," *BDG*, Feb. 24, 1929; "Killing of 7 Laid to Chicago Police," *NYHT*, Feb. 16, 1929; Michael Willrich, *City of Courts: Socializing Justice in Progressive Era Chicago* (Chicago, 2003), 289.

2. "A New Hoover is Heard," *NYT*, Mar. 5, 1929, 1; 7; Herbert Hoover, Inaugural Address, Mar. 4, 1929, American Presidency Project, http://www.presidency.ucsb.edu.

3. Deok-Ho Kim, "A House Divided: The Wickersham Commission and National Prohibition," (PhD diss., SUNY Stony Brook, 1992), 107. For Wickersham funding, see James D. Calder, *The Origins and Development of Federal Crime Control Policy: Herbert Hoover's Initiatives* (Westport, CT, 1993), 84; "Senate Yields on Wickersham Fund; Votes All," *CDT*, July 4, 1930, 2; Franklin E. Zimring, "Barrock Lecture: The Accidental Crime Commission: Its Legacies and Lessons, *Marquette Law Review* 96 (2013): 995–1013. On the enforcement acts, see Eric Foner, *Reconstruction: America's Unfinished Revolution, 1863–1877* (New York, 1988), esp., 412–557.

4. For Coolidge's views, see "Coolidge Deplores Rise in Crime, Religion is the only Remedy," *NYT*, Oct. 21, 1925; see also Zimring, "Barrock Lecture: The Accidental Crime Commission."

5. "Hoover Demands Respect for Law," *NYT*, Apr. 23, 1929, 1. James Calder offers the most extensive discussion of Hoover's crime control initiatives: see Calder, *The Origins and Development of Federal Crime Control Policy: Herbert Hoover's Initiatives* (Westport, CT, 1993); see also Glen Jeansonne, *The Life of Herbert Hoover, Fighting Quaker, 1928–1933* (New York, 2012), 89–112.

6. Legal scholars have done more than others to grapple with Prohibition; see Robert Post, "Federalism, Positive Law and the Emergence of the American Admin-

istrative State: Prohibition and the Taft Court Era," *WMLR* 48 (2006); Lawrence Friedman, *Crime and Punishment in American History* (New York, 1993), 256–66; William Stuntz, *Collapse of American Criminal Justice* (Cambridge, MA, 2011); Ken Kersch, *Constructing Civil Liberties: Discontinuities in the Development of American Constitutional Law* (New York, 2004), esp. 66–88; see also James Marone, *Hellfire Nation: The Politics of Sin in American History* (New Haven, 2003), 318–49.

7. Kim, "A House Divided," 112–17; "Mrs. Sabin Resigns Republican Post," *NYT*, Mar. 9, 1929, 3. On Sabin, see *American Women and the Repeal of Prohibition* (New York, 1996); Grace C. Root, *Women and the Repeal: The Story of the Women's Organization for National Prohibition Reform* (New York, 1934), 3.

8. Calder, *The Origins and Development of Federal Crime Control Policy*, 5; "Hoover Demands Respect for Law," *NYT*, Apr. 23, 1929, 1.

9. Post, "Federalism, Positive Law," 103 (Beck quotation); Albert J. Harno, "Crime and Punishment," in *American Law Institute Proceedings* (May 20, 1954): 45; C. P. Connolly, "America—Land of the Lawbreaker," *McClure's Magazine*, July 1923, 40; Harry Elmer Barnes, "Reflections on the Crime Wave," *Bookman*, Sept. 1926, 44, quoted in Post, "Federalism, Positive Law," 103 n. 348.

10. See, for example, "A Carnival of Crime," *HC*, Oct. 6, 1929; "Redlands Carnival of Crime," *LAT*, Oct. 9, 1922; Claire Potter, *War on Crime: Bandits, G-Men, and the Politics of Mass Culture* (New Brunswick, NJ, 1998), 69; Willrich, *City of Courts*, 290.

11. Daniel Okrent, *Last Call: The Rise and Fall of Prohibition* (New York, 2010), 276; Calder, *The Origins and Development of Federal Crime Control*, 130; John Landesco, "Prohibition and Crime," in Annals of the American Academy of Social Science, *Prohibition: A National Experiment* 163 (Sept. 1932), 127; Willrich, *City of Courts*, 290–91, Douglas Bukowski, "William Dever and Prohibition: The Mayoral Elections of 1923 and 1927," *Chicago History* (Summer 1978): 7, 114.

12. Sam Bass Warner, *Crime and Criminal Statistics in Boston* (Cambridge, MA, 1934); Survey of Crime and Criminal Justice in Boston (Cambridge, MA, 1934), 3–34.

13. Friedman, *Crime and Punishment*, 340; United States, National Commission on Law Observance and Enforcement, *Report on the Enforcement of the Prohibition Law* (Washington, DC, 1931), 4; Arthur Evans Wood, "Crime," in *American Journal of Sociology* 35 (May 1930): 1031; see also Marone, *Hellfire Nation*, 324–33.

14. *Missouri Crime Survey* (New York, 1926), 5; Friedman, *Crime and Punishment*, 340 (E. W. Burgess quotation); Landesco "Prohibition and Crime," 125; Post, "Federalism, Positive Law," 103 n. 349 (*New York Times* letter).

15. Landesco, "Prohibition and Crime," 128; Harno, "Crime and Punishment," 522.

16. Rebecca McLennan, *The Crisis of Imprisonment: Protest Politics and the Making of the American Penal State, 1776–1941* (New York, 2008), 450–55; see also Prison Association of New York, Annual Report (New York, 1929), 95–102; Cornelius F. Collins, "Crime: A Critical Analysis," *NAR* 226 (July 1928): 27–36; Norman Clark, *Deliver Us from Evil: An Interpretation of American Prohibition* (New York, 1976), 194–96.

17. Raymond Moley, *An Outline of the Cleveland Crime Survey* (Cleveland, 1922); see also Sheldon Glueck and Eleanor T. Glueck, "One Thousand Juvenile Delinquents," *Survey of Crime and Criminal Justice in Boston*, conducted by the Harvard Law School, introduction by Felix Frankfurter (Cambridge, MA, 1931), 1–24; Warner, *Crime and Criminal Statistics in Boston*; *Missouri Crime Survey* (New York, 1926).

18. Kim, "A House Divided," 153, 172. The commission researchers were some of the best-known social scientists of their day. On social science and its intersection with social policy, see Dorothy Ross, *The Origins of American Social Science* (New York, 1991), esp. 143–470. For the New Deal period, see Alan Brinkley, *The End of Reform: New Deal Liberalism in Recession and War* (New York, 1996).

19. Simon A. Cole, *Suspect Identities: A History of Fingerprinting and Identification* (Cambridge, MA, 2001), 161–66; Potter, *War on Crime*, 29.

20. Warner opinion cited in "Progress Report," 1–5, Oct. 24, 1929, Reel 99, *FFP*; Ronald H. Beattle, "Sources of Statistics on Crime and Correction," *Journal of the American Statistical Association* 54 (Sept. 1959): 582–92: Lent D. Upson, Report on Criminal Statistics: Comment, *Michigan Law Review* 30 (Nov. 1931): 70–71: Sam Bass Warner, "Survey of Criminal Statistics in the United States," USNC, Report on Criminal Statistics, 3 (Washington, DC, 1931); Calder, *The Origins and Development of Federal Crime Control*, 88–93; Felix Frankfurter to Max Lowenthal, July 1, 1929, Reel 48, *FFP*. See also Kim, "A House Divided," 204.

21. Beattle, "Sources of Statistics on Crime and Correction," 582–92; Upson, "Report on Criminal Statistics," 70–71; Calder, *The Origins and Development of Federal Crime Control*, 88–93; Felix Frankfurter to Max Lowenthal, July 1, 1929, Reel 48, FFP. For another discussion of the Uniform Crime Report's creation, but not the internal debate on statistical gathering, see Lawrence Rosen, "The Creation of the Uniform Crime Report," *SSH* 19 (Summer 1995): 215–38.

22. Friedman, *Crime and Punishment*, 270; NCLOE, *Report on Enforcement of the Prohibition Laws of the United States* (Washington, DC, 1931), 58; "Dry Law Violators Most Numerous, Says U.S. Prison Official," *CDT*, May 19, 1931, 12 (Moore quotation). Drug violators were never far behind liquor-law violators as the leading class of federal prisoners, in some years surpassing them. Despite this variability, Volstead and narcotics violators made up the core of the problem of prison overcrowding; see NCLOE, *Report on Enforcement of the Prohibition Laws*, 58. See also Department of Justice, Bureau of Justice Statistics, *Historical Correctional Statistics in the United States, 1850–1985* (Rockville, MD, 1986), 29–30.

23. David F. Musto, *American Disease: Origins of Narcotic Control* (New Haven, 1973), 204; "3,700 Convicts Riot at Leavenworth," *NYT*, Aug. 2, 1929, 1; see also "3 Convicts Die," *NYHT*, Dec. 12, 1931, 1. On Hoover's call for prison growth in the wake of the riot, see *NYT*, Aug. 7, 1929, 1. See also Calder, *The Origins and Development of Federal Crime Control*, 48–49; Arthur Evans Wood, "Crime," *American Journal of Sociology* 35 (May, 1930): 1027, 1028; "Convicts Kidnap Warden," *NYT*, Dec. 12, 1931, 1.

24. Friedman, *Crime and Punishment*, 309 ("There is less room"); Calder, *The Origins and Development of Federal Crime Control*, 44–45. On Texas prison conditions, see Paul M. Lucko, "A Missed Opportunity: Texas Prison Reform during the Dan Moody Administration, 1927–1931," *Southwestern Historical Quarterly* 96 (July 1992): 27–52. Lucko found that African-Americans made up 40 percent of the Texas prison population although they made up only 15 percent of state residents, 36. "Georgia Convict Rolls Increasing," *AC*, Dec. 6, 1921, 1; William Stuntz, *The Collapse of American Criminal Justice* (Cambridge, MA, 2011), 43, 49; Arthur W. James, *The State Becomes a Social Worker: An Administrative Interpretation* (Richmond, VA, 1942), 162–63; Ethan Blue, *Doing Time in the Great Depression* (New York, 2012), 3.

25. Calder, *The Origins and Development of Federal Crime Control*, 154, 167–73; see also "Hoover Backs Mass Drive . . . Need of More Prisons is Stressed," *NYT*, Apr. 30, 1930, 1. See also "Hoover Demands Passage of Dry Enforcement Bills," *NYT*, Apr. 29, 1929, 1. For number of facilities, see Federal Bureau of Prisons, History, http://www.allgov.com/departments/department-of-justice/federal-bureau-of -prisons-bop?agencyid=7204, accessed Nov. 29, 2014.

26. Calder, *The Origins and Development of Federal Crime Control*, 154. The United States Bureau of the Census issued its new annual series *Report on Prisoners in State and Federal Prison and Reformatories* in 1926. Early reports were unreliable and incomplete, relying on voluntary reporting from wardens on "conditions of crowding." Their numbers included only individuals housed in federal and state prisons, excluding those in state and county jails, prison farms, and road forces, and underestimated the numbers of incarcerated. For a discussion of statistics, see Ronald H. Beattle, "Sources of Statistics on Crime and Correction," 582–92.

27. "All Time High Set for U.S. Prisoners," *NYT*, Oct. 20, 1935, E7; Calder, *The Origins and Development of Federal Crime Control*, 170. On the number of prisoners in state and federal facilities across the decades, see United States Bureau of the Census, *Historical Statistics of the United States: Colonial Times to 1970* (Washington, DC, 1975); "Federal and State Institutions, Prisoners, 1926–1970," Series 1135-1143, p. 420; see also "Federal Prison System," in *Encyclopedia of Prisons and Correctional Facilities* (Thousand Oaks, CA, 2004), 312–19; Department of Justice, Bureau of Justice Statistics, *Historical Correctional Statistics in the United States, 1850–1985* (Rockville, MD, 1986), 29–30. Certain states, such as California, pardoned whole classes of Volstead violators after repeal in 1933 to relieve prison overcrowding, but other violators had to appeal to their governors for pardons. See, for example, Alabama, Governor's Office, Benjamin Miller, Board of Pardons, "Executive Orders for the Remission of Fines and Forfeitures, 1931–1939, Alabama," Dept. of Archives and History. Liquor offenders also continued to be sentenced after repeal for failure to pay the reinstituted alcohol tax. Criminologists have noted the relatively flat rates of growth proportional to population from 1940 to 1970, but with the exception of few scholars, they have not charted the earlier leap during Prohibition, not least because systematic annual reports only began in 1926 as a result of rising rates of incarceration. William Stuntz is an exception in noting this first phase of growth. See Stuntz, *The Collapse of American Criminal Justice*, 43, 158–314. On the spike in state prison populations such as in Illinois, Ohio, Tennessee, and Kentucky from the 1920s to 1940 and the subsequent decline in rates of incarceration, see the charts in Alfred Blumstein and Soumyo Moitra, "An Analysis of the Time Series of the Imprisonment Rate in the States of the United States: A Further Test of the Stability of Punishment Hypothesis," *Journal of Criminal Law and Criminology* 70 (Autumn 1979): 384, 385, 388. Blumstein and Moitra interpret their data to point to overall stability by looking at 1925 and 1970, but their stability theory neglects the sharp historical fluctuation—first the spike that began earlier with Prohibition and peaked in 1940 and subsequent decline and the sharp rise once again beginning in 1970 that would put to rest their static analysis of "stability."

28. By 1925 only Virginia and Mississippi did not have laws providing for the release of prisoners on parole. See Illinois, Committee on the Study of the Workings of the Indeterminate-Sentence Law and Parole, *The Workings of the Indeterminate-Sentence*

Law and the Parole System in Illinois (1928), 48; William G. Brown, "State Cooperation in Enforcement," American Academy of Political and Social Science, Prohibition: A National Experiment 163 (Philadelphia, 1932), 30–38; Friedman, Crime and Punishment, 305; L. W. Kolakoski and T. W. Broecker, "The Pennsylvania Parole System in Operation," Journal of Criminal Law and Criminology 23 (Sept. 1932): 427–38; Calder, The Origins and Development of Federal Crime Control, 175.

29. Friedman, Crime and Punishment, 266; "44,022 Liquor Law Violators Convicted," WP, Sept. 29, 1926, 9; Willrich, City of Courts, 285–86; Calder, The Origins and Development of Federal Crime Control, 218. See also "Hoover Will Investigate Federal Court System," BDG, Mar. 9, 1929, 1.

30. See John F. Padgett, "Plea Bargaining and Prohibition in the Federal Courts, 1908–1934," Law & Society Review 24 (1990): 413–50; George Fisher, Plea Bargaining's Triumph: A History of Plea Bargaining in America (Stanford, CA, 2003), 6–7; Kenneth M. Murchison, Federal Criminal Law Doctrine: The Forgotten Influence of National Prohibition (Durham, NC, 1994), 22, 41, 170; Post, "Federalism, Positive Law," 47–103.

31. Post, "Federalism, Positive Law," 66, 58.

32. This discussion draws upon Robert Post's arguments on Prohibition and the Taft Court. See Post, "Federalism, Positive Law," 3.

33. Charles Merz, The Dry Decade (New York, 1931), 233–234; Randall Holcombe, "The Growth of the Federal Government in the 1920s," Cato Journal 18 (Fall 1996): 175–99.

34. Potter, War on Crime, 20, 196; Francisco E. Balderrama and Raymond Rodriguez, Decade of Betrayal: Mexican Repatriation in the 1930s (Albuquerque, NM, 1995), 9; Merz, The Dry Decade, 236, 259; see also NCLOE, Report on the Enforcement of the Prohibition Laws, 16.

35. Potter, War on Crime, 26.

36. According to John Landesco, the Washington Herald reported 1,550 killed from 1920 to 1930, including 494 officers and aides and 1,056 civilians. See Landesco, "Prohibition and Crime," 120–29, 127; Colonel Charles Askins, Unrepentant Sinner: Autobiography of Colonel Charles Askins (Boulder, CO, 1985), 52–53. Herbert Hoover declared that the Border Patrol's charge was to impede the entry of both illegal "people and goods." The Border Patrol took up this mandate; NCLOE, Report on the Enforcement of the Prohibition Laws, 19. See also Kelly Lytle Hernandez; Migra! A History of the U.S. Border Patrol (Berkeley, CA, 2010), 59–63; Askins, Unrepentant Sinner, 53; NCLOE, Report on the Enforcement of the Prohibition Laws, 19; "Border Patrol Plan to Mean New National Military Force," BDG, Jan. 15, 1930, 32; "Hoover Plan Wins" BDG, July 2, 1930, 17; "Proposed Armed Border Guard Becomes Hoover's Stepchild," Baltimore Sun, Jan. 24, 1930, 1.

37. Potter, War on Crime, 22, 33, 33–44.

38. Calder, The Origins and Development of Federal Crime, 86, 149 (Loesch quotation).

39. On Hoover's statement on "aliens," see "Hoover, Annual Message to Congress," WP, Dec. 3, 1930; Calder, The Origins and Development of Federal Crime Control, 144; John C. McWilliams: The Protectors: Harry J. Anslinger and the Federal Bureau of Narcotics, 1930–1962 (Newark, 1990), 57–58; see also Jeansonne, The Life of Herbert Hoover, 89–112.

40. Walter Earl Pittman, Jr., "Richmond P. Hobson, Crusader," (PhD diss., Univ. of

Georgia, 1969), 168; Musto, *American Disease*, 121–32, 260–61; Peter Andreas, *Smuggler Nation: How Illicit Trade Made America* (New York, 2013), 253–90.

41. "Simon Says Drugs Cause Crime Wave," *NYT*, Dec. 19, 1920, 2; Musto, *American Disease*, 121–32, 155, 157, 260–61.

42. Andreas, *Smuggler Nation*, 264. For the government campaign, see, for example, "Halt that Demon Drug, Cry of Uncle Sam," *WP*, Apr. 27, 1924, SM 3.

43. Pittman, "Richmond P. Hobson, Crusader," 174–79; "The Struggle of Mankind Against his Deadliest Foe," broadcast, Mar. 1, 1928, *Narcotics Education* 1, 51–54 (1928), in Musto, *American Disease*, 168; Richmond P. Hobson, "The Peril of Narcotics," *Western Osteopath* 18 (Apr. 1924); Musto, *American Disease*, 190–91; see also James Inciardi, *The War on Drugs: Heroin, Cocaine, Crime, and Public Policy* (Berkeley, 1986), 98.

44. Hobson, "The Peril of Narcotics"; Musto, *American Disease*, 190–91; "America Must Lead in the World War Against the Illicit Narcotic Drug Traffic," transcript by Richmond P. Hobson, Oct. 16, 1930, Box 67, 3, RHP; Pittman, "Richmond P. Hobson, Crusader," 179; Ida B. Wise to Richmond Hobson, Jan. 31, 1936; "Remarks . . . on the radio broadcast of WCTU President Ida Smith," Box 66, 6, RHP; see also "Officers of Oklahoma Narcotic Educational Association," Box 68, 7, RHP; "Special issue on Narcotics Education Week," *US*, Jan. 25, 1936; "Drug Addicts are One Answer to Why Kidnappings and Other Brutal Crimes," *US*, Jan. 30, 1937; and "Federal Bureau of Narcotics asks WCTU Help," *US*, Jan. 30, 1937, 69, 72; Inciardi, *The War on Drugs*, 98.

45. On earlier drug entrepreneurs, see Musto, *American Disease*, 1–120; Richmond P. Hobson to Josiah K. Lilly, Apr. 25, 1930; Josiah K. Lilly to George W. March, Dec. 3, 1930; June 4, 1930; Apr. 22, 1936; Hobson to Irénée du Pont, Apr. 17, 1931; Herbert Hoover to Richmond P. Hobson on the occasion of the INEA annual conference, Box 33, RHP; see also "A message from the White House," Box 67. Hobson, proposed resolutions at the semiannual meeting of the World Narcotics Defense Association, 1935, Box 69. Richmond P. Hobson, Mar. 15, 1935, Box 66, RHP; "Remarks . . . on the radio broadcast of WCTU President Ida Smith," Box 66, 6, RHP.

46. Proposed resolutions at the semiannual meeting of the World Narcotics Defense Association, 1935, Box 69, RHP; Hobson to Roosevelt, Oct. 19, 1933 and Nov. 6, 1933; Roosevelt to Hobson, Nov. 11, 1933, Box 68, 8, RHP; Hobson to Homer Cummings, Mar. 14, 1935; Speech by Homer Cummings and Homer Cummings to Hobson, Mar. 15, 1935, Box 66, RHP.

47. "Report of the Centre de l'Association Internationale de Défense contre les Stupéfiants, Summary of Activities, July–Dec. 1931"; "Projet de Programme du Centre," 1932, Box 65, 6, RHP. In Latin America, Hobson's outfit gained the support of the Pan American Union. See Pan American Union Director General L. S. Rowe to Hayne Davis, Mar. 31, 1933; L. S. Rowe to Richmond Hobson, June 20, 1933; telegram from Richmond P. Hobson to L. S. Rowe, Dec. 20, 1935, Box 69, 2, RHP. For an excellent discussion of the U.S. role in the formation of an international drug-control regime, see William B. McAlister, *Drug Diplomacy in the Twentieth Century: An International History* (London, 2000); see also Musto, *American Disease*, 202–9; Kathleen Frydl, *The Drug Wars in America, 1940–1973* (New York, 2013), 22–27. These otherwise quite excellent studies do not trace the linkages between the alcohol and drug prohibition regimes, their borrowed logics

and shared moral entrepreneurs. See also Calder, *The Origins and Development of Federal Crime Control*, 118.

48. "Report of the Centre de L'Association Internationale de Défense contre les Stupéfiants, Summary of Activities, July–Dec. 1931"; "Projet de Programme du Centre," 1932, Box 65, 6; Raymond Mage to Georgina Brewster, Apr. 26, 1932, Box 65, 6; Raymond Mage to Richmond P. Hobson, Feb. 20, 1936, Box 65, 8, RHP. See also "A Brief Survey of the Activities of the INEA, the World Conference on Narcotic Education, the WNDA, their Center of International Relations and their National Committees" presented to the League of Nations Commission on Opium and Other Dangerous Drugs, Mar. 1936, Box 65, 8; Roosevelt telegram to Richmond Hobson, Dec. 8, 1933, Box 68, 8; Attorney General Homer Cummings Speech, 1935, 2; Roosevelt to Richmond Hobson, Mar. 31, 1935; Hayne Davis to Homer Cummings, Oct. 13, 1934, Box 66, 6, RHP. On the importance of these agreements as the foundational edifice for later agreements, see McAllister, *Drug Diplomacy*, 79–101; 208–9.

49. Levi Nutt was quickly demoted, but a grand jury investigation gave the Narcotics Unit a clean bill of health: see McWilliams, *The Protectors*, 42. By way of comparison to Narcotics Bureau funding, the Prohibition Bureau received $15 million in 1929 to suppress the far larger and more profitable liquor trade: Musto, *American Disease*, 190–212; NCLOE, *Report on the Enforcement of the Prohibition Laws*, 18.

50. Lawrence Spinelli, *Dry Diplomacy: The United States, Great Britain and Prohibition* (Wilmington, DE, 1989), 59–83; McWilliams, *The Protectors*, 30–34.

51. Musto, *American Disease*, 212; McWilliams, *The Protectors*, 78; Harry Anslinger, "Organized Protection Against Organized Predatory Crime: Drug Peddling Narcotic Drugs," *Journal of Criminal Law and Criminology* 24 (Sept.–Oct. 1933): 636–55; "Roosevelt Asks Narcotic War Aid," *NYT*, Mar. 22, 1935, 7.

52. Homer Cummings, transcript of radio address drafted by Richmond Hobson, Mar. 1935, Box 66, 6, RHP; Frank Smith, "Narcotic Law Enforcement," *American Journal of Nursing* 48 (Oct. 1939): 1117–9.

53. Francisco E. Balderrama and Raymond Rodriguez, *Decade of Betrayal: Mexican Repatriation in the 1930s* (Albuquerque, NM, 1995).

54. McWilliams, *The Protectors*, 82–90; see also McAllister, *Drug Diplomacy in the Twentieth Century*, 156–211.

55. McWilliams, *The Protectors*, 82–90; McAllister, *Drug Diplomacy in the Twentieth Century*, 156–211; Frydl, *The Drug Wars in America*, 59–119. Between 1947 and 1950 an average of only 115 prisoners entered California prisons annually on drug charges. In contrast, the figure for 1985 was 3,609 and for 1990, 13,751: see Friedman, *Crime and Punishment*, 356–57.

56. Kenneth O'Reilly, "A New Deal for the FBI: The Roosevelt Administration, Crime Control, and National Security," *JAH* 69 (Dec. 1982): 638–58; American Association Against the Prohibition Amendment, "Government Lawlessness," (Westerville, OH, 1929), 2 (Addams quotation); O'Reilly, "A New Deal for the FBI," 643.

57. O'Reilly, "A New Deal for the FBI," 643.

58. Kim, "A House Divided," 114, 184, 187; Felix Frankfurter Memo, June 16, 1929, Reel 99; Felix Frankfurter Memo, June 2, 1929, Reel 48; Felix Frankfurter to Monte Lemann, May 23, 1929, Reel 46, FFP.

59. George Wickersham to Felix Frankfurter, June 4, 1929, Reel 48; Memo, June 16, 1929, Reel 99; Memo, "Outline of Commission Work," June 4, 1929, Reel 48; Felix Frankfurter to Monte Lemann, June 2, 1929, Reel 46; Felix Frankfurter to Max Lowenthal, July 1, 1929, Reel 48; FFP; see also Kim, "A House Divided," 114, 184, 187.

60. See, for example, Robert Oppenheimer, "Deportation of Aliens," *NCLOE*, *Report on the Enforcement of the Deportation Laws of the United States* 5 (Washington, DC, 1931), 177.

61. Morris M. Ploscowe, "Some Causative Factors in Criminality," in NCLOE, *Report on the Causes of Crime* 13, v. 1 (Washington, DC, 1931), 137; NCLOE, *Report on Lawlessness in Law Enforcement* 11 (Washington, DC, 1931), 1; Michael Palmiotto and Prabha Unnithan, *Policing and Society: A Global Approach* (Clifton, NY, 2010), 253–54; NCLOE, *Report on Lawlessness in Law Enforcement* 11, 19, 153–55.

62. See Sanford Bates, "Have Our Prisons Failed Us?" *Journal of Criminal Law and Criminology* 23 (Nov./Dec. 1932): 562; NCLOE, *Report on Penal Institutions, Probation, and Parole* 9 (Washington, 1931), 171.

63. Sanford Bates, "Have Our Prisons Failed Us?" 562; Calder, *The Origins and Development of Federal Crime*, 158–59; Blue, *Doing Time in the Great Depression*.

64. NCLOE, *Report on Crime and the Foreign Born* 10 (Washington, DC, 1931).

65. NCLOE, *Report on the Cost of Crime* 12 (Washington, DC, 1931), 444, 447–48; Monte Lemann to Felix Frankfurter, Jan. 27, 1931, Reel 46, *FFP*; "Ada Louise Comstock: Some of her memories of her life up to 1943," by Roberta Yerkes Blanshard, Ada Louise Comstock, Box 1, 1, Ada Louise Comstock Papers, Schlesinger Library, Radcliffe Institute, Harvard University; Kim, "A House Divided," 327; NCLOE, *Report on the Enforcement of the Prohibition Laws*, iv.

66. NCLOE, *Report on the Causes of Crime* 13, v. 1 (Washington, DC, 1931), 193–218, 312 ("the conclusion"); 330 ("security of employment").

67. NCLOE, *Report on the Causes of Crime*, 167, 222, 233, 237–38, 249.

68. NCLOE, *Report on the Causes of Crime*, 250–51.

69. See, for example, "U.S. Oppresses Aliens . . . Deporting Methods Called 'Tyrannic,'" *CDT*, Aug. 8, 1931, 4; "Brutal Third Degree Practices by Police Denounced in Report," *HC*, Aug. 11, 1931, 1; "Wickersham Commission Hits Third Degree and Brutal Police," *NYT*, Aug. 11, 1931, 1; "Law Body Hits Brutal Police Third Degrees," *WP*, Aug. 11, 1. In response to the commission's deportation findings, Hoover's labor secretary called for "practical legislation that will strengthen the hands of the Department of Labor to deport 'criminal aliens,'" *NYT*, Aug. 9, 1931, 5.

70. "An Apple of Discord," *NYT*, July 20, 1929, 6; "A Strong Subcommittee," *NYT*, Aug. 10, 1929, 12; the New Republic reported that the proposals of the commission would "sound the death knell" of the noble experiment, and, despite the "duality of thinking," it "marks the beginning of the end," "Four Aspects of the Wickersham Report," *New Republic*, Feb. 4, 1931, 313. New York congressman Robert Wagner similarly noted that it signaled the beginning of the end: see Wagner quoted in *Congressional Record*, Seventy-First Congress, Third Session, 5162; see also Harry G. Levine and Craig Reinarman, "From Prohibition to Regulation: Lessons from Alcohol Policy for Drug Policy," *Milbank Quarterly* 69 (1991): 461–64; Kyvig, *Repealing National Prohibition* (1979; Kent, OH, 2000), 115.

71. NCLOE, *Report on the Cost of Crime* 12, 447.

8. Repeal

1. *RTD,* June 19, 1932, 3, 4; Arthur Schlesinger, *The Crisis of the Old Order* (1957; Boston, 2003), 302. The slogan "Bread Not Booze" revived the earlier World War I dry slogan. For its use during the 1932 campaign, see, for example, "Bread Not Booze: The Issue," *Eugene Register-Guard,* Oct. 24, 1932.
2. Robert Post, "Federalism, Positive Law and the Emergence of the American Administrative State: Prohibition and the Taft Court Era," *WMLR* 48 (2006): 11 (Taft quotation); George Wickersham to the members of the Commission, Jan. 29, 1930; Box 1, 1, WCR (traveling salesman quotation); Sept. 24, 1930, *WP,* in Deok-Ho Kim, "A House Divided: The Wickersham Commission and National Prohibition," (PhD diss., SUNY Stony Brook, 1992), 273; Howard Lee McBain, *Prohibition Legal and Illegal* (New York, 1928), 14 (MacIntosh quotation); "National Prohibition" Women's Committee For Repeal of the Eighteenth Amendment, Box 1, LGP.
3. Felix Frankfurter, "A National Policy for Enforcement of Prohibition," *Annals of the American Academy of Political and Social Science* 109 (Sept. 1923): 193; Louise Gross, "Short History of the Women's Committee for Repeal of the Eighteenth Amendment"; George Stratham to Louise Gross, Oct. 5, 1928, Box 1, LGP.
4. Louise Gross, "National Prohibition," unpublished article, n.d., Box 1, LGP.
5. Pound views cited in Max Lowenthal to Felix Frankfurter, Mar. 21, 1930, Box 1, 2, Max Lowenthal Papers, Harvard Law School; Norman Clark, *Deliver Us from Evil: An Interpretation of Prohibition* (New York, 1976), 197 (Hearst quotations); Temperance or Prohibition? The Hearst Temperance Contest Committee, ed. Francis J. Tietsort (New York, 1929); see also David Kyvig, *Repealing National Prohibition* (1979; Kent, OH, 1986); George Wickersham to Members of the Commission, Jan. 29, 1930, Box 1, 1, WCP.
6. NCLOE, *Report on the Enforcement of the Prohibition Laws of the United States* (Washington, DC, 1931), iv; Kim, "A House Divided," 242–51, 313–14. Walter Lippman attacked a Hoover "plot" to change the report. For a discussion, see Kim, "A House Divided," 313–23; "Statement of Board of Managers of the Voluntary Committee of Lawyers," Mar. 22, 1931, Folder 10, Voluntary Committee of Lawyers Papers, Baltimore, MD, Maryland Historical Society; "Four Aspects of the Wickersham Report," *New Republic,* Feb. 4, 1931, 313; *CR,* Seventy-First Congress, Third Session, Feb. 17, 1931, 5158 (Wagner quotation); Henry Stimson Diaries, Nov. 24, 1930, Reel 2, Sterling Library, Yale University, in Kim, "A House Divided," 323; see also Harry G. Levine, "The Birth of Alcohol Control: Prohibition, the Power Elite, and the Problem of Lawlessness," *Contemporary Drug Problems* (Spring 1985): 63–115.
7. NCLOE, *Report on the Enforcement of the Prohibition Laws,* iv; see also Kyvig, *Repealing Prohibition,* 115; Schlesinger, *Crisis of the Old Order,* 250 (quotation).
8. Statement of Nes Alifas, president of District 44 of the IAM, NCLOE, *Report on Enforcement of the Prohibition Law* 3, 60. Alifas mentioned the "decided resentment among millions of people against an unjust and unfair law." See also Matthew Woll, Statement before the Wickersham Commission, transcript, 19, Box 24, 9, WCR; Levine, "The Birth of Alcohol Control," 63–115.
9. Levine, "The Birth of American Alcohol Control," 74 ("decidedly soothing tendency").

10. Letter from Robert W. Kenney to "Repealers," Box 19, California Crusaders Papers, Bancroft Library, Berkeley, California; "Voluntary Committee of Lawyers, Inc.," pamphlet; see also George Betts to Thomas Dunlop, Mar. 4, 1929, Folder 7, and "Certificate of Incorporation of the Voluntary Committee of Lawyers, Folder 2, Dec. 1928, Voluntary Committee of Lawyers Papers, Maryland Historical Society. On Pauline Sabin and the Women's Organization for National Prohibition Reform, see Kenneth D. Rose, *American Women and the Repeal of Prohibition* (New York, 1997); Levine, "The Birth of American Alcohol Control," 63–115.

11. See http://www.drugpolicy.org/docUploads/RockefellerLetter1937.pdf, accessed July 22, 2014. See also Levine, "The Birth of American Alcohol Control," 63–115; Kyvig, *Repealing National Prohibition*, 154, 155; Donald Ritchie, *Electing FDR: The New Deal Campaign of 1932* (Lawrence, KS, 2007), 98; Republican Party Platform, 1932, American Presidency Project, www.Presidency.ucsb.edu; Schlesinger, *Crisis of the Old Order*, 296 (Mencken quotation); conference observer quoted from "Convention Spotlights," undated memo by A.M., Box 376, Memorandum and Correspondence, 1928–1932, DNC.

12. Republican Party Platform, 1932.

13. Claire Potter, *War on Crime: Bandits, G-Man, and the Politics of Mass Culture* (New Brunswick, NJ, 1998), 122; "Convention Spotlights"; see also Republican Party Platform, 1932.

14. On Hoover's government activism, see, for example, David Kennedy, *Freedom from Fear: The American People in Depression and War* (New York, 1999), esp. 10–103; Republican Party Platform, 1932; "Scrapbooks," 1932 campaign material, Molly Dewson Papers, FDR.

15. David Farber, *Everybody Ought to be Rich: The Life and Times of John J. Raskob, Capitalist* (New York, 2013), 486–90.

16. Joseph Guffey to Roosevelt, Sept. 30, 1931, Box 297, DNC; Frank Freidel, *Franklin D. Roosevelt: The Triumph* (Boston, 1956), 288–90.

17. Schlesinger, *Crisis of the Old Order*, 157; Freidel, *Franklin D. Roosevelt*, 288–90; Elizabeth Tilton Diary, July 29–Aug. 1, 1932, Reel 994, ETP; see also, "Big Majority for Repeal," *NYT*, June 30, 1932, 1; E. J. Huyge to Roosevelt, June 3, 1932; Roosevelt to Huyge, June 13, 1932, Box 81, DNC.

18. "Big Majority for Repeal," *NYT*, June 30, 1932, 1; see also "Roosevelt Victory Predicted," *NYT*, June 30, 1932, 13; "Plank for Dry Law Repeal Accepted by Democrats," *LAT*, June 30, 1932, 1.

19. Tilton, Diary, June 29–July 1, 1932, Reel 994, ETP; NCLOE, Enforcement of the Prohibition Laws, Official Records of the National Commission on Law Observance and Enforcement 1, 400–409; NCLOE, Report of the Enforcement of the Prohibition Laws, 54–55.

20. Schlesinger, *Crisis of the Old Order*, 310–11; Tilton Diary, June 29–July 6, 1932, Reel 994, ETP.

21. Roosevelt, Acceptance Speech, Democratic National Convention, 1932, American Presidency Project, www.presidencyproject.ucsb.edu.

22. Louis McHenry Howe, "Roosevelt Wrote 140,000 Letters to Campaign Workers," *BDG*, Dec. 11, 1932; C. O. Jaynes to Roosevelt, Box 81; Christa Jensen to Roosevelt, Sept. 19, 1932, Box 85; "Report on Chicago Meeting," Sept. 12, 1932, Box 87; James T. Frazier to Roosevelt, Sept. 12, 1932, Box 142; Chas Macdonald

to Roosevelt, Aug. 17, 1932; Martin W. Melahn to Roosevelt, Sept. 20; George Luker to Roosevelt, Sept. 7, 1932; Box 87, DNC.

23. Letter to Roosevelt, Sept. 1932, Box 302, DNC; scrapbook, campaign material 1932, "Why Wage Earners Want Roosevelt and Garner," Box 21, Molly Dewson Papers, FDR.

24. Michael P. Weber, *Don't Call Me Boss: David L. Lawrence, Pittsburgh's Renaissance Mayor* (Pittsburgh, 1988); Davin, *Crucible of Freedom: Workers Democracy in the Industrial Heartland, 1914–1960* (Lanham, MD, 2010), 20; 111.

25. David L. Lawrence to Colonel Louis M. Howe, Oct. 7, 1932; David Lawrence to Roosevelt, Oct. 7, 1932, Box 304, DNC; Franklin D. Roosevelt, campaign address on the federal budget at Pittsburgh, PA, Oct. 19, 1932, American Presidency Project, www.presidency.ucsb.edu; Davin, *Crucible of Freedom*, 171–72.

26. Roy V. Peel and Tomas Claude Donnelly, *The 1932 Campaign: An Analysis* (New York, 1935), 108.

27. Tilton Diary, Nov. 6–7, 1932, Reel 994, ETP.

28. "House Votes on Beer Bill," *NYHT*, Mar. 14, 1933, 11; Kyvig, *Repealing National Prohibition*, 177.

29. C. O. Jaynes to Roosevelt, May 25, 1932, Box 81, DNC.

30. NCLOE, Report on the Enforcement of the Prohibition Laws, 79, 104–5; United States Senate, *The National Prohibition Law: Hearings before the Subcommittee of the Committee on the Judiciary, Sixty-Sixth Congress*, April 5–24, 1926, 1, 24, 416; Kim, "A House Divided," 344.

31. Kyvig, *Repealing National Prohibition*, 187–90; see also Levine, "The Birth of Alcohol Control," 76–115; "Distilling Control by Federal Board Fixed by New Board," *NYT*, Nov. 23, 1933, 1.

32. Here I draw on Harry G. Levine's discussion, see Levine, "The Birth of Alcohol Control," esp. 90–110.

33. Levine, "The Birth of Alcohol Control, esp. 90–110.

34. Ronald Reagan, "Speech to the Nation on the Campaign Against Drug Abuse," Sept. 14, 1986, Miller Center, President Speeches, www.millercenter.org/president/speeches; see also http://www.drugpolicy.org/new-solutions-drug-policy/brief-history-drug-war, accessed Aug. 28, 2014.

35. Michelle Alexander, *The New Jim Crow: Mass Incarceration in the Age of Colorblindness* (New York, 2010); Christian Parenti, *Lockdown America: Police and Prisons in the Age of Crisis* (London, 2000). See also Ruth Gilmore, *Golden Gulag; Prisons, Surplus, Crisis and Opposition in Globalizing California* (Berkeley, 2007); Marc Mauer, *Race to Incarcerate* (New York, 1999); William Stuntz, *The Collapse of American Criminal Justice* (Cambridge, MA, 2011), esp. 158–95. Stuntz's comparative analysis of prison rates in the United States and Europe reveals in stunning terms the extremely punitive policies in the United States.

36. http://www.washingtonpost.com/blogs/wonkblog/wp/2013/08/13/wonkbook-11-facts-about-americas-prison-population/, accessed Aug. 29, 2014. On the rise of women in prison and its relationship to drug trafficking, see Chloe Constant, "Trajectories et Dynamiques carcérales au féminin: Le Cas de Lima" (PhD diss., Paris III Sorbonne Nouvelle, 2013). See also Chloe Constant and C. Boutron, "Gendering Transnational Criminality: The Case of Female Imprisonment in Peru," *Signs: Journal of Women in Culture and Society* (2013): 39, 177–95.

37. For racial disparities and uneven sentencing, see Alexander, *The New Jim Crow*;

Craig Reinarman and Harry G. Levine, eds., *Crack in America: Demon Drugs and Social Justice* (Berkeley, 1997); Kimberly Streeter, "Coin Blood into Gold: A History of the Prison Industrial Complex in Georgia and Tennessee (MLA thesis, Univ. of North Carolina-Asheville, 2004); Human Rights Watch, *Modern Capital of Human Rights? Abuses in the State of Georgia*, Human Rights Watch Report, (New York, July 1996), 7.

38. For a discussion of the U.S. role in the creation of the international drug Prohibition regime, see William B. McAllister, *Drug Diplomacy in the Twentieth Century: An International History* (New York, 2000).

39. "Short History of the Women's Committee for Repeal of the 18th Amendment" Box 1, LGP; Eleanor Roosevelt to Mrs. Charlotte Wilkinson, Apr. 12, 1930, Box 9, Eleanor Roosevelt papers, FDR; "Coalition Urges Nations to Decriminalize Drugs and Drug Use," *NYT*, Sept. 9, 2014; Coletta Youngers and Eileen Rosin, eds., *Drugs and Democracy in Latin America: The Impact of U.S. Policy* (Boulder, CO, 2005); Organization of American States, *Scenarios for the Drug Problem in the Americas, 2013–2015* (Cartagena, Colombia, 2012).

INDEX

Report on Prisoners in State and Federal Prison and Reformatories (Census Bureau), 298n

Report on the Cost of Crime (Wickersham Commission), 225

Report on the Enforcement of the Prohibition Laws of the United States (Wickersham Commission), 225–26

Republican National Convention, of 1932, 237–38, 239–40

Republican Party, Republicans, 15, 16, 47, 102, 139, 157, 159, 162–63, 170, 173, 175, 176, 177, 178, 179, 180, 181, 183, 184, 185–86, 187–88, 189, 208, 235, 239–40, 243, 244, 245, 246, 293n, 294n

    corporate and manufacturing support for, 161

    German Americans in, 161–62

    national politics dominated by, 162

    Prohibition repeal and, 237–38

    and war on crime, 238–39

Republican Party National Committee, 158, 192

    and 1928 election, 158

restaurants, bootleg liquor in, 105–6

Rhode Island, 35, 174

Richmond, Va., xvii, 73, 75, 76, 84–86, 87, 97, 157, 195

Richmond Chamber of Commerce, 73

Richmond Planet, 87, 90

Richmond Times-Dispatch, 73, 84, 231

Rio Grande, 209

Ritchie, Albert C., 240

Ritz-Carlton, 105

roadhouses, 121, 127

Robinson, Joseph T., 169

Rockefeller, John D., 29

Rockefeller, John D., Jr., 237–38

Rodriguez, John, 92–93

Rome Club, 146

Roosevelt, Eleanor, 174, 254

Roosevelt, Franklin D., xiii, xx, xxii, 33, 102, 159, 163, 170, 173, 174, 179, 183, 184, 186, 188, 198, 215, 216, 217, 219–20, 234, 247, 248, 294n

    New Deal legislation of, *see* New Deal

    at 1932 convention, 240–43

    in 1932 election, 235, 243–45

    Prohibition repeal and, 240, 241–43, 246

Roosevelt, Theodore, 162

Rotary Club, 152

Rothstein, Arnold, 114, 216, 282n

Rubio, Ortiz, 93

Ruggeri, Alex, 149

Russia, 32

    liquor-control laws in, 30

Russian immigrants, 14, 162

Sabath, Adolph, 175

Sabin, Pauline, 192

Saint Joseph County, Ind., 140

St. Louis, Mo., 112, 149, 152, 168

St. Valentine's massacre, 189

Salem, Mass., 26

saloons, 107, 144

    African-American, 17, 74–75

    "athletic clubs" as replacement for, 48, 50

    campaign against, 11–12, 15–18, 20–21, 25, 46, 274n

    illicit, 49

    as immigrant social centers, 42

    leisure-time competition to, 46

    party politics and, 15–16

    poor and, 74–75

    Prohibition as demise of, 46–48, 271n

    prostitution and, 15

    as symbols of social upheaval, 12, 14–15

    working class as patrons of, 11–12, 14, 42

Salvation Army, 133

Sánchez, Pedro, 93

Sanchez, Tanya Marie, 278n